Readings in
Child and Adolescent Psychology
Contemporary Perspectives

Harper & Row's
CONTEMPORARY PERSPECTIVES READER SERIES
Phillip Whitten, Series Editor

Readings in Child and Adolescent Psychology
Contemporary Perspectives

edited by

Paul Henry Mussen
University of California, Berkeley

John Janeway Conger
University of Colorado School of Medicine

Jerome Kagan
Harvard University

HARPER & ROW, PUBLISHERS, New York
Cambridge, Hagerstown, Philadelphia, San Francisco,
London, Mexico City, São Paulo, Sydney

1817

Sponsoring Editor: George A. Middendorf
Project Editor: Jo-Ann Goldfarb
Senior Production Manager: Kewal K. Sharma
Compositor: Maryland Linotype Composition Co., Inc.
Printer & Binder: The Murray Printing Company
Cover Photo: Biggs, DPI

Readings in Child and Adolescent Psychology:
Contemporary Perspectives

Library of Congress Cataloging in Publication Data
Main entry under title:
Readings in child and adolescent psychology.

   (Harper & Row's contemporary perspectives reader series)
  1. Child psychology—Addresses, essays, lectures.
2. Adolescent psychology—Addresses, essays, lectures.
I. Mussen, Paul Henry. II. Conger, John Janeway.
III. Kagan, Jerome.
BF721.R327   155.4   80–13235
ISBN 0–06–041888–5

SUMMARY OF CONTENTS

CONTENTS

V. ADOLESCENCE

PREFACE

This anthology is intended to be a distinctive one. Its dintinctiveness lies in the fact that the selection of articles has been determined primarily by the needs and interests of beginning students in child psychology, who are so easily turned off by the relentless jargon of many articles in more conventional readers. The aims of this anthology are to reveal the breadth of the discipline; to demonstrate the direct relevance of child psychology to the students' lives, both personally and professionally; and to capture and retain the interest of the student. Moreover, the publisher has made every effort to keep down the cost of the book to the student by reproducing articles in facsimile form wherever this procedure does not detract from the overall design of the book; it has thus been possible to include an unusually large number of selections in relatively inexpensive form.

The editors of this book are three of the most distinguished developmental psychologists in North America. Paul Mussen is professor and director of the Institute of Human Development at the University of California at Berkeley. John Conger is professor of clinical psychology at the University of Colorado Medical Center. Jerome Kagan is professor of psychology at Harvard University. The editors chose the articles included in this anthology in accordance with several basic criteria. First, they must be sound psychology. Second, they must be highly readable. Third, they must appeal to the student through their intrinsically interesting and challenging content. Fourth, they must relate to the introductory course in child and adolescent psychology as it is taught in most American colleges. And fifth, they must have relevance to the student as a parent, potential parent, or potential member of the helping professions. All of the articles in this book, forty in number, meet these criteria.

Readings in Child and Adolescent Psychology: Contemporary Perspectives has been structured chronologically to make it as flexible a book as possible. It can be used in conjunction with Mussen, Conger, and Kagan's *Essentials of Child Development and Personality* (1980), their longer text, *Child Development and Personality* (Fifth Edition, 1979), with any of the other leading textbooks in the discipline, or, indeed, as the sole text in a brief course.

The articles in this book were carefully selected from a broad range of contemporary sources—books, journals, and semipopular magazines. Three-quarters of the articles were published in 1978 or later, while fully 95 percent were published after 1970. Thus the articles reflect the current interests, issues, concerns, and controversies of the discipline. The work of some of today's top developmental psychologists has been included—articles by Joseph Adelson, Diana Baumrind, Urie Bronfenbrenner, Jerome Bruner, Thomas J. Cottle, John J. Conger, Elizabeth Douvan, David Elkind, Daniel G. Freedman, E. Mavis Hetherington, Jerome Kagan, Paul Mussen, Ross D. Parke, and Dan I. Slobin, among others. Distinguished academics in related disciplines—such as John Money and Arlene Skolnick—have also contributed articles, as have some of today's top professional writers writing about the social sciences. The range of issues covers virtually every topic taught in contemporary introductory courses, and it should provide a thorough and readable background introduction to the fascination of the discipline.

This anthology will be revised regularly—not only in response to changes in the discipline itself, but also as a result of the suggestions and criticisms of students and instructors who use it. For this reason, we have included a response card, located in the back of the book. Please take a moment to fill out the card and send it to the publisher after you have used the book. Your comments will be much appreciated and gratefully received.

PHILLIP WHITTEN
Series Editor

Readings in
Child and Adolescent Psychology
Contemporary Perspectives

I. The Prenatal Period

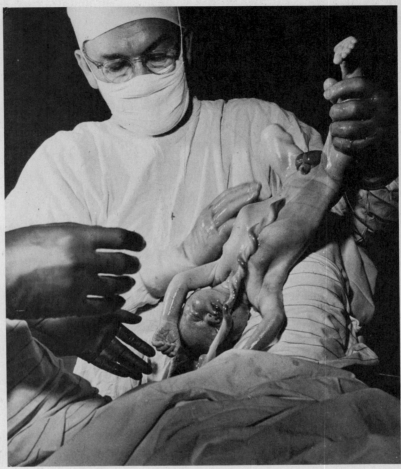

Photograph by Wayne Miller, Magnum

The development of the child during the period prior to birth is a remarkably well-buffered process. Despite wide variations in climate and in the diet and life-style of the mother, most newborn babies display remarkably similar psychological characteristics and are potentially capable of adapting to their environments. One reason for the similarity in competence among newborns is that nature prunes potentially unfit embryos early in pregnancy. It is estimated that at least 50 percent of all conceptions are spontaneously aborted before the sixth month of pregnancy. Additionally, modern medicine has found ways to detect potential problems and to neutralize the danger of conditions like blood incompatibility and breech birth. However small the variation among live babies, variation still remains, and some babies begin life with psychological risk, mainly originating from premature birth and birth with some degree of oxygen deprivation before the child begins to breathe.

The major causes of prematurity are psychological and physiological stress to the mother, especially chronic disease, infection, poor diet, and psychologi-

1

cal tension. Since these undesirable events are more common in mothers who live under economic privation than in those from more affluent homes, premature births are more common among the working and lower classes than among middle and upper middle class mothers. Most scientists and physicians agree that if we could initiate health programs that would guarantee the health of the pregnant mother, we could reduce the incidence of prematurity by a considerable amount.

Anoxia—or lack of sufficient oxygen—at birth is often due to mechanical difficulties; for example, if the placenta tears away from the uterine wall prematurely or the breathing mechanisms that normally operate at birth fail to operate when the child is born. If the child is deprived of oxygen for too long a time—say, several minutes—some neurons in the central nervous system may possibly be permanently destroyed, thus making the child a risk for motor paralysis. In more severe cases, damage to the cortex can impair cognitive processes. Fortunately, modern medicine has developed ways to diagnose some of these problems early in pregnancy and to prepare for or eliminate them. Of course, mothers can help by trying to maintain a good diet and to avoid smoking, alcohol, and drugs; for each of these can increase the probability of difficulty in the birth process.

PREGNANCY: THE CLOSEST HUMAN RELATIONSHIP

NILES NEWTON
AND
CHARLOTTE MODAHL

During its life within the uterus, a baby develops from a single fertilized cell and becomes a human being who, though still immature and dependent, can survive in the outside world. In the course of those 38 weeks, the baby depends on its mother for all its physical needs. She, in turn, is aware that she carries within her a living being. As her baby grows, the mother undergoes profound physical and emotional changes. From conception to birth, the pair deeply affect each other, and their relationship may establish attitudes and ways of interacting that persist for years.

Life begins when sperm and egg unite, and a woman's sexual enjoyment may make it more likely that the sperm will reach the egg. After a woman experiences orgasm, her cervix descends and enlarges, increasing the size of the passageway into the uterus and making it easier for the sperm to ascend and meet the egg. Orgasm also makes her vaginal secretion more alkaline, and according to obstetrician Landrum Shettles, sperm travel more easily in an alkaline environment than in the normally acid vaginal secretion.

At the same time, prostaglandins — substances that are found throughout the body but that are concentrated in the fluid that surrounds the sperm — enter the vaginal wall and are absorbed into the bloodstream. Oxytocin, a hormone, is produced by the woman's own body. In response to these substances the uterus contracts, then relaxes, and this sequence may help the sperm move into the uterus. By remaining relaxed and recumbent after intercourse a woman also helps the sperm make their way into the uterus.

The feeling of closeness that most couples have after intercourse may be the direct result of uterine responses to such substances as prostaglandins and oxytocin, which is released by the pituitary gland during sexual stimulation. Our own pilot studies, in which we measured the moods of both sexes immediately after intercourse, suggest that there is a postcoital decrease in anxiety and depression. The drop was sharper in men than in women. Learning by gradual conditioning also contributes to the closeness of a couple. Because the intense emotions involved in orgasm are extremely pleasurable, the experience of intercourse is reinforcing. Repeated intercourse tends to condition the two people to each other, binding them into a reproductive partnership and providing a foundation for family life and the nurture of the baby.

Of course, orgasm is not necessary for conception, nor is any affection for one's partner. However, there is a strong relationship between a woman's feelings toward her mate and the course of her pregnancy.

Frances K. Grossman and her colleagues at Boston University studied 98 pregnant women in an attempt to assess the effects of their emotions. They f that women with good m ships were less li anxious during

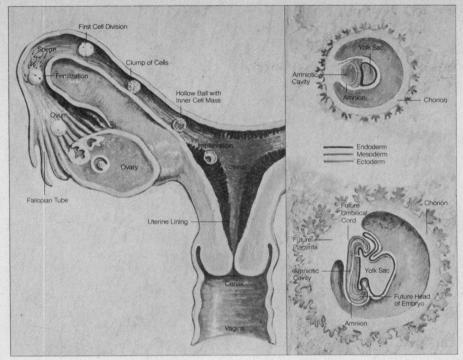

First Cell Division
Sperm
Fertilization
Ovum
Clump of Cells
Hollow Ball with Inner Cell Mass
Ovary
Implantation
Uterine
Fallopian Tube
Uterine Lining
Cervix
Vagina

Yolk Sac
Amniotic Cavity
Amnion
Chorion
Endoderm
Mesoderm
Ectoderm

Future Umbilical Cord
Chorion
Future Placenta
Amniotic Cavity
Yolk Sac
Future Head of Embryo
Amnion

The fertilized egg divides many times on its way to the uterus. In the small drawings of the zygote on the right, cells in the red band will develop into the digestive system; those in the green band, into the heart, muscles, and skeleton; those in the blue band, into the skin and nervous system.

with unhappy marriages.

Whether the good marital relationships led to low levels of anxiety and depression or whether women who are anxious and depressed generally have unhappy marriages cannot be determined. But Grossman did find that women who said, early in their pregnancies, that they had wanted to become pregnant were much less likely to have complications during labor and delivery than women who had not consciously wanted to become pregnant.

Conception does not occur for some time after intercourse and takes place without the awareness of the woman. Sperm travel at only 0.5 cm per minute, but with the aid of muscular contractions and natural chemical and hormonal assistance, they may reach the Fallopian tubes within a few minutes after they are deposited in the vagina.

Although the egg may survive for approximately 72 hours after it is released from the ovary, it probably can be fertilized only during the first 24 hours. Some of the 400,000,000 sperm that are ejaculated by the man may survive within the woman for as long as seven days, although it is unlikely that they can penetrate and fertilize the egg after the first two days.

Planning the date of intercourse may help determine the baby's sex. About half the sperm released during intercourse carry an X chromosome; they will produce a girl. The other half carry a Y chromosome and they will produce a boy. The male-producing sperm are lighter and move faster, but they die sooner than the sperm that produce females. Because male-producing sperm tend to reach the fertilization site first, intercourse at the time the woman ovulates favors the conception of a boy. Because male-producing sperm die first, intercourse a day or two before ovulation increases the chances of the couple's conceiving a girl.

The first two weeks of a baby's life are called the germinal phase, and the fertilized egg is called a zygote. After the sperm penetrates the egg, the zygote spends three or four days traveling down the length of the Fallopian tube and then another three to four days floating free in the uterus.

By the time the zygote is about nine days old, it has developed two sacs that surround it completely. The inner one is a fluid-filled sac that protects the zygote from injury, and the outer sac is the one from which the tendrils will grow that attach the zygote to the mother. Throughout this period, the cells of the zygote are dividing rapidly.

By the end of the second week, the zygote is firmly implanted in the uterine wall and has developed three layers of cells. The outer layer will produce the baby's skin, sense organs, and nervous system; the middle layer will develop into the baby's heart and blood vessels, muscles, and skeleton; the inner layer will become the digestive system and related organs such as the liver, the pancreas, and the thyroid gland.

The placenta, which transmits nourishment from mother to baby and takes away all waste products, is also developing at this stage.

Although the mother is unaware of the spectacular growth that is taking place within her, her body is responding to the implanted zygote. Instead of sloughing off its lining in a menstrual period as it normally does when an egg remains unfertilized, her uterus accepts the zygote in its thickened wall, and the dense network of blood vessels that has developed since ovulation begins to join the placenta.

The end of the baby's germinal phase coincides with the mother's expected menstrual period. At first she may think her period is only delayed, but soon her breasts begin to feel full, heavy, and tender, and she may start each day with nausea and vomiting.

Not all women become sick at the same time of day and many never feel nausea at all. Recently, Marilyn Theotokatos and Niles Newton collected information from over 500 women who were breast-feeding their babies. Sixty-eight percent of them reported experiencing nausea during their pregnancies, although only 16 percent said it had been severe. Among those who became nauseated, 40 percent also vomited.

By now the zygote has become an

The embryo pictured below is eight weeks old. It is about an inch long and has a recognizable brain, heart, stomach, liver, kidneys, and endocrine system. Its tail will recede and become the tip of its spine. Although its head is enormous, it is obviously a developing human being.

embryo, a term that describes the baby for the next six weeks. The placenta becomes more developed and from it the umbilical cord runs to the baby's navel. During this phase, the embryo develops its major organs.

At eight weeks, the baby is not much more than an inch long. It has a recognizable brain, a heart that pumps blood through tiny veins and arteries, a stomach that produces digestive juices, a liver that manufactures blood cells, kidneys that function, and an endocrine system. In the male embryo the testes produce androgens. The baby now has limbs and an enormous head with ears, nose, eyes, and mouth. Its eyelids have not yet developed and it has a definite tail, which will recede and become the tip of the spinal column. Nevertheless, it looks human.

Although the mother does not yet look pregnant, her baby has begun to react to its environment. It holds its hands close to its face; should they touch its mouth, the embryo turns its head and opens its mouth wide.

The behavior of the mother has also begun to change in response to changes in hormone production, to her bodily growth, and to her expectations that her way of life will soon be different. She may be unusually tired and sleep a good deal. As the growing embryo presses on her bladder, she may find herself urinating frequently.

Her eating habits are likely to change, perhaps in response to local custom. Many women have cravings for strange food at this time. S. M. Tobin asked 1,000 Canadian mothers "Did you have any peculiar food craving in pregnancy?" and 640 of them said "Yes." Sometimes these cravings may be intense but usually they involve milder yearnings.

Craving for cornstarch or clay is common among poor groups in the United States, whereas affluent women may crave ice cream or strawberries in winter. The reasons for these cravings are unknown, though they have been attributed to dietary deficiencies, anxiety, or conformity to cultural expectations.

With the appearance of bone cells at about the ninth week of development, the embryo is called a fetus, which will remain its technical name until birth. For the rest of its gestational period, the fetus is protected from the outside world by the amniotic fluid that fills the space between the inner and outer sacs that developed eight weeks earlier. The amniotic fluid provides a stable, buffered environment, and the fetus floats in a state of relative weightlessness. The fetus urinates directly into the fluid, and its waste products travel from the fluid through the placenta, from which they enter the mother's bloodstream. Exchange between the fetus and the amniotic fluid is slow, while exchange be-

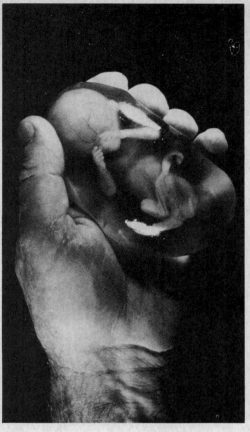

The features of the developing fetus show plainly in these photographs by radiologist Roberts Rugh. The three-month-old fetus (left) can bend its finger and swallow; the 17-week-old fetus (below, right) is so active within the uterus that its mother can now feel the separate life within her.

tween the mother and the fluid is rapid. The fluid is completely replaced every two or three hours.

By the end of the third month, counting from the mother's last menstrual period, the fetus has grown to a length of three inches and weighs about half an ounce. It shows one of the signs of humanity — its thumb and forefinger are apposed so that, theoretically, it could grasp objects. It bends its finger when its palm is touched; it swallows. It has taste buds, sweat glands, and a prominent nose. By now it has eyelids, but they are sealed shut.

It is during the first trimester that the developing baby may be most sensitive to such influences as drugs, x-rays, disease, and the lack of essential nutrients. Mark Safra and Godfrey Oakley, Jr., of the Georgia Center for Disease Control found that women who take diazepam (a tranquilizer marketed as Valium) during the first trimester are four times as likely to have babies with cleft lips or cleft palate as mothers who do not take the tranquilizer.

During the 1960s, before the sedative was banned, mothers who took thalidomide during the first trimester sometimes gave birth to babies whose arms and legs were nothing more than rudimentary flippers. Other drugs can cause abnormalities ranging from yellowed nails and teeth, which may follow the use of an antibiotic like tetracycline, to blindness, deafness, and gross malformations.

Only within the past six years has the existence of "fetal alcohol syndrome" been established. Kenneth L. Jones and his colleagues at the University of California at San Diego, have followed the pregnancies of alcoholic mothers and report that their babies are likely to be smaller and lighter than most babies, and that they are more likely to have slight facial, limb, and cardiovascular malformations. Some babies who are born to alcoholic mothers have conical heads and are mentally retarded. Animal research indicates that even the regular consumption of moderate doses of alcohol can affect the physical condition of offspring, but such a connection has not yet been established in human beings.

Heroin also affects the fetus. Babies whose mothers take heroin regularly will be born addicted to the drug and soon after birth must endure acute symptoms of heroin withdrawal.

Some minor illnesses may have profound effects. Some mothers who contract rubella (German measles) during the first trimester produce babies who are blind, deaf, mentally retarded, or have diseased hearts.

The fetus depends on its mother for all vitamins, minerals, and nutrients. In ex-periments with animals, severe protein shortages in early pregnancy have been associated with fetal brain damage. Stephen Zamenhof and his colleagues at the University of California School of Medicine, Los Angeles, found significantly fewer brain cells and cells with lower protein content in rats whose mothers had been placed on a protein-restricted diet before mating. They suggest that protein deprivation leads directly to mental retardation in children.

Research that severely restricts prenatal diets cannot be done on human beings, but records kept during the 1940s, when Germany occupied the Netherlands and Dutch diets were reduced below the minimum requirements for good health, showed an increase in stillborn babies and premature births. As soon as diets returned to normal, the rates dropped. In depressed areas of the United States and in countries where the customary diet is deficient, infant mortality rates are high. In such places, dietary supplements have reduced mortality rates.

During the second trimester, the mother first feels her baby's movements. It is this quickening that makes many women acutely aware that they are carrying a living human being. Fetal movement patterns often give rise to maternal fantasies and expectations for the new baby. Women who reject the idea of motherhood when they first discover they have conceived generally come to accept the idea during this period of pregnancy.

The second trimester is generally a time of physical and emotional well-being. The mother no longer finds it necessary to sleep so much, her nausea has gone, and her appetite has returned. She has lost the continual urge to urinate, and she often feels better than she did when not pregnant. Her condition is now apparent, and each time she looks at herself in the mirror, she has visible evidence of her baby's existence.

Her major worry at this stage may be in regard to her weight, for this is the period of most rapid weight gain. A few years ago, obstetricians urged their patients to restrict weight gain during pregnancy, and many mothers found themselves put on strict diets at a time when they both wanted and needed more nutrients.

Today it is realized that mothers who fail to gain adequately during pregnancy may have less healthy babies. According to the Committee on Maternal Nutrition of the National Research Council, the desirable weight gain during pregnancy is 24 pounds. The extra weight includes, in addition to the baby and the placenta, amniotic fluid, water that enlarges breast tissue, and extra blood needed for circulation. Some of the 24 pounds — on the average, about three and a half pounds — is stored as fat and protein to act as a buffer against the stresses of the postnatal period.

By the time the fetus is five months old, it appears in many ways to be a fully developed human being, but if it were taken from its mother, it could not survive. Only 10 inches long and weighing about half a pound, it has well-formed lungs that are not ready to function and a digestive system that cannot handle food.

This miniature being is often quite active within the uterus and seems to squirm or writhe slowly. Sometimes, by placing a hand on the mother's abdomen, it is possible to identify an elbow, a knee, or a tiny bottom. At this time, if one presses gently on the fetus, it is likely to respond with movements.

At the end of the second trimester, the six-month-old fetus wakes, sleeps, and has sluggish periods. It is likely to nap in a favorite position. It will open and close its eyes, look in all directions, and even hiccup. The grasp reflex is developed, and the fetus is capable of supporting its own weight with one hand. It is about 13

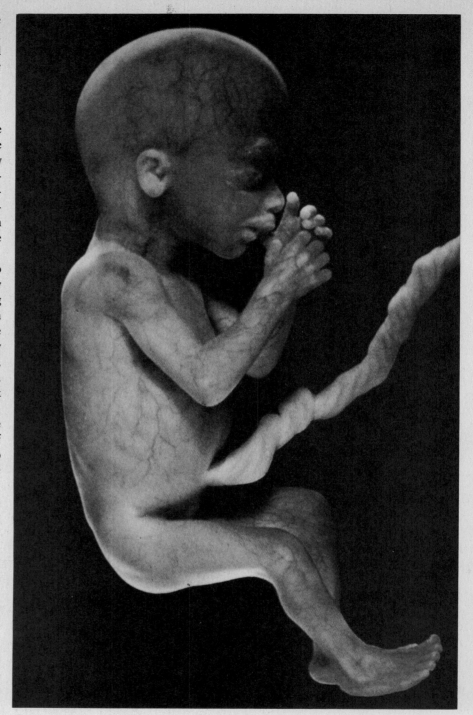

inches long and weighs about one and a half pounds. With intensive care — regulated temperature, intravenous feeding, and oxygen supplementation — the fetus might now be able to survive outside its mother's body.

At Northwestern University, Marcia Jiminez studied 120 women who were pregnant for the first time, and examined their attitudes toward their jobs and their moods during the last three months of pregnancy. She found that women who expressed satisfaction with their work also felt less anxious, depressed, tired, and guilty and had less difficulty coping with their situation than did women who were dissatisfied.

Although it has been suggested that

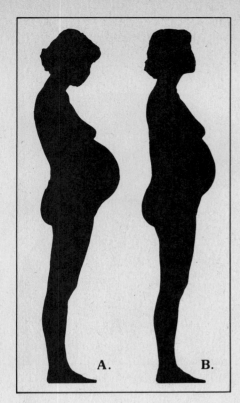

A.   B.

Women who stand improperly may be extremely uncomfortable during their pregnancies. The woman on the left, who is eight months pregnant, complained of pain in her abdomen and lower back. When shown how to stand correctly, she experienced immediate relief, and as the silhouette on the right shows, appeared less pregnant.

women who have strong career interests find it difficult to adapt to motherhood, Jiminez' work suggests that a woman's enjoyment of her occupation and her enjoyment of her pregnancy may both be part of a generally positive attitude toward life.

During the last trimester of pregnancy, the mother may respond with pride to the bulge of her enlarging uterus as a sign of fertility. In a society that advocates strict birth control measures, a woman's feelings about her pregnant body may be mixed. A mother who has seen few pregnant women in her life may feel that her body is uncomfortably different. The difference is accentuated if she wears shoes with high heels and stands in a poor posture. Her baby now may kick or punch sharply and sometimes uncomfortably, which can be an annoyance in the middle of the night.

The demand for nutrients is especially heavy at this time, and the baby will absorb 84 percent of all the calcium the mother eats, and 85 percent of the iron. The rapidly developing fetal brain also requires extra protein.

By the last trimester, the baby is aware of events outside its own body. The fetus lives in a noisy environment. Small microphones inserted through the cervix into the uterus of pregnant women whose babies were due any day have detected a loud whooshing sound in rhythm with the mother's heartbeat. The sound is produced by blood pulsing through the uterus and is the constant companion of the fetus, which also hears the occasional rumbling of gas in its mother's intestines.

The unborn baby may also respond to outside sounds. Some mothers have complained that they cannot attend symphony concerts because their babies respond to the music and applause with violent movement. Lester Sontag of the Fels Research Institute placed a small block of wood over the abdomens of women whose babies were due in about five weeks. When the board was struck with a doorbell clapper, about 90 percent of the fetuses immediately began kicking and moving violently. Their heart rates also increased. Besides responding to loud sounds, the fetus responds to the reaction of its mother's heart to such sounds.

Fetuses show individual differences in activity level and heart rate. Like people, some have heart rates that fluctuate greatly while others have hearts that tend to beat more regularly. Sontag has followed a dozen people from their fetal existence to adulthood and discovered that those whose heart rates showed wide variation within the uterus generally show the same wide variation as adults.

On the basis of three-hour interviews with a large group of children and adults, Sontag's colleagues have found that men with highly fluctuating heart rates tend to be reluctant to depend on people they love, to be in conflict over dependency, to be more compulsive, introspective, and indecisive than men with more stable heart rates. They have no explanation for this, but speculate whether they have discovered a genetic component of personality or an example of the influence of the uterine environment.

The relationship between a mother and her unborn baby is so close that the mother's emotions affect her baby's behavior, and the effect may persist after the baby is born. There is no way to ascertain when maternal emotions begin to influence a fetus, because there is no way to measure the effect in early pregnancy. But when a mother is emotionally upset, her body responds with physical changes.

Sontag has observed women in the last trimester of pregnancy who were suddenly faced with grief, fear, or anxiety. One young woman, whose fetus he was checking weekly for activity level and heart rate, came to him terrified after her husband suffered a psychotic breakdown and threatened to kill her.

Most obstetricians recommend that their patients gain about 24 pounds during pregnancy. Extra interstitial fluid, distributed throughout body tissues, contributes to weight gain. The weight that is not accounted for in the chart on the right is stored as fat and protein and helps the new mother withstand the stresses of the postnatal period.

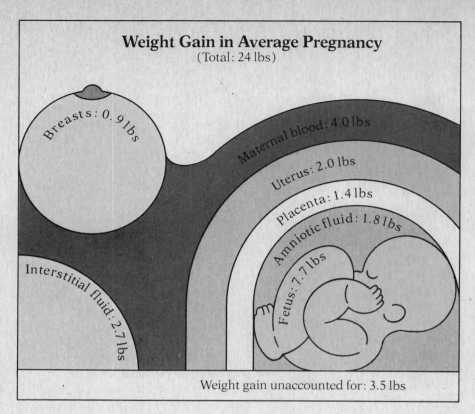

Weight Gain in Average Pregnancy
(Total: 24 lbs)

Breasts: 0.9 lbs

Maternal blood: 4.0 lbs

Uterus: 2.0 lbs

Placenta: 1.4 lbs

Amniotic fluid: 1.8 lbs

Fetus: 7.7 lbs

Interstitial fluid: 2.7 lbs

Weight gain unaccounted for: 3.5 lbs

Her baby began kicking so violently that she was in pain, and recordings showed that its activity was 10 times greater than it had been in earlier recordings. The unborn baby of a woman whose husband was killed in an accident showed the same sharp rises in activity. Six other pregnant women who took part in Sontag's studies suffered similar emotional crises. In every case, their babies responded with violent activity. Sontag followed these babies and found that, although they were physically and mentally normal, they were irritable and hyperactive, and three had severe feeding problems.

The link between mother and child has other postnatal effects. During the last three months of pregnancy, the mother confers on her baby immunity to a number of diseases that she may have contracted in the past. The antibodies manufactured by her immune system cross the placenta and circulate in the baby's bloodstream as well. If the mother has developed such immunities, the baby will have some resistance to measles, mumps, whooping cough, scarlet fever, colds, or influenza for the first few months of its life.

Other substances also cross the placental bridge. Women who smoke on a regular basis give birth to babies who are smaller and lighter than average. Recent studies by Gerhard Gennser and his colleagues showed that when such women smoke a single cigarette, the nicotine concentration in their blood quadruples and their heart rates increase. Within 30 minutes their unborn babies, all at eight months of development, showed a decrease in chest movements and short periods during which they did not

"breathe" at all.

When the fetus has completed its 38 weeks in the uterus, the birth process begins. The exact sequence of the physiological changes that initiate labor is not clearly understood, but several substances — oxytocin, vasopressin, progesterone, and prostaglandins — are believed to be involved. Both the mother and the baby produce hormones, and some investigators believe that the fetus initiates the process, or at least gives the signal that tips the balance of factors that start labor.

The experience of childbirth varies from culture to culture. In societies that look upon birth as a fearful and secret experience, women often have long, difficult labors. In societies that are open about childbirth and expect it to be simple, women usually have short, uncomplicated labors. In normal deliveries, a relaxed, undisturbed environment, the presence of trusted helpers, and a minimum of medical interference encourage the mother and infant to interact successfully.

Fear and disturbance may increase the mother's discomfort, and the excessive amounts of adrenaline that fear can place in a woman's bloodstream may counteract the work of hormones like oxytocin that help labor progress. Anxiety may cause the mother's muscles to become tense, converting simple contractions into painful cramps. Studies have shown that women who have a high level of anxiety during pregnancy are also likely to have complications during delivery.

In the first stage of labor, which may last from two to 16 hours or more, the uterus contracts at regular intervals while the cervix slowly dilates to allow the baby to pass into the birth canal. During this stage, the uterine contractions are faint at first and gradually increase in strength. The mother may not realize that she is in labor until she notices the regular rhythm of the contractions.

In the second stage of labor, the baby usually passes headfirst down the vagina and into the world. This stage may last only a few minutes in women who have previously given birth. With first babies, it generally lasts more than an hour and varies greatly from woman to woman. This is the expulsive stage of labor, and

Women who choose the Lamaze method of childbirth attend exercise classes with their husbands, where they learn how to breathe and push at proper times during the second stage of labor. Their husbands, who will be present at the birth, learn how to give assistance and comfort.

the mother generally helps by bearing down during contractions. General or regional anesthesia may interfere with her efforts to push. The presence of the father in the labor and delivery room often helps the mother relax between contractions and enables the parents to be involved as a couple in the baby's arrival.

In the third stage of labor, the placenta is expelled. This stage can be described as a minilabor that ends with the delivery of the placenta. It usually lasts only a few minutes.

Drugs, even spinal injections, given to relieve a mother's pain or discomfort pass through the placenta to the baby and may interfere with the early bonding process. The baby may receive such a heavy dose that it spends its first few days in a drugged condition. Pediatrician T. Berry Brazelton of Harvard University found that drugged babies had trouble learning to suck and began to gain weight 24 hours later than a control group of unmedicated babies.

Heavily drugged babies may have slow heart and circulatory rates, bluish extremities, and an impaired ability to clear mucus from air passageways. The stimulation of the birth process may wake them, but only for a short time. Brazelton reports that some drugged babies seem alert in the delivery room, only to lapse into a drugged state in the nursery.

Obviously, a drugged mother and a drugged baby have a hard time relating to each other during the first few days. When Ester Conway and Yvonne Brackbill followed a group of babies, they found that, a year after delivery, babies whose mothers had received medication during labor were still performing much more poorly on standard tests of behavior than babies of undrugged mothers.

And the more heavily drugged the mother had been, the worse the infant performed. Mothers who had required heavy medication differed from mothers requiring less medication, but Conway and Brackbill also discovered that the performance of the baby was related to the type of medication administered, and that the poorest performance levels followed the use of inhalant drugs. Whether the effects are permanent is still unknown.

In the United States, childbirth is often expected to be long and painful, even repellent. Our obstetrical procedures seem based on the premise that labor and birth are not natural experiences but a serious disease. Until recently, women have responded with deliveries that bore out the premise. Now research and practice have begun to dispel the image of suffering.

Women who have been prepared for childbirth, and who are allowed to go through the birth with a minimum of disturbance and with the support of their husbands, often describe their experience in terms that bear little resemblance to deliveries based on the pain and suffering model. Even women who report a good deal of pain also report feelings of joy, bliss, rapture, and ecstasy.

My own studies have noted a similarity between a woman's behavior during orgasm and at the birth of a baby. In both conditions there is fast, deep breathing in the early stages, the holding of breath at the climax, a tendency to make gasping noises, facial contortions, upper uterine contractions, contraction of abdominal muscles, the loss of sensory perception as delivery or orgasm approaches, and a sense of euphoria at the end.

A mother's emotional attachment to her baby appears to intensify in the few hours after birth if she is awake and allowed to hold the baby. Breast-feeding is a powerful process that conditions both the mother and the child to a mutually pleasant and healthful interaction. When a baby sucks at the breast, sensory impulses go to the mother's pituitary gland, causing the release of oxytocin. Oxytocin causes the mother's uterus to contract, helping it return to normal size. The hormone also causes the grapelike alveoli in the breast, which hold milk, to contract, letting down milk for the baby.

Research on the nature of pregnancy is beginning to demonstrate what sensitive parents have long known. When pregnancy begins with a rich emotional and sexual relationship, mother and growing fetus continue the pattern. Many psychological and physiological patterns learned in the parents' relationship with each other are carried over to create a bonding between parents and child.

The nutrients, heartbeat, and sleeping patterns that are shared by the mother and the fetus during pregnancy continue after the baby has been born. Hormones such as oxytocin that are present during intercourse, childbirth, and lactation provide a similar physiological basis for these processes, and the emotional reactions appear to be parallel in all. The result of these emotional patterns is the bonding of parents' and baby into patterns of mutual pleasure and caring that promote the survival of the species. ☐

For further information:

Brackbill, Yvonne. "Obstetrical Medication and Infant Behavior." *Handbook of Infant Development*, ed. J. D. Osofsky. John Wiley & Sons, 1978.

Gennser, Gerhard, Karel Marshal, and Bo Brantmark. "Maternal Smoking and Fetal Breathing Movements." *American Journal of Obstetrics and Gynecology*, Vol. 123, No. 8, 1975.

Jacobson, H. N. "Nutrition." *Scientific Foundations of Obstetrics and Gynecology*, ed. Elliot E. Philipp, Josephine Barnes, and Michael Newton. William Heineman Ltd., 1977.

Jones, Kenneth L., David W. Smith, Christy N. Ulleland, and Ann Pytkowicz Streissguth. "Pattern of Malformation in Offspring of Chronic Alcoholic Mothers." *The Lancet*, June 9, 1973, pp. 1267-1271.

Mead, Margaret, and Niles Newton. "Cultural Patterning of Perinatal Behavior." *Childbearing: Its Social and Psychological Aspects*, ed. S. A. Richardson and A. F. Guttmacher. The Williams & Wilkins Co., 1967.

Newton, Niles. "Emotions of Pregnancy." *Clinical Obstetrics and Gynecology*, Vol. 6, 1963, pp. 639-668.

Newton, Niles. "On Parenthood." *Handbook of Sexology*, ed. John Money and Herman Musaph. Elsevier/North Holland Biomedical Press, 1977.

Sontag, Lester W. "Implications of Fetal Behavior and Environment for Adult Personalities." *Annals New York Academy of Sciences*, Vol. 134, 1966, pp. 782-786.

Walker, David, James Grimwade, and Carl Wood. "Intrauterine Noise: A Component of the Fetal Environment." *American Journal of Obstetrics and Gynecology*, Vol. 109, No. 1, 1971.

Niles Newton *is professor of psychology at Northwestern University Medical School in Chicago. She has been studying childbirth and reproduction for many years. With Margaret Mead, she investigated the way different cultures treat reproduction. She conducted some of the first research in this country on human lactation. In one series of experiments she served as a subject, nursing her seven-month-old baby in a study that established oxytocin as the hormone responsible for the reflex that lets down milk in human beings. Newton also has studied the effects of stress during labor, and has surveyed women to discover their reactions to their hysterectomies. Her latest research explores the role of the hormone oxytocin in coitus, childbirth, and lactation. Newton is associate editor of* Birth and Family Journal *and a member of the executive board of the International Society of Psychosomatic Obstetrics and Gynecology.*

Charlotte Modahl *is a doctoral student in psychology at Northern Illinois University. She is collaborating with Newton on a study of hormonal similarities in coitus, childbirth, and lactation. Modahl is also working on a longitudinal study of sex-related legal cases, exploring sexual symbolism in psychic trauma. With Newton, she recently wrote an article on mood differences between mothers who nurse their babies and those who bottle-feed them.*

2

Crucial Questions of an Expectant Mother

"Will My Belly Button Ever Be the Same?"

By Maryann Bucknum Brinley

For several months after Senior Editor Maryann Brinley walked into the office last November and announced with some disbelief that she was pregnant, we all responded somewhat like proud, overanxious, doting in-laws. "Are you eating enough?" we asked. "Sit down and rest!" we ordered. "Here are some crackers for your morning sickness," we offered.

"I have no morning sickness," she told us time and time again. "I'm eating plenty. I feel great. I don't need any more rest."

As the months went by, she seemed to defy all the standard symptoms of pregnancy, leaving the staff with the strange problem of having a very cheerful pregnant editor around with no leg aches, no morning sickness, no fatigue—no complaints at all.

Finally, one day she deposited herself in my office and, with panic in her eyes, allowed as she had one horrifying thought plaguing her. She had heard that now that she was five months along, a strange and terrifying thing was about to happen: Her stomach, about to be stretched to its limit over the next four months, was going to become so distended that her belly button would spread, flatten out and disappear entirely. It was an unthinkable possibility; a problem no ordinary human being should have to contend with.

We were so pleased to have something to worry about that we suggested she jot down all her particular, personal responses to her pregnancy so that other expectant mothers with none of the usual symptoms could have something to relate to.

And she did. As you read this, Maryann will be days-close to giving birth. We will let you know in a subsequent issue whether her belly button ever returned.

–The Editor

The New York subways are full of them. It's not that you can't find them in any town or city in the United States, it's just that I seemed to be noticing them more and more. In fact, I was compelled to take stock of all of them that day on the way home from my visit to my obstetrician's office.

At one end of the car, an elderly woman with wild, matted hair and at least 14 ratty shopping bags sat cooing and mumbling to herself, thoroughly engrossed in her own smelly world . . . a world that must have been lonely if the empty seats around her were any indication. When was the last time she had taken a bath? The two teenage boys with the fresh crops of pimples who

> **"Am I happy?" my husband had asked on the phone when I called him with the positive news of my pregnancy test. "Yes, yes, ecstatically!"**

were slouching on the seats across from her couldn't contain their ugly laughter and were even throwing bits of wadded up newspaper, wet with their saliva, across the aisle. The old man in the ripped, rumpled suit clutching his pint of cheap wine—I could just about make out the label because

its brown paper camouflage wasn't working too well—could barely keep his eyes open as he slurped and sipped and sprawled across three seats. And coughed. I think he tried to smile at me.

I sat and I stared up and down the length of the train as it bumped and jerked downtown. Creeps, weirdos, nose-pickers, the *haaarrrummpers* who were constantly clearing their throats, the diseased, deformed, miserable, warty, stinky . . . all manner of humankind. Ugh.

I understand full well that it takes all types to make an interesting, vital world. And yes, I do love humanity with its endless variety. But this sudden fixation on the weirdest ones—the shopping bag lady and the drunken derelict—was new to me. I used to simply avoid eye contact or not even look at all. That day, though, I was gaping, unable to avert my eyes. But it was also that day, at the obstetrician's, that I had heard my unborn baby's heartbeat for the first time. And I wondered, amid my excitement: Did I really want to bring a child into this strange cross-section of humanity? More important, would my little girl end up with 14 shopping bags and dirty hair; my little boy with a bottle of cheap whiskey in a torn breast pocket?

"Am I happy?" my husband had asked tentatively on the phone when I called him several months before with the positive news of my pregnancy test. Well, well—in spite of a new job, 1,001 other commitments, or what our childless friends might think—yes, yes, ecstatically!

From the very beginning, my emotions had been in flux. Me? Pregnant? But that's incredible. I had always firmly believed that pregnancy only occurred in *other* women—women who had thought long and hard about the exact timing for becoming mothers . . . that even though the biology books told me that conception was the logical end result of sexual intercourse,

13

it just wouldn't happen to *me* that way . . . that it was something I would try some day at the *right* time in my life, my career, my marriage . . . that I would carefully plan my family when that *right* time arrived. But would there ever have been a perfectly *right* time for me?

For most normal human females, pregnancy lasts approximately 280 days. (Statistics tell us that 95 percent of all babies are born between the 266th and 294th day after their conception.) Two hundred and eighty days doesn't sound like a very long time, and it isn't. Actually, it is definitely a short spell when one considers the monumental changes that a woman must go through—physically and psychologically.

ic! With all the babies, both wanted and unwanted, being born all the time, baby-making odds are still incredible to me. A sperm cell has an average life of about 48 hours inside the female reproductive tract. Meanwhile, an unfertilized egg lives for about 12 to 24 hours once a month. If sexual intercourse doesn't take place exactly on target, when both egg and sperm are ready, nothing will happen. A couple really only has about three days each menstrual cycle to make a child of their own, according to research studies. And, in spite of temperature calculating and various other methods of geometric configuring that promise to predict the perfect moment, it can still be quite a match game to hit this

(that's the only thing that was "showing" at that point), she guessed my own joy. That was all there was—two knowing glances exchanged. However, the episode signaled the beginning of something downright odd. At least, it seemed so to me at the time. In the next few weeks, my ability to pick out other pregnant women on the streets, in supermarkets, on buses—they were all over—became uncanny.

But my moods can and do swing. On the down days, I've been known to cry about an overripe banana. At those times, I also worry and see the hurt side of humanity, the people who make life, especially the prospect of a new one, difficult to swallow.

My friend Fran tells me that when she was pregnant, she received a piece of mail one day announcing that one out of every 87 children was born with some dread deformity. Instead of putting her check in the mail for such a worthy cause, she was stricken, like I was on the subway. What could she do? She promptly walked down the street to the nearest schoolyard in her Brooklyn neighborhood and began counting the youngsters at play. After she had reached number 86, she paused, wondering—the way I did as I stared at the shopping bag lady—would her little one be number 87? Of course, it wasn't.

On the up days, though, I'm untouchable, "impregnable." There's none of that subway stuff or hysterical head counting; only my clear conviction that I am carrying a beautiful, healthy child.

At my first visit to the doctor—an excitable, opinionated, wonderful woman—when I asked her if I would be nauseated in the morning and tired in the evening, she answered: "You are not going to be sick. Pregnancy is not an illness. You, Maryann, are going to be happy and healthy." Well, there's nothing like the power of positive thinking to ward off disease and disability—with a little help from prenatal vitamins, extra iron tablets and an unwavering appetite. Last winter, everyone I know suffered through colds, intestinal flus, coughs, viruses. Not me. Nothing more than an occasional stomach fluttering demanding a cracker before it would settle and go away. Still, I was the one people asked, sometimes in stuffed-up, hacking voices, "How are you feeling?"

Along with my "impregnable" days come the doubts. About the time my unborn baby began sucking his or her thumb (around 14 weeks), I suddenly thought: "But I don't feel motherly. I'm not one of those women who peeks at babies in carriages and beams. Also, what happens to *me* after the baby comes? Will I still be able to be a separate person or must I be—for the rest of my life and to the exclusion of all else—someone's mother?"

And, as the doubts increase, so does the

Illustration by Peter Bramley

Flooded with thoughts of what my baby would be like, I became obsessed with all the weirdos on the streets of New York.

The physical side of this transformation—though it may be the most obvious, the most well recorded in books and magazines (and obstetrical charts) and in many ways, the more interesting part of pregnancy for others—is only half of what happens. My growing belly may be my statement to the rest of the world, but more amazing to me are the funny feelings, quirks, heady stirrings and the very new ways I look at life.

For months now, I've been walking, talking, acting the same as I used to. But I am changed. I watch events with the knowing eyes of a person with a secret. I am harboring a little human being. What mag-

nail on the head. I often wonder why odds-maker "Jimmy the Greek" hasn't gotten involved.

But, never mind the odds and statistics: The plain and ever-growing fact is that it did work for my husband, me and our little person who has been given a start—with nary a nod or helping hand from any Greek gambler, I might add.

Most of the time, we are a secret three. On occasion, however, I can give this secret away, without ever opening my mouth. It happened once. Suddenly, there she was, looking big and pregnant but so, so happy. I understood her smile and, perhaps from my wide-eyed expression action. The movements around week 20, called "quickening," when the little person is exploring and swimming about the warm, wet world of the womb, are awesome. They just can't be dismissed as intestinal rumblings. Sitting in an elegant French restaurant at a staff luncheon with my hands on my stomach, my little one instantly comes to life and vigorously pushes my hands up and away from what has now been declared his or her territory. I jump and realize that I am not the only one who is contented with my meal.

At week 24, though, I am shocked when the skin on my belly is stretching and itching and I think, my god, what will happen to my belly button? No one ever explained *that* part to me before! By week 30, it just may flatten out altogether, as the books predict. I am dumbstruck. My husband tells me to look on the brighter side and be thankful that this will be the year I can finally clean all the lint out of my navel; but, for some profound reason, I can't laugh. While others are concerned about the snowstorms and preparing their taxes, I sit there, almost humorless, hung up on my belly button. Will it return next summer and be the same one I have always known?

(A young doctor in a midwestern hospital became fascinated by the different ways women's navels change during pregnancy. He was so taken by what appeared to be two distinct patterns—some flatten out, others pop up—that he decided to keep a record to see whether these variations had any bearing on the sex of the future offspring. Would outies be boys and flatties girls? Unfortunately for me, since I do seem to be more interested in this research than my not-pregnant colleagues, he found absolutely nothing.)

Other unusual side effects mysteriously appear. My ears ache whenever I put on a pair of pierced earrings (even the hypo-allergenic kind). After the doctor could find no rational, medical explanation, and after I had asked in the right circles, looking for an applicable old wives' tale, I came across someone else who had suffered the same agony. Bonnie, a friend with three children, assured me that after delivering each baby, her ears returned to normal. Which is great news, since I was beginning to wonder just what I would do with one slightly used but much-loved collection of pierced earrings.

One of the most disconcerting aspects of later pregnancy is directly related to my rapidly expanding waistline. Though my body is awkwardly different, I don't always see myself as others do: I'm still the same person despite the fact that I look like I've swallowed a basketball. (For some women, it seems more like a watermelon; mine is a basketball.)

I remember one morning on the train when I was about five and a half months along and had to stand in the aisle because of an overcrowded run. Liberated as I've become, I saw nothing unusual about not receiving an offer from a gentleman for a seat. It was winter and warm in the car and I had taken off my coat. When the train went through a darkened tunnel, I glimpsed my reflection in the opposite window. Why, I looked like a pregnant lady! Could it really be me? (And though this isn't the point of my tale, if it was me with the pronouncedly pregnant belly, why *didn't* someone offer me a seat?)

My body does indeed shock even me, its owner. And my shock of recognition on the train is nothing compared to the bemused wonder with which my husband and I watch the bare-naked changes that are taking place. Bob assures me that I am still the same desirable woman he fell in love with, but . . . when my bikini underpants ripple down (they just won't cover that basketball anymore) and are straddling the tops of my thighs, it's hard to walk right, let alone feel sexy. It's also difficult to concentrate on love because our little creation tries to join in with kicks and punches at those intimate times. Already he or she doesn't want to be left out of anything! (Research has shown that this miniature human being, who from six months on, wakes, sleeps, relaxes, naps in favorite spots, opens and closes his or her eyes, and even hiccups, also responds to the mother's emotional ups and downs.) Nevertheless, they tell me that if I can retain my sense of humor, love will survive.

And there are other things that "they"—those pregnant, formerly pregnant and "authorities" on pregnancy—say. I know because I have canvassed them all, and have learned that at the end of these ten lunar months (technically speaking), my husband and I will rediscover more than an intact love affair. "They" explain comfortingly that all my normal, predictable doubts, frustrations, ups and downs will be worth it . . . that the *me* I am worried about losing will still be here after my baby arrives . . . and that, in fact, this *me* may be thoroughly enriched by the state called motherhood. It is all very reassuring but I'm not quite assured . . . yet.

Maybe by Mother's Day, I'll understand what "they" mean—especially because that second Sunday in May is supposed to take on a different meaning . . . one that can only be fully appreciated by those who have run this nine-month gauntlet called pregnancy. This particular prediction, by the nameless authorities that be, does fascinate me since as holidays go, I've never fully grasped how it could bring so much joy to my own mother.

As one of the six children she bore, I have enjoyed the day as a fun, family get-together time, but she, as the mother of us all, seems to reap so much from it . . . more than the crazy cards, dinners, celebrations or homemade gifts actually warrant. The only year I can recall understanding a good measure of what she was going through was the year we, her six grown youngsters, gave her a bicycle. When we pointed her toward her present, she was positively stunned by the sight of it on the front lawn. The fact that she had never ridden a bicycle in her life might have been reason enough for her amazement! I could comprehend that much. But as soon as she had become used to the idea that we were going to teach her to ride a bike and she was comfortably seated behind the handle bars, her look turned from one of fearful amazement to positive, unfathomable happiness. A kind of happiness the rest of us couldn't begin to know.

This year, since I am due to give birth in mid-May, I just may discover a small part of those mysterious but apparently wondrous feelings she feels. At least that's what "they" tell me. ■

II. The First Two Years

Photograph by Leslie E. Palmer

The period of infancy has traditionally been of great interest to psychologists as well as to parents, because many believe that the differential experiences of children during the first two years lead to psychological qualities that may last for years to come. Undoubtedly, the way the infant is treated in the home has an obvious and significant effect on the child at that time. The infant who is spoken to and played with frequently is livelier and more alert than one who lies in the crib for most of the day. The child who is abused or abandoned is less stable emotionally than one who has nurturant care. However, there is some controversy regarding the stability of these first dispositions in the face of important changes in future environments.

Despite the variation among children that is a product of different treatment, the maturation of the central nervous system guarantees that certain milestones will appear in all children with an intact nervous system. Discovering these milestones and their time of appearance is one of the important tasks of developmental psychology. Some of these include the attachment of the baby to its caretaker, the enhanced ability to recall the past, and the fear of strangers and separation, which appear during the last half of the first year; symbolic play and understanding of language at the end of the first year; the emergence of the first intelligible words at 18 to 22 months; and, as the second year ends, the appearance of standards and the first sense of self-awareness.

A second controversy concerns the function of differences in infant temperament. Many psychologists have noted that during the opening days and months of life, babies differ in level of irritability, activity level, placidity, timidity, and ease with which sleeping and feeding cycles are established. But psychologists do not know how stable each of these tendencies is. Of course, there is an interaction between the child's temperamental qualities and the kind of handling he or she receives. An irritable child with a mature, understanding mother is less likely to suffer from this irritability than the same child born to an immature parent who has a low frustration tolerance. The psychological outcome of a particular temperamental attribute will always be a function of the kind of family environment the child encounters.

A third controversy concerns attachment. Although all infants become attached to their caretakers to some degree, some psychologists and psychiatrists believe that during the first year of life the infant should have an uninterrupted and unshared relationship with a single caretaker, preferably the biological mother. Deviations from this ideal are expected to produce an anxious and emotionally insecure infant who will be vulnerable to psychological difficulties at a later age. This assumption leads some parents to be wary about surrogate care for their children and makes some mothers question whether they can pursue a full-time career while raising a young child.

Many psychologists regard the appearance of language as the most significant development of the first two years of life. Although most children begin to understand language early in the second year and to speak single words sometime before their second birthday, the reasons for the first appearance of language during the last half of the second year and the lawful growth of language within a particular society are still unknown. For example, the child understands more than he or she can say; the first words typically describe objects (a bottle, a ball) rather than actions (jump, sit). Moreover, just before the second birthday the child begins to replace words that name objects with descriptions of his or her own actions. Although maturation of the central nervous system is as necessary for the comprehension and speaking of language as it is for motor development, such as sitting, standing, or walking, the reasons for the particular sequence of language forms remains very much a mystery.

In sum, maturation of the central nervous system, differences in temperament, and experiences in the family are three important factors that promote development and introduce subtle variations among children. Although there is great interest in the psychological differences between boys and girls, between different ethnic groups, and between healthy and less healthy children, we need to remember that the similarities among two-year-olds around the world are far more striking than the differences.

3

Growing By Leaps:
The Form of Early Development

by Jerome Kagan

The cooling of Cape Cod in autumn is gradual; the first snowstorm is more abrupt. The thickening of the lens of the eye in the development of the embryo is gradual, cumulative and continuous, but the appearance of the neural crest is relatively sudden and discontinuous. In viewing developmental phenomena, whether biological or psychological, we can assume one of two complementary attitudes. One favors continuity, cumulativeness and a long history; the alternative favors emergence, discontinuity and a shorter history. Both patterns are plentiful in nature, but the tradition in Western thought favors a long chain of connected causes and effects and is prejudiced against discontinuities. Modern developmental psychologists share this view and typically posit a closely connected set of stages in describing the acquisition of psychological competencies.

Keeping the Faith

There are several considerations that maintain a faith in the connectivity of psychological structures. These include our desire to attain an egalitarian society through proper management of the early experiences of children. We believe we can prepare for the future and we urge mothers to engage in certain practices with their infants, implying that such behaviors will have a permanent effect on the child's future psychological health.

A quite different basis for belief in connectivity comes from the nature of our language. The adjectives we select to describe people rarely refer to the age of the actor or to the context of the action. Like the names of colors they imply stability over time and location. We use words like "passive" or "intelligent" to describe infants and adults as if the meanings of those words were not altered by maturation. The belief in a material link between infancy and later childhood is also a consequence of entrenched practices in our society, especially a tendency to rank children on valued traits. When children begin school they are ordered on academic ability and it is

From *The Sciences*, April 1979 © 1979 by The New York Academy of Sciences.

a fact that most retain their rank order for at least a decade.

Finally, psychological science, which is strongly dependent on the natural sciences, is reductionistic. The belief that experience produces a permanent change in the central nervous system, added to the corollary that the brain directs thought and behavior, leads the average citizen to conclude that early experience must be connected to later experience: The iron filings on the fresh tape that serves as a metaphor for the infant's mind will be permanently altered and if no one erases the message it will be preserved with fidelity for an indefinite period.

Yet although there are both historically near and far bases for the belief in connectiveness and continuity in human development, recent investigations of infants are suggesting that some psychological functions emerge rather suddenly as a result of maturational changes in the central nervous system. And I suspect that future research will reveal that there are a great many competencies that appear with relative suddenness, much as a large rose bush successively reveals its blossoms during the first three weeks of May.

In the First Year

Consider, for example, the changes that occur between the ages of eight and twelve months. A decade of empirical inquiry by many investigators has revealed a remarkable group of events that seem to emerge together during the last three or four months of the first year of life.

Toward the end of the first year the infant frequently displays greater attention to a variety of interesting occurrences than he or she did at the age of six or seven months. If masks or drawings of human faces are shown to children four to 36 months of age, the infants' attention is prolonged at four months, markedly lower at seven to eight months, then increases through the second and third years. This U-shaped developmental function holds not only for North American children but also for rural Mexican and Guatemalan children as well.

18

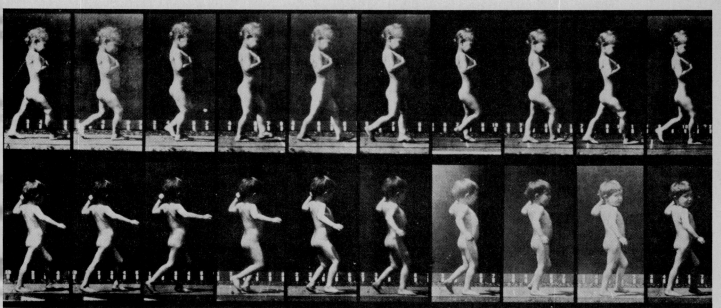

Plate 540 from the series *Animal Locomotion* (c. 1887), by Eadweard Muybridge. The Museum of Modern Art, N.Y.

But increased attention is only part of the picture. Before seven months of age the infant typically reaches at once for a novel object that is unexpectedly presented after repeated presentations of a different object. An eleven-month old, however, typically shows a short but obvious delay before reaching for the novel object—an inhibition response. It also appears that infants who can crawl do not always show avoidance of the deep side of what looks to them like a cliff until after seven months of age, even though these infants are capable of perceiving the difference between the deep and shallow sides. Finally, inhibition is the predominant reaction of one-year olds to the introduction of an unfamiliar child: The child suddenly stops playing, stops vocalizing, and may retreat to a familiar caretaker.

Toward the end of the first year there is also a dramatic increase in the likelihood of signs of stress—or anxiety—to unusual or unfamiliar events. The effect of the appearance of an unfamiliar adult has been investigated many times and the consensus from these studies is that crying and other signs of anxiety to the stranger appear at seven months, grow dramatically between that time and the end of the first year, and then decline. The course of development of separation anxiety is similar among children being raised in the United States, the barrios of urban Guatemala, subsistence farming Indian villages in the Guatemalan highlands, Israeli kibbutzim, !Kung San bands in the Kalahari desert, and among infants diagnosed as suffering from failure to thrive. Crying following maternal departure in an unfamiliar setting tends to emerge at about eight months, rises to a peak at thirteen to fifteen months and then declines. This pattern appears to be so universal that even in blind children the developmental course of anxiety in response to both strangers and maternal separation is not seriously different from that noted in sighted children.

Finally, one of the most reliable phenomena of the first year of life is the emergence of what the Swiss psychologist Jean Piaget has called object permanence: Prior to eight months of age most children will not retrieve a toy or prized object that they have watched being hidden under a cover. After eight months the retrieval is reliable.

Enhanced Memory

I believe that the nearly simultaneous appearance of these phenomena—increased attentiveness, inhibition, distress at strangers and separation, and object permanence—results from the maturation emergence of several related cognitive abilities. Perhaps the most important of these is the enhanced ability to retrieve a schema related to present experience, and the ability to retain the old schema and the new experience in active memory while the child compares the two pieces of information in an attempt to resolve their potential inconsistency. Following departure of the mother, the ten-month-old generates from memory the schema of her former presence in the room and holds that knowledge in active memory while comparing it with the present. If the child cannot resolve the inconsistency inherent in that comparison, he or she becomes uncertain and may cry. Thus, I believe the universal growth function for separation distress, as well as other fears, is related to an enhancement of memory.

Still, my hypothetical sequence is not completely satisfactory for several reasons. First, the one-year-old occasionally cries when his or her caretaker merely walks toward the exit without leaving. Second, the child does not cry or become upset in similar situations of comparing past and present and being unable to resolve the discrepancies they contain. So additional processes must be postulated if we are to explain the separation findings.

One possibility is that the enhanced ability to retrieve and hold a representation of past experience is correlated with the ability to generate anticipations of the future—representations of possible events. I believe that the nine-month-old has a new capacity we might describe as "the disposition to predict future events and to generate responses to deal with discrepant situations." The child, for the first time, tries to cope with unfamiliar experiences rather than just assimilate them. If children cannot generate a prediction or instrumental response, they become vulnerable to uncertainty and, therefore, distress. If they can successfully generate the prediction they may laugh, and laughter during anticipation of a novel event increases after eight months of age.

We are left with one final puzzle. Why does the presence of either a familiar person — such as the parent — or a familiar setting so dramatically reduce the occurrence of uncertainty and crying in response to maternal departure, the presence of strangers, or any discrepant event?

The interpretation I prefer is that the presence of the familiar person or setting provides the child with opportunities for responses when uncertainty is generated. Recognition of the opportunity to issue a familiar action buffers uncertainty. Distress does not occur when the mother leaves the child with the father because the father's presence provides the child with a potential target for his behaviors. That knowledge keeps uncertainty under control. This interpretation is profoundly cognitive; the infant does not have to move toward the father, the infant has only to know that he is present. The blind one-year-old does not have to see the mother to be protected against distress, only know that the mother is in the room.

Freud's Prophetic Insight

This increased ability to hold past and current experience in active memory, and the ability to deal cognitively with the past, the present, and the unexpected, may be direct consequences of maturational changes in the central nervous system. Since many physiologists believe neural control of sleep shifts from the brainstem to forebrain mechanisms during the first year, it is reasonable to suggest that the diverse behavioral changes that suddenly and rather uniformly appear toward the end of the first year are caused by structural or biochemical events that

are essential components of the individual's biological development.

Apparently, Freud was approaching a similar insight toward the end of his career. In a prophetic paragraph he questioned the formative power he had assigned earlier to variation in infant experience with a caretaker and suggested that maturational forces would guarantee that infants would display some common developmental profile. Freud wrote, "The phylogenetic foundation has so much the upper hand over personal accidental experience that it makes no difference whether a child has sucked at the breast or has been brought up on the bottle and never enjoyed the tenderness of a mother's care. In both cases the child's development takes the same path."

Other Milestones

There appear to be other periods of infancy that are characterized by the relatively sudden emergence of psychologicial competencies. These milestones are more recent discoveries than the phenomena that characterize the period eight-to-twelve months, and they are presented with considerably more tentativeness. They are, however, inductions from data and not *a priori* expectations based on some sophisticated theory of the first two years of life.

These later milestones were discovered in the context of a study involving two groups of infants: the younger group was seen monthly from thirteen to twenty-two months of age; the older group was seen every month between the ages of twenty and twenty-nine months. There were sixteen infants in each group.

One of the questions we wanted to answer was whether children in the second year of life are capable of dealing with perceptual categories such as symmetry, seriation and number. To find this out we showed all the children a screen on which we projected pairs of chromatic slides, each illustrating a particular category. Each of the first ten pairs illustrated a different example of the same category, but the two pictures presented on any one trial were identical. For example, if the category being tested was *seriation,* on the first trial the child might see a pair of identical slides each showing four trees seriated with respect to size. On the second trial the child might see a pair of slides illustrating four seriated dolls. Then on the eleventh trial—the critical one—the child was shown a pair of slides in which one picture was a new instance of the category with which the child was being familiarized, while the other was a new instance of the complementary category. The complementary categories we explored were man/dog, same/different, two/four, seriation/non-seriation, child/self, and symmetry/asymmetry. Thus, if the relevant series had to do with seriation, the child might be shown a set of seriated dogs along with a non-seriated arrangement of dogs on the critical eleventh trial.

The important variable in this context is the change in the child's heart rate during the familiarization series. When a child's attention is engaged by an event he or she is trying to assimilate, the child's heart rate tends to stabilize; that is, the difference between the fastest and slowest heart rate during a period of attention is low—usually under five or six beats.

During our chromatic slide trials we coded the fixation time of each child to each picture and monitored their heart rates continually. When we looked at the mean heart rate range of the children across all concepts and across the entire period from thirteen to 29 months of age, we discovered that the heart rate was most stable at the age of seventeen months.

I believe that this result implies that the age of seventeen months is the approximate time when the middle-class American children in our sample began to shift from a perceptual to a more symbolic-linguistic mode of processing stimuli. Marvin Minsky of MIT has used the word "frame" to capture the meaning I intend. Human beings approach an experience with a dominant frame or *Aufgabe*. Adults have several frames they can adopt. Faced with a printed essay one can "read" it for meaning, for typographical errors, or for grace of style. And while we are operating under one frame it is possible—though difficult—to process it at another level.

Infants are not as versatile. It is likely that before sixteen or seventeen months of age they use only one frame in processing our pictures; they attend to the perceptual qualities of the event. But by the middle of the second year they have shifted frames and are attending to the linguistic meaning of the event. A hypothetical eighteen-month-old faced with a picture of four seriated giraffes is prompted to ask privately, "What is that?" That orientation subdues the attention to pattern that the infant used a few months earlier. Support for this idea comes from the fact that more younger than older children behaved as if they detected concepts involving perceptual pattern, such as symmetry and seriation.

There are other data that lend support to the notion that seventeen to twenty months is a critical developmental era. We recorded the child's spontaneous speech during two play sessions that occurred on two different days each month. Roger Brown of Harvard has found that the mean length of the child's utterance demonstrates lawful growth. There is a sharp rise in mean length of utterance at about seventeen months—the time when most children begin to speak for the first time. Thus, the marked decrease in heart rate range that we observe in response to the pictures occurs at about the same time that these children are first beginning to speak spontaneously.

The reasons why children begin to speak in the middle of the second year are still unclear. Children thirteen to fifteen months of age know the meanings of many words, even though they are usually not yet talking. It is likely that several factors are relevant including the ability to gain access to the word (that is, to recall the words they wish to use), the realization that words name things in the real world, and the desire to fix the names of objects correctly. This leads us to our last milestone.

Meeting Their Own Standards

Each month we observed our same 32 children in a twenty-minute session in which they were first permitted to play with some toys while their mother and a familiar woman sat on a couch talking quietly. At the end of ten minutes the woman came to the child, sat down on the floor and indicated she was going to play. While the child sat on the mother's lap the woman modelled three different action sequences in front of the child. The sequences were appropriate to the age of the child; that is, they were neither too easy nor too difficult for the child to understand or implement. For example, when the children were thirteen, fourteen and fifteen months old, the woman would feed a toy zebra with a toy bottle, put a doll to bed, and wash a doll's face. At 22 months the three acts were a little more difficult. For children this age the model put a telephone to a doll's ear; simulated a cooking sequence with two dolls, two plates and a toy pot; and made three animals walk and then made them hide under a cover to avoid some rain. All the actions were accompanied by appropriate verbal explantions. After completing the actions the woman said that it was the child's turn to play and returned to the couch. It is important to note that the woman never told the child to imitate the behaviors he or she had just seen.

To our surprise we found that as the children approached their second birthdays they began to show unambiguous signs of distress during the minute after the model completed her actions. Many children would cry, cling to their mothers and refuse to play; some had tantrums. We interpret this to indicate that the 22-to-23-month-olds felt an obligation to imitate the model but experienced uncertainty over their ability to do so. The failure to meet a self-generated standard led to distress.

If this explanation is valid then it would appear that by the age of twenty to 23 months children come to recognize that there are correct and incorrect—proper and improper—responses. This display of distress to the model's actions may be the earliest form of what in later childhood will be called fear of failure. If the child of 22 or 23 months has become concerned with correct behavior, other changes might be seen at this time, especially an enhancement of language and more intense motivation to solve problems.

The relatively sudden enhancement of memory we have seen between eight and twelve months, the adoption by the child of a symbolic frame in the middle of the second year, and the appreciation of standards of competence and correctness that appears near the second birthday are different functions. One source of theoretical controversy surrounding these phenomena concerns the degree of connectivity among them

and their link to the competencies of the first year of life.

Do these processes have short histories and emerge as a function of the maturation of special areas in the central nervous system? Or does each of these trace part of its origin to competencies and events that go back many months, perhaps even to the first half year? The distress that follows the model's actions requires, as a prerequisite, that the child attempt to remember what the model has done. We have suggested that this competency appears between the ages of eight and twelve months. Thus the enhanced memory competency at one year appears to be a necessary precondition for the anxiety following the model's actions seen at two years of age. But that statement is different from one that

declares that the distress at age two is part of a connected sequence that began with the earlier enhancement of memory. There is nothing in the earlier memory ability that implies the experience of distress following the failure to meet a standard one year later.

This is not to deny that there is connectivity and stability of structures in a child's development. I believe that there is a great deal of such continuity despite surface change. Cognitive structures representing motives, standards, knowledge and beliefs about the self, I am certain, exhibit considerable stability over time. But such structures typically emerge after the period of infancy—following the initial establishment of the executive function we call the "self."   □

Jerome Kagan is professor of human development at Harvard University. His most recent book, with Richard Kearsley and Philip Zelazo, is INFANCY: ITS PLACE IN HUMAN DEVELOPMENT *(Harvard University Press, 1978).*

ETHNIC DIFFERENCES IN BABIES

4

Striking differences in temperament and behavior among ethnic groups show up in babies only a few days old.

DANIEL G. FREEDMAN

The human species comes in an admirable variety of shapes and colors, as a walk through any cosmopolitan city amply demonstrates. Although the speculation has become politically and socially unpopular, it is difficult not to wonder whether the major differences in physical appearances are accompanied by standard differences in temperament or behavior. Recent studies by myself and others of babies only a few hours, days, or weeks old indicate that they are, and that such differences among human beings are biological as well as cultural.

These studies of newborns from different ethnic backgrounds actually had their inception with work on puppies, when I attempted to raise dogs in either an indulged or disciplined fashion in order to test the effects of such rearing on their later behavior.

I spent all my days and evenings with these puppies, and it soon became apparent that the breed of dog would become an important factor in my results. Even as the ears and eyes opened, the breeds differed in behavior. Little beagles were irrepressibly friendly from the moment they could

detect me; Shetland sheepdogs were very, very sensitive to a loud voice or the slightest punishment; wire-haired terriers were so tough and aggressive, even as clumsy three-week-olds, that I had to wear gloves while playing with them; and finally, Basenjis, barkless dogs originating in Central Africa, were aloof and independent. To judge by where they spent their time, sniffing and investigating, I was no more important to them than if I were a rubber balloon.

When I later tested the dogs, the breed indeed made a difference in their behavior. I took them, when hungry, into a room with a bowl of meat. For three minutes I kept them from approaching the meat, then left each dog alone with the food. Indulged terriers and beagles waited longer before eating the meat than did disciplined dogs of the same breeds. None of the Shetlands ever ate any of the food, and all of the Basenjis ate as soon as I left.

I later studied 20 sets of identical and fraternal human twins, following them from infancy until they were 10 years old, and I became convinced that both puppies and human babies begin life

along developmental pathways established by their genetic inheritance. But I still did not know whether infants of relatively inbred human groups showed differences comparable to the breed differences among puppies that had so impressed me. Clearly, the most direct way to find out was to examine very young infants, preferably newborns, of ethnic groups with widely divergent histories.

Since it was important to avoid projecting my own assumptions onto the babies' behavior, the first step was to develop some sort of objective test of newborn behavior. With T. Berry Brazelton, the Harvard pediatrician, I developed what I called the Cambridge Behavioral and Neurological Assessment Scales, a group of simple tests of basic human reactions that could be administered to any normal newborn in a hospital nursery.

In the first study, Nina Freedman and I compared Chinese and Caucasian babies. It was no accident that we chose those two groups, since my wife is Chinese, and in the course of learning about each other and our families, we came to believe that some character

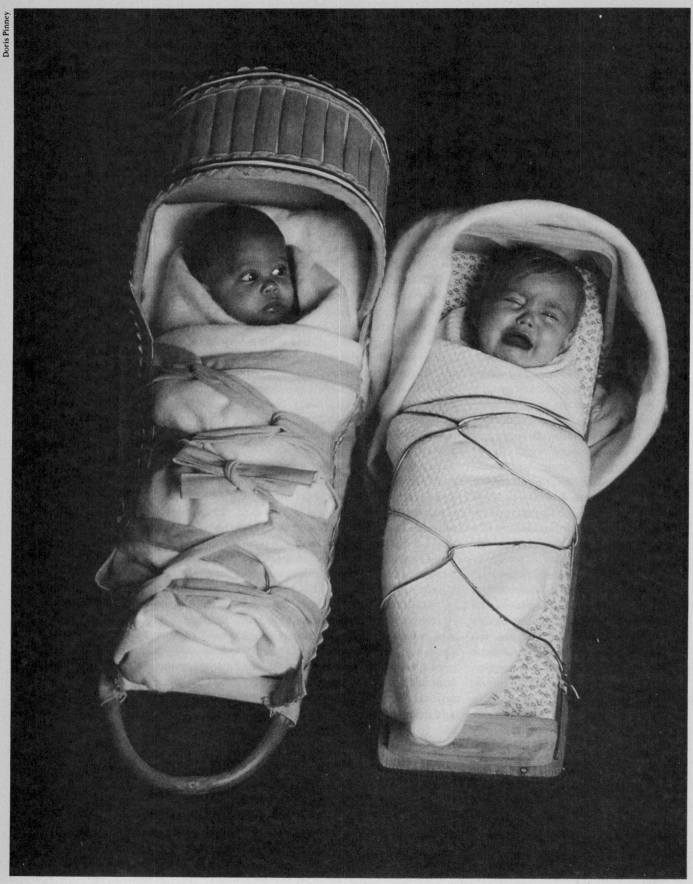

Most Navaho babies calmly accept the cradle board; Caucasian babies protest vigorously when strapped in one.

It was almost immediately clear that
we had struck pay dirt; Chinese and Caucasian babies indeed
behaved very differently.

differences might well be related to differences in our respective gene pools and not just to individual differences.

Armed with our new baby test, Nina and I returned to San Francisco, and to the hospital where she had borne our first child. We examined, alternately, 24 Chinese and 24 Caucasian newborns. To keep things neat, we made sure that all the Chinese were of Cantonese (South Chinese) background, the Caucasians of Northern European origin, that the sexes in both groups were the same, that the mothers were the same age, that they had about the same number of previous children, and that both groups were administered the same drugs in the same amounts. Additionally, all of the families were members of the same health plan, all of the mothers had had approximately the same number of prenatal visits to a doctor, and all were in the same middle-income bracket.

It was almost immediately clear that we had struck pay dirt; Chinese and Caucasian babies indeed behaved like two different breeds. Caucasian babies cried more easily, and once started, they were harder to console. Chinese babies adapted to almost any position in which they were placed; for example, when placed face down in their cribs, they tended to keep their faces buried in the sheets rather than immediately turning to one side, as did the Caucasians. In a similar maneuver (called the "defense reaction" by neurologists), we briefly pressed the baby's nose with a cloth. Most Caucasian and black babies fight this maneuver by immediately turning away or swiping at the cloth with their hands, and this is reported in most Western pediatric textbooks as the normal, expected response. The

average Chinese baby in our study, however, simply lay on his back and breathed through his mouth, "accepting" the cloth without a fight. This finding is most impressive on film.

Other subtle differences were equally important, but less dramatic. For example, both Chinese and Caucasian babies started to cry at about the same points in the examination, especially when they were undressed, but the Chinese stopped sooner. When picked up and cuddled, Chinese babies stopped crying immediately, as if a light switch had been flipped, whereas the crying of Caucasian babies only gradually subsided.

In another part of the test, we repeatedly shone a light in the baby's eyes and counted the number of blinks until the baby "adapted" and no longer blinked. It should be no surprise that the Caucasian babies continued to blink long after the Chinese babies had adapted and stopped.

It began to look as if Chinese babies were simply more amenable and adaptable to the machinations of the examiners, and that the Caucasian babies were registering annoyance and complaint. It was as if the old stereotypes of the calm, inscrutable Chinese and the excitable, emotionally changeable Caucasian were appearing spontaneously in the first 48 hours of life. In other words, our hypothesis about human and puppy parallels seemed to be correct.

The results of our Chinese-Caucasian study have been confirmed by a student of ethologist Nick Blurton-Jones who worked in a Chinese community in Malaysia. At the time, however, our single study was hardly enough

evidence for so general a conclusion, and we set out to look at other newborns in other places. Norbett Mintz, who was working among the Navaho in Tuba City, Arizona, arranged for us to come to the reservation in the spring of 1969. After two months we had tested 36 Navaho newborns, and the results paralleled the stereotype of the stoical, impassive American Indian. These babies outdid the Chinese, showing even more calmness and adaptability than we found among Oriental babies.

We filmed the babies as they were tested and found reactions in the film we had not noticed. For example, the Moro response was clearly different among Navaho and Caucasians. This reaction occurs in newborns when support for the head and neck suddenly disappears. Tests for the Moro response usually consist of raising and then suddenly dropping the head portion of the bassinet. In most Caucasian newborns, after a four-inch drop the baby reflexively extends both arms and legs, cries, and moves in an agitated manner before he calms down. Among Navajo babies, crying was rare, the limb movements were reduced, and calming was almost immediate.

I have since spent considerable time among the Navaho, and it is clear that the traditional practice of tying the wrapped infant onto a cradle board (now practiced sporadically on the reservation) has in no way induced stoicism in the Navaho. In the halcyon days of anthropological environmentalism, this was a popular conjecture, but the other way around is more likely. Not all Navaho babies take to the cradle board, and those who complain about it are simply taken off. But most Navaho infants calmly accept the

Navaho and Chinese newborns may be so
much alike because the Navaho were part of a relatively
recent emigration from Asia.

board; in fact, many begin to demand it by showing signs of unrest when off. When they are about six months old, however, Navaho babies do start complaining at being tied, and "weaning" from the board begins, with the baby taking the lead. The Navaho are the most "in touch" group of mothers we have yet seen, and the term mother-infant *unit* aptly describes what we saw among them.

James Chisholm of Rutgers University, who has studied infancy among the Navaho over the past several years, reports that his observations are much like my own. In addition, he followed a group of young Caucasian mothers in Flagstaff (some 80 miles south of the reservation) who had decided to use the cradle board. Their babies complained so persistently that they were off the board in a matter of weeks, a result that should not surprise us, given the differences observed at birth.

Assuming, then, that other investigators continue to confirm our findings, to what do we attribute the differences on the one hand, and the similarities on the other? When we first presented the findings on Chinese and Caucasians, attempts were made to explain away the genetic implications by posing differences in prenatal diets as an obvious cause. But once we had completed the Navaho study, that explanation had to be dropped, because the Navaho diet is quite different from the diet of the Chinese, yet newborn behavior was strikingly similar in the two groups.

The point is often still made that the babies had nine months of experience within the uterus before we saw them, so that cultural differences in maternal attitudes and behavior might have

been transferred to the unborn offspring via some, as yet unknown, mechanism. Chisholm, for example, thinks differences in maternal blood pressure may be responsible for some of the differences between Navahos and Caucasians, but the evidence is as yet sparse. Certainly Cantonese-American and Navaho cultures are substantially different and yet the infants are so much alike that such speculation might be dismissed on that score alone. But there is another, hidden issue here, and that involves our own cultural tendency to split apart inherited and acquired characteristics. Americans tend to eschew the inherited and promote the acquired, in a sort of "we are exactly what we make of ourselves" optimism.

My position on this issue is simple: We are totally biological, totally environmental; the two are as inseparable as is an object and its shadow. Or as psychologist Donald O. Hebb has expressed it, we are 100 percent innate, 100 percent acquired. One might add to Hebb's formulation, 100 percent biological, 100 percent cultural. As D. T. Suzuki, the Zen scholar, once told an audience of neuropsychiatrists, "You took heredity and environment apart and now you are stuck with the problem of putting them together again."

Navaho and Chinese newborns may be so much alike because the Navaho were part of a relatively recent emigration from Asia. Their language group is called Athabaskan, after a lake in Canada. Although most of the Athabaskan immigrants from Asia settled along the Pacific coast of Canada, the Navaho and Apache contingents went on to their present location in about 1200

A.D. Even today, a significant number of words in Athabaskan and Chinese appear to have the same meaning, and if one looks back several thousand years into the written records of Sino-Tibetan, the number of similar words makes clear the common origin of these widely separated peoples.

When we say that some differences in human behavior may have a genetic basis, what do we mean? First of all, we are *not* talking about a gene for stoicism or a gene for irritability. If a behavioral trait is at all interesting, for example, smiling, anger, ease of sexual arousal, or altruism, it is most probably polygenic—that is, many genes contribute to its development. Furthermore, there is no way to count the exact number of genes involved in such a polygenic system because, as geneticist James Crow has summarized the situation, biological traits are controlled by one, two, or *many* genes.

Standing height, a polygenic human trait, can be easily measured and is also notoriously open to the influence of the environment. For this reason height can serve as a model for behavioral traits, which are genetically influenced but are even more prone to change with changing environment.

There are, however, limits to the way that a given trait responds to the environment, and this range of constraint imposed by the genes is called a *reaction range*. Behavioral geneticist Irving Gottesman has drawn up a series of semihypothetical graphs illustrating how this works with regard to human height; each genotype (the combination of genes that determine a particular trait) represents a relatively inbred human group. Even the most favorable environment produces little change in

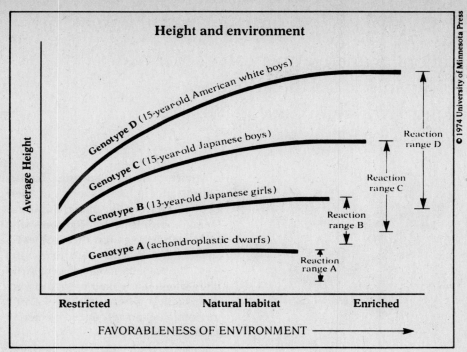

Height and environment

Average Height

Genotype D (15-year-old American white boys)

Genotype C (15-year-old Japanese boys)

Genotype B (13-year-old Japanese girls)

Genotype A (achondroplastic dwarfs)

Reaction range D

Reaction range C

Reaction range B

Reaction range A

Restricted   Natural habitat   Enriched

FAVORABLENESS OF ENVIRONMENT

© 1974 University of Minnesota Press

The concept of reaction range shows clearly in this comparison of adolescent groups: the better the environment, the taller the person. Although some groups show considerable overlap in height, no matter how favorable the environment, height cannot exceed the possible reaction range.

height for genotype A, whereas for genotype D a vast difference is seen as nutrition improves.

When I speak of potential genetic differences in human behavior, I do so with these notions in mind: There is overlap between most populations and the overlap can become rather complete under changing conditions, as in genotypes D and C. Some genotypes, however, show no overlap and remain remote from the others over the entire reaction range, as in genotype A (actually a group of achondroplastic dwarfs; it is likely that some pygmy groups would exhibit a similarly isolated reaction range with regard to height).

At present we lack the data to construct such reaction-range curves for newborn behavior, but hypothetically there is nothing to prevent us from one day doing so.

The question naturally arises whether the group differences we have found are expressions of richer and poorer environments, rather than of genetically distinguishable groups. The similar performance yet substantial difference in socioeconomic status

between Navaho and San Francisco Chinese on the one hand, and the dissimilar performance yet similar socioeconomic status of San Francisco Chinese and Caucasians on the other favors the genetic explanation. Try as one might, it is very difficult, conceptually and actually, to get rid of our biological constraints.

Research among newborns in other cultures shows how environment—in this case, cultural learning—affects reaction range. In Hawaii we met a Honolulu pediatrician who volunteered that he had found striking and consistent differences between Japanese and Polynesian babies in his practice. The Japanese babies consistently reacted more violently to their three-month immunizations than did the Polynesians. On subsequent visits, the Japanese gave every indication of remembering the last visit by crying violently; one mother said that her baby cried each time she drove by the clinic.

We then tested a series of Japanese newborns, and found that they were indeed more sensitive and irritable than either the Chinese or Navaho

babies. In other respects, though, they were much like them, showing a similar response to consolation, and accommodating easily to a light on the eyes or a cloth over the nose. Prior to our work, social anthropologist William Caudill had made an extensive and thorough study of Japanese infants. He made careful observations of Japanese mother-infant pairs in Baltimore, from the third to the twelfth month of life. Having noted that both the Japanese infants and their mothers vocalized much less to one another than did Caucasian pairs, he assumed that the Japanese mothers were conditioning their babies toward quietude from a universal baseline at which all babies start. Caudill, of course, was in the American environmentalist tradition and, until our publication appeared, did not consider the biological alternative. We believe that the mothers and babies he studied were, in all probability, conditioning each other, that the naturally quiet Japanese babies affected their mothers' behavior as much as the mothers affected their babies'.

With this new interactive hypothesis in mind, one of my students, Joan Kuchner, studied mother-infant interactions among 10 Chinese and 10 Caucasian mother-infant pairs over the first three months of life. The study was done in Chicago, and this time the Chinese were of North Chinese rather than South Chinese (Cantonese) ancestry. Kuchner started her study with the birth of the babies and found that the two groups were different from the start, much as in our study of newborns. Further, it soon became apparent that Chinese mothers were less intent on eliciting responses from their infants. By the third month, Chinese

Fourth-generation Japanese-American babies, like babies in Japan, sucked their fingers less and were less playful than Caucasian babies.

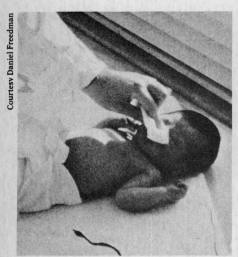
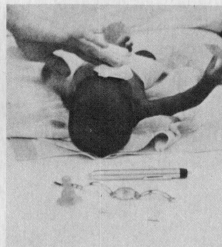

Courtesy Daniel Freedman

The Japanese newborn (left) does not struggle when a cloth covers his nose; the Australian aborigine (right), like the Caucasian, protests.

infants and mothers rarely engaged in bouts of mutual vocalizing as did the Caucasian pairs. This was exactly what the Caudill studies of Japanese and Caucasians had shown, but we now know that it was based on a developing coalition between mothers and babies and that it was not just a one-way street in which a mother "shapes" her infant's behavior.

Following our work, Caudill and Lois Frost repeated Caudill's original work, but this time they used third-generation Japanese-American mothers and their fourth-generation infants. The mothers had become "super" American and were vocalizing to their infants at almost twice the Caucasian rate of activity, and the infants were responding at an even greater rate of happy vocalization. Assuming that these are sound and repeatable results, my tendency is to reconcile these and our results in terms of the reaction-range concept. If Japanese height can

change as dramatically as it has with emigration to the United States (and with post-World War II diets), it seems plausible that mother-infant behavior can do the same. On a variety of other measures, Caudill and Frost were able to discern continuing similarities to infant and mother pairs in the old country. Fourth-generation Japanese babies, like babies in Japan, sucked their fingers less and were less playful than Caucasian babies were, and the third-generation mothers lulled their babies and held them more than Caucasian American mothers did.

A student and colleague, John Callaghan, has recently completed a study comparing 15 Navaho and 19 Anglo mothers and their young infants (all under six months). Each mother was asked to "get the attention of the baby." When video tapes of the subsequent scene were analyzed, the differences in both babies and mothers were striking. The Navaho babies showed greater

passivity than the Caucasian babies. Caucasian mothers "spoke" to their babies continually, using linguistic forms appropriate for someone who understands language; their babies responded by moving their arms and legs. The Navaho mothers were strikingly silent, using their eyes to attract their babies' gaze, and the relatively immobile infants responded by merely gazing back.

Despite their disparate methods, both groups were equally successful in getting their babies' attention. Besides keeping up a stream of chatter, Caucasian mothers tended to shift the baby's position radically, sometimes holding him or her close, sometimes at arm's length, as if experimenting to find the best focal distance for the baby. Most of the silent Navaho mothers used only subtle shifts on the lap, holding the baby at about the same distance throughout. As a result of the intense stimulation by the Caucasian mothers, the babies frequently turned their heads away, as if to moderate the intensity of the encounter. Consequently, eye contact among Caucasian pairs was of shorter duration (half that of the Navaho), but more frequent.

It was clear that the Caucasian mothers sought their babies' attention with verve and excitement, even as their babies tended to react to the stimulation with what can be described as ambivalence: The Caucasian infants turned both toward and away from the mother with far greater frequency than did the Navaho infants. The Navaho mothers and their infants engaged in relatively stoical, quiet, and steady encounters. On viewing the films of these sequences, we had the

In a Chinese-American nursery school, the noise level stayed low and the emotional atmosphere projected serenity, not bedlam.

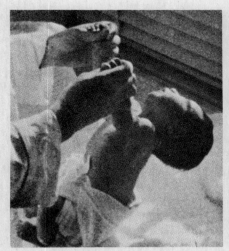
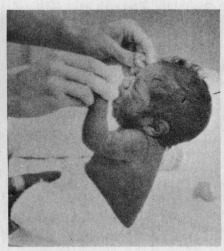

The Japanese newborn (left), like the Caucasian, cannot support his head; the Australian aborigine (right) has an exceptionally strong neck.

feeling that we were watching biocultural differences in the making.

Studies of older children bear out the theme of relative unexcitability in Chinese as compared to Anglos. In an independent research project at the University of Chicago, Nova Green studied a number of nursery schools. When she reached one in Chicago's Chinatown, she reported: "Although the majority of the Chinese-American children were in the 'high arousal age,' between three and five, they showed little intense emotional behavior. They ran and hopped, laughed and called to one another, rode bikes and roller-skated just as the children did in the other nursery schools, but the noise level stayed remarkably low, and the emotional atmosphere projected serenity instead of bedlam. The impassive facial expression certainly gave the children an air of dignity and self-possession, but this was only one element effecting the total impression.

Physical movements seemed more coordinated, no tripping, falling, bumping, or bruising was observed, nor screams, crashes or wailing was heard, not even that common sound in other nurseries, voices raised in highly indignant moralistic dispute! No property disputes were observed, and only the mildest version of 'fighting behavior,' some good-natured wrestling among the older boys. The adults evidently had different expectations about hostile or impulsive behavior; this was the only nursery school where it was observed that children were trusted to duel with sticks. Personal distance spacing seemed to be situational rather than compulsive or patterned, and the children appeared to make no effort to avoid physical contact."

It is ironic that many recent visitors to nursery schools in Red China have returned with ecstatic descriptions of the children, implying that the New Order knows something about child rearing that the West does not. When the *New Yorker* reported a visit to China by a group of developmental psychologists including William Kessen, Urie Bronfenbrenner, Jerome Kagan, and Eleanor Maccoby, they were described as baffled by the behavior of Chinese children: "They were won over by the Chinese children. They speak of an 'attractive mixture of affective spontaneity and an accommodating posture by the children: of the 'remarkable control of young Chinese children'— alert, animated, vigorous, responsive to the words of their elders, yet also unnervingly calm, even during happenings (games, classroom events, neighborhood play) that could create agitation and confusion. The children 'were far less restless, less intense in their motor actions, and displayed less crying and whining than American children in similar situations. We were constantly struck by [their] quiet, gentle, and controlled manner . . . and as constantly frustrated in our desire to understand its origins.' "

The report is strikingly similar to Nova Green's description of the nursery school in Chicago's Chinatown. When making these comparisons with "American" nursery schools, the psychologists obviously had in mind classrooms filled with Caucasian or Afro-American children.

As they get older, Chinese and Caucasian children continue to differ in roughly the same behavior that characterizes them in nursery school. Not surprisingly, San Francisco schoolteachers consider assignments in Chinatown as plums—the children are dutiful and studious, and the classrooms are quiet.

A reader might accept these data and

We have studied newborns in Nigeria, Kenya, Sweden, Italy, Bali, India, and Australia, and in each place have observed unique behavior.

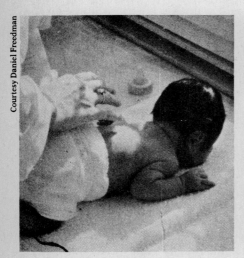
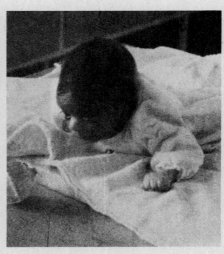

Courtesy Daniel Freedman

Placed on his stomach, the Japanese newborn (left) remains in position; the Australian aborigine (right) lifts up his head and looks around.

observations and yet still have trouble imagining how such differences might have initially come about. The easiest explanation involves a historical accident based on different, small founding populations and at least partial geographic isolation. Peking man, some 500,000 years ago, already had shovel-shaped incisors, as only Orientals and American Indians have today. Modern-looking skulls of about the same age, found in England, lack this grooving on the inside of their upper incisors. Given such evidence, we can surmise that there has been substantial and long-standing isolation of East and West. Further, it is likely that, in addition to just plain "genetic drift," environmental demands and biocultural adapta-

tions differed, yielding present-day differences.

Orientals and Euro-Americans are not the only newborn groups we have examined. We have recorded newborn behavior in Nigeria, Kenya, Sweden, Italy, Bali, India, and Australia, and in each place, it is fair to say, we observed some kind of uniqueness. The Australian aborigines, for example, struggled mightily against the cloth over the nose, resembling the most objecting Caucasian babies; their necks were exceptionally strong, and some could lift their heads up and look around, much like some of the African babies we saw. (Caucasian infants cannot do this until they are about one month old.) Further, aborigine infants were easy to calm,

resembling in that respect our easy-going Chinese babies. They thus comprised a unique pattern of traits.

Given these data, I think it is a reasonable conclusion that we should drop two long-cherished myths: (1) No matter what our ethnic background, we are all born alike; (2) culture and biology are separate entities. Clearly, we are biosocial creatures in everything we do and say, and it is time that anthropologists, psychologists, and population geneticists start speaking the same language. In light of what we know, only a truly holistic, multidisciplinary approach makes sense. ☐

For further information:

Caudill, W., and N. Frost. "A Comparison of Maternal Care and Infant Behavior in Japanese-American, American, and Japanese Families." *Influences on Human Development*, edited by Urie Bronfenbrenner and M. A. Mahoney. Dryden Press, 1972.

Chisholm, J. S., and Martin Richards. "Swaddling, Cradleboards and the Development of Children." *Early Human Development*, in press.

Freedman, D. G. "Constitutional and Environmental Interaction in Rearing of Four Breeds of Dogs." *Science*, Vol. 127, 1958, pp. 585-586.

Freedman, D. G. *Human Infancy: An Evolutionary Perspective*. Lawrence Erlbaum Associates, 1974.

Freedman, D. G., and B. Keller. "Inheritance of Behavior in Infants." *Science*, Vol. 140, 1963, pp. 196-198.

Gottesman, I. I. "Developmental Genetics and Ontogenetic Psychology." *Minnesota Symposia on Child Psychology*, Vol. 8, edited by A. D. Pick. University of Minnesota Press, 1974.

Daniel G. Freedman, *professor of the behavioral sciences at The University of Chicago, spent last fall in Australia as a visiting fellow in the department of anthropology at the Australian National University in Canberra. There he extended his research into the new-* *born capacities of Australian aborigines. His doctorate in psychology from Brandeis University was followed by a postdoctoral fellowship at Mt. Zion Psychiatric Clinic and the Langley Porter Neuropsychiatric Institute in San Francisco. Much of the information in*

this article appears in an expanded form in Freedman's new book, Human Sociobiology.

5

India's mobile crèches

An imaginative experiment in child-care

by Meera Mahadevan

MEERA MAHADEVAN, *founder and director of the "Mobile Crèche" child care programme in India, died in July 1977. This article, an edited version of a study published in Unesco's educational quarterly* Prospects *(Vol. VII, N° 4, 1977), appears with the kind permission of Unicef's journal* Assignment Children.

From *Unesco Courier*, May 1978.

INDIA is developing fast in every field. The country is mobilizing all its resources to accelerate its transformation from the bullock cart era to the space age; yet millions of our children still live in conditions of poverty.

The Mobile Crèche programme specializes in caring for children from the poorest sections of Indian society—construction labourers who travel from site to site, many thousands of whom are women and mothers, coal-scavengers, rag-pickers and others like them are the parents of our young charges.

The origins of the Mobile Crèche programme go back to 1969, when we opened a crèche in a tent for children under three left to fend for themselves while their mothers worked on a construction site in Delhi. In the next eight months, three more centres for children under three were opened. At that time we had neither transport facilities nor an office and the work of setting up a skeleton programme, gathering meagre supplies and scouting around for urgently needed help and finance was all carried out from the homes of volunteers or from central meeting points.

By the end of 1970, the number of crèches had grown to five and funds had been found for a small base office. In the next six months, five more centres were opened. The programme was gathering momentum and by mid-1971 we were pro-

Photo © Abigail Heyman, Unicef

A mobile crèche set up on a New Delhi building site provides basic health and education services for the young children of unskilled construction workers. Forever on the move from one building site to another, and therefore the responsibility of no one local authority, these young urban nomads were left to look after themselves as best they could until the mobile crèche organization took a hand.

viding care for 1,000 children, dealing with ten building contractors and negotiating with a large number of officials who could sanction funds, water supplies or sanitation for the work-sites.

Construction workers are not the only ones compelled to leave their young ones to look after themselves. Every poor working mother has to leave the household and the babies in the charge of the older children. It is not uncommon, for example, to find a girl of six, herself in need of care, bringing up her baby brothers and sisters.

The first lesson we learned was that a child cannot be isolated either from its family or from the community. We started the programme with a crèche because that was the first priority as we saw it. But the moment we took in the babies, the older children who had been looking after them had nothing to do and they came along to our centres as well. Their nomadic way of life and the fact that they had been obliged to look after their siblings meant that most of them had never been to school.

So today we are involved not only in crèche and nursery services but also in elementary education. Our centres have three sections: a crèche, nursery classes, and elementary classes for children between the ages of six and twelve.

Furthermore, as we gained experience, we felt a great need for contact with parents and this led us to launch an adult

education programme. We realized that it was impossible to cater only for this or that age group, and took the whole community as our target.

Our equipment is simple and familiar to the mothers. For example we use improvised cradles of a type that is found throughout rural India and costs next to nothing. Other basic equipment for a crèche includes mats, a table for changing babies' clothes, and a cupboard for medicines, plates and other utensils. A stock of toys for a section of some 50 children costs no more than 10 rupees.

The accommodation allotted to us is usually drab. It may be in a basement or on the 18th floor of an unfinished skyscraper. To mellow the harsh surroundings, the staff decorate the crèche with the children's colourful drawings. The babies' cots and cradles have lovely mobiles hanging on them.

The babies, who come to us from the age of 3 or 4 weeks are generally malnourished. They receive a preliminary medical examination and are prescribed a diet by the visiting doctor. Most of them are given vitamin drops, milk, and other high-protein food according to need. Although the doctor visits a centre only once a week, the supervisors and nutritionists keep a close watch on the children's progress. Many babies are given half an egg as a special diet. Once they show signs of progress,

their mothers come forward to share the cost of an egg.

We try to make our crèches a home from home. Every effort is made to develop the child physically as well as emotionally, intellectually and socially. The crèches resound with the traditional songs familiar to children.

In our nursery sections there is nothing unfamiliar or alien to either the children or their teachers and the educational methods we use are carefully adapted to Indian experience.

Nursery schools are often considered a luxury in poor countries, mainly because they are thought to need elaborate and expensive facilities.

We have shown the fallacy of this belief by making imaginative use of cheap, locally available materials to provide equipment for children aged between three and six. In the nursery section the materials used are cardboard, chart paper, glazed paper, kite paper, wooden beads, scissors, blackboard, stones, leaves, flowers, potters' clay (to replace plasticine), rag dolls, old saris, wooden blocks and other inexpensive items.

Our most important achievement is to have produced model nursery equipment suitable for a country like India that has to think of children in millions. With few variations, the same equipment can be used throughout the country.

Having found an answer to the problem of children under six, we realized that it was impossible not to cater for deprived children aged between six and twelve.

In Delhi, primary education is free and poor children are entitled to get free books and uniform. Unfortunately, many of the poorest members of our society, who are completely illiterate, are not even aware of these opportunities. In spite of the best intentions, the government does not always succeed in reaching the poorest people in the country. This is where the role of an agency like Mobile Crèches becomes vital. When we take care of the babies and the nursery-age children, we prepare the older children in our elementary sections to join the local elementary school.

We had to educate our own staff. We need teachers who will attend to a child's sores and bathe him before settling down to teach. We also need teachers who will convince the parents that they should send their children to the school. Thus a worker in a Mobile Crèche must be a social worker, a teacher and a mother.

The training has to be very basic and simple. A standard routine of bathing, feeding and giving medicine to babies had to be worked out and suitable equipment provided. The role of the dustbin had to be dramatized. Working in unhygienic surroundings without sanitation, we have an enormous task to maintain standards of cleanliness in our centres. We have to improvise little places which babies can use as toilets and then find methods of disposing of the waste in a hygienic way.

Higher secondary school girls form the bulk of our staff, but over the past three or four years we have also started recruiting boys. They bring a different atmosphere with them and children love to have a male teacher around.

From the beginning, the Mobile Crèche programme had wholehearted support from the children on construction sites and in the slums. Seeing their children so happy with our staff, parents also accepted us, although they were a little suspicious at the beginning.

Each child is charged a nominal fee. They all have to buy slates, notebooks, pencils, erasers and other materials at subsidized rates.

When the idea of charging fees was introduced, many mothers refused to pay for nursery children on the grounds that this age group did nothing but play and sing. It was quite understandable, and we decided to organize a mothers' meeting to explain all our nursery school activities. This meeting was a great success and we now always hold this type of meeting when a new centre is opened.

Mothers' meetings are a very common feature of our activities today. In 1969 and 1970, when we were new in the field, we tried to bring the mothers together but they were always busy with their household chores. Then we tried cooking demonstrations and these attracted a group of mothers who began to meet regularly. We provided them with education in nutrition and taught other topics related to child care, hygiene, weaning foods, and the diet of pregnant and nursing mothers.

Today our main point of contact with the parents is our Adult Education Programme, which has helped us considerably in improving our services to children. Before carrying out immunization or vaccination programmes we hold parents' meetings at which we explain, with the aid of films, flash cards, etc., what we want to do and why. In this way we retain the parents' goodwill and they do not get the impression that the programme is being high-handedly imposed on them.

In its Fifth Plan, the Government of India has given priority to crèche programmes and the Mobile Crèche programme now receives a substantial grant from the Welfare Department. This has enabled us to work at certain sites even when the building contractors have refused to contribute financially. Our aim is to educate the community by our work. We want the contractors and the authorities concerned to be convinced that there is no ulterior motive and that our sole concern is the welfare of the children.

■ **Meera Mahadevan**

Photo © J.L. Nou, Unicef.

Crèche and nursery school programmes have been given high priority by the Indian Government over recent years. At this nursery school in Madras carefully selected toys help stimulate the imagination and develop manual dexterity.

6

How Love Begins Between Parent and Child

by Stephen P. Hersh
and Karen Levin

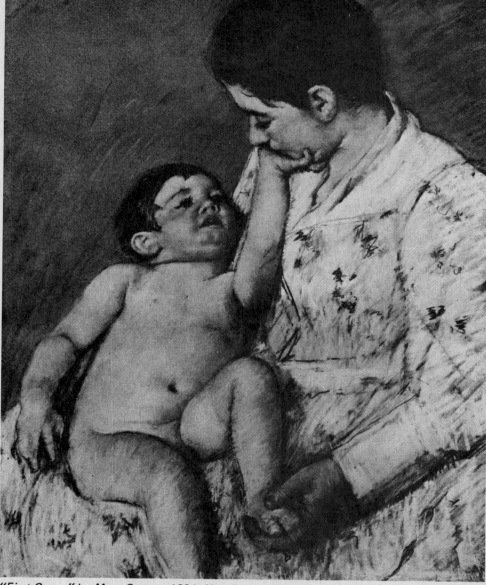

"First Caress" by Mary Cassatt, 1891, New Britain Museum of American Art (Harriet Russell Stanley Fund).

The expectant mother, no less than the father, often finds it hard to imagine how she is going to feel about the unborn infant. But once the child arrives the mother love that so strongly shapes the infant's future unfolds in a complex and wonderful pattern. This mysterious process begins before birth. As our knowledge increases, all who bother to look at the process find themselves instilled with awe and respect.

The newborn, it turns out, is not the passive creature most people have assumed him to be. Recent research shows that the newborn comes well-endowed with charm and a full potential for social graces. His eyes are bright and equipped with surprisingly good vision. Shortly after birth, he likes to watch the human face. He looks at his mother and soon recognizes and prefers her. Dr. Robert Emde, of the University of Colorado Medical School, observes, "Little in life is more dramatic than the mother's moment of discovery that the baby is beaming at her with sparkling eyes." This is the time,

Stephen P. Hersh, M.D., a psychiatrist, is Assistant Director for Children and Youth, NIMH. Karen Levin is director of science writing, Biospherics, Inc., Rockville, Md.

From *Children Today* Magazine, March/April 1978. U.S. Department of Health, Education and Welfare.

mothers often say, when affection begins. The infant's cry alerts her and causes a biological as well as emotional reaction. Swedish studies using thermal photography have shown that the cry increases the flow of blood to her nipples, increasing milk secretion. The newborn hears the mother's or caretaker's voice and turns his head towards that person. The infant's ability to cling and cuddle communicates a pleas-

urable warmth to the mother. The infant's odor, too, is pleasant and uniquely his own. Although some experts say the smile is not "real" until some weeks after birth, the newborn does smile. Dr. Burton L. White of Harvard University says, "God or somebody has built into the human infant a collection of attributes that guarantee attractiveness."

Some argue about whether the

child sparks the development of love, or whether a special physiological state of the mother prompts her to interact with the new infant. Each view probably offers a partial explanation. In any case, a number of researchers agree that the infant does mold or trigger adult behavior. Dr. Michael Lewis, Director of the Infant Laboratory, Educational Testing Service, Princeton, N.J., believes that "The neonate organizes the mother by crying, starting, and by eye to eye contact." When an infant opens his mouth to feed, the mother automatically opens hers, too. When the infant smiles, she smiles back.

The newborn's cry almost always causes an adult reaction. To prove his point, one researcher played a record of a newborn in his office, and secretaries from nearby rooms came running in to find out what was "wrong" with the baby.

To get a close look at what happens between mother and the new infant, Dr. T. Berry Brazelton of Harvard has studied video-tapes of their interactions. Frame-by-frame "micro-analysis" of the pictures shows that the baby moves in smooth, circular "ballet-like" patterns as he looks up at the mother. The baby concentrates his attention on her while body and limbs move in rhythm; the infant then withdraws briefly, but returns his attention, averaging several cycles a minute. The mother falls in step with the baby's cycles by talking and smiling, in a kind of "dance." If the mother falls out of step and disappoints the infant by presenting a still, unresponsive face when he gazes at her, the baby becomes "concerned" and keeps trying to get her attention. If he fails, the baby withdraws into a collapsed state of helplessness, face turned aside, and body curled up and motionless. If the mother becomes responsive again, the baby looks puzzled but returns to his cyclical motions.

Intrigued by these patterns, Dr. Louis W. Sander, professor of psychiatry at the University of Colorado Medical Center, Denver, had mothers of 7-day-old babies wear masks while they fed and cared for their infants. The babies became disturbed, and for 24 hours their rhythms of sleep and feeding were completely off schedule.

Indeed, even before birth, the infant is a responsive creature. We know that the fetus can see and hear during the third trimester. A soft red light or certain kinds of sound cause the fetus to slowly turn; a bright light or certain noises can startle the unborn child. Some fetuses seem to signal their personalities to the mother ahead of time by being active or quiet. All third trimester fetuses appear to be somnolent at some times and very alert or "hypervigilant" at others. Over the next five years, investigations in this area may allow for prediction (and hence possible earlier remediation) of certain vulnerabilities and difficulties now too subtle to detect.

Is it any wonder, given the above information, that the experienced and much-loved clinician, teacher and researcher, Dr. Brazelton, laments: "Why do we still embrace the passive model of the newborn, plunging him/her into a delivery room hardly safe for adults and immediately thereafter into an over-stimulating neonatal nursery?"

Curiosity about how mothers begin to love their babies grew out of observations of premature infants. Separated from their families at birth for weeks and sometimes months, "premies" often have no opportunity to interact with their mothers. The mothers find it hard to feel a close tie to these infants in the beginning. This suggests to some that one important milestone in mother-child love takes place soon after birth.

A number of pediatricians began to look for hard evidence that the mother-infant tie starts early, and how it benefits the child. Drs. Marshall H. Klaus and John H. Kennell of Case Western Reserve University School of Medicine divided 28 mothers and their first-borns into two matched groups. In one, mothers were given their nude babies to nurse and care for in bed for one hour in the first two hours after delivery, and for five extra hours on each of the next three days of life. The other group of mothers received the care that is routine in most U.S. hospitals: a glimpse of the baby at birth, brief contact for identification at six to eight hours, then visits of 20 to 30 minutes for feedings every four hours.

When the mothers and infants returned to the hospital a month later, there were marked differences in the two groups. The "early contact" mothers showed a closer tie to their infants. They were more concerned, more soothing, fondled their infants more, and were more reluctant to leave them with others than the second group. At one year, the same differences were observed between the two groups of mothers. Two years after birth, the mothers who had early and extended contact with their infants asked them more questions, and issued fewer commands, than the second group. The scientists decided that the children had made an impact on the mothers' behavior for two years. But what was the effect on the children? A recent comparison of the two groups of children at five years of age shows that the "early contact" youngsters had significantly higher I.Q.'s and a better command of language than the control group.

Studies of mothers and newborns in other cultures showed similar results. In Guatemala, Dr. Deborah Hales (of Montifiore Hospital and Medical Center, New York City) attempted to pinpoint the time when the mother-child tie was made. One group of mothers lay next to their infants for 45 minutes right after leaving the delivery room; the second spent the same amount of time with their new babies, but at 12 hours after delivery. A third group received routine hospital care. When the mothers were observed a day and a half later, the first group showed significantly more affectionate behavior than the other mothers. They spent more time talking to the infant and fondling, kissing and smiling at him or her.

Recent Swedish research also suggests the importance of early mother-child contact in the hospital. First-time mothers who held their naked infants one hour immediately after birth showed more affection to the babies when observed several days later. In another Swedish study, new mothers were given their infants for 15 to 20 minutes right after birth. Three months later, these mothers showed more affection than those routinely separated from their infants by the hospital. The babies smiled and laughed more, and cried less.

Early exposure to the new infant seems to have an effect on the father

as well as the mother. When he attends the birth, sees the newborn in the first hours, and holds him, the father remains more closely tied to the child, researchers report.

In America, the father is playing an increasingly important part in caring for the infant. The work of Dr. Ross D. Parke at the University of Illinois, Urbana-Champaign dispels some common myths about the father— that he is not interested in the newborn, does not nurture him, prefers leaving him to the mother, and is not so competent as she. Dr. Parke has found that when left alone with the infant, the father is very sensitive to his needs, and shows affection and considerable skill in handling him. Nine months later, infants cope better with stress (when a stranger appears) if the father has

taken part early in his care. Dr. Parke concludes, "There are very few differences between mother-child and father-child interactions."

Keeping the newborn and the father as well as the mother together in the earliest hours apparently improves the child's outlook in a number of problem families. Dr. Peter Vietze of the National Institute of Child Health and Human Development, NIH, recently reported on a large study of infants born in a large city hospital to disadvantaged families. Half of the infants roomed-in with their mothers seven hours after birth and remained there throughout the hospital stay. Fathers were encouraged to visit at all hours and to handle the new child. The rooming-in infants were held more, cried less, and were more alert than those kept in the hospital nursery. When observed months later, the rooming-in infants enjoyed better general health and a closer tie with their mothers than the control children. There were also fewer cases of inadequate child care, neglect and abuse. Dr. Vietze believes that rooming-in with the mother right after birth plus the frequent visiting by the father "means that the child will have a better chance in life."

The new research has prompted doctors to identify developmental differences among newborns, and to take preventive steps early if something is wrong. Some pediatricians go beyond the usual physical examination of the newborn to check him or her for a number of personal qualities. They include alertness, cuddliness, irritability, persistence and determination. Some infants are more active or more cuddly than others, and doctors think they can help parents get a better understanding of their infant's personality in the earliest days. By identifying the infant's special characteristics, mental health professionals think they can help prevent emotional problems later on.

In June 1976, child specialists

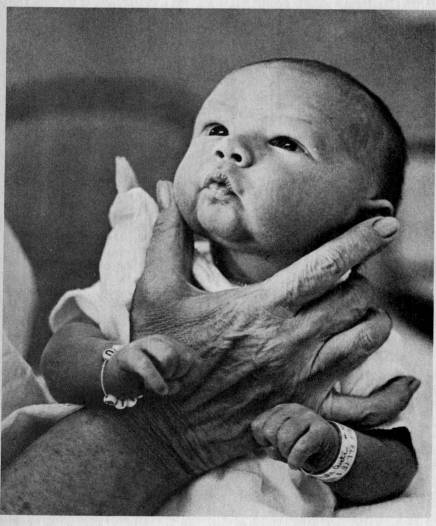

A nurse holds a newborn.

gathered in Washington, D.C., at the White House for a Conference on the Prevention of Psychosocial Disabilities in Infancy. New infant research was reviewed in that setting for the purpose of calling to the attention of the executive branch of government the hypothesis that major preventive mental health measures could be launched at relatively modest costs in the perinatal period. Research and information reviewed at that meeting included:

• The results of a 10-year study by Dr. Elsie Broussard, professor of psychiatry, University of Pittsburgh, demonstrating that maternal attitude towards an infant *when consistent* between two and 30 days after birth is highly correlative with future adjustment difficulties in the children studied.

• Studies by Dr. Gordon Bronson, professor of psychology, Mills College, Oakland, Calif., showing that about 20 percent of infants appear to be temperamentally disposed to avoid or at least to have difficulty with new situations; such infants were found to respond to new stimuli by avoidance or by stopping their activity, pouting and crying.

• Some infants seem naturally happy, lively and without fear; others seem naturally subdued and easily made uncomfortable; such differences in behavioral responses may be due to actual differences in neurological and hormonal endowments.

As a result of research documentation of the profound effects of interaction between infants and their mothers, the National Institute of Mental Health has organized, under the leadership of Drs. Stanley Greenspan, Reginald Lourie and Robert Nover, a clinical infant research program to help develop multidisciplinary approaches to prevent problems in the newborn. In addition, based on the encouragement of a distinguished panel of researchers and clinicians,[1] a private non-profit National Center for Clinical Infant Programs has been estab-

lished in Washington, D.C. The center will convene experts in the field and transmit new knowledge as it is produced to physicians, child development centers and interested others throughout the nation.[2]

The new findings have already contributed to some major changes in the nation's maternity wards. More and more hospitals are altering their services to give parents more information and a bigger role in decision making and to provide more homelike settings. As one hospital administrator put it, "We are treating birth as a normal process rather than a disease."

Hospitals are offering a variety of approaches to keep the mother and child together, and to bring the father and the rest of the family into the nursery. A decreasing use of anesthesia is encouraged and breast feeding is again being recommended whenever possible. Human milk has special infections-disease control attributes not found in formulas; in addition, being low in protein and fat, it resembles that of many mammals who constantly suckle their newborns. This means, according to some experts, that the human infant, too, was meant to suckle frequently and to remain close to the mother after birth, enhancing maternal-infant bonding.

Four examples of the varied new approaches follow.

In San Francisco, the Kaiser-Permanente Medical Center offers a Family Centered Perinatal Care Program that begins with prenatal courses for both parents. A team of obstetricians, pediatricians and nurse practitioners work with the family throughout the birth period. The father attends the delivery and stays with the mother directly afterward. The mother and child are examined 12 hours after birth and are permitted to return home if all is well; in some cases, they remain for 24 hours, then are released. The nurse practitioner who was originally assigned to the mother makes daily home visits for four days afterwards

and is available for two weeks to assist the family in caring for the infant. Besides being economical and safe, the program provides concentrated and personalized care. But most important, it expedites parent-child attachment.

The Washington Hospital Center in Washington, D.C., provides a delivery room with a relaxed, home atmosphere. If a birth is normal, the mother delivered in that setting may return home in four to six hours. Such an approach to delivery, however, remains at this time most unusual in the United States.

A form of primary nursing care in which the same group of nurses works with the new mother is offered by the Alexandria Hospital in Alexandria, Virginia. There, the baby rooms with the mother, and father and siblings are welcome.

The Booth Maternity Center in Philadelphia offers prenatal training and delivery services during labor by nurse-midwives. The physician is present only at the end of labor for infant delivery in about half the births. Full support and instruction for infant care and breast feeding are provided. Mothers are encouraged to establish physical contact with the infant as soon as possible and to nurse him or her within the first hour. An interview-questionnaire administered to new mothers indicates that the program is a success. As one mother put it, "Booth has the most natural and pleasant approach to childbirth that I have heard of in these . . . clinical times."

The lessons of early parental contact for normal infants are also being applied in the care of premature infants. As recently as 1970, only one-third of the nurseries for premature babies permitted families to visit because of the fear of infection. When studies showed that parents "scrubbed up" thoroughly when asked, and that infection did not break out when they visited, a number of hospitals began to permit them to touch and to care for the premie. Most parents, anxious and

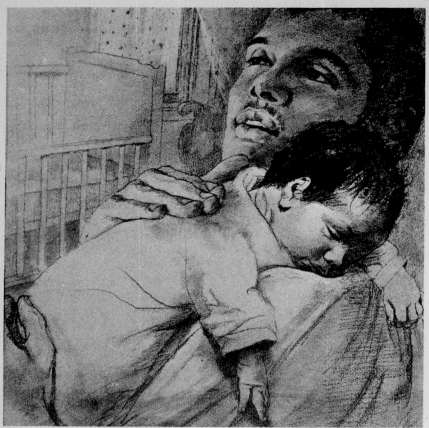

*Drawing by Symeon Shimin for "A New Baby! A New Life!"
by Erma Brenner (McGraw-Hill, 1973). © 1973 Symeon Shimin.*

fearful about the child's chance of survival, gain confidence when the staff encourages them to visit.

One hospital permits visits 24 hours a day, explaining:

"We would like to welcome and encourage all parents to come into the nursery. You may touch your baby now and help to care for him or her. At certain times, the nursery appears a bit busy, sometimes hectic; even at these times there is always room for you. If you have any concerns when you go home, please do not hestitate to call. The nurses enjoy talking with you . . . Someone is always here."

Studies of these new practices show big benefits for the premie. If he is touched, rocked and cuddled daily while in the nursery, he thrives and gains more weight. Parents feel a closer bond to the infant, who is then more responsive and closer in behavior to a full-term child.

More intensive care units for high risk infants are now permitting parents to visit as often as they like. Dr. Rita Harper of North Shore University Hospital in Manhasset, N.Y., studied parental reactions to the new, liberal nursery policies. She reports that although many parents felt anxious about entering the intensive care facility, more than half came long distances to visit every day; most spent their time caring for their babies and most felt the new program was a good idea.

Some hospitals are training personnel to help the mother grow closer to her infant. The University of Colorado Medical Center in Denver trains Child Health Associates (CHAs) in an intensive three-year program to teach new mothers how to care for their infant. In one study, Dr. Claibourne I. Bungy quoted a mother as saying, "The CHA was there when I needed questions answered . . . I felt much better after talking to her. She told me what to expect when getting home." Working with physicians, the CHAs can also help spot problems that are sometimes overlooked in normal births.

Ann Clark, R.N., of the University of Hawaii, is helping train nurses to strengthen maternal attachment to the infant when things are not going well between mother and child. She has developed a "Degree of Bother" inventory to find out how much the mother is annoyed by the infant and why, so that a nurse may suggest what can be done to restore harmony.

A number of American families are attempting to avoid the hospital altogether and to have their babies at home. Some mothers say they get to know the infant better in the home setting and that they like the support of other family members. Proponents include individuals from a variety of belief systems and human service backgrounds. Their perspectives and data are often attractive but further evaluation of home deliveries is needed.

One group, midwives of a commune network called The Farm, presents summary data from almost seven years of experience. These women delivered 722 babies, 94 percent of them in the home. The neonatal death rate was 11.1 per 1,000—better than the national average.

Lewis E. Mehl, research director of a Berkeley, California group called the National Association of Parents and Professionals for Safe Alternatives in Childbirth, claims to have compared home and hospital deliveries. In a recent book, *21st Century Obstetrics Now!*, he says that after studying more than 2,000 cases he thinks home delivery may be a reasonable alternative for *"low* medical risk" women.

Still, some authorities caution that too little medical help at birth is risky. They point out that infant mortality in the United States dropped from 140 deaths per 1,000 births in 1900 to 16 per 1,000 today because of hygienic, hospital-based births. Despite this claim, the extent and quality of prenatal care also has been documented as contributing importantly to lowered infant mortality.

In even the most carefully arranged home births, emergencies can occur. Although everything seems to be normal, infants may have difficulty in breathing promptly or other unexpected problems. In a British study, of 150 infants born at home, 20 percent ran into trouble during labor; 18 babies took more than one minute to breathe properly and 11 took more than two minutes. Another infant was rushed to the hospital as an emergency. Nearly everything went well after birth, although a few diagnostic problems among newborns were missed. Dr. C.A. Cox, who conducted the study at West Middlesex Hospital, concluded that home delivery can "never provide a completely safe alternative to hospital births . . . because of unpredictability of events during childbirth. Half the babies with problems at birth occurred in the obstetrical low risk group, and although there were no perinatal deaths, there were occasional potentially hazardous situations which may have prejudiced the child's optimal development." Nevertheless, many of the British mothers preferred to have their babies at home. Dr. Cox's solution is to encourage mothers to give birth in the hospital, but to try to humanize "austere impersonal labour wards and inflexible hospital routines."

Research documentation of the value of mother-infant contact in the minutes and hours right after birth has caused a stir among parents and professionals alike, one that has all the enthusiasm of a revival. As the specialness of infants is "discovered," parents are reawakening to the critical importance of their role. It is ironic that an ancient truth has been rediscovered through the vehicle of the scientific method, but somehow this process helps us evolve further. However, the enthusiasm inspired by the new research poses some dangers for a country and people much entranced by "science."

Thus, some child experts and parents are concerned about the other side of the story. If close early contact with the mother enhances a baby's development, will lack of such contact or reduced amounts harm a child? As one professional said, "Won't the new findings make the parents hyperanxious about what they do? Will they feel guilty if they don't follow the new practices?"

Parents hunger for new information about infant and childrearing, so some caution is in order. Dr. Jerome Kagan of Harvard says, "The question of how to rear the better baby is so glamorous, so attractive to Americans and so fraught with emotionalism that it invites precipitous judgments and ungrounded speculations."

Dr. Klaus explains, "Most of us were not brought up in early contact with our mothers, and we have survived. It is important, but certainly not critical . . ."

Dr. Brazelton insists that the early mother-infant, father-infant interaction "provides the groundwork for the child's competence later on . . . Still if a mother asks me 'What steps should I take to ensure that my child will be a competent person?' I would immediately begin to wonder if she's fallen into one of the traps that some psychologists have laid for young women in our society. They say you've got to do the right thing at the right time or you're going to be in trouble. I think that's a trap."

Within the new research lies the message that an infant is programmed to begin to love the parent in a certain time period. Such a "message" bears watching since biological systems are not so rigid. It is true that one can identify periods in the life span when an individual is certainly more impressionable, or more vulnerable. However, studies of behavior and mental health show the human to be surprisingly flexible and adaptable.

We now have a new understanding of how interesting and complex the newborn is. We also know from studies within the various mental health disciplines that the family has an impact on the young person throughout childhood and adolescence, as well as in infancy. Whatever form the family takes, children are one of the principal reasons for its existence. The ways parents and children learn to adapt to the realities of life within the family has produced throughout human history a high tensile strength among families—a truly remarkable ability to deal with stress and change over a child's lifetime. Because of this, even when all the "right" things don't always happen on schedule, most of the three million children who are born in the United States each year will develop into productive individuals capable of autonomy, reciprocal caring and love. ∎

[1]The panel members were T. Berry Brazelton, Selma Fraiberg, Peter Neubauer, Sally Provence, Julius Richmond, Albert J. Solnit, Joseph Stone and Leon Yarrow.

[2]The National Center was incorporated in 1977. Information concerning its planned activities can be obtained by writing to Ms. Sharon Alperovitz, Executive Secretary, National Center for Clinical Infant Programs, 3000 Connecticut Ave., N.W., Washington, D.C. 20008.

7

The Father of the Child

by Ross D. Parke

Photograph by Barbara Bengen, New York

Fathers are taking a more active role in caring for their newborn babies

The days when fathers were only permitted a glance at their new offspring through the nursery window are past. Hospital practices are changing and many more fathers are now permitted to have direct contact with their babies in the hospital rather than waiting until they go home. Now that fathers and newborns are getting together more frequently, researchers are watching more often. The aim is to determine how fathers and mothers differ in their early interactions with young infants. Our own observations, which began in 1970, revealed that fathers were just as involved with their newborn infants as mothers. They looked at the infants, touched and rocked them and vocalized to them just as often as mothers. Fathers were just as active when they were alone with the babies as when their wives were present. Mothers surpassed fathers in only one way—smiling. However, the reason for the higher rate of mothers' smiling may be that females simply smile more than males—not just at babies, but at all kinds of people.

One of my students, David Phillips, has recently taken a closer look at one part of the early parent-infant exchange—the types of speech that mothers and fathers use in talking to their newborns. Fathers, as well as mothers, change their styles of speech when addressing their new offspring. They speak in shorter phrases—about half as long as the phrases used when speaking with adults. They repeat their messages much more often and slow their rate of talking. All of these changes in the style of speaking are likely to increase the extent to which the baby pays attention or looks at the parent. In turn, the changes may make it easier for the infant to learn to recognize his caregivers.

The social setting makes a difference in the behavior of fathers. When we observe fathers and mothers together, fathers smile and explore (count fingers and toes, check eyes and ears, etc.) more

Ross D. Parke is professor of psychology at the University of Illinois at Champaign-Urbana. He is the editor of RECENT TRENDS IN SOCIAL LEARNING THEORY *(Academic Press, 1972),* READINGS IN SOCIAL DEVELOPMENT *(Holt, Rinehart & Winston, 1969), and co-author with Mavis E. Hetherington, of* CHILD PSYCHOLOGY: A CONTEMPORARY VIEWPOINT *(McGraw-Hill, 1975, 1979).*

From *The Sciences,* April 1979 © 1979 by The New York Academy of Sciences.

than when they are alone with the baby. Mothers show a similar pattern of increased interest when their husbands are present.

Fathers are active and involved, but are they involved in all aspects of early newborn care? Apparently not. Our studies indicate that fathers' involvement is selective even in the earliest interactions. Consistent with our cultural stereotypes, fathers are less likely than mothers to be actively involved in caretaking activities such as feeding or changing diapers. Fathers are more likely to play with a baby (vocalize, touch, imitate) than to feed it. These findings suggest that parental roles as caretaker or playmate begin to emerge even in the earliest days of the infant's life. This pattern may be part of a general shift toward a more traditional division of responsibilities that occurs in most families after the birth of a baby. Even in families where there is an egalitarian sharing of household tasks before a child arrives, this shift toward traditionally defined roles seems to occur, according to a recent study by Carolyn Cowan and her co-workers at Berkeley.

Are fathers less competent to care for infants? If so, this would easily explain their limited involvement in caretaking. This hypothesis, however, is wrong. Fathers are just as competent and capable of taking care of infants, according to our research. We define competence as the parent's ability to correctly "read," interpret and respond to the infant's cues or signals. To assess fathers' feeding skills, we determined how sensitively fathers reacted to infant distress signals, such as spitting up, sneezing and coughing. Fathers reacted just as quickly and appropriately as mothers did. Fathers, like mothers, adjusted their behavior by momentarily ceasing feeding the infant, looking more closely to check on the infant, and vocalizing to the infant. Moreover, babies drank about the same amount of milk from their fathers and mothers.

Play

Nearly all fathers play regularly with their infants and spend four to five times as much time playing as they spend in caretaking.

Fathers not only play more, they play differently than mothers. Based on home observations, fathers play more physically stimulating games, such as rough and tumble play and other types of unpredictable or idiosyncratic play. Mothers stimulate their infants verbally, rather than physically, use toys in their infant play, and choose conventional games such as peek-a-boo and pat-a-cake.

To examine fathers' play more closely, Harvard pediatricians Michael Yogman and T. Berry Brazelton and their colleagues videotaped playful interchanges between infants and their mother, father, and a strange adult in a laboratory setting. By slow motion analyses of the videotapes, Yogman found a number of differences in the patterns of infant play with different partners. Mothers spoke in a soft, repetitive and imitative fashion more often than fathers, while fathers did so more than strangers. Fathers poked and touched with rhythmic tapping patterns more often than mothers. The temporal pattern differed as well. Father-infant play shifted more rapidly from accentuated peaks of maximal infant visual attention and excitement to valleys of minimal attention. Mother-infant play had a less jagged and sawtooth quality; it was characterized by more gradual and modulated shifts.

Play patterns of fathers are, however, influenced by the amount of time that they spend with their infants. In a recent study, Tiffany Field of the University of Miami compared the play of fathers who served as primary caretakers for their infants to that of fathers who were secondary caretakers—the traditional father role. The primary caretaker fathers smiled more often, imitated their infants' facial expressions and their high-pitched vocalizations. These play patterns were similar to those of mothers who are primary caretakers. Probably mothers and fathers who spend a good deal of time with their infants recognize that infants of this age (four months) enjoy being imitated.

One important implication of the finding that primary caretakers—whether male or female—are similar, is that father-mother differences are not necessarily biologically fixed. Instead, these differences might be due to cultural factors such as the amount of experience males and females typically have with their infants. Biological sex of the caretaker may be a less important determinant of caretaker behavior than experience with infants.

Fathers and Sons

Although it is a common cultural stereotype that fathers want a boy, there is considerable truth to this view. Not only in our own culture, but in a wide variety of other cultures, fathers have a three-to-one preference for a boy over a girl—at least for their first-born. These preferences affect reproduction patterns. According to psychologist Lois Hoffman of Rutgers University: "Couples are more likely to continue to have children if they have only girls. They will have more children than they originally planned to try for a boy."

After the birth of their infant, parents, especially fathers, have clear stereotypes concerning the particular type of behavior that they expect of boy and girl babies. Even before the opportunity to hold their infants, fathers rated their sons as firmer, larger featured, better co-ordinated, more alert, and stronger, while they rated their daughters as softer, finer featured, weaker, and more delicate.

Not only do men prefer to have sons and expect them to be different, fathers treat them differently as well—even in the newborn period. In our own hospital-based observations of father-infant interaction, we found that fathers touched first-born boys more than either later-born boys or girls of either ordinal position. Fathers vocalize more to first-born boys than first-born girls. Nor are the differences in fathers' behavior with boy and girl infants restricted to the newborn period. Various investigators report that fathers look at their year-old male infants more, vocalize more to their sons, and play more with their sons than their daughters, particularly their first-born sons. Mothers, on the other hand, do not show as strong preferences, but if they do discriminate, they show heightened involvement with girls. Cross-cultural and comparative data tell a similar story. In studies of the Israeli kibbutzim, fathers were found to visit for longer periods in the children's house with their four-month-old sons than with their infant daughters. Even adult male rhesus monkeys play with male infants more than female infants while female adult monkeys interact more with female infants. Whether this pattern of heightened involvement of fathers with sons reflects what the sociobiologists, such as E.O. Wilson and Robert L. Trivers of Harvard University, call gene investment, or whether it is an outcome of cultural shaping, is still an open question.

Fathers' Effects on Infants and Mothers
Even though fathers spend less time with their infants than mothers, the quality rather than the quantity of parent-infant interaction is the important predictor of infant development. Not surprisingly, then, variations in father-infant interaction patterns do affect the infant's social and cognitive development. However, boys are generally affected more than girls.

The majority of infants develop a positive social relationship or "attachment" (a preference or desire to be close to a specific person) to both their fathers and their mothers by the end of the first year. This is an important finding which directly challenges the popular assumption of the influential British ethologist, John Bowlby, that infants should prefer or even be uniquely attached to their mothers. Clearly both fathers and mothers are important "attachment" objects for infants. As we have already seen, the roles that father and mother play in the infant's social world may be different. What behavior affects the strength of the father-infant relationship?

According to one study, the strength of the father-infant relationship—assessed by the infant's responsiveness to his father—is related to the degree of the father's involvement in routine caretaking and the stimulation level of paternal play. This relation was especially true for boys in this study of eight-month-old infants. Confirming this relationship are studies which show that social responsiveness of five-month-old male infants is lower where the father is absent than in homes where he is present. Not only is high involvement related to a stronger father-infant bond, but a high degree of father-infant interaction helps a child cope more adequately in other social situations as well. Children react to the stress of being left alone with a stranger better if their fathers are active and involved caretakers. Children who are not cared for by their fathers show extensive distress in the laboratory situation when left alone.

Cognitive progress is affected by the father-infant relationship as well. Scores on standard tests of infant mental development were positively related to the amount of contact with the father in five-to-six-month-old lower class black infants. However, variations in father interaction were unrelated to cognitive development of female infants. Similarly, infants from homes where fathers were absent performed less well on the tests of cognitive development. Other studies with older infants suggest that fathers and mothers contribute to their infants' cognitive development in different ways. While the quality of father-infant play patterns was related to higher cognitive progress, for mothers it was verbal stimulation that was the best predictor of infant cognitive status. In short, both parents may contribute, but in unique ways, to their developing infant.

The father's involvement, however, cannot be adequately understood independently of his role as part of the family. Fathers affect infants not only in the direct ways that we have described, but in a variety of indirect ways as well. For example, a father may affect his child by modifying his wife's attitudes and behaviors toward the child. Recent studies by Frank A. Pedersen and his colleagues at the National Institute of Child Health and Development in Washington, D.C. have shown that the adequacy of a mother's feeding skill was related to the degree of emotional support provided by her husband.

Cultural Supports for Father
Just as mothers can benefit from opportunities to learn and practice caretaking skills, in a time when fathers are increasingly being expected to share caretaking responsibilities, these learning opportunities need to be available for fathers as well.

Supportive intervention for fathers might assume a variety of forms. First, an increase in opportunities for learning caretaking skills is needed.

Such opportunities might be provided through pre- and post-partum training programs for fathers. Second, fathers need increased opportunities to practice and implement these skills. Paternity leaves would help provide these opportunities. Opportunities for contact with the infant in the early post-partum period could alter subsequent parent-infant interaction patterns. Preliminary evidence from recent studies suggests that father-infant interaction patterns can be modified by hospital-based interventions. John Lind, a Swedish obstetrician, found that fathers who were provided the opportunity to learn and practice caretaking skills during the post-partum hospital period were more involved in the care of the infant three months later at home.

My colleagues Shelley Hymel, Thomas Power and Barbara Tinsley and I recently presented to American fathers a videotape of father-infant interaction during the early post-partum hospital period. The videotape provided information concerning the newborn infant's perceptual and social competence, play techniques and caretaking skills. Fathers were observed during feeding and play. Fathers who viewed the film were better able to maintain infant feeding and vocalized more to their infants—especially their first-born sons—during play. In addition, the fathers who saw the film in the hospital participated in feeding and diapering activities at home when their infants were three months old. However, the film increased the amount of caretaking only for fathers of boys; fathers of girls were unaffected by the film intervention. This selective effect of our intervention for boys is similar to earlier findings that fathers are more involved with sons than daughters.

Considerable care must be taken in the implementation of these support systems. One must consider parents' rights. The aim is not to impose on all families an implicit scenario of the liberated family and an endorsement of egalitarian family organization. Too often "more" is equated with "improvement." However, in many families, increased participation by the father may cause conflict and disruption as a result of the threat to well-established and satisfying role definitions. Intervention, therefore, should be sensitively geared to the needs of individual families, and the dynamics and beliefs of the couple should be recognized at the outset.

Fathers play a unique and important role in infancy. As social standards continue to change it is likely that fathers will be assuming an increasingly larger role in the care and feeding of infants and young children. Our evidence suggests that not only can they assume these responsibilities competently, but that the result is likely to be beneficial for all—infants, mothers and fathers.   □

8

"And the whole earth was of one language and of one speech"

GENESIS. 11:1

Children and Language

They Learn The Same Way All Around The World

by Dan I. Slobin

ACCORDING TO THE ACCOUNT of linguistic history set forth in the book of Genesis, all men spoke the same language until they dared to unite to build the Tower of Babel. So that men could not cooperate to build a tower that would reach into heaven, God acted to "confound the language of all the earth" to insure that groups of men "may not understand one another's speech."

What was the original universal language of mankind? This is the question that Psammetichus, ruler of Egypt in the seventh century B.C., asked in the first controlled psychological experiment in recorded history—an experiment in developmental psycholinguistics reported by Herodotus:

"Psammetichus . . . took at random, from an ordinary family, two newly born infants and gave them to a shepherd to be brought up amongst his flocks, under strict orders that no one should utter a word in their presence. They were to be kept by themselves in a lonely cottage. . . ."

Psammetichus wanted to know whether isolated children would speak Egyptian words spontaneously—thus

proving, on the premise that ontogeny recapitulates phylogeny, that Egyptians were the original race of mankind.

In two years, the children spoke their first word: *becos*, which turned out to be the Phrygian word for bread. The Egyptians withdrew their claim that they were the world's most ancient people and admitted the greater antiquity of the Phrygians.

Same. We no longer believe, of course, that Phrygian was the original language of all the earth (nor that it was Hebrew, as King James VII of Scotland thought). No one knows which of the thousands of languages is the oldest—perhaps we will never know. But recent work in developmental psycholinguistics indicates that the languages of the earth are not as confounded as we once believed. Children in all nations seem to learn their native languages in much the same way. Despite the diversity of tongues, there are linguistic universals that seem to rest upon the developmental universals of the human mind. Every language is learnable by children of preschool-age, and it is becoming apparent that little

children have some definite ideas about how a language is structured and what it can be used for:

Mmm, I want to eat maize.
What?
Where is the maize?
There is no more maize.
Mmm.
Mmm.
[Child seizes an ear of corn]:
What's this?
It's not our maize.
Whose is it?
It belongs to grandmother.
Who harvested it?
They harvested it.
Where did they harvest it?
They harvested it down over there.
Way down over there?
Mmm. [yes]
Let's look for some too.
You look for some.
Fine.
Mmm.
[Child begins to hum]

The dialogue is between a mother and a two-and-a-half-year-old girl. Anthropologist Brian Stross of the University of Texas recorded it in a

"The basic operations of grammar all are acquired by about age four, regardless of native language or social setting."

thatched hut in an isolated Mayan village in Chiapas, Mexico. Except for the fact that the topic was maize and the language was Tzeltal, the conversation could have taken place anywhere, as any parent will recognize. The child uses short, simple sentences, and her mother answers in kind. The girl expresses her needs and seeks information about such things as location, possession, past action, and so on. She does not ask about time, remote possibilities, contingencies, and the like—such things don't readily occur to the two-year-old in any culture, or in any language.

Our research team at the University of California at Berkeley has been studying the way children learn languages in several countries and cultures. We have been aided by similar research at Harvard and at several other American universities, and by the work of foreign colleagues. We have gathered reasonably firm data on the acquisition of 18 languages, and have suggestive findings on 12 others. Although the data are still scanty for many of these languages, a common picture of human-language development is beginning to emerge.

In all cultures the child's first word generally is a noun or proper name, identifying some object, animal, or person he sees every day. At about two years—give or take a few months—a child begins to put two words together to form rudimentary sentences. The two-word stage seems to be universal.

To get his meaning across, a child at the two-word stage relies heavily on gesture, tone and context. Lois Bloom, professor of speech, Teachers College, Columbia University, reported a little American girl who said *Mommy sock* on two distinct occasions: on finding her mother's sock and on being dressed by her mother. Thus the same phrase expressed possession in one context (*Mommy's sock*) and an agent-object relationship in another (*Mommy is putting on the sock*).

But even with a two-word horizon, children can get a wealth of meanings across:

IDENTIFICATION: *See doggie.*
LOCATION: *Book there.*
REPETITION: *More milk.*
NONEXISTENCE: *Allgone thing.*
NEGATION: *Not wolf.*
POSSESSION: *My candy.*
ATTRIBUTION: *Big car.*
AGENT-ACTION: *Mama walk.*
AGENT-OBJECT: *Mama book* (meaning, "Mama read book").
ACTION-LOCATION: *Sit chair.*
ACTION-DIRECT OBJECT: *Hit you.*
ACTION-INDIRECT OBJECT: *Give papa.*
ACTION-INSTRUMENT: *Cut knife.*
QUESTION: *Where ball?*

The striking thing about this list is its universality. The examples are drawn from child talk in English, German, Russian, Finnish, Turkish, Samoan and Luo, but the entire list could probably be made up of examples from two-year-old speech in any language.

Word. A child easily figures out that the speech he hears around him contains discrete, meaningful elements, and that these elements can be combined. And children make the combinations themselves—many of their meaningful phrases would never be heard in adult speech. For example, Martin Braine studied a child who said things like *allgone outside* when he returned home and shut the door, *more page* when he didn't want a story to end, *other fix* when he wanted something repaired, and so on. These clearly are expressions created by the child, not mimicry of his parents. The matter is especially clear in the Russian language, in which noun endings vary with the role the noun plays in a sentence. As a rule, Russian children first use only the nominative ending in all combinations, even when it is grammatically incorrect. What is important to children is the *word*, not the ending; the *meaning*, not the grammar.

At first, the two-word limit is quite severe. A child may be able to say *daddy throw, throw ball*, and *daddy ball*—indicating that he understands the full proposition, *daddy throw ball*—yet be unable to produce all three words in one stretch. Again, though the data are limited, this seems to be a universal fact about children's speech.

Tools. Later a child develops a rudimentary grammar within the two-word format. These first grammatical devices are the most basic formal tools of human language: intonation, word order, and inflection.

A child uses intonation to distinguish meanings even at the one-word stage, as when he indicates a request by a rising tone, or a demand with a loud, insistent tone. But at the two-word stage another device, a contrastive stress, becomes available. An English-speaking child might say BABY *chair* to indicate possession, and *baby* CHAIR to indicate location or destination.

English sentences typically follow a subject-verb-object sequence, and children learn the rules early. In the example presented earlier, *daddy throw ball*, children use some two-word combinations (*daddy throw, throw ball, daddy ball*) but not others (*ball daddy, ball throw, throw daddy*). Samoan children follow the standard order of possessed-possessor. A child may be sensitive to word order even if his native language does not stress it. Russian children will sometimes adhere strictly to one word order, even when other orders would be equally acceptable.

Some languages provide different word-endings (inflections) to express various meanings, and children who learn these languages are quick to acquire the word-endings that express direct objects, indirect objects and locations. The direct-object inflection is one of the first endings that children pick up in such languages as Russian, Serbo-Croatian, Latvian, Hungarian, Finnish and Turkish. Children learning English, an Indo-European language, usually take a long time to learn locative prepositions such as *on, in, under,* etc. But in Hungary, Finland, or Tur-

"Mothers in other cultures do not
speak to children very much—children hear
speech mainly from other children."

key, where the languages express location with case-endings on the nouns, children learn how to express locative distinctions quite early.

Place. Children seem to be attuned to the ends of words. German children learn the inflection system relatively late, probably because it is attached to articles (*der, die, das,* etc.) that appear before the nouns. The Slavic, Hungarian, Finnish and Turkish inflectional systems, based on noun suffixes, seem relatively easy to learn. And it is not just a matter of articles being difficult to learn, because Bulgarian articles which are noun suffixes are learned very early. The relevant factor seems to be the position of the grammatical marker relative to a main content word.

By the time he reaches the end of the two-word stage, the child has much of the basic grammatical machinery he needs to acquire any particular native language: words that can be combined in order and modified by intonation and inflection. These rules occur, in varying degrees, in all languages, so that all languages are about equally easy for children to learn.

Gap. When a child first uses three words in one phrase, the third word usually fills in the part that was implicit in his two-word statements. Again, this seems to be a universal pattern of development. It is dramatically explicit when the child expands his own communication as he repeats it: *Want that . . . Andrew want that.*

Just as the two-word structure resulted in idiosyncratic pairings, the three-word stage imposes its own limits. When an English-speaking child wishes to add an adjective to the subject-verb-object form, something must go. He can say *Mama drink coffee* or *Drink hot coffee,* but not *Mama drink hot coffee.* This developmental limitation on sentence span seems to be universal: the child's mental ability to express ideas grows faster than his ability to formulate the ideas in complete sentences. As the child learns to con-

struct longer sentences, he uses more complex grammatical operations. He attaches new elements to old sentences (*Where I can sleep?*) before he learns how to order the elements correctly

Work Done

INDO-EUROPEAN FAMILY
Romance Branch:
Italian, Spanish, French, Romanian
Germanic Branch:
English, Dutch, German, Danish,
Swedish, Norwegian
Slavic Branch:
Russian, Polish, Czech, Slovenian,
Serbo-Croatian, Bulgarian
Baltic Branch:
Latvian

OTHER FAMILIES
SEMITIC FAMILY
   Hebrew, Arabic
URALIC FAMILY
   Finnish, Hungarian
TURKISH FAMILY
   Turkish
SOUTH CAUCASIAN FAMILY
   Georgian (spoken in Georgian Soviet
   Socialist Republic)
EASTERN SUDANIC FAMILY
   Luo (spoken in Kenya)
KOREAN FAMILY
   Korean
JAPANESE-RYUKYUAN FAMILY
   Japanese
HAN CHINESE FAMILY
   Mandarin
BODO-NAGA-KACHIN FAMILY
   Garo (spoken in Assam, India)
AUSTRONESIAN FAMILY
   Samoan
MAYAN FAMILY
   Tzeltal (spoken in Yucatan)

The available material varies greatly, from detailed observational and experimental studies to brief and anecdotal reports. We have reasonably firm data on about 18 of these languages. In addition, I am aware of ongoing research on the acquisition of the following native languages: Kurdish, Persian, Armenian, Albanian, Ukranian, Swahili, Koya, Tagalog and Quechua. The language classification in this table comes from the University of Indiana language archives (C. F. Voegelin and F. M. Voegelin).
          —Dan Slobin

(*Where can I sleep?*). When the child learns to combine two sentences he first compresses them end-to-end (*the boy fell down that was running*) then finally he embeds one within the other (*the boy that was running fell down*).

Across. These are the basic operations of grammar, and to the extent of our present knowledge, they all are acquired by about age four, regardless of native language or social setting. The underlying principles emerge so regularly and so uniformly across diverse languages that they seem to make up an essential part of the child's basic means of information processing. They seem to be comparable to the principles of object constancy and depth perception. Once the child develops these guidelines he spends most of his years of language acquisition learning the specific details and applications of these principles to his particular native language.

Lapse. Inflection systems are splendid examples of the sort of linguistic detail that children must master. English-speaking children must learn the great irregularities of some of our most frequently used words. Many common verbs have irregular past tenses: *came, fell, broke.* The young child may speak these irregular forms correctly the first time—apparently by memorizing a separate past tense form for each verb—only to lapse into immature talk (*comed, falled, breaked*) once he begins to recognize regularities in the way most verbs are conjugated. These over-regularized forms persist for years, often well into elementary school. Apparently regularity heavily outranks previous practice, reinforcement, and imitation of adult forms in influence on children. The child seeks regularity and is deaf to exceptions. [See "Learning the Language," by Ursula Bellugi, PT, December 1970.]

The power of apparent regularities has been noted repeatedly in the children's speech of every language we have studied. When a Russian noun

"Every normal child masters his particular native tongue, and learns basic principles in a universal order common to all children."

appears as the object of a sentence (*he liked the story*), the speaker must add an accusative suffix to the noun—one of several possible accusative suffixes, and the decision depends on the gender and the phonological form of the particular noun (and if the noun is masculine, he must make a further distinction on whether it refers to a human being). When the same noun appears in the possessive form (*the story's ending surprised him*) he must pick from a whole set of possessive suffixes, and so on, through six grammatical cases, for every Russian noun and adjective.

Grasp. The Russian child, of course, does not learn all of this at once, and his gradual, unfolding grasp of the language is instructive. He first learns at the two-word stage that different cases are expressed with different noun-endings. His strategy is to choose one of the accusative inflections and use it in all sentences with direct objects regardless of the peculiarities of individual nouns. He does the same for each of the six grammatical cases. His choice of inflection is always correct within the broad category—that is, the prepositional is always expressed by *some* prepositional inflection, and dative by *some* dative inflection, and so on, just as an English-speaking child always expresses the past tense by a past-tense inflection, and not by some other sort of inflection.

The Russian child does not go from a single suffix for each case to full mastery of the system. Rather, he continues to reorganize his system in successive sweeps of over-regularizations. He may at first use the feminine ending with all accusative nouns, then use the masculine form exclusively for a time, and only much later sort out the appropriate inflections for all genders. These details, after all, have nothing to do with meaning, and it is meaning that children pay most attention to.

Bit. Once a child can distinguish the various semantic notions, he begins to unravel the arbitrary details, bit by bit. The process apparently goes on below

the level of consciousness. A Soviet psychologist, D.N. Bogoyavlenskiy, showed five- and six-year-old Russian children a series of nonsense words equipped with Russian suffixes, each word attached to a picture of an object or animal that the word supposedly represented. The children had no difficulty realizing that words ending in augmentative suffixes were related to large objects, and that those ending in diminutives went with small objects. But they could not explain the formal differences aloud. Bogoyavlenskiy would say, "Yes, you were right about the difference between the animals—one is little and the other is big; now pay attention to the words themselves as I say them: *lar-laryonok.* What's the difference between them?" None of the children could give any sort of answer. Yet they easily understood the semantic implications of the suffixes.

Talk. When we began our cross-cultural studies at Berkeley, we wrote a manual for our field researchers so that they could record samples of mother-child interaction in other cultures with the same systematic measures we had used to study language development in middle-class American children. But most of our field workers returned to tell us that, by and large, mothers in other cultures do not speak to children very much—children hear speech mainly from other children. The isolated American middle-class home, in which a mother spends long periods alone with her children, may be a relatively rare social situation in the world. The only similar patterns we observed were in some European countries and in a Mayan village.

This raised an important question: Does it matter—for purposes of grammatical development—whether the main interlocutor for a small child is his mother?

The evidence suggests that it does not. First of all, the rate and course of grammatical development seem to be strikingly similar in all of the cultures we have studied. Further, no-

where does a mother devote great effort to correcting a child's grammar. Most of her corrections are directed at speech etiquette and communication, and, as Roger Brown has noted, reinforcement tends to focus on the truth of a child's utterance rather than on the correctness of his grammar.

Ghetto. In this country, Harvard anthropologist Claudia Mitchell-Kernan has studied language development in black children in an urban ghetto. There, as in foreign countries, children got most of their speech input from older children rather than from their mothers. These children learned English rules as quickly as did the middle-class white children that Roger Brown studied, and in the same order. Further, mother-to-child English is simple—very much like child-to-child English. I expect that our cross-cultural studies will find a similar picture in other countries.

How. A child is set to learn a language—any language—as long as it occurs in a direct and active context. In these conditions, every normal child masters his particular native tongue, and learns basic principles in a universal order common to all children, resulting in our adult Babel of linguistic diversity. And he does all this without being able to say how. The Soviet scholar Kornei Ivanovich Chukovsky emphasized this unconscious aspect of linguistic discovery in his famous book on child language, *From Two to Five:*

"It is frightening to think what an enormous number of grammatical forms are poured over the poor head of the young child. And he, as if it were nothing at all, adjusts to all this chaos, constantly sorting out into rubrics the disorderly elements of the words he hears, without noticing as he does this, his gigantic effort. If an adult had to master so many grammatical rules within so short a time, his head would surely burst. . . . In truth, the young child is the hardest mental toiler on our planet. Fortunately, he does not even suspect this."

9

Twins With a Language All Their Own

Cynthia Gorney

Photograph by Stephen Kelley, copyright Union-Tribune Publishing Co.

SAN DIEGO—The film is two years old now, and still riveting.

Two 6-year-old girls, faces alight, are rearranging furniture in a large dollhouse. They have short brown hair, little print dresses and eyes that scrunch with concentration as they examine each new piece of furniture. Their conversation, to the untrained ear, sounds like this:

"Genebene manita."

"Nomemee."

"Eebedeebeda. Dis din qui naba."

"Neveda. Ca Baedabada."

"Ga."

The film was made in July 1977 at a San Diego hospital, and was the first recorded study of two animated

twin sisters whose case has fascinated experts ever since the bewildered parents first brought the girls in for help. Grace and Virginia Kennedy, apparently healthy and energetic identical twins, spoke to each other in a rapid-fire language that nobody else understood.

It was not English.

It was not German, which was their mother's native language, and which their grandmother had spoken to them while caring for them during the day.

Somehow, in the extended privacy of a world without regular visitors, the sisters had made a language of their own—a "twin language," which occurs fairly often in very young twins, but rarely in children so old, and almost never to the exclusion of any other tongue. The Kennedy girls' only concession to English was an occasional request for certain items ("Want water," they would say, or "Want juice"), although it was obvious that they understood both English and German when someone spoke directly to them.

They called each other Poto, for Grace, and Camenga, for Virginia. They had never been to school, or played much with other children. Until they arrived two years ago at the San Diego Children's Hospital Speech, Hearing and Neurosensory Center, the girls had never been examined by speech experts; their father, then an unemployed accountant, had been referred to specialists only after he told the state unemployment office, in response to a routine question, that his daughters were not in school because they could not talk to others.

And when strangers spoke to them in their own language, after careful transcription of what seemed to be the twins' words, the girls looked utterly blank—"like we are crazy," one of their therapists said.

"They call me Camenga," Virginia Kennedy says, bending over a sheet of paper in her sister's bedroom to print the word.

Why do they call her that?

"Cause."

Because what?

"Poto," Ginny says, pointing at Grace. And that is all she will say about that. The twins know a photographer is coming to take their picture—"When is the camera man coming?" Grace keeps asking—but they do not seem to know why. Their language is leaving them, and if they understand their extraordinary history at all, they do not talk about it with strangers.

At 8½, the Kennedy twins are second graders in special San Diego public school speech handicap classes. They have been intentionally separated, attending different schools and the language they now speak, both in school and to each other, seems to be mostly a simplified and very fast English—a sort of speeded-up pidgin. Tenses, conjugations and subordinate clauses—all the stubborn agonies of high school Latin and French—still give them trouble, and there is no way of knowing how quickly, if ever, they will pick up the more complicated nuances of standard English speech.

For the last two years, ever since the twins' much publicized arrival at the San Diego hospital, linguist and speech pathologists have been examining their private language in great detail, trying to understand where it came from and how it works. Three linguists at the University of California's San Diego campus have listened over and over to the videotapes of the twins, spending as much as an hour on each minute of tape, unscrambling vocabulary and charting syntax like the military analysts of some complex maritime code.

Grace and Virginia Kennedy were born in Columbus, the first children of a Georgia-born accountant named Thomas Kennedy and the German woman he had met while traveling in Munich. (Kennedy has three other

children from a previous marriage.) The day after the twins were born, as Kennedy remembers it, Grace suddenly raised her head and stared at him as she lay in her hospital crib. She was having a convulsive seizure. Ginny had a similar seizure the following day.

"The pediatrician went into the brain area to see what was causing the seizures," Kennedy says. He says the doctor's tests showed a slight accumulation of fluid on the brain of each baby. The fluid was released and although the twins were given anticonvulsion drugs, they continued to have seizures off and on for the first six months of their lives.

Then at about six months the convulsions stopped in both girls. Neither the Kennedys nor their doctor understood exactly why (and there is still no certainty what effect the seizures may have had), but Christine Kennedy says the doctor, very tentatively, pronounced both girls healthy. "He said they were too small to actually say they would come out normal," she says. "He said it would take all the way up to their fifth or sixth year before they (the doctors) could see."

When the girls began to talk, they did what most children do. They rattled along, making noises that sounded like language, and they said "mommy" and "daddy" in distinct English. By the time they were 6, when the family had moved to California, they were still doing precisely that. They stayed at home most days, cared for by a German-speaking grandmother who attended to their needs but apparently did not talk to them much. Kennedy says both he and his wife would spend their days out looking for work, and that when they came home and watched their daughters in animated but unintelligible conversation with each other, they simply did not know what to think.

"We had been cautioned that they might be mentally retarded, and we wouldn't know until they were 6 years old," he says. "We just thought it was a childhood thing between them."

It was not until the Children's Hospital therapists first talked about private languages, Kennedy says, that he began to think about what he had sometimes seen as the girls played together. Grace—the first born, by five minutes, and the more dominant of the two—would say a word to Ginny while holding up an object, as though naming it.

"Our best guess," says Chris Hagen, chairman of the speech pathology department that took on the Kennedy twins' therapy, "would be that it had something to do with the communicative environment."

"Or the lack thereof," adds Donald Krebs, director of the speech, hearing and neurosensory center.

What the children apparently did, as far as speech pathologists and linguists can determine, was to latch onto the English and German sounds they heard spoken around them and reshape the familiar noises into words of their own. It took months of listening to the children's voices, sometimes replaying tapes again and again, before certain words began to make sense: "pinit" meant "finished," "gimba" meant "camper," "buda" meant "butter." The girls could pronounce words quite differently from one moment to the next, which made understanding them even harder; Richard Meier, a University of California, San Diego, psycholinguistics graduate student who worked on the language, recorded 26 different pronunciations of the twins' word for "potato"—ranging from "puhed" to "pandaydooz"—in one 15 minute videotape.

There were some words that took longer still. "Toolenis," for example, had them stumped for a long time. They had figured out by watching the children that the word meant "spaghetti," but they could not imagine why. Finally the pathologists asked Mrs. Kennedy where the word might have come from, and she brightened immediately. "While cooking spaghetti, now and then, she had sung "O Sole Mio.""

Their syntax, Meier says, was basically simple English —subject, verb, object—with a few striking exceptions. When the girls used the word "anmet," which seemed to be a distortion of the German word "enmechen," meaning to fasten or to fix, they stuck the verb at the end of the sentence, German-style.

The most maddening part of the Kennedy twins' story is that they may never be able to explain it either. There is no way to tell whether Ginny and Grace will ever remember the sound or the secrets of the private language—or whether they have any idea, right now, about why these large people fell over themselves just to hear twins converse.

10 Childhood: The Last Frontier in Sex Research

by John Money

If scientists were permitted to study childhood sexuality we might be better equipped to raise healthy children

You don't know how difficult it is to do postpubertal—let alone prepubertal—sex research until you try to finance it. Then you crash, head-on, into the major taboo of our society, the sex taboo, which is diligently guarded by politicians, bureaucrats, and others who guard public and private funds.

Consider what happened before a 1976 conference on the ethics of sex research and sex therapy held under the auspices of Masters and Johnson. The organizers were advised to delete the term *sex* from the title of their application for Public Health Service supporting funds. Imagine the expurgated title: "Ethics of S . . Research and S . . Therapy," as prim as if the unmentionable word were F . . .

S . . research is equated with f . . . research by professional and lay people alike, especially in the sexology of childhood. In consequence, childhood sexuality remains a research frontier, unopened to empirical and operational study. Any attempt to cross the frontier is subject to condemnation, as if juvenile sexology constituted a branch of pornography, which, in turn, is stigmatized as illicit and immoral. The social mechanisms for maintaining the taboo on juvenile sex research include the withholding of funds, academic ostracism and the mouthing of falsely pious platitudes about the "informed consent" of infants and children as subjects of research. (For their protection, participants in clinical investigative treatment must now sign a consent form after receiving a complete explanation of what will be done, and what the risks are. Children, it is claimed, have no legal rights, and therefore no capacity to give this informed consent.)

The hidden assumption behind the common attitude toward juvenile sex research is that childhood is an age of sexual innocence that would be tarnished by research. Innocent children must be protected from the depravity of sexologists. Paradoxically, another hidden assumption is that because children are conceived in iniquity and born in original sin, they are programmed for sexual depravity unless supervised and disciplined. In consequence, juvenile sex research encourages juvenile sexual depravity.

What proponents of the doctrine of original sin define as sexual depravity in childhood is, in fact, nothing more than the sexual rehearsal play that is typical in the development of the young of many, if not all, species of primates. Not only is early sexual rehearsal play typical in the behavioral development of most primate species, it is a prerequisite to the proper maturation of adult sexual behavior.

The evidence in support of this proposition has been well established in rhesus monkeys. In late infancy and early childhood, these animals engage in presenting and mounting play. Initially, they mount the head end and the sides, as well as the tail end. Gradually they acquire directional orientation. The males become accustomed to mounting and the females to presenting. When the males first accustom themselves to mounting the female's rear, they stand with their feet on the floor. Later, they achieve

John Money, Professor of Medical Psychology and Associate Professor of Pediatrics at The Johns Hopkins University and Hospital, is a prominent sexologist. Among his books is MAN AND WOMAN, BOY AND GIRL, *originally published by The Johns Hopkins University Press and now available in paperback from Mentor.*

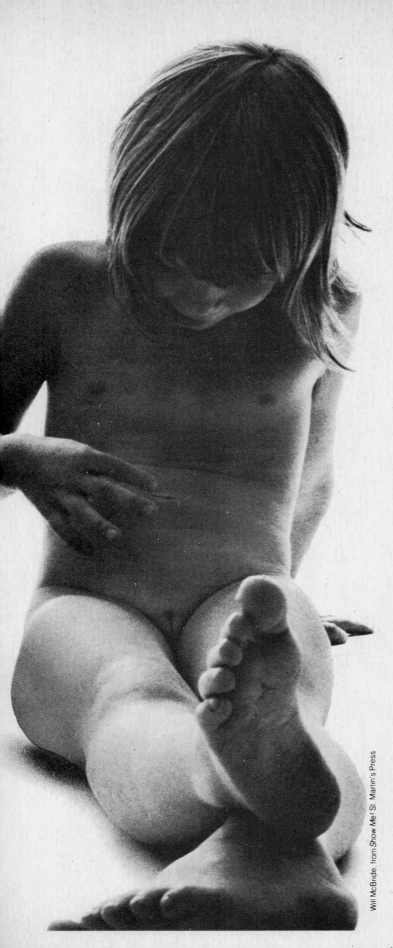

adult positioning with their feet clasping the legs of the female above the ankle.

When infant monkeys are reared in social isolation without playmates and without even a mother in place of playmates, they are deprived of all social and sexual rehearsal play. Then, after puberty, they are unable to establish a sexual partnership. Even with a gentle and experienced partner, the deprived animal—male or female—is unable to get properly positioned for copulation. They do not breed. If pregnancy is experimentally induced, the female becomes an abusing mother—so abusive, in fact, that she almost certainly will kill her baby. Atypical and bizarre sexual behavior associated with excessive isolation in captivity has been recorded also in a higher primate, the chimpanzee. But infantile deprivation in chimpanzees has not yet been systematically documented, as it has been in rhesus monkeys.

Human children, like the young of other primates, also engage in sexual rehearsal play. In our culture, the natural history of sexual rehearsal play cannot be ascertained, because free sexual expression among children is prohibited. In some children the prohibition takes effect successfully, and sexual play is suppressed. In others, the prohibition simply sends sexual play underground where it may never become known to adults. Thus, we know only about sexual play, such as infantile masturbation, which occurs before the prohibition takes effect, or play which is intruded upon by adults and, typically, subject to further prohibition.

Beyond our own culture, we can glimpse at what may be the natural way in which children's sexual rehearsal play evolves. The Aboriginal inhabitants of Arnhem Land on the Australian north coast, for example, traditionally have no taboo against infantile sexuality, and, despite Westernization, some of the old traditions survive. Once in a while in nursery school at nap-time a boy may press up against a girl, his body making pelvic thrusting movements, an innocuous rhythmic contentment resembling in significance the thumb-sucking of other children nearby.

Aboriginal children a year or two older, aged five or six, may play at more explicit coital positioning when going to sleep outdoors around the campfire. Adults often laugh their approval, as if to say: "Isn't it cute? They will know how to do it right when they grow up." It is not clear whether these children would invent such positioning in play if they had no model to copy or whether they mimic the play of older children. They may see adolescents and adults copulating, but that is not likely, since Aboriginal adults typically copulate in private, usually in the dark.

Rehearsal of pelvic thrusting and coital positioning is not the beginning of sexuality in childhood. In fact, the first phase of sexual rehearsal may begin even before birth with erections in boys. Certainly erections occur neonatally and throughout infancy and childhood. Even if erections are not observed during waking hours, they can be seen to occur from birth onwards during REM sleep (when rapid eye movements indicate that the sleeper is dreaming). The corresponding phenomenon in girls has not been fully identified and documented.

The first postnatal phase of sexual rehearsal is sensuous rather than sexual and it is not play so much as part of living—the haptic sensuousness of skin contact in clinging, cuddling and hugging. If children are delivered by natural childbirth methods, skin contact begins at birth when the baby emerges from the vagina and lies on the mother's belly. In the first few hours after delivery the pair-bond between mother and infant is established, partly through the sense of sight, but chiefly through the haptic, or tactual, sense. This bonding is not only of great importance to the well-being of mother and child; it is a rehearsal, so to speak, of the pair-bonding of romantic love, which usually happens for the first time in adolescence or young adulthood.

John Money

Sensuous pair-bonding in infancy is essential for human behavioral development. It continues during breast-feeding, lessens gradually during weaning, is maintained during childhood, and has a great resurgence as an erotic pair-bond at or after puberty. The infant's first pair-bond is necessarily with the mother, but a parallel bond is established between infant and father, beginning even at delivery if the father is present.

When Freud formulated his theory of infantile sexuality, he overlooked the haptic phase, possibly because it is initially contemporaneous with what he termed the oral phase. Freud's second, or anal phase, is not exclusively sensuous. It also coincides with the onset of sphincter control and is a programmed phase of learning in which a connection is established between the stimulus to eliminate and the response of finding a place to eliminate.

The genital phase proposed by Freud is the beginning of authentic sexuality in that the child experiences the sensuousness of the sex organs. In Europe until the eighteenth century, parents and guardians soothed fretful children by masturbating the genitals. In the aftermath of the Inquisition, however, masturbation came to be viewed as the cause of insanity and other symptoms of degeneracy, and adults who played with children's genitals were punished as child molesters.

In modern terms, Freud's oedipal phase of late infancy and early childhood does not relate only to genital and erotic sexual rehearsal but also to differentiation of gender identity and role as masculine, feminine, or in some cases, ambivalent. The two principles involved are identification and complementation. Identification is *with* people of the same sex—chiefly parents. Complementation is *to* people of the opposite sex—also chiefly parents. At kindergarten age it is common to observe daughters flirting with their fathers, and sons with their mothers, in a way that clearly rehearses the flirtation of what, in adolescence and adulthood, will be known as the proceptive phase. Proception is a new term for erotic invitation, solicitation, or courtship which postpubertally leads up to the phase of acception (copulation), which then may or may not be followed by the phase of conception. Prior to puberty, flirtation in infancy may become frankly erotic, but actual erotic rehearsal during this phase is more likely to be enacted with peers.

Such rehearsal ensures that the behavioral sex differences that are bona fide sexual and erotic will be amalgamated with those differences which are sex-coded by tradition and are actually optional rather than imperative. If rehearsal of the bona fide sex differences—those that ultimately will be associated with impregnation in the male, and menstruation, gestation and lactation in the female—is thwarted, there is a risk that disordered or anomalous erotic, sexual, and psychosexual function will evolve. Such disorders or anomalies come into full bloom when the hormones of puberty lower the threshold for their expression.

As far as sexual rehearsal play is concerned, the middle years of childhood are not latency years as Freud believed. On the contrary, in cultures where sexual play is not forbidden, children express their sexuality from time to time, but not obsessively or excessively. During this phase, children may establish romantic pair bonds or love affairs in play rehearsal, but there is not enough evidence for a firm statement to be made about such behavior.

At puberty, sexual rehearsal play gradually relinquishes its rehearsal function and emerges as the finished performance. The hormones of puberty are the chief agent of this change. Apart from producing obvious changes in the body, these hormones also lower the barrier or threshold to the expression of sexuality in imagery and dreams, and in practice. Puberty does not determine what will be expressed. Rather, it releases that which has already been determined by rehearsals during infancy and childhood.

Nature's ideal developmental program of sexual rehearsal play in childhood is not known; nor do we know all the noxious influences that can misdirect it. Noxious influences on sexuality need not themselves be explicitly sexual. The death of a parent, sibling, or other close relative, for example, may adversely affect a child's psychosexual development. By contrast, a childhood sexual experience, such as being the partner of a relative, or of an older person, need not necessarily affect the child adversely. If violence or trauma are involved, however, the probability of an adverse effect is increased.

What may be important in some cases is not the event itself, but the context in which it is experienced. If a child intrudes on copulating parents—the so-called primal scene—the effect may be adverse if, as is common in our middle class society, the parents have no formula ("playing the mommy-daddy game," for example) for coping with the interruption. In scores of other societies, however, children sleep in the same room with their parents and inevitably see coitus. They know about copulation from as far back as they can remember—even if convention dictates that they not talk about it.

Although there is no firm knowledge of what constitutes a natural program of sexual rehearsal, nor what effect various experiences may have on sexual development, it is almost certain that human beings, like the other primates, require a period of early sexual rehearsal play in order to ensure the maturation and manifestation of functional mating behavior during puberty and later. It could well be that the dysfunctional mating behavior that is prevalent among us as adults comes as an unplanned, unbargained-for result of the imposition of the taboo on sex play in childhood.

Whether this hypothesis is true or false cannot be decided by armchair speculation or doctrinal moralizing. It can be decided only by evidence—the hard-science evidence of well-planned, systematic, and long-term observational research.

It would not be technically difficult to test whether harsh, negative attitudes toward childhood sexuality produce sexual abnormality or inadequacy at puberty, and in adolescence and adulthood.

One could follow two groups of children, one group with a closed-minded, punitive sexual upbringing, and the other raised in an open-minded unpunitive sexual atmosphere. By keeping complete and systematic records, year by year, until puberty and adolescence, one would learn how many children in each group became sexually and psychosexually normal, and how many abnormal. There are already some parents in our society who are openminded about their children's sexual upbringing, as well as many who are not. It would be possible to do this study at any university or medical school in the country.

An even more attractive research possibility would be to compare two or more different cultures in a cross-sectional rather than longitudinal experiment. One would select each culture on the basis of preliminary evidence that it was either open-minded, or closed-minded with respect to childhood sexuality. Then, one would collect further evidence on the sexual rearing of children in each society. One would also collect evidence on how well or how poorly the adults in these societies were getting along in their sex lives—frequency of marital problems, sexual dysfunction, sex offenses, so-called perversions, and other psychosexual anomalies.

There is a dearth of even preliminary evidence of this type, for cultural anthropologists, by and large, have been as prudish as most other scientific and medical people and have not thoroughly recorded sexual matters. In addition, cultural anthropologists are not trained in sexology. No university in the U.S. has a department of sexology. In fact, in all of the Western Hemisphere, only the University of Quebec, in Montreal, Canada, has a department of sexology. And that department is not yet affiliated with a medical school or hospital.

Clearly, information on childhood sex is lacking. Parents do not have sound facts and good theory to guide them in child-rearing. All they have is the folk belief that children's sex play, if discovered, should be severely disciplined, that children should be made to feel guilt and shame, and that the sensuous pleasure found in the sex organs is sinful. Whether they accept or reject this belief, parents must do so as an act of faith, not of reason.

Further research into childhood sexuality could provide the much needed information on which to base reasoned decisions. Why then, does society stand in the way of childhood sex research?

No final and complete answer can be given to this question. It essentially asks why our society has a strong sexual taboo. Not only is that taboo of great an-tiquity, it is also only one manifestation of a total social order. Perhaps, far back in history, our forebears' ruler-priests invented the sex taboo as a principle of child rearing. Inculcation of a taboo ensures the presence of guilt, anxiety and shame, which can be used as a lever to control all sorts of behavior.

Whatever the origin of the sex taboo, one major rationale for maintaining it has today begun to disappear, and that is the prevention of premarital pregnancy. With the invention of the crude rubber condom last century, and the improvement of birth control in this century, the sex play of children and the continuation of that play in actual sex among adolescents need not pose the danger of pregnancy.

The strength of the taboo on sex is evident in that birth control technology alone has not eliminated it. Society's ability to separate recreational and procreational sex is still a source of cultural and moral indigestion.

The sex taboo resists extinction. Punitive treatment of childhood sexuality is the norm. And it is practiced in ignorance. Parents do not know whether punishing sexual rehearsal play may make their children paragons or sexual cripples in adulthood. They do not know whether treating sexual play with dignity and respect will benefit their children, allowing them to lead more fulfilling sexual lives as adults. They need to know, and research into childhood sexuality can help provide the answers—provided, that is, that society, the Congress, and the private foundations will change their timid policy and allocate funds for research into sexuality and its development at all ages, childhood included.   □

11

GOOD SAMARITANS AT AGE TWO?

illustration by Brock Newman

Freud and Piaget did not foresee it. A new government-sponsored
study shows that, as early as one year, some babies are capable
of comforting others who are crying or in pain. Before age two or three,
some children display even more sophisticated altruistic behavior.
But not all mothers want their kids to be Good Samaritans.

By Maya Pines

A two-year-old boy hits a small girl's head accidentally. He looks aghast. "I hurt your hair," he tells the little girl. "Please don't cry."

Another child, a girl only 18 months old, sees her grandmother lying down for a rest. She toddles over to her crib, grabs her own blanket, and covers her grandmother with it.

Those children are normal Americans, neither angelic nor exceptional, says Marian Radke Yarrow, chief of the Laboratory of Developmental Psychology at the National Institute of Mental Health. After a detailed study of children between the ages of 10 months and two-and-a-half years, she *expects* infants to show empathy for the feelings of others. Babies have amazingly generous impulses, she says, and many children perform acts of altruism at a surprisingly early age.

Such findings challenge traditional theories of child development, which hold that young children are totally self-centered and selfish creatures, quite unable to act altruistically before the age of five or six. Yet Yarrow and psychologist Carolyn Zahn-Waxler are very sure of their evidence. Their data show clearly that children have a capacity for compassion and for various kinds of prosocial behavior from at least the age of one, though it may coexist with the capacity for aggression and rage that psychologists have emphasized ever since Freud.

"This precocity gives one pause," declares Yarrow. Although she is not proposing a new theory about the innate goodness of man, the very fact that altruism is possible in such young children comes as a shock at a time when many people seem to be preoccupied with self-gratification above all. Indeed, Yarrow's research project may force us to revise our view of human beings. It leads to some interesting hypotheses about how altruism could be encouraged by parents and society, as well as to questions about the extent to which parents really *want* to foster altruism—some deliberately avoid promoting Good Samaritanism in their children, as we shall see.

Altruism began getting more attention as a research topic about 15 years ago, shortly after Kitty Genovese was murdered on a New York City street. A *New York Times* reporter vividly described the scene: 38 witnesses heard the young woman scream as she was fatally stabbed, many actually saw her being murdered, and yet none did anything to help her, or even tried to call the police, until she was dead. The report stirred up a great deal of discussion about the passivity of the bystanders. Why had so many people failed to act?

A number of psychologists started to investigate the prosocial behavior of adults and older children in different circumstances. By contrast, Marian Yarrow decided to look for the origins of such behavior, turning to young children. A meticulous researcher with a long-standing interest in child development, she wanted to discover how children learn kindness and altruism. She also wanted to find out whether those traits could be developed through training.

Yarrow's idea was to study children before and during the emergence of altruistic behavior, which she defines as actions designed to help someone who is in distress. She started out with three- to five-year-olds in a Washington nursery school. It was a rather daring move, since, according to Jean Piaget's theories of cognitive development, young children are too egocentric to understand anyone else's point of view—and therefore cannot have genuine concern for others—until the age of six or seven.

And, although Freud did not touch on the development of altruism in his writings, traditional Freudians believe that altruistic behavior requires a superego—an internalized representation of morality—that children develop at the age of five or six, when they resolve the Oedipus complex and begin to identify with their parents.

Nevertheless, Yarrow and Waxler set out to observe how preschool children reacted to pictures of distressed children and animals and to some staged events portraying people or animals in trouble. For example, the children were shown a picture of a girl who looked sad while all the other children around her were eating ice cream cones. Or, they were shown a picture of a boy falling off a bike. "What would you do if you were there?," the children were asked. "Give her a lick" or "Get him a Band-aid" were the kind of responses coded as altruistic. The researchers also studied the children's behavior when a kitten was brought into the room entangled in a net of yarn. The same children were studied again after their teachers had modeled various kinds of altruistic behavior for them. While showing the children a three-dimensional scene of a monkey trying to reach a banana, for example, the teacher might turn to the monkey and say, "Oh, you can't reach your food. I'll help you. Here's your banana" (and she would give him the cardboard banana). "Now, you won't be hungry." The teacher would then uncover a picture of a similar dilemma and tell one of the children it was his or her turn.

It became clear right away that some children stood out for their compassion and their willingness to help others, even at the age of three or four. These individual differences were so extreme, both before and after the modeling in nursery school, that Yarrow realized she had actually arrived too late. To find the source of those differences, she would have to start even earlier, with babies in their first and second years of life.

Babies are very inconvenient subjects to study. Their homes are scattered, they don't go to school. "We couldn't get the data we needed about their responses if we just brought them into the lab for short sessions," Yarrow explains. "On the other hand, plenty of distress occurs naturally every day at home—someone falls, another child bites, somebody chokes on food and coughs." To make the most of those incidents, Yarrow tried a novel approach: she enlisted the aid of the mothers.

Soon, 24 women who had answered ads in local newspapers became Yarrow's eyes and ears in an ambitious study. They were told only that it would be a study of children's responses to other people's emotions. (In fact, the researchers wished to study a whole range of responses that might or might not be related to the development of altruism.) All high school or college graduates, the young women started out with a training period during which they learned to become more aware of their own babies' cries, startles, and facial expressions. Then, Yarrow gave each woman a tape recorder and instructed her to dictate a brief report every time someone in the baby's immediate environment showed either affection, happiness, physical pain, respiratory discomfort, sorrow (sadness or crying), anger, or fatigue. The mother was asked to describe exactly what her baby did or said on such occasions, as well as to record her own actions, taping her report as soon as possible after the event.

For nine months, the mothers observed and recorded faithfully. "It became a way of life," one of the women said. "I just kept the recorder plugged in at all times, and dictated whenever anything happened." Some entered the project when their babies were only 10 months old, others when their babies were 15 or 20 months old. Every three weeks, a researcher visited the homes to make independent observations, answer questions, and pick up the tapes, which were later transcribed and analyzed by those in the research group.

It was a revelation for some of the mothers to see how sensitive their babies were to everything that went on around them. Several of them remarked that taking part in the study had made them much more attuned to their children. "It's the best thing that ever happened to me in my relationship to my child," said one mother. Meanwhile, Yarrow, Waxler, and psychiatrist Robert A. King collected a treasure trove of 1,500 incidents, hundreds of which illustrated how young children react to other people's miseries, as well as how their parents shape those reactions.

When faced with someone else's distress, the youngest babies—those less than one year of age—do little more than give a small cry, startle, or stare at the source of trouble. Yet they react. One mother reported that her 10-month-old son heard her choking on some food at the dinner table; he stared at her intently with a worried look. A 10-month-old girl saw her father tickle her mother, who squealed, "Stop it! Don't do that!" Obviously startled, the child let out a small cry.

One of the study's most surprising findings was that as early as the age of one, some babies actually try to comfort people who are crying or in pain. They snuggle up to them, pat them, or hug them. Sometimes they even attempt to help them. When one of the mothers went to a doctor with a sore throat, she had her throat swabbed and made a strangling noise. At once, her small son, only 50 weeks old, tried to knock the swab out of the nurse's hand to defend her.

Another mother told of her 13-month-old son who was hungrily eating his cereal when his father came home, obviously tired, and sat down, resting his head in his hand, next to the boy. The child immediately pulled the father's hand away and tried to feed him some cereal. ("A noble gesture," his mother noted, "because he wanted cereal himself.")

The babies' attempts to help may be somewhat ambiguous. When one 15-month-old boy saw that his mother was very tired, for instance, he patted her gently and offered her his own bottle. But when she refused the bottle, he lay down on her and drank it himself—a mixture of giving and getting comfort that Yarrow finds typical of children at that stage.

At approximately 18 months, it becomes very common for children to imitate other people's laughter, crying, or grimaces. One woman who had accidentally bit her cheek and winced reported that her daughter's face was "an exact mirror of the pain." Another child saw a newborn cry; she watched for a minute as tears welled up in her eyes and she began to cry, too. "Some of these imitations seem almost reflexive," Yarrow says. "They are much like our definition of empathy—a shared emotional response. Others appear more deliberate and studied, as if the child were 'trying on' an emotional expression to see how it feels."

By "trying on" such emotions, children may also test the distinction between themselves and others. When one woman bumped her elbow and said "Ouch," her 20-month-old son at once screwed up his face, rubbed his own elbow, and said, "Ow." Only then did he begin to rub *her* elbow. He seemed to be trying to understand what kind of hurt was involved, and

===

> ## "It became clear that some children stood out for their compassion and their willingness to help others."

===

in whom—in preparation for helping his mother by rubbing her elbow.

Imitation does not always lead to altruism, however. Once a child figures out that "it's somebody else's pain—and thank goodness it's not my own," as Yarrow puts it, he can become either more sensitive to others (and therefore more altruistic) or, on the contrary, more self-centered and unfeeling. Yarrow and Waxler are now studying how the choice is made. "We speculate that this is a critical point in life, when the behavior of parents can be particularly influential," says Yarrow.

The children who are on the path to altruism develop many different ways of helping others. Even before their second birthday, some of them have an impressive repertoire of altruistic behavior, and if one thing doesn't work, they'll try another. That flowering can be seen, as in time-lapse photography, through progressive reports on one little girl whose mother often did baby-sitting for the neighbors' children in her home.

When Laura was 14 months old, her mother reported, she never did anything for children who happened to cry in their house. Once, when a three-year-old boy cried loudly, she seemed upset and puckered up her face, raising her arms to show her mother that she wanted to be picked up and comforted; but she was concerned only for herself. Her mother hugged her and stroked her hair.

About a month later, Laura heard another child cry. She started to cry, too, in full-blown imitation. At 17 months, she made her first move toward a child who was crying. She approached tentatively, pulled back, then approached again and offered the child a Kleenex.

By the time she was 18 months old, she had become a very inventive altruist. When a six-month-old baby began to cry after throwing his cookie from his high chair, Laura picked up the cookie and gave it back to him, looking concerned (she usually tried to eat everything she could lay her hands on, her mother noted). But the baby went on crying—he missed his own mother. So Laura patted him on the head. When that didn't work, she tried speaking to him: "Baby, baby." He went on crying. Laura then started to whimper and insisted that her mother come over. She even put her mother's hand on the baby's head. The baby calmed down a little, but Laura still looked worried. She continued to bring him toys and stroked his hair (as her mother had done for her) until he was completely pacified.

Yarrow is quite sure that such behavior shows altruism and that the little girl really wanted to comfort the baby, though of course it is very difficult to impute motives to children at that age. If Laura had found the crying a mere nuisance, she could have walked away from the baby and gone to another room, the researcher points out. Instead, she kept approaching the baby with new remedies. If she had wanted to stop the noise of the crying, she could have put her hand over the baby's mouth. Instead, she brought him cookies and toys and stroked his hair.

Such findings give strong support to a theory of altruistic motivation developed in 1975 by psychologist Martin Hoffman. Hoffman argues that there are no grounds for the widespread Western assumption that all altruism can ultimately be explained in terms of egoistic, self-centered motives. He believes that altruism derives from a primitive involuntary feeling of distress in the presence of others' distress—an "empathic distress" response—which can be seen even in infants and appears to be inborn. Two-day-old infants in hospital nurseries often become agitated and cry loudly at the sound of another infant's cry, much more so than at other loud sounds, he notes. Empathic distress is so unpleasant that children are driven to help others in order to relieve it.

There are many reasons why an innate capacity for altruism would be an asset from an evolutionary point of view. Altruism toward one's children and other close relatives brings obvious benefits to one's own genetic line. And, as Edward O. Wilson and other sociobiologists have argued, reciprocal altruism toward nonrelatives may also increase one's own chances of survival. In other words, some measure of altruism is good for you.

The capacity for altruism and the "gut feeling" of empathy that underlies it may depend on the prefrontal cortex, the newest part of the human brain, suggests the eminent brain researcher Paul D. MacLean of NIMH. For the first time, nature has designed a creature who shows concern for the suffering of other living things, he says. MacLean believes we can expect human beings to become increasingly empathic and altruistic, since "we seem to be acquiring the mental stuff of which we imagine angels are made." But he warns that "if neural circuits of the brain are not brought into play at certain critical times of development, they may never be capable of functioning. Chimpanzees reared in darkness may be forever blind. Is it possible that if empathy is not learned at a critical age, it may never become fully developed?"

The children whose empathy and altruism have a good start become increasingly helpful as they learn to speak more clearly, around the age of two. At that point, the reports of the mothers in Yarrow's study also become much richer. One woman told of a long-distance call from her elderly parents during which she learned that her father had a serious illness. She hung up and started to cry. Her 20-month-old son, Billy, came over with a very sad look on his face, she

reported. "He put his arm around me, hugged me, and said, 'I love you.' Then, he gave me a big kiss."

Another woman described how her child tried to comfort one of the characters in a storybook. They had been looking at a book with a picture of a boy crying, and her son exclaimed, "He'll be happy when his daddy comes home; his daddy will come home soon."

Such altruism is not always consistent, however. The same child who seems compassionate one day may be totally insensitive to another's pain the next, or may even inflict hurt on some occasions. Siblings are particu-

---

"One theory argues that altruism derives from an 'empathic-distress' response that appears to be inborn."

---

larly prone to developing a strange mixture of empathy and jealousy. Typically, says Yarrow, a boy who expresses concern when his brother's hand is hurt will hate to see his brother get all the attention and will keep shouting something like, "Look at *my* boo-boo," inventing an imaginary hurt, if necessary, to distract his mother from the task of caring for his brother's real injury.

After all the children in the program had been observed for a period of nine months (they were then between 19 months and two-and-a-half years old), the researchers began to analyze their material. Some items seemed to defy classification. For example, one woman reported that when the family dog sneezed, her 18-month-old son ran off to get a Kleenex and then wiped the dog's nose with it. Was that altruism? ("That's the kind of thing that makes me tear my hair out," confesses Waxler, who ended up putting it into a special category: "Treating animals like people.") For the most part, though, the incidents described by the mothers fell into fairly clear patterns.

The NIMH group found that

neither the children's sex nor the size of their families made any difference in the amount of sympathy or help they offered to people in distress. However, there were enormous individual differences in altruism among the children—differences that became increasingly clear in the period between 18 and 24 months, and that could be related to different styles of child-rearing.

The most powerful factor appeared to be the intensity with which mothers conveyed the message that their children must not hurt others. Parents who made it clear that they cared tremendously about that, and who portrayed the consequences of their children's hitting or otherwise harming others more dramatically, had children who would be more likely to give help or comfort to those in need. Neutral, calmly reasoned explanations such as "Sarah is hurt now" or "Tom's crying because you pushed him" had little effect. But forceful explanations and prohibitions ("*Look* what you did!" or "You must *never* poke anyone's eyes"), physical restraint, even physical punishment and love withdrawal ("When you act like that, I don't want to be near you") seemed to lead to altruism.

The researchers emphasize that physical restraint or punishment alone, without any explanation of how the children had hurt others, did not lead to altruism. And just saying "No!" or "Stop!" without giving any clarifying information was actually counterproductive; apparently, it taught children to refrain from any activity at all when confronted with another's distress. The parents' message had to have cognitive content, as well as emotional force, to be effective.

The researchers also found that neither the mothers' permissiveness nor the amount of time they played with their children was related to altruism in their children. The mothers themselves apparently engaged in few instances of altruism toward others, so that modeling did not appear to have any significant impact, either.

The only other factor that seemed related to altruism in children—besides the intensity of the mothers' message about not hurting others—was the mothers' altruism toward their own children. The hugs and kisses, the soothing words, the Band-aids and the Kleenexes proffered by mothers when their children were hurt frequently reappeared, almost as a mirror image, in the children's actions toward others.

"Altruism" generally refers to good deeds that are performed by innocent bystanders—not by the offenders themselves. "Reparations" to one's victims are usually considered matters of guilt or conscience rather than altruism. Yet Yarrow and Waxler investigated both kinds of prosocial acts. "The core of moral behavior is the child's sense of concern and responsibility for the welfare of others," they believe; both reparations and altruism share that core, and reparations play an especially important role in children's moral development.

At first, young children are not quite sure of cause and effect when someone is hurt—they may not know who is actually responsible for it—they or someone else. Surprisingly, they get the clearest lesson on the subject when they hurt their own mothers. That apparently happens in the best of families. The baby may be nursing and may bite the mother, or a small child may kick and bruise her. Naturally, the mother reacts with intensity of feeling ("Ouch!" or "This hurts—don't do it again"). The child generally understands. He may apologize or express sympathy, and eventually that understanding extends to other kinds of distress, too.

What children learn from incidents in which they are innocent bystanders to other people's suffering is less clear. Far from conveying intense messages about children's responsibilities in such times, the mothers tend either to ignore the suffering or—more frequently—to reassure their children and tell them not to worry about it! This lack of involvement in others' pain, when their own children have not had a hand in it, is startling. "It's part of the way we rear children in this culture," says Waxler. "It may be different in other cultures, but we have no information. There have been no cross-cultural studies."

Judging from the mothers' reports, some of the children actually fight their parents' reluctance to intervene in the troubles of others. An 18-month-old girl riding in a supermarket cart as her mother shopped for groceries heard a baby crying very loudly; she became very agitated and pointed in the direction of the noise. "Baby crying, baby crying," she told her mother. "I just kept on pushing my cart and picking up the things I wanted," the mother reported later. "I said, 'Yes, there's a baby crying.' But she seemed to want me to do something about it. She wasn't satisfied that I just agreed with her there was a baby crying."

Sometimes parents also teach their children not to be too generous—they do not want their children to give away toys, clothes, or other possessions that might have to be replaced. At the same time, the parents' reac-

---

"The intensity of the mother's message that the child must not hurt others was a powerful factor in altruism."

---

tions to television programs—and the programs themselves—often teach young children callousness, in the opinion of Yarrow and Waxler. When the baker in a "Sesame Street" skit is shown carrying cakes, falling down a flight of steps, and getting cake all over him, for instance, some young children don't find it funny. "He gets very upset about it," reported one mother about her son. "He says, 'Man fall down,' and comes running to get me. Then he puts his thumb in his mouth and just stands there very large-eyed. So I've taken to saying to him, 'He'll be all right, Timmy.'"

In other families, the television set is on so often that scenes of pain and bloodshed are disregarded. "Ginny is sitting in front of the TV with her family eating dinner," reported one of the NIMH researchers after a home visit. "The news program parades on-the-spot coverage of the bloody death and destruction of street fighting in a current war. The family goes on with the dinner conversation as the news continues. Ginny chews her food and drinks her milk, all the time watching. At one point she grimaces, but she is almost immediately caught up in comments about the family car."

Obviously, many parents don't want their children to be overburdened with altruism: it's too inconvenient and too demanding. "People have little use for altruism in this society, except when it's institutionalized, as through charities and volunteer services," says Yarrow. Parents generally want their children to be able to compete successfully—and how can they compete if they're altruists? There are also strong feelings of privacy that many fear to invade.

Under those circumstances, how do children ever learn to give aid and comfort to others? Fortunately, they seem to profit a great deal from the forceful explanations that they receive from their mothers whenever they do anything that hurts anyone else. The mothers' scolding carries such a strong emotional wallop that it produces both reparations and altruism, according to the study.

Occasionally, those intense explanations are carried too far, however, and children become overanxious. Yarrow points to several instances of the "misplaced responsibility" that sometimes results. Upon seeing his mother cry (for reasons that had nothing to do with him), one small boy asked apologetically, "Did I make you sad?" Another told his mother, "Sorry, I be nice." Young children are especially vulnerable to "guilt-induction," Yarrow notes. They may end up feeling responsible for all kinds of disasters unrelated to them.

Yarrow and Waxler conclude that parents may be making a serious mistake if they focus so exclusively on their children's transgressions. They wish parents would give their children equally clear messages when they are just witnesses to others' pain. If parents used "bystander" events for deliberate teaching about other people's grief, that might be less guilt-inducing, the researchers believe. It might also lead to more altruism. For example, when another child falls down near them and is hurt, parents should intervene and help, Yarrow suggests, and if such intervention is impossible, they should at least show their children that they care.

According to Yarrow, such teaching may be particularly important when children are around 18 months of age—a critical time, when their discovery of the separateness of others'

THE BABY ALTRUISTS FIVE YEARS LATER

Do children become altruistic as they grow up, between the ages of two and a half and seven? Usually not, according to the Yarrow study. So far, her subjects have shown a remarkable constancy in the degree of their willingness to help others.

For a period of three months recently, 22 out of the 24 mothers who had observed their children as babies took out their tape recorders and once again dictated what happened when their children—now six to seven years old—witnessed other people's distress. In addition, all 24 children came to the National Institute of Mental Health in Bethesda, Maryland, for further laboratory tests of altruism.

As in the original study, those laboratory sessions were used to confirm the results of the parents' observations. But after watching one of the sessions in the small house that serves as NIMH's lab for the project, I realized there are many limitations to research of this kind. The children may feel constrained by the unfamiliar surroundings, and the researchers are hard put to provide situations that call for altruism yet do no harm to anyone involved.

Some of the situations are staged by research assistants whose "act" may not be totally convincing. While showing a seven-year-old girl how to do a test exercise involving push-ups, for instance, the researcher suddenly started moaning, "*Ooh*, my back," and pretended to roll on the floor in pain. But there was something a little phony about it, and the child who was being tested for altruism reacted mostly with puzzlement. (Watching behind a one-way mirror, with her mother's permission, I felt I would have been equally puzzled.)

The seven-year-old was also observed as she heard the sound of a crash and wailing from another room, where she knew another child was stacking books. The little girl was alone at the time. Obviously startled, she frowned and fidgeted,

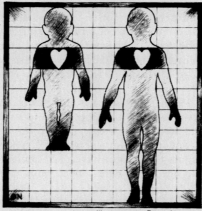

Illustration by Brock Newman

as if torn between a desire to go see what was happening and the need to stay where she was apparently supposed to be. It seemed less a test of altruism than a choice between assertiveness and obedience, in a relatively intimidating atmosphere.

Most of the lab tests were simpler and more revealing, however. Many were questions about picture stories in which various characters were shown in trouble, helping each other, or failing to help. One set of pictures showed a boy and girl fighting over a bicycle. The boy fell down and started to cry; the girl at once let him have the bike and even gave him a stick of bubble gum. "What are they really thinking or feeling?" the researcher asked the little girl. "She's scared that she might get into trouble for fighting with him," the child replied. In other stories, the little girl recognized that various children were trying to help their parents when they were hurt, or wanted to share something with friends.

According to Yarrow and Waxler, the findings from the lab tests proved generally consistent with those from the mothers' taped reports—still the researchers' primary source, since they were far more detailed and natural than any lab research could be. About two-thirds of the children clearly had not changed their particular patterns of response to other people's distress, the researchers found. Children who had

been notable for their empathy as toddlers were still exceptionally empathic. Those who tended to flee from the scene of trouble or to plug up their ears in response to cries at 18 months of age still did so. Among the remaining one-third of the children, some had definitely changed their styles of response, and others had no clearly definable patterns.

Of course, the older children understood a great deal more of what was going on around them, and the *form* of their altruism had changed. One six-year-old pretended to like the present her father had given her, for instance; she explained to her mother that she "didn't want him to be disappointed." A precocious seven-year-old who saw that his grandmother was feeling sick called a doctor for her (as a small child, he might have tried to help her with his play doctor's kit).

Nevertheless, the *frequency* of helping behavior—the number of times each child actually helped, compared with the number of times he might have helped—did not seem to change. There was no developmental progression between the ages of two and seven.

The general lack of change leads one to believe that for empathy and altruism, as for so much else, important patterns are set within the first two or three years of life. Since most of the children stayed with their mothers between the ages of two and seven, and their mothers' personalities or methods of child-rearing also remained basically the same, it is not yet clear how lasting the patterns may be. After the age of seven, children are exposed to many other influences besides their parents'. Perhaps a change in their environment, particularly an extreme change, would radically alter the children's behavior. But other things being equal, the child's willingness to give aid and sympathy—or to disregard other people's troubles—seems firmly established by the age of two or three.

—**M. P.**

pain can lead them to either altruism or fundamental selfishness.

Unfortunately, "there is an expectation in our culture that young children are not able to behave altruistically," says Yarow. That expectation is not only wrong, but also probably harmful, since it may be self-fulfilling. It is reflected in current books for children. To their dismay, Yarrow and Waxler were unable to find any children's books that dealt with children's responses to the problems or feelings of others. Even a series of books written in cooperation with the Menninger Foundation, such as *Sometimes I'm Jealous* and *Sometimes I Get Angry*, shows children resenting other children, ignoring their needs, and focusing solely on "Me, me, me!"

Different societies clearly produce different levels of caring and altruism. Among the Ik of Uganda, for example, there is no compassion at all, not even for one's own children or parents, and people laugh at one another's misfortunes. By contrast, among the Hopi Indians, nothing is more important than to be helpful to others and to have a "Hopi good heart."

Yarrow's study shows that, regardless of culture, the *capacity* for empathy and altruism exists at a remarkably early age. Many people resist the idea, she has found. "They quote Freud and other authorities and insist it can't be true." Some may feel guilty because, if selfishness is not the norm, they have no excuse for their own lack of altruism (or that of their children).

Others question whether mothers are sufficiently reliable reporters of their own children's behavior. Obviously mothers want to present their children in the best possible light, which may lead them to see good qualities even where none exist. However, the mothers did not know precisely which responses the researchers were studying, and on many occasions that apparently called for altruism, they reported that their children did nothing to help. The researchers found, moreover, that the mothers tended to underreport their children's altruism; on the average, the mothers reported only one out of every three such acts.

To control for inaccurate reporting, the NIMH investigators who went into the children's homes every three weeks always simulated some incident—they pretended to bang their ankles or to find something extremely funny in a book—and then sent in independent reports on the child's reactions, which could be compared with the mothers' reports. On all those grounds, Yarrow believes that the mothers gave generally reliable descriptions of their children's responses and of their capabilities.

A surprising number of followers of Freud and Piaget are now edging closer to her view about those early capabilities because of recent research in their own fields. "Early altruism is probably genuine, as far as it goes,"

"Some children actually fight their parents' unwillingness to intervene in the troubles of others."

---

declares John Flavell of Stanford University, a leading interpreter of Piaget. "Piaget overestimated how egocentric young children are. In certain circumstances, three-year-olds behave in a patently nonegocentric fashion." While some of the classic Piagetian tests of role-taking skills may have been too complicated for young children, simpler tests give a more favorable view of their ability, he says. For example, if you show a card with a dog on one side and a cat on the other to a child of two or three, and then hold it up so that he sees only one side, and you see the other, the child will be able to tell you correctly what animal you see, disregarding the one that faces him, Flavell points out. "Though young children may not completely understand, they can pay some attention to how other people feel," he says.

Freudians, too, have begun to revise their timetable for the appearance of the Oedipus complex and the superego. "The Oedipal complex has its origins long before it's called a stage," says Reginald Lourie, senior research psychiatrist at NIMH's Mental Health Study Center in Adelphi, Maryland. "You can see its beginnings even by the age of one and a half or two. The superego also has its beginnings much earlier than was previously thought, though it isn't crystallized until five or six. And the development of altruism is also a gradual process, advancing through various stages."

Lourie, who describes himself as a "real Freudian who keeps moving and changing with new information that emerges in the field, just as Freud did," points out that classical Freudian theories were formed on the basis of what people who were in analysis could remember—and very few people remember the first three years of their lives. "Psychoanalysis didn't really begin to look at children until the middle of the 1920s, with Anna Freud," he says. "Even then, it didn't have access to children in their first years of life, since it looked at three- to four-year-olds in nursery school. So this is an evolving field."

Yarrow's information adds "a new dimension," according to Lourie. He was delighted with the opportunity to weld together classical Freudian and child-development approaches. As for children's early capacity for altruism, he says, "It's good to know it's there." If more parents become aware of its existence, perhaps they can find ways of encouraging it. Children's natural talent for empathy and acts of kindness would then have a better chance to flower. ⋂

Maya Pines is the author of *The Brain Changers: Scientists and the New Mind Control* (Harcourt Brace Jovanovich, 1973), and winner of the National Media Award of the American Psychological Association; a 1976 article on memory won the Claude Bernard Science Journalism Award. Pines writes regularly on science and behavior for a number of major periodicals.

For further information, read:

Hoffman, Martin L. "Developmental Synthesis of Affect and Cognition and Its Implications for Altruistic Motivation," *Developmental Psychology*, 11(1975):607-622.

Mussen, Paul, and Nancy Eisenberg-Berg. *Roots of Caring, Sharing & Helping*, W. H. Freeman, 1977, $12 , paper, $4.95.

Staub, Ervin. "Helping a Person in Distress: The Influence of Implicit and Explicit 'Rules' of Conduct on Children and Adults," *Journal of Personality and Social Psychology*, 17(1971)137-144.

Yarrow, Marian Radke, and Carolyn Zahn-Waxler. "The Emergence and Functions of Prosocial Behaviors in Young Children," in *Readings in Child Development and Relationships*, 2nd ed., Russell Smart and Mollie Smart, eds., Macmillan, 1977, $7.50.

Yarrow, Marian Radke, Phyllis Scott, and Carolyn Zahn-Waxler. "Learning Concern for Others," *Developmental Psychology*, 8(1973):240-260.

III. The Preschool Years

Youngsters between two and five years old are particularly interested in exploring the world around them, testing their newly acquired skills, asking question after question about all kinds of things, enriching their understanding of the world, and interpreting what they see and hear. Biological maturation interacts with learning to produce great increases in motor agility and coordination. By three, most children can ride their tricycles, draw a circle, button and unbutton some of their clothes. By four, they can skip, hop, climb a ladder, and catch a ball.

According to Piaget, one of the leading developmental psychologists of this century, interaction between maturation and experience advances the child's cognitive abilities from the *sensorimotor period,* which lasts from birth until the age of two, to the *preoperational stage* which lasts from about two to seven. The preschool child, in the preoperational stage, uses symbols to represent objects and people—a box becomes a ship, for example—and his or her ability to solve complex problems improves enormously. Several factors contribute to these changes: more efficient, more selective, and more accurate perceptions; heightened ability to accommodate to new information; improved memory; increased skill at maintaining focused attention. However, the preschool child's perspective is egocentric; things cannot readily be seen from others' points of view.

The average two-year-old has mastered a vocabulary of approximately 200 to 300 words and combines two words into simple sentences. At first, grammatical structures tend to be rather rudimentary and the sentences omit important "little words" such as *the, a,* and *in.* Gradually, sentences become longer, and by three or four, children show an excellent understanding of grammar or syntax—although, of course, they cannot state the rules. Apparently, children learn the rules for speaking grammatically correct sentences early in childhood by actively processing the speech they hear, searching for similarities and irregularities, and thus forming rules.

Preschool children's improved motor and cognitive skills pave the way for greater emphasis on *socialization,* the process by which children acquire those behaviors, beliefs, standards, and motives that are considered appropriate, or at least acceptable, in their own social, ethnic, or religious group. Although many people and institutions contribute to the child's socialization, the parents are the principal and most influential agents, especially during the early years. They usually have the most contact with the child, interacting intensely and frequently, thus regulating and modifying the child's behavior continually. Much of socialization is accomplished through *learning*—the strengthening of certain responses by means of direct rewards and reinforcements—and through imitation of others' behavior. By their child-rearing techniques, parents provide learning settings conducive to the development of specific personality characteristics. In addition, they serve as models whose behavior children are likely to imitate. For example, authoritative parental control, which is characterized by high control and positive encouragement of the child's autonomous and independent strivings, tends to produce mature, competent, socially responsible preschool children. High degrees of permissiveness (lax discipline, accompanied by relatively few and only weak demands for mature behavior), together with warmth, are antecedents of immaturity, lack of independence, and lack of self-reliance in preschool children.

Many of the child's complex behavior patterns, personality characteristics, motivations, ideals, and attitudes are acquired by means of identification with parents or other models. A child is said to be identified with the model when he or she feels similar to the person; this feeling of similarity may be increased through the child's adoption of the model's attributes. Both positive and negative characteristics of parents may be acquired through *identification.* As Mussen's article in this section demonstrates, identification is of major significance in the development of prosocial behavior, including honesty, generosity, kindness, altruism, obedience to rules and regulations, and consideration of the rights and welfare of others. Individual differences in some personality and behavioral characteristics that emerge during the preschool period—for example, aggressiveness in boys, dependency in girls, and achievement motivation in both sexes—tend to be stable; that is, they persist (often in changed form) into later childhood or adolescence, or even into adulthood.

Under some conditions, socialization is a particularly difficult process. Maladjusted parents may not be able to give their children the warmth and nurturance they need for adequate emotional growth. Parents who suffered abuse and neglect when they were children are likely to become highly aggressive and socially isolated. Children who are sickly or mentally impaired, as well as those who suffer severe emotional maladjustments, present special problems, and their parents may need professional help in the socialization process. As three articles in this section demonstrate, fortunately, families can be taught techniques that may help substantially in socializing deviant and disturbed children, including those who are diagnosed as autistic.

Emergent Themes in Human Development

12

Some basic assumptions about the development of cognitive and affective structures and their stability from infancy to later childhood are reexamined in light of new evidence from a variety of sources

Jerome Kagan

Every scientific discipline during successive eras in its growth rests on a small set of presuppositions which are either unproven or, in some cases, not amenable to confirmation or refutation. Many of these presuppositions have a complementary opposite and the discipline is loyal to one or the other member of the pair during successive historical periods. Holton (1973) has called these polarized pairs of assumptions "themata." Controversy over whether matter is particulate or wavelike, whether the universe is

Jerome Kagan is Professor of Human Development in the Department of Psychology and Social Relations at Harvard University. His work over the last twenty years has been concerned with the development of cognitive, motivational, and affective systems during the opening decade of life. Currently his research is focused on the complementary relation between maturation and experience and its effect on cognitive development. Dr. Kagan is the author of Birth to Maturity, Change and Continuity in Infancy, *and* Understanding Children. *He is a Fellow of the American Academy of Arts and Sciences.*

The research summarized in this paper was supported over the past 18 years by grants from the National Institute of Child Health and Human Development, National Institute of Mental Health, National Science Foundation, Carnegie Corporation of New York, Spencer Foundation, Office of Child Development, Foundation for Child Development, and the Grant Foundation. The paper was originally presented as the Presidential Address to the Annual Meeting of the Eastern Psychological Association, New York City, 4 April 1975. Address: Department of Psychology and Social Relations, Harvard University, William James Hall, 33 Kirkland St., Cambridge, MA 02138.

steady-state or expanding, whether growth is continuous or discontinuous are among the themes that scientists have debated in the past and will continue to discuss in the future because, as Bohr (1934) wisely noted, the twin propositions are likely to be complementary rather than incompatible.

This paper considers three themata in developmental psychology whose polarities are shifting as a result of fresh empirical information. Theory is, of course, the energy cell of science. Facts, even elegant ones, isolated from relevant assumptions are lovely but unappreciated flowers. But facts have a refereeing function; they prevent presuppositions from becoming dogma. That is why Karl Popper (1962) insists that the primary function of mature empirical science is to refute, not to affirm, hypotheses—a directive that is occasionally annoying to psychologists who have many young candidates vying for affirmation but very few hardy enough to withstand rigorous examination and possible failure.

The recent crest of interest in developmental psychology has produced a tiny corpus of moderately firm facts that invite reexamination of the presuppositions that have guided so much past work. Three changing themes are (1) the shift from a less to a more maturational interpretation of early cognitive and affective phenomena; (2) the

shift from a less to a more continuous view of stages in cognitive development; (3) the shift from less to more faith in the potential resilience of human cognitive growth.

The maturation of early cognition

The Western conception of psychological events has been plagued by an inability to regard body and mind as components of one idea. We do not want to believe in two different life processes but cannot seem to find the right set of sentences that will pierce the semantic barrier separating the two constructs and permit each to nestle alongside the other. Although many historical forces have contributed to this epistemological tension, the most obvious was the need of renaissance scholars to accommodate to both the new science of matter and the still powerful church. Despite half a millennium of debate we continue to struggle with that conceptual issue, which has taken a specific form in developmental psychology.

Because the development of muscle, bone, and myelinization of the nervous system are guided by a maturational program, we acknowledge that the motor behaviors of reaching, sitting, standing, and walking must be under rather strict maturational control. But because mental phenomena are supposed to be of a different quality—not part of soma—we have supposed that they are under the stewardship of experience. As a result we have looked to Locke rather than Darwin to explain the development of perception, thought, and emotion in the young child. Hence many parents and developmental psychologists believe that the probability of a one-year-old's crying as he watches his mother leave him alone in a strange room is a function of his past nurturant experience with her—his attachment to his mother. But whether or not he walks to her as she enters his bedroom with a toy is regarded as a function of whether he is motorically mature enough to locomote.

Recent research in many laboratories has made more credible both Piaget's assertion that maturation exerts strong control over mental competence and the ethologists' contention that biology has prepared the young organism to be selectively alerted by special classes of stimulus information. Movement and amount of contour contrast are particularly potent in attracting and maintaining the visual attention of the very young infant (Haith 1966; Karmel, Hoffmann, and Fegy 1974; Kessen, Salapatek, and Haith 1972; Salapatek and Kessen 1973). In fact, there is a curvilinear relation between both the duration of the young child's attention or the amplitude of the positive peak component of the visual evoked potential, on the one hand, and the square root of the density of contour in the stimulus pattern, on the other (Karmel 1969; Karmel, Hoffman, and Fegy 1974).

Bornstein (1975) has shown that 4-month-old infants attend longer to wavelengths corresponding to red and blue than to other hues. And the young infant's pattern of attention suggests categorical perception for wavelengths that correspond to blue, green, yellow, and red—a finding that confirms the earlier, elegant work of sensory physiologists.

It also appears the infant is more excited by circularity than by linearity. Ruff and Birch (1974) showed pairs of stimuli to infants 13 weeks old and quantified their attentional preferences (see Fig. 1). Concentric patterns were studied

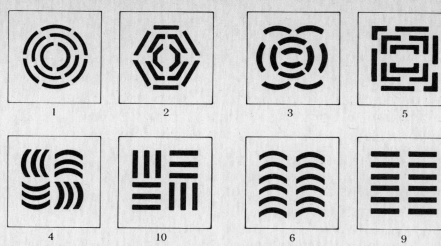

Figure 1. When 13-week-old infants were shown pairs of patterns composed of curves and straight-line segments, they were found to prefer forms constructed of arcs to forms constructed of straight lines and they studied concentric patterns longer than nonconcentric ones. The numbers below each pattern refer to the relative power of that stimulus to maintain the infant's attention; stimulus 1 elicited the most attention, stimulus 10 the least. (From Ruff and Birch 1974.)

longer than nonconcentric ones, and when pattern was similar, forms constructed of arcs were looked at longer than identical patterns constructed of straight-line segments.

In our laboratory Hopkins (Ph.D. thesis, 1974) permitted 10-month-old infants to view one of four simple three-dimensional segments each time they pressed a bar in front of them. When they became habituated to one of these simple stimuli (i.e. the rate of operant bar-pressing fell below an *a priori* criterion), children in nine experimental groups were shown a different stimulus while control children continued to see the same event. Infants who were familiarized on the straight-line segment and dishabituated on a curved one showed the greatest recovery of both bar-pressing and attention. Infants who experienced the opposite change, from a curve to a straight-line segment, showed some recovery but significantly less than that displayed by the former group (Fig. 2).

This special effect of curvature on attention is present in the newborn but in less sturdy form (Fantz and Miranda 1975). By two months of age, however, following maturation of acuity and scanning patterns, the infant displays a more consistent

attraction to circularity and attends longer to a bull's-eye than to a checkerboard (Fantz 1965). Since the spiral is one of nature's favorite and most versatile forms, it is not unreasonable to suppose that evolution would have prepared each of us to be sensitive to this pattern.

Maturational influences on cognition are not limited to perceptual dynamics but seem to touch affective phenomena that have traditionally been viewed as a consequence of specific parent-child experiences. We have recently found that occurrence of both separation distress and apprehension to an unfamiliar peer emerge between 9 and 12 months, peak between 13 and 20 months, and then decline. Our explanation for this growth function involves the assumption that a new cognitive competence emerges during the last third of the first year.

Before we name this competence let us list some of the major phenomena that are also first displayed during the last three months of the first year. They include Piagetian object permanence, increases in excited babbling in response to speech, increased attention to discrepant events, and a shift from simple play with one object at a time to play in which the child actively relates two objects. In addition, the 8- to 12-month-old begins to show wariness, inhibition, and cardiac acceleration to a variety of unusual or unpredictable events that elicited approach and cardiac deceleration a few months earlier (Kagan 1972; Parry 1973; Scarr and Salapatek 1970; Schwartz, Campos, and Baisel 1973). For example, signs of wariness to a strange adult, a jack-in-the-box, a moving mechanical dog, or the appearance of depth on the visual cliff, to name a few, emerge at about 7 to 8 months and reach peak intensity between 11 and 18 months. This is about the same time that an infant begins to show inhibition to novelty, as reflected in a delay in reaching for a new object after repeated presentations of another object. The wariness and inhibition cannot be due to a new ability to detect discrepancy, to cry, or to display motor inhibition to a change in stimulation, for each of these responses is present in the 2-month-old.

It seems necessary, therefore, to posit a new competence. Although each of these phenotypically different phenomena might be due to separate mechanisms, our affection for parsimony tempts us to suggest that perhaps they can be accounted for by positing a competence we have called "activation of relational structures." The 9- to 12-month-old child is capable of actively generating representations of previously experienced absent events—as well as potential future ones—and comparing these representations with the perceptions generated by the situation he is in at the moment. The one-year-old seems to be able to generate structures *about* events, not just *of* events, that represent possible causes and sequelae of fresh experience, as well as the relations of that experience to his knowledge. Unlike the 4-month-old, who attempts only to assimilate a discrepant event, the 1-year-old attempts to interpret that event—to generate structures that resolve questions about the relation of the event to his past experience, possible future states of the event, and possible behaviors the child might initiate toward the event.

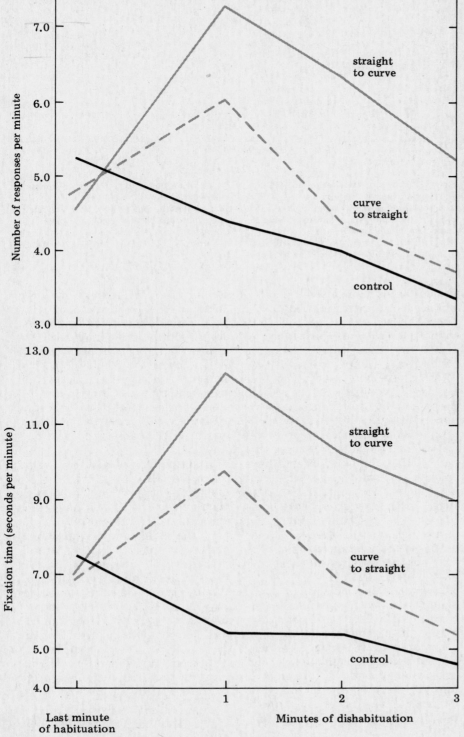

Figure 2. In another experiment involving curves and straight-line segments, groups of 10-month-olds were shown one of 4 simple 3-dimensional line segments each time they pressed a bar. When the infants became bored with the familar form, some groups were shown a different stimulus: babies habituated on a curve were shown straight lines, those habituated on a straight line were shown curves. As the graphs reveal, those who had been familiarized on the straight segments and shifted to the curves showed greatest recovery of both bar-pressing (responses per minute) and attention (seconds per minute spent gazing at the stimulus).

Schaffer (1974) has also suggested that a new cognitive competence emerges at this time; he views it as the ability to activate from memory schemata for absent objects and to use them to evaluate a situation: "Initially each stimulus is treated in isolation; and although the memory store may be checked for representations of that same stimulus, it is not compared with different stimuli or their representations. In time, however, the infant becomes capable of relating stimuli to one another ... as a result the strange stimulus can be considered simultaneously with the familiar standard, even though the latter is centrally stored and must therefore be retrieved."

In the classic object-permanence situation, the face of a one-year-old announces surprise when the toy is not under the cloth, because he actively compares his schema for the object he saw hidden moments ago with his perception of its absence, and he tries to relate the two. Forgive me if I add that he seems to be trying to understand what has happened. The one-year-old shows prolonged attention to events that are discrepant transformations of his knowledge, compared with his minimal attentiveness at 7 months, because he is trying not only to assimilate the event, as he did earlier, but to understand how the discrepant event in front of him could have been transformed into the schema for the class of event he brought to the situation.

The mental work involved in that process is likely to be accompanied by cardiac acceleration, for in school-age children and in adults, cardiac acceleration tends to occur when subjects are instructed to reason or memorize; whereas heart-rate deceleration tends to follow instructions that ask the subject simply to listen or look at an interesting event (Lacey 1967; Van Hover 1974). It is of interest, therefore, that a discrepant transformation on a familiarized standard, which typically elicits cardiac deceleration in infants under 9 months, is a little more likely to elicit acceleration after 9 months. Moreover,

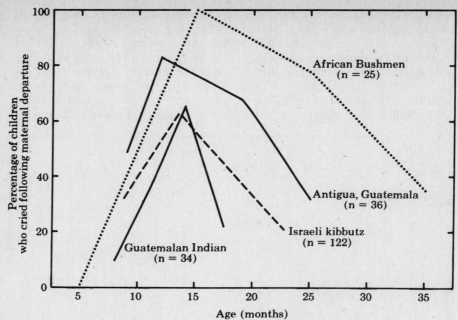

Figure 3. Studies of "separation protest" as a function of age yielded remarkably similar results in 4 independent samples outside the U.S. In all studies, the values represent the percentage of children in each age group who cried when their mothers left them alone with an unfamiliar woman. The response seems to be the result of a new competence that emerges in the last third of the first year, when the child is mature enough to raise questions about the consequences of an unexpected event such as the mother's departure but not mature enough to resolve them.

5-month-olds show a small deceleration when they are placed on the deep side of a visual cliff, while 9-month-olds show a 6-beat acceleration in the same situation (Schwartz, Campos, and Baisel 1973). Since there were no age differences in vocalizing or crying, it is possible that the increased heart rate reflects the fact that the older infants were activating representations of the possible. For those who believe that the older infants were "afraid" and the younger ones were not, it is not unreasonable to suggest that it was the representations activated by the 9-month-old in response to the deep side that produced the subsequent apprehension, not the raw physical event.

This suggestion would help to explain why a 1-year-old, but not a 6-month-old, is likely to become distressed if his mother leaves him alone or with a stranger—a phenomenon that has come to be called "separation anxiety." There are two quite different aspects of this phenomenon. The first is the growth function for separation distress; the second concerns individual differences in the intensity of distress during the period of its display. We are primarily concerned with the former. Our view is that distress to separation is the result of the new ability to generate a question or representation concerning the discrepant quality of the separation experience coupled with the temporary inability to resolve it.

We have performed a series of related studies (Kagan 1974) in which the setting was either a laboratory playroom or the child's home, and the actors were the mother, the father, the child, and an unfamiliar woman. In the first study (Kotelchuck, Ph.D. thesis, 1972), six cross-sectional samples of firstborn infants were observed in the laboratory at 6, 9, 12, 15, 18, and 21 months of age, with 12 boys and 12 girls at each of the six ages. Initially the infant sat in the middle of a large room surrounded by many interesting toys and with his mother and father sitting at one end of the room. Every three minutes, one of the adults entered or left the room.

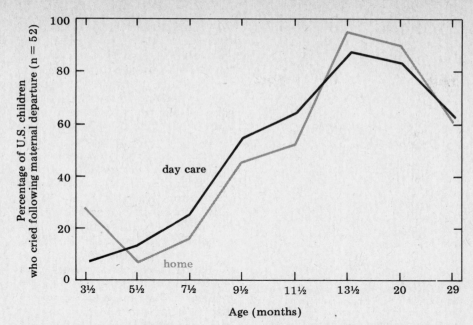

Figure 4. Studies of separation protest in two groups of U.S. children showed results comparable to those summarized in Fig. 3. In these studies, groups of day-care and home-reared children were left alone by their mothers in an unfamiliar room. In both groups, the percentage of children who cried after the mother's departure peaked at about 13 months.

Thus the child was by turns with all three adults, alone with mother, alone with father, with father and stranger, mother and stranger, or alone with the stranger. He was never totally alone in the room. The child's play and crying, as well as other behaviors, were coded throughout each of the 13 three-minute episodes. The main result was that there was no significant decrease in play—a sensitive sign of apprehension—or occurrence of crying following the departure of either parent until the child was about 9 to 12 months old. These two signs of apprehension or distress increased linearly until 18 months and then declined at 21 months. Moreover, the child showed apprehension only when he was alone with the stranger, and there was very little difference in his reactions to the departure of mother or father.

Since that original study we have gathered additional observations on the developmental course of separation protest over the first 2½ years of life in children from four settings outside the United States—lower-class Ladino families living in the city of Antigua, Guatemala; Indian families residing in the isolated agricultural village of San Pedro on Lake Atitlan in northwest Guatemala; Israeli kibbutzim where infants spend most of the day in an infant house, and Bushmen families living in the Kalahari Desert. In all four samples, the occurrence of crying following maternal departure when left with a stranger was minimal prior to 9 months, increased to a peak value between 12 and 15 months, and then declined (Lester et al. 1974; Fox et al., MS in prep.).

Additionally, we recently completed a study in which children attended a research day-care center five days a week from 3½ to 29 months of age. Each child in the day-care group was paired with a control child of the same sex, social class, and ethnic group who was being raised at home. The child's reactions to his mother's leaving him alone in a strange room were observed regularly from 3½ to 29 months of age. The growth function was identical for both the day-care and home-reared children for both probability of crying and the delay between departure and distress and, as in the earlier studies, separation fear did not occur reliably until 9 to 12 months of age and peaked during the second year (Kearsley et al. 1975). Moreover, the latency to distress was greater than five seconds for about one-third of those who cried, which suggests that the child was thinking about the separation event before he began to fret. Figures 3 and 4 illustrate the developmental course of separation protest for these studies.

It is probably not a coincidence that the growth function for separation distress resembles closely the child's increasing tendency to relate external information to himself. After the mothers of children 9 to 24 months unobtrusively rubbed a little rouge on their child's nose, the child was brought in front of a mirror. The probability that the child would touch his nose was very low at 9 months but increased linearly through the second year—paralleling the growth curve for separation protest (Lewis and Brooks 1975). We believe that the older but not the younger children were relating the discrepant information in the mirror to their schema of selfhood. In attempting to resolve the uncertainty resulting from that cognitive process, they touched their noses. This interpretation resembles the one proposed for separation protest; namely, the child tries to relate the departure of the caretaker to possible consequences for himself. In the case of the rouge on his nose, the 20-month-old answers the question and does not become upset; in the case of the departure he cannot answer the question and becomes apprehensive.

The complete corpus of data suggests that "separation anxiety" is being monitored closely by maturational factors, for it does not emerge until the last third of the first year, peaks during the middle of the second, and then declines in samples differing widely in rearing conditions. However, it is possible, even likely, that during the 12-month period when the distress is most likely to occur the intensity of crying and inhibition covaries with the quality of the mother-child interaction. For example, in the kibbutz study firstborns were significantly more distressed by the separation than children born later, even though the growth function was the same for both groups (Fox, Ph.D. thesis, 1975). Observations in the infant house suggest that mothers of firstborns are anxious about leaving their infants at the end of the day and vacillate in that decision. Hence they reward the child's crying by returning to the child's side.

We suggest that the maturational event that mediates the separation response is primarily but not solely cognitive in nature. It is the new ability to activate representations about the discrepant event contained in the parental departure. Separation distress occurs when the child is mature enough to ask questions about the parental departure and his response to it—Where is mother? Will she return? What should I do? What will the stranger do?—but is not mature enough to answer those queries. As a result he becomes uncertain and stops playing. If he is temperamentally prone to irritability, he may also cry. When he is mature enough to resolve those questions, his distress disappears.

Support for this interpretation of separation distress is found in a recent, quite unexpected finding regarding the development of apprehension to an unfamiliar child. The relevant data come from the day-care project mentioned earlier. The children were observed in three pairs of play sessions (solo and peer play) when they were 13½, 20, and 29 months of age. During the first play session, the child was with his mother and a set of interesting, age-appropriate toys. During the peer-play session which followed, an unfamiliar peer of the same sex and age and the peer's mother were in the room with the subject and his mother. The variable of interest was change in play from the solo to the peer session. The greatest inhibition of play, comparing solo with peer sessions, occurred for most children at 20 months of age and seems due to the presence of the

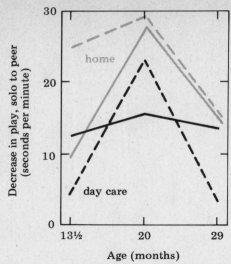

Figure 5. Another aspect of behavior that may be comparable to separation anxiety is the young child's apprehension when confronted by an unfamiliar peer. One indication of this distress is that the child's play is inhibited when he is with an unfamiliar child. In studies of both boys (*solid lines*) and girls (*dashed lines*) in both day-care and home settings, inhibition of play peaked at about 20 months. In the graph, the ordinate shows the average decrease in play from solo to peer conditions in number of seconds playing per minute over a 15-minute period of observation. That is, if a child was playing an average of 50 seconds out of every minute before the stranger's entry, and only 20 seconds per minute after, the average decrease is 30 seconds per minute.

peer, not the peer's mother, because the child stared at the peer significantly more often than he stared at the unfamiliar woman (Kagan, Kearsley, and Zelazo 1975) (see Fig. 5).

There is a parallel between the inhibition of play to an unfamiliar peer at 20 months and the growth function for separation anxiety. Although this curvilinear function for apprehension to a peer characterized children in both rearing conditions, the day-care children were a little less uncertain than those reared at home, suggesting that the group experience had theoretically anticipated effects. Maturational forces may determine the basic developmental function for initial uncertainty, inhibition, and apprehension to unfamiliar events, while experience and temperament monitor the intensity of distress and the time when it declines.

We suggest that apprehension to the peer does not peak until late in the second year because the primary source of the apprehension is the inability to resolve questions like "What do I do with that person?" What will that person do to me?" Can I still play with the toys?" This interpretation resembles the one offered for separation anxiety. It is interesting to note that Mary Shirley, in her classic monograph summarizing a longitudinal investigation of 25 Minneapolis children (1933), reported a wave of timidity at 18 months which lasted about 3 months and was displayed by more than three-quarters of her subjects. It may not be a coincidence that macaque monkeys display a generally fearful posture in a variety of contexts at about 5 months of age. Since development in macaques proceeds at a rate approximately four times faster than in human children, the expected age of peak apprehension for the human infant would be about 20 months—the time when inhibition of play to the introduction of another child and to separation was maximal.

The concept of stage

The second theme, which we will consider in less detail, is concerned with the popular concept of stage. The idea of a developmental stage refers to a special hierarchical organization of psychological processes that is part of an invariant sequence of theoretically related competences. Flavell (1971) has recently argued that we should take a softer view toward stage and regard emerging competences as much more gradual and less discontinuous than we have in the past. I should like to phrase that suggestion in a slightly different way, although the idea is similar to the one put forward by Flavell.

The Western mind is friendly to abstract attributes that are minimally constrained by context. We speak of hostile people or achievement motivation and do not feel it necessary to specify target and occasion. Mischel's (1968) cogent criticism of this pan-situational traitism reflects the growing corpus of empirical data which implies that we must specify the target and occasion of motivational and attitudinal dimensions. The same criticism applies to cognitive competences, although few, except for Guilford (1967), have acted on it. Generalizations about memory, reasoning, planfulness, or perceptual analysis rarely specify the problem context in detail or restrict developmental principles to classes of problem situations.

Decades of research on short-term memory for digits reveal that 3-year-olds can remember two to three items; 4-year-olds, four numbers; 10-year-olds, six or seven items. This literature implies that the short-term memory span of a 3-year-old is two to three items. Although that statement may be true for numbers, it is not true for locations. We recently administered the following task to a group of 2½- to 3-year-olds. A familiar object is hidden under a hollow receptacle. The receptacle is screened for five seconds, the screen is then removed, and the child is asked to retrieve the object. The number of objects and receptacles is gradually increased to five, as the child comes to realize that he is supposed to reach for the object the examiner requests. Under these conditions the average 30-month-old is able to remember the location of one of four or five different objects, no matter which receptacle it was placed under. One-third of the children correctly retrieved the requested object when five different toys were hidden under five different receptacles. In this context the 2½-year-old has a short-term memory for four or five independent items of information—not two or three as is true for numbers.

Quality of recognition memory is also dependent on the information to be remembered. Recognition memory for photographs of natural scenes was assessed by showing 6-year-olds pairs of pictures, one of which was the originally inspected photo, the other a transformation

that involved either addition of an element, rearrangement of elements, or a change in perspective. Performance was close to chance if the original photograph depicted a coherent group of objects—say, three bicycles leaning against a rack in front of a building—but close to 90 percent if the original photo showed a unitary object like a television set or a pocketbook.

As a final example, consider the ability to anticipate the requirements of a problem and adjust one's effort so that it is in accord with task difficulty. This competence, which might be called planfulness, is also highly dependent on problem context. Although 4-year-olds are planful in the building of difficult toy constructions, they are less planful when the task involves long-term recognition memory. We told groups of 4, 6, and 8-year-olds that they would have to remember some pictures for a few minutes, a day, or a week, after first convincing ourselves that the children appreciated the duration of the three time intervals. The index of planfulness was the initial inspection time for each of the 40 photographs. The eight-year-olds who were told they had to remember the information for one or seven days studied the pictures almost twice as long as those who were to be tested after a short delay. The four-year-olds in all three groups displayed equally short inspection times (Rogoff, Newcombe, and Kagan 1974). We interpret this result to mean that the ability of a 4-year-old to adjust his effort so that it is in accord with task demands is not an abstract competence that emerges at some particular age, but rather one that appears very early in some problem contexts, later in others.

It may be useful to regard basic cognitive competences as having long developmental histories. Each of the basic processes—habituation, detection of discrepancy, activation of relational structures, ability to recall four independent items of information or recognize forty pictures, planfulness, and multiplication of classes—emerges in very

narrow problem contexts early in development. With growth, each is applied—or generalized—to an increasing array of problem situations until that competence is reliably activated in most relevant situations. It is likely that the postulation of a stage by theorists has corresponded to the age when the hypothetical ability was successfully activated in 80 to 90 percent of appropriate contexts. Development of cognition might be conceptualized as a series of growth functions, one for each competence, in which the ordinate is the number of contexts in which that competence is activated and the abscissa is age. At the least, we should stop talking about cognitive competences like short-term memory, perceptual analysis or defect, reflection-impulsivity, and spatial reasoning in the abstract. We must specify, as we should for attitudes and motives, the class of problem in which that competence is being manifested.

Resilience in development

The final theme of resilience in development, which we discussed in an earlier paper (Kagan and Klein 1973), has generated some controversy. The suggestion was made then that early environments that are not beneficial to psychological growth do not necessarily produce deficits that cannot, under more benign conditions, be reversed. Resistance to that view is based on loyalty to what might be called a "tape recorder" theory of development, which assumes that from the first day of life every salient experience is recorded somewhere in the brain and is never erased. This view is consonant with modern man's desire to solve the mind-body problem by adopting a materialistic view of psychological experience. Early experience alters the iron filings on the hypothetical tape in our brains, and these material changes remain with us throughout life. Although the young infant is influenced by his environment from the moment he is born—there is no quarrel with that statement—the additional assumption that the effects of those early experiences ordinarily extend long into the future has equivocal support.

There are many reasons why a majority has favored the view that the products of early experience are difficult to alter. The influence of psychoanalytic theory and early data from animal laboratories form the modern scientific basis for the belief. But Darwinian theory also made a contribution. Darwin created a paradox by positing a continuum between animal and man. Since animal behavior was regarded by nineteenth-century scientists as instinctive and resistant to change, how was it possible for man to be so varied, flexible, and progressive?

One way to resolve the dilemma was to award a special function to what appeared to be a prolonged period of infant helplessness in humans as compared with animals. Since evolutionary theory made scholars sensitive to the idea that all qualities of living things had a purpose, it was reasonable to ask about the purpose of man's prolonged infancy. Most concluded that infancy was the period of maximal plasticity, the time when adults were to teach children skills, habits, and ideas they would carry with them throughout life. In a lecture at Harvard in 1871, Fiske argued that man's power to control his environment and to make progress was due to his educability. The purpose of infancy was to educate and to train the child, because he was most malleable to training during the early years (Fiske 1883). That assumption was congruent with a belief in continuity from infancy to later childhood, it served to keep parents affectively concerned with their actions toward their babies, and it was an argument for creating good schools.

Additionally, each of us feels a compelling sense of continuity when we reflect on the experiences of our own childhood. The sense of the past's contribution to the present derives from our need to regard our life as coherent and past decisions as a part of a rationally causal chain. More speculatively, faith in the permanent effects of early experience may be a derivative of one of the central maxims of Protestantism, namely, preparation for the future. Application of that principle to child-rearing would lead parents to believe that if children were treated optimally during the early years, healthy attitudes, talents, and behaviors established then would provide protection against trauma during adolescence and adulthood. Proper early experience, like vaccination, was expected to inoculate a child against vulnerability to future psychic distress. Finally, faith in the permanent influence of early experience is in accord with the commitment to political egalitarianism which is strong in Protestant democracies. If society treats children properly during the opening years, there is at least the hope that the distress, sense of hopelessness, and lack of technical skills that prevent full participation by all adult citizens can be eliminated and a truly egalitarian society established.

There is, however, good reason to begin to question the nonerasability of the tapes and, therefore, the strong version of the doctrine of irreversibility. Perhaps the least persuasive are clinical reports and naturalistic studies of children who have experienced destructive environments during infancy but, following removal to benevolent family contexts, develop more normative profiles. Several years ago I interviewed a 14½-year-old girl who spent most of the first 30 months of her life in a crib in a small bedroom with no toys and a sister one year older than herself. She was removed to a foster home at 2½ years of age, severely retarded in both weight and height, without language, and, of course, completely untestable. She has remained with the same foster family for 12 years. Her full-scale IQ was 88 and she performed normatively on a wide battery of standard and nonstandard cognitive tests. Koluchova (1972) has reported a similar history for twin Czechoslovakian boys who were isolated from 18 months until 7 years of age, when they were sent to a foster home. Their full-scale Wechsler IQs at age 11 were 95 and 93, and the clinician noted that they appeared psychologically normal for their age.

These clinical data are affirmed by two recent follow-up studies of institutionalized infants. Dennis (1973) assessed 16 children who had been adopted from institutions in Lebanon by middle-class families when the children were between 12 and 24 months of age and had an average developmental quotient of 50 on the Cattell scale. The average Stanford-Binet IQ obtained when these children were between 4 and 12 years of age was 101, and 13 of the 16 children had IQ scores of 90 or above. Tizard and Rees (1974) assessed 65 4½-year-olds who had spent their first two to four years in an institution in which an exclusive relation between an infant and one caretaker was actively discouraged. Of the original group of 65, 15 were now living with their natural mothers, 24 had been adopted, and 26 were still living in the institution. There was no difference in Wechsler IQ scores among the three groups at 4½ years of age (means ranged from 100 to 115). Although the institutionalized children had been retarded in language development when they were 2 years old, they were not retarded with respect to British norms at 4½ years (Tizard and Rees 1974; see also Dennis 1938; Rheingold and Bayley 1959).

A third source of information is the animal laboratory. Suomi and Harlow (1972) have reported that even the stereotyped and bizarre social behavior shown by 6-month-old macaque isolates can be altered by placing them with female monkeys three months younger than themselves over a 26-week therapeutic period. Generally, investigators have reported that, although the isolate-reared animal is initially inhibited and deficient on test performance, after continued exposure to the test situation his behavior approaches that of the normally reared animal, often in a short time. Wild-born or isolate chimpanzees were placed with a passive human for 10 minutes a day for 13 days.

Each day, after the initial 10 minutes, the person spent 50 minutes encouraging the chimpanzee to socialize by making gentle social contacts. The wild-born chimps contacted the human throughout the 13 days. The isolates were initially inhibited but by the last session made as much contact as the wild-born animals (Mason, Davenport, and Menzel 1968).

Even imprinting toward a nonnatural object in a laboratory context seems to be reversible. Hess, in an attempt to imprint ducklings to human beings in the laboratory, exposed newly hatched ducklings to adults for 20 continuous hours; before long, they followed the adults. The ducks were then given to a female mallard that had hatched a clutch of ducklings several hours before. After only an hour and a half of exposure to the female, the human-imprinted ducklings followed her on her first exodus from the nest (Hess 1972).

This phenomenon is analogous to changes in the object of primary attachment among primates. Rhesus monkeys were raised from birth with cloth surrogates, their mothers, or a peer monkey for 3 to 10 months. All the monkeys were then separated from these objects of primary attachment and gradually exposed to spayed adult female dogs. Initially most of the monkeys were fearful, but this behavior disappeared quickly, and after seven hours all monkeys approached the dogs and eventually clung to them. Soon the monkeys displayed the classic signs of attachment—clinging and following. The initial attachment had been changed (Mason and Kenney 1974; see Elias lecture MS and Ader 1970 for additional support for the rehabilitative properties of proper experience following early insult).

These alterations of behavior are in accord with reports of recovery of visual functioning in monkeys and cats deprived of patterned light soon after birth (Baxter 1966; Chow and Stewart 1972; Wilson and Riesen 1966)—although this conclusion is controversial (see Wiesel and Hubel 1965). Even complex cognitive functions like spatial-delayed alternation seem to recover following removal of areas of frontal cortex in infant monkeys (Goldman 1974).

A more controversial source of support comes from our studies of children growing up in the small, isolated village of San Marcos in the highlands of western Guatemala. During the first year of life these infants are restricted to dark huts, are not talked to or played with very much, and are malnourished and ill for much of the time. As a result of the combination of these factors, the 1- and 1½-year-olds are retarded in the time of emergence of the standard developmental milestones of reactivity to discrepancy, activation of relational structures, object permanence, stranger and separation anxiety, and onset of speech. In addition, the children have extremely depressed and withdrawn appearances.

During the second year, however, they are allowed outside the hut and begin to encounter the greater variety of the external world. At 8 to 9 years of age they are assigned chores and adult responsibilities like working in the field, caring for infants, cooking, and cleaning. Prior to 10 or 11 years of age, their performance on culturally fair tests of perceptual analysis, memory, and reasoning is markedly inferior to that of children in the United States and to the performance of children in a nearby village who are not restricted during the first year. But with each successive year their competence improves, until by adolescence they perform on tests of perceptual analysis of pictures, memory for familiar objects, and conceptual inference at a level that approaches that of children tested in Cambridge, Massachusetts.

My colleagues and I have continued to work in this and other villages in this area and have administered more difficult memory tests to children 6 through 18 years of age. The results are generally in accord with the original findings. Although the children 6 to 12 years of age perform less well than Cambridge children and those from San Pedro, a more modern Indian village nearby, by adolescence their performance begins to approach that of the other groups. In one of the memory tasks the child must remember the orientation of a series of identical dolls (placed either right side up or upside down). The series begins with 2 dolls and gradually increases to 12 as the examiner adds a doll each time the child successfully reproduces the series. A similar task involves remembering the order of a series of pictures of familiar objects, and a third involves memory for a list of familiar words. Examination of the average performance of children from three settings—the isolated village of San Marcos, the more modern Indian village of San Pedro, and Cambridge reveals that the North Americans reached maximum performance on all three tests by age 9 to 10. Although the Indian children had difficulty remembering the words, on the other two tasks the children in the less isolated village of San Pedro approached maximum performance by age 12, and the San Marcos children by 17 to 18 years of age (Fig. 6) (see also Scribner 1974).

Finally, longitudinal studies of American children fail to provide convincing support for the view that aspects of infant behavior and early experience are strongly predictive of adolescent or adult behavior. In a longitudinal study of the middle-class Fels Institute population (Kagan and Moss 1962), we found very little relation between aspects of the maternal treatment of the child during the first three years of life and a variety of psychological dispositions displayed during adolescence or adulthood. There was, for example, no consistent relation between maternal hostility toward the child and anger-arousal or aggressive behavior in adulthood; no relation between early maternal overprotection or restriction and the adult's dependence on parents or friends or the tendency to with-

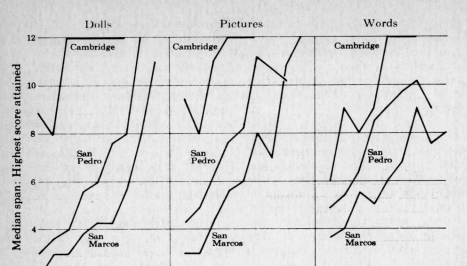

Age (years)

Figure 6. Three tests of memory—for orientation of a series of dolls, order of a series of pictures of familiar objects, and a list of familiar words—were given to three groups of children 6 to 18 years of age. The groups came from disparate cultural backgrounds: the city of Cambridge, Massachusetts, the village of San Pedro, Guatemala, and the isolated Indian village of San Marcos, Guatemala. Each test series began with 2 items and gradually increased to a maximum of 12 as one item was added each time the child successfully recalled the series. The Cambridge children reached maximum performance on all three tests by 9 to 10 years of age. The Indian children performed least well on memory for words. On the doll and picture tests, however, the San Pedro children approached maximum performance by age 12, and the isolated San Marcos children by age 18. These tests provide some support for the view that early environments that are not optimal for aspects of psychological growth do not necessarily stunt the child's cognitive development permanently.

draw in times of stress.

However, if one examined the social class of the parents rather than the mother's specific behaviors, the correlations with adult behavior were much stronger (about 0.5 and 0.6). Since social class represents a complex and continuing set of experiences that influences values and beliefs about the self and others throughout the life span, it is possible that the experiences during later childhood were as influential or even more so than the maternal treatments experienced during the first three years (Kagan and Moss 1962).

With the exception of infant passivity, there was little relation between the infant's behavior during the first three years and his adult profile. Occurrence of temper tantrums during infancy was unrelated to aggressive behavior in adulthood; mastery attempts with objects during the first three years were unrelated to achievement or fear of failure in adulthood; fearfulness toward strangers did not predict social anxiety. Generally, a moderately strong predictive relation between child and adult behavior did not emerge until the child was about 10 years old.

A similar conclusion was reached by Jean Macfarlane who, after a lifetime of study of the Berkeley Growth Study subjects, concluded that the forces that shape behavior are subject to continuous modification: "Many of our most mature and competent adults had severely troubled and confusing childhoods and adolescences. Many of our highly successful children and adults have failed to achieve their predicted potential" (Macfarlane 1964). Macfarlane believes she awarded too much power to early habits, expecting excessive durability for behaviors that seemed so

fixed and stable in childhood: "It appears that no matter how habitual these patterns were, if they were coping devices or instrumental acts that no longer were effective for desired ends in changed situations . . . they were dropped or modified" (Macfarlane 1963).

We recently conducted a more focused longitudinal investigation on a large sample of firstborn white children from intact families who were seen on four occasions from 4 to 27 months of age (Kagan 1971). One might have expected that this short developmental period would have yielded stronger instances of continuity. There was minimal continuity (in the rank-order sense) from 4 or 8 months to 27 months of age but suggestive stability from 13 to 27 months for attentiveness to human faces and forms. But active 8-month-old babies were not excessively motoric twenty months later; fretful 4-month-olds were not irritable 2-year-olds; frightened 8-month-olds were not anxious 2½-year-olds. We are currently evaluating these children at age 10, and preliminary analyses of the data do not reveal much phenotypic or genotypic continuity for dimensions like irritability, activity, or attentiveness. Moreover the 10-year-old child's intelligence and reading ability are more clearly related to the social class of his family than to his behavior profile in the first 27 months of life.

The few infants who showed extremely deviant patterns of behavior (e.g. stereotyped rocking behavior) were not psychologically unusual at age 10, suggesting a disposition to grow toward health. The child tries to grow toward adaptation, not away from it, and early dispositions that interfere with adaptation seem to be vulnerable to change, if the proper environmental events occur. This suggestion is in accord with Block's study of change and stability from adolescence to adulthood. The adolescents who changed the most were characterized as passive, brittle, and negativistic—traits that are valued by neither the society nor the self. The intellectually productive adolescents changed the least (Block 1971).

One reason for the weak support for continuity from infancy to later childhood is that the behaviors displayed during the first year or two are particularly suited to the problems of that developmental era and not to those of later childhood. It would be maladaptive for a child to retain for too long a time the hierarchical organization of cognitive and behavioral structures that are characteristic of the first year. And nature will not permit him that luxury, for maturational forces replace old behaviors with new abilities that permit, indeed demand, a different interaction with the world.

Each phase of development is marked by changing clusters of dominant reactions toward objects and people. As cognitive and motor systems mature, early behaviors are replaced by more mature ones. Mouthing of other monkeys is an act frequently displayed by macaque rhesus during the early weeks of life. By four months, rough-and-tumble play has replaced this initial class of simpler behaviors. This sequence is analogous to the human progression from the display of crying in distress, seen at 6 months, to requests for help at 18 months, as speech replaces fretting in a frustrating context. We do not know why the new behavior appears. Some assume, I think gratuitously, that greater variety, efficiency, and pleasantness accompany display of the new form. But it is not clear that a motivational interpretation is helpful. Although the butterfly inevitably follows the caterpillar, each form seems equally efficient, happy, or distressed. It is not obvious that adding a statement about pleasure to explain the emergent response enhances understanding, especially since the macaque displays a decrease in rough-and-tumble play—an act that appears to be such great fun—after his first birthday and begins to spend more time sitting and grooming—acts which appear, at least to a human observer, to contain less variety, vigor, and excite-

ment. Observations of early behavioral development in both monkey and man suggest that, during the early years, the frequent changes in response classes are based, in part, on changing cognitive and motor competences.

A useful metaphor for early development is waves of emerging, plateauing, and declining behavioral systems which dominate the scene for a time until they are displaced by a new set. This view suggests that there will be, at any one age, two important sources of individual differences in behavior. One source is individual variation in rates of development; the other, experience combined with temperamental factors that make one class of action prepotent over another. In general, the older the child, the longer the period between the emergence of new sets of cognitive competences; hence, the more likely it is that individual differences will be experiential in origin. But during the first few years of life, when there are frequent maturational changes in basic competences, individual differences are just as likely to be the result of differences in rates of development as they are to be a product of experience. Perhaps that is why there is so little predictive validity for most behaviors from infancy to later childhood.

The total corpus of information implies that the young mammal retains an enormous capacity for change and, therefore, for resilience in the growth of psychological competences *if environments change;* if an initial environment that does not support psychological development becomes more beneficial. The existing data—clinical, longitudinal, institutional, cross-cultural, and animal—do not support the belief that certain events during the first year can produce irreversible consequences in either human or infrahuman infants. For most of this century many parents and some developmental psychologists have favored the irreversibility pole of the irreversibility-reversibility theme. The extreme form of that position is as likely to be incorrect as its opposite,

which assumes complete capacity for alteration of any disposition at any age.

Available knowledge is certainly not firm enough to assert that there is no relation between structures established during infancy and the victories of the next three, five, or ten years. Further, the data do not imply that caretakers need not be concerned with the experiences of their infants. Infants recover from colds, but we still try to protect them from this distress. Rather, these data invite a slightly more critical attitude toward the strong version of the tape-recorder view of development. We should entertain the possibility that there is less inevitability between infancy and later childhood than has been traditionally assumed.

Young sciences suffer the combined disadvantages of ambiguous propositions and weak methodology—a condition that makes it likely that original suppositions, usually loose metaphors taken from the philosophy of the larger culture, will be difficult to disconfirm. As a result these suppositions live longer than they should. It is useful to remain critically skeptical of the unexamined premises of an emergent discipline. We should expect that many of psychology's early advances will be disconfirmations of old prejudices and it is wise, therefore, to heed Parmenides' prophecy:

But you also shall learn how it was that elusive opinion
Forcing its way through all things was destined to pass for the real.

References

Ader. R. 1970. The effects of early life experiences on developmental processes and susceptibility to disease in animals. In J. W. Hill, ed., *Minnesota Symposium on Child Psychology,* vol. 4, pp. 3–35. Univ. of Minneapolis Press.

Baxter, B. L. 1966. Effect of visual deprivation during postnatal maturation on the electroencephalogram of the cat. *Exper. Neurol.* 14:224–37.

Block, J. 1971. *Lives through Time.* Berkeley: Bancroft.

Bohr, N. 1934. *Atomic Theory and the Description of Nature.* Cambridge Univ. Press.

Bornstein, M. H. 1975. Qualities of color vision in infancy. *J. Exper. Child Psych.* 19: 401–19.

Chow, K. L., and D. L. Stewart. 1972. Reversal of structural and functional effects of long-term visual deprivation in cats. *Exper. Neurol.* 34:409–33.

Dennis, W. 1938. Infant development under conditions of restricted practice and of minimum social stimulation: A preliminary report. *J. Genetic Psych.* 53:149–158.

———. 1973. *Children of the Creche.* NY: Appleton-Century-Crofts.

Elias, M. F. Rehabilitation erases behavioral effects of nutritional and rearing restriction in infant monkeys. Paper presented at Federation of American Societies for Experimental Biology, Atlantic City, NJ, April 1974.

Fantz, R. L. 1965. Visual perception from birth as shown by pattern selectivity. *Annals of the New York Academy of Sciences* 118:793–814.

———, and S. B. Miranda. 1975. Newborn infant attention to form of contour. *Child Devel.* 46:224–28.

Fiske, J. 1883. *The Meaning of Infancy.* Boston: Houghton Mifflin.

Flavell, J. H. 1971. Stage-related properties of cognitive development. *Cognitive Psych.* 2:421–53.

Fox, N. Separation distress in kibbutz-reared children. Ph.D. thesis, Harvard University, 1975.

———, J. Kagan, M. Konner, and M. Kotelchuck. Maturation of separation protest. MS in prep.

Goldman, P. S. 1974. An alternative to developmental plasticity: Heterology of CNS structures of infants and adults. In D. G. Stein, J. J. Rosen, and N. Butters, eds., *Plasticity and Recovery of Function in the Central Nervous System,* pp. 149–74. NY: Academic Press.

Guilford, J. P. 1967. *The Nature of Human Intelligence.* NY: McGraw-Hill.

Haith, M. M. 1966. The response of a human newborn to visual movement. *J. Exper. Child Psych.* 3:235–43.

Hess, E. H. 1972. Imprinting in a natural laboratory. *Sci. Am.* 227:24–31.

Holton, G. 1973. *Thematic Origins of Scientific Thought.* Harvard Univ. Press.

Hopkins, J. R. Curvature as a dimension in infant visual perception. Ph.D. thesis, Harvard University, 1974.

Kagan, J. 1971. *Change and Continuity in Infancy.* NY: Wiley.

———. 1972. Do infants think? *Sci. Am.* 226:74–83.

———. 1974. Discrepancy, temperament, and infant distress. In M. Lewis and L. A. Rosenblum, eds., *The Origins of Fear,* pp. 229–48. NY:Wiley.

———, and H. A. Moss. 1962. *Birth to Maturity.* NY:Wiley.

———, and R. E. Klein. 1973. Cross-cultural perspectives on early development. *Am. Psychol.* 28:947–61.

———, R. B. Kearsley, and P. R. Zelazo. 1975. The emergence of initial apprehension to unfamiliar peers. In M. Lewis and L. A. Rosenblum, eds., *Friendship and Peer Relations,* pp. 187–206. NY:Wiley.

Karmel, B. Z. 1969. The effect of age, complexity, and amount of contour on pattern preferences in human infants. *J. Exper. Child Psych.* 7:339–54.

———, R. F. Hoffman, and M. J. Fegy. 1974. Processing of contour information by human infants evidenced by pattern-dependent evoked potentials. *Child Devel.* 45:39–48.

Kearsley, R., P. R. Zelazo, J. Kagan, and R. Hartmann. 1975. Differences in separation protest between day-care and home-reared infants. *J. Pediatrics* 55:171–75.

Kessen, W., P. Salapatek, and M. Haith. 1972. The visual response of the human newborn to linear contour. *J. Exper. Child Psych.* 13:9–20.

Koluchova, J. 1972. Severe deprivation in twins. *J. Child Psychology and Psychiatry* 13:107–11.

Konrad, K. W., and M. Bagshaw. 1970. The effect of novel stimuli on cats reared in a restricted environment. *J. Comp. and Physiol. Psych.* 70:157–64.

Kotelchuck, M. The nature of a child's tie to his father. Ph.D. thesis, Harvard University, 1972.

Lacey, J. I. 1967. Somatic response patterning and stress: Some revisions of activation theory. In M. H. Appley and R. Trumbull, eds., *Psychological Stress: Issues in Research,* pp. 14–44. NY: Appleton-Century-Crofts.

Lester, B. M., M. Kotelchuck, E. Spelke, M. J. Sellers, and R. E. Klein. 1974. Separation protest in Guatemalan infants: Cross-cultural and cognitive findings. *Devel. Psych.* 10:79–85.

Lewis, M, and J. Brooks. 1975. Infants' social perception: A constructivist view. In L. B. Cohen and P. Salapatek, eds., *Infant Perception: From Sensation to Cognition,* vol. 2, pp. 101–48. NY: Academic Press.

Macfarlane, J. W. 1963. From infancy to adulthood. *Childhood Ed.* 39:336–42.

———. 1964. Perspectives on personality consistency and change from the guidance study. *Vita Humana* 7:115–26.

Mason, W. A., R. K. Davenport, and E. W. Menzel. 1968. Early experience in the social development of rhesus monkeys and chimpanzees. In G. Newton and S. Levine, eds., *Early Experience in Behavior,* pp. 440–80. Springfield, IL: C. C. Thomas.

———, and M. D. Kenney. 1974. Redirection of filial attachments in rhesus monkeys: Dogs as mother surrogates. *Science* 183: 1209–11.

Mischel, W. 1968. *Personality and Assessment.* NY: Wiley.

Parry, M. H. 1973. Infant wariness and stimulus discrepancy. *J. Exper. Child Psych.* 16:377–87.

Popper. K. R. 1962. *Conjectures and Refutations.* NY: Basic Books.

Rheingold, H. C., and N. Bayley. 1959. The later effects of an experimental modification of mothering. *Child Devel.* 30:363–72.

Rogoff, B., N. Newcombe, and J. Kagan. 1974. Planfulness and recognition memory. *Child Devel.* 45:972–77.

Ruff, H. A., and H. G. Birch. 1974. Infant visual fixation: The effect of concentricity, curvilinearity, and number of directions. *J. Exper. Child Psych.* 17:460–73.

Salapatek, P., and W. Kessen. 1973. Prolonged investigation of a plane geometric triangle by the human newborn. *J. Exper. Child Psych.* 15:22–29.

Scarr, S., and P. Salapatek. 1970. Patterns of fear development during infancy. *Merrill Palmer Quarterly* 16:53–90.

Schaffer, H. R. 1974. Cognitive components of the infant's response to strangeness. In M. Lewis and L. A. Rosenblum, eds., *The Origins of Fear,* pp. 11–24. NY: Wiley.

Schwartz, A. N., J. J. Campos, and E. J. Baisel. 1973. The visual cliff: Cardiac and behavioral responses on the deep and shallow sides at 5 and 9 months of age. *J. Exper. Child Psych.* 15:86–99.

Scribner, S. 1974. Developmental aspects of categorical recall in a West African society. *Cognitive Psych.* 6:475–94.

Shirley, M. M. 1933. The first two years: A study of 25 babies, vol. 2. *Institute of Child Welfare Monograph Series,* no. 7. Univ. of Minneapolis Press.

Suomi, S. J., and H. F. Harlow. 1972. Social rehabilitation of isolate-reared monkeys. *Devel. Psych.* 6:487–96.

Tizard, B., and J. Rees. 1974. A comparison of the effects of adoption, restoration to the natural mother, and continued institutionalization on the cognitive development of 4-year-old children. *Child Devel.* 45: 92–99.

Van Hover, K. I. 1974. A developmental study of three components of attention. *Devel. Psych.* 10:330–39.

Wiesel, T. N., and D. H. Hubel. 1965. Extent of recovery from the effects of visual deprivation in kittens. *J. Neurophysiol.* 28: 1060–72.

Wilson, P. D., and A. H. Riesen. 1966. Visual development in rhesus monkeys neonatally deprived of pattern light. *J. Comp. and Physiol. Psych.* 61:87–95.

13

PIAGET

by DAVID ELKIND

"He is advocating a revolutionary doctrine about human knowing that undermines the assumptions of much of contemporary social science."

Perhaps no living scholar has contributed more to our knowledge of how we learn and grow than Jean Piaget. As he nears 80, he has surely earned the right to rest on his considerable laurels. But in fact, he has barely slowed down.

It is probably fair to say that the single most influential psychologist writing today is famed Swiss developmentalist Jean Piaget. His work is cited in every major textbook on psychology, education, linguistics, sociology, psychiatry and other disciplines as well. There is now a Jean Piaget Society that each year draws thousands of members to its meetings. And there are many smaller conferences, both here and abroad, that focus upon one or another aspect of Piaget's work. It is simply a fact that no psychologist, psychiatrist or educator today can claim to be fully educated without some exposure to Piaget's work.

The man who has made this tremendous impact upon social science is now in his 79th year and shows no signs of letting up his prodigious pace of research, writing and lecturing. In the last few years, he has published more than a half-dozen

Photograph by John Sotomayor, The New York Times

books, has traveled and lectured extensively (he received an honorary degree from the University of Chicago last fall) and continues to lead a year-long seminar attended by interdisciplinary scholars from around the world. The seminar is held in Geneva at Piaget's Center for Genetic Epistemology, which he founded more than 15 years ago. Each year Piaget invites scholars from all over the world to attend the Center for a year.

My first extensive exposure to Piaget occurred when I spent the 1964–65 year at the Center and learned

something of Piagetian psychology firsthand. Although I have never been among the small intimate group of colleagues and students who surround Piaget, we have remained good friends over the years. I last visited with him about two years ago in New York when he came to America to receive the first International Kittay Award (of $25,000) for scientific achievement. The ceremony was held at the Harvard Club and was attended by a small group of invited guests, many of whom, like myself, had worked with or been associated with Piaget in some way. He presented a paper in the afternoon and a brief acceptance speech at the formal dinner that evening.

When Piaget arrived, he wore his familiar dark suit and vest with the remarkably illusionary sweater that somehow seems to keep appearing and disappearing as you watch him. He is of average height, solid in build and looks a little like Albert Einstein, a resemblance that is heightened by the fringe of long white hair that surrounds his head and by the scorched meerschaum that is inevitably in his hand or in his mouth. Up close, his most striking feature is his eyes, which somehow give the impression that they possess great depth and insight. My fantasy has always been that Freud's eyes must have looked something like that. (Piaget's eyes are remarkably keen as well, despite his glasses. A year before the Kittay

79

ceremony, I visited him in Geneva and we took a walk together. As we climbed the small mountain in the back of his home, he pointed out wild pigeons and flora and fauna towards the top that I could not see at all!)

That afternoon, Piaget talked about his research on conscious-awareness. As one has come to expect from him and his co-workers, the studies were most original. In one investigation, he asked children to walk upon all fours and then describe the actions they had taken. "I put my left foot out, then my right hand" and so on. What he found was that young children have great difficulty in describing their actions and that it is not until middle childhood that they can describe their actions with any exactness. Piaget also said (but was most probably joking) that he also asked some psychologists and logicians to perform the same task. The psychologists did very well but the logicians, at least according to Piaget, constructed beautiful models of crawling that had nothing to do with the real patterning of their actions.

At the dinner meeting that evening, Piaget accepted the award. In his talk, he related his fantasy of the committee meeting at which it was decided that the award should go to him. He imagined, he said, that the physicians on the committee were reluctant to give the award to a neurologist or physiologist who in turn were reluctant to see it go to a neurochemist or molecular biologist. Piaget appeared as the compromise candidate because he belonged to no particular discipline (except to the one he himself created, although he did not say this) and was, therefore, the only candidate upon whom everyone could agree. The speaker who gave Piaget the award assured him that while his fantasy was most amusing, it had no basis in fact, and that Piaget was the first person nominated and unanimously chosen by the selection committee.

There was not much chance to talk to Piaget after the dinner, but it was probably just as well. He does not really like to engage in "small talk," and at close quarters it is often difficult to find things to say to him other than discussion of research, which seems rather inappropriate at dinner parties. Yet his difficulty with small talk does not seem to extend to women, and with them he can be most charming in any setting. He is even not above clowning a bit. It should be said, too, that on formal social occasions, when he is officiating or performing some titular function, he is most gracious and appropriate. It is the small interpersonal encounters, such as occur at the dinner table, that seem most awkward for him. Perhaps his total commitment to his work has produced this social hiatus. It is certainly a small price to pay for all that he has accomplished.

Despite the enormity of his collected works, the extent of Piaget's influence is surprising for several reasons. For one thing, it has been phenomenally rapid and recent. Although Piaget began writing in the early decades of this century, his work did not become widely known in this country until the early 1960s. It is only in the past 10 years that Piaget's influence has grown in geometric progression from his previous recognition. Piaget's influence is also surprising because he writes and speaks only in French; so all of his works have had to be translated. Moreover, his naturalistic research methodology and avoidance of statistics are such that many of his studies would not be acceptable for publication in American journals of psychology. But most surprising of all is the fact that Piaget is advocating a revolutionary doctrine regarding the nature of human knowing that, if fully appreciated, effectively undermines the assumptions of much of contemporary social science.

What then is it about Piaget's work and theory that has made him so influential despite his controversial ideas and his somewhat unacceptable (at least to a goodly portion of the academic community) research methodology? The fact is that, theory and method aside, his descriptions of how children come to know and think about the world ring true to everyone's ear. When Piaget says that children believe that the moon follows them when they go for a walk at night, that the name of the sun is in the sun and that dreams come in through the window at night, it sounds strange and is yet somehow in accord with our intuitions. In fact, it was in trying to account for these strange ideas (which are neither innate, because they are given up as children grow older, nor acquired, because they are not taught by adults) that Piaget arrived at his revolutionary theory of knowing.

In the past, two kinds of theories have been proposed to account for the acquisition of knowledge. One theory, which might be called *camera* theory, suggests that the mind operates in much the same way as a camera does when it takes a picture. This theory assumes that there is a reality that exists outside of our heads and that is completely independent of our knowing processes. As does a camera, the child's mind takes pictures of this external reality, which it then stores up in memory. Differences between the world of adults and the world of children can thus be explained by the fact that adults have more pictures stored up than do the children. Individual differences in intelligence can also be explained in terms of the quality of the camera, speed of the film and so on. On this analogy, dull children would have less precise cameras and less sensitive film than brighter children.

A second, less popular theory of knowing asserts that the mind operates not as a camera but rather as a projector. According to this view, infants come into the world with a built-in film library that is part of some natural endowment. Learning about the world amounts to running these films through a projector (the mind), which displays the film on a blank screen—the world. This theory asserts then that we never learn anything new, that nothing really exists outside of our heads and that the whole world is a product of our own mental processes. Differences between the world of adults and the world of children can be explained by arguing that adults have projected a great many more films than have children. And individual differences can be explained in terms of the quality of the projection equipment or the nature and content of the films.

The projector theory of knowing has never been very popular because it seems to defy common sense. Bishop Berkeley, an advocate of this position, was once told that he would be convinced that the world was not all in his head if, when walking about the streets of London, the contents of a slop bucket chanced to hit him on the head. The value of the projector, sometimes called the *idealistic* or *platonic* theory of knowing, has been to challenge the copy theorists and

"When he was 10, his observations on a sparrow were published in a science journal, initiating a publications career equalled by few."

to force them to take account of the part that the human imagination plays in constructing the reality that seems to exist so independently of the operations of the human mind.

In contrast to these ideas, Piaget has offered a nonmechanical, creative or *constructionist* conception of the process of human knowing. According to Piaget, children construct reality out of their experiences with the environment in much the same way that artists paint a picture from their immediate impressions. A painting is never a simple copy of the artist's impressions, and even a portrait is "larger" than life. The artist's construction involves his or her experience but only as it has been transformed by the imagination. Paintings are always unique combinations of what the artists have taken from their experience and what they have added to it from their own scheme of the world.

In the child's construction of reality, the same holds true. What children understand reality to be is never a copy of what was received by their *sense* impressions; it is always transformed by their own ways of knowing. For example, once I happened to observe a friend's child playing at what seemed to be "ice-cream wagon." He dutifully asked customers what flavor ice cream they desired and then scooped it into make-believe cones. When I suggested that he was the ice-cream man, however, he disagreed. And when I asked what he was doing, he replied, "I am going to college." It turned out his father had told him that he had worked his way through college by selling Good Humor ice cream from a wagon. The child has recreated his own reality from material offered by the environment. From Piaget's standpoint, we can never really know the environment but only our reconstructions of it. Reality, he believes, is always a reconstruction of the environment and never a copy of it.

Looked at from this standpoint, the discrepancies between child and adult thought appear in a much different light than they do for the camera and projector theories. Those theories assume that there are only quantitative differences between the child and adult views of the world, that children are "miniature adults" in mind as well as in appearance. In fact, of course, children are not even miniature adults physically. And intellectually, the child's reality is qualitatively different from the adult's because the child's means for constructing reality out of environmental experiences are less adequate than those of the adult. For Piaget, the child progressively constructs and reconstructs reality until it approximates that of adults.

To be sure, Piaget recognizes the pragmatic value of the copy theory of knowing and does not insist that we go about asserting the role of our knowing processes in the construction of reality. He does contend that the constructionist theory of knowing has to be taken into account in education. Traditional education is based on a copy theory of knowing that assumes that if given the words, children will acquire the ideas they represent. A constructionist theory of knowing asserts just the reverse— that children must attain the concepts before the words have meaning. Thus Piaget stresses that children must be active in learning, that they have concrete experiences from which to construct reality and that only in consequence of their mental operations on the environment will they have the concepts that will give meaning to the words they hear and read. This approach to education is not new and has been advocated by such workers as Pestalozzi, Froebel, Montessori and Dewey. Piaget has, however, provided an extensive empirical and theoretical basis for an educational program in which children are allowed to construct reality through active engagements with the environment.

Piaget's concern with the educational implications of his work comes naturally because he has, for the whole of his career, been associated with the J. J. Rousseau Institute, which is essentially a training school for teachers. And Rousseau made explicit a theme that has permeated Piaget's work, namely, that child psychology is the science of education.

The union of child development and educational practice is thus quite natural in Switzerland, particularly in Geneva where Rousseau once lived and worked. Indeed, Piaget's Swiss heritage, while it does not explain his genius, was certainly an important factor in determining the directions towards which his genius turned.

Besides its beauty, perhaps the most extraordinary thing about Switzerland is the number of outstanding psychologists and psychiatrists it has produced in relation to the modest size of its population (two million people). One thinks of Claparède who preceded Piaget at the Institut de Rousseau in Geneva; of Carl Gustav Jung, the great analytic psychologist; of Herman Rorschach, who created the famed Rorschach inkblot test; and of Frederich Binswanger, the existential psychiatrist. And then, of course, there is Jean Piaget. But it is important to recognize that there appears to be something in the Swiss milieu and gene pool that is conducive to producing more than its share of exceptional social scientists.

Piaget himself was born in a small village outside Lausanne. His father, a professor of history at the University of Lausanne, was particularly well-known for his gracious literary style. Piaget's mother was an ardently religious woman who was often at odds with her husband's free thinking and lack of piety. Growing up in this rather conflictual environment, Piaget turned to intellectual pursuits, in part because of his natural genius, but perhaps also as an escape from a difficult and uncomfortable life situation.

As often happens in the case of true genius, Piaget showed his promise early. When he was 10, he observed an albino sparrow and wrote a note about it that was published in a scientific journal. Thus was launched a career of publications that has had few equals in any science. When Piaget was a young adolescent, he spent a great deal of time in a local museum helping the curator, who had a fine collection of mollusks. This work stimulated Piaget to undertake his own collection and to make systematic observations of mollusks on the shores of lakes and ponds. He began reporting his observations in a series of articles that were published in Swiss journals of biology. As a result, he won an international reputation as a mollusciologist, and, on the basis of his work, he was offered, sight unseen, the curatorship of a museum in Geneva. He had to turn the offer down because he was only 16 and had not yet completed high school.

Although Piaget had a natural bent for biological observation, he was not inclined toward experimental biology. The reason, according to Piaget, was that he was "maladroit" or not well coordinated enough to perform the delicate manipulations required in the laboratory. But Piaget had other intellectual pursuits. He was very interested in philosophy, particularly in Aristotle and Bergson, who speculated about biological and natural science. Piaget was initially much impressed by the Bergsonian dualism between life forces (*élan vital*) and physical forces, but he eventually found this dualism unacceptable. More to his liking was the Aristotelian position that saw logic and reason as the unifying force in both animate and inanimate nature. What living and nonliving things have in common is that they obey rational laws. Not surprisingly, Piaget came to regard human intelligence, man's rational function, as providing the unifying principle of all the sciences—including the social, biological and natural disciplines. It was a point of view that was to guide him during his entire career.

In 1914, Piaget had intended to go to England for a year to learn English as many young Europeans did, but the war intervened. Consequently, despite rumors to the contrary, Piaget does not speak or understand spoken English very well, although he has a fair command of written English.

At the University of Lausanne, Piaget majored in biology and, not surprisingly, conducted his dissertation on mollusks. Early in his college career, Piaget took what Erik Erikson might call a "moratorium"—a period away from his studies and his family. Piaget's moratorium was spent in a Swiss mountain spa. There, he wrote a novel that described the plan of research he intended to pursue during his entire professional career. To a remarkable degree, he has followed the plan he outlined in that book.

After obtaining his doctorate, Piaget explored a number of traditional disciplines seeking one that would allow him to combine his philosophical interest in epistemology (the branch of philosophy concerned with how we know reality) and his interest in biology and natural science. He spent a brief period of time at the Burgholzli in the psychiatric clinic in Zurich where Carl Gustav Jung had once worked. In those years, he was much impressed by Freudian theory and even gave a paper on children's dreams in which Freud showed some interest. But he never had any desire to be a clinician and left the Burgholzli after less than a year.

From Zurich, Piaget traveled to Paris where he worked in the school that had once been used as an experimental laboratory by Alfred Binet. Piaget was given the chore of standardizing some of Sir Cyril Burt's reasoning tests on French children. Although the test administration was boring for the most part, one aspect of the work did capture his interest: often when children responded to an item, they came up with unusual or unexpected replies. Although these replies were "wrong" or "errors" for test purposes, they fascinated him. In addition, when children came up with the wrong answer to questions such as "Helen is darker than Rose and Rose is darker than Joyce, who is the fairest of the three?" Piaget was curious about the processes by which the wrong response was arrived at. It seemed to him that the contents of the children's errors and the means by which they arrived at wrong solutions were not fortuitous but systematic and indicative of the underlying mental structures that generated them.

These observations suggested to Piaget that the study of children's thinking might provide some of the answers he sought on the philosophical plane. He planned to investigate them, then move on to other problems. Instead, the study of children's thinking became his lifelong preoccupation. After Paris, Piaget moved permanently to Geneva and began his investigations of children's thinking at the J. J. Rousseau Institute. The publication of his first studies in the field, *The Language and Thought of the Child*, and later, *Judgment and Reasoning in the Child*, *The Child's Conception of the World* and *The Moral Judgment of the Child*, gained

worldwide recognition and made Piaget a world-renowned psychologist before he was 30. Unfortunately, these books, which Piaget regarded as preliminary investigations, were often debated as finished and final works.

When Claparède retired from his post as director of the Institute of Educational Science at the University of Geneva, Piaget was the unanimous choice to succeed him. Piaget retained this post, as well as his professorship at that university, until his recent retirement. As Piaget's work became more well-known, many students came to work with him and collaborate in his research efforts. One of these students was Valentine Châtenay, whom Piaget proceeded to court and to wed. In due course they had three children, Jacqueline, Laurent and Monique. These children, all grown now, have been immortalized by Piaget in three books that are now classics in the child-development literature, *The Origins of Intelligence in the Child*, *The Construction of Reality in the Child* and *Play, Dreams and Imitation in Childhood*.

The books came about in this way. After Piaget's initial studies of children's conceptions of the world, he turned to the question of how these notions came to be given up and how children arrive at veridical notions about the world. What he was groping for was a general theory of mental development that would allow him to explain both the "erroneous" ideas he had discovered in his early works and the obviously valid notions arrived at by older children and adults. It seemed clear to Piaget that the mental abilities by which children reconstruct reality have to be sought in the earliest moments of psychic existence; hence, the study of infants.

In his study of infants, Piaget, as had other investigators such as Milicent Shinn and Bronson Alcott, used his own children as subjects. However, Piaget's infant studies were unusual in several respects. Perhaps the most novel aspect had to do with his own perspective. He did not assume that there was an external reality for the infant to simply copy and become acquainted with. Rather, he saw the construction of reality as being the basic task of the infant. This way of looking at infant behavior allowed him to observe and study aspects of the infants' reactions that had previously been ignored or the significance of which had not been fully appreci-

"Piaget took a novel tack: he didn't posit an outer reality for the infant; he saw construction of reality as the infant's basic task."

ated. Piaget noted, for example, that infants do not search after desired objects that disappear from view until about the end of the first year of life. To him, this meant that young infants had not yet constructed a notion of objects that continue to exist when they are no longer present to their senses.

Traditional psychology has been very harsh towards any hint, in psychological writings, of anthropomorphism, the readings of feelings and thoughts into others without full justification. Piaget wanted to conjecture as to what the infants' experience of the world was, but he also wanted to do this in a scientifically acceptable and testable way. His solution to this difficult problem is another testament to his genius.

In *The Origins of Intelligence in Children*, Piaget describes the evolution of children's mental operations from the outside, as it were. In this book, he introduced some of the basic concepts of his theory of intelligence, including *accommodation* (changing the action to fit the environment) and *assimilation* (changing the environment to fit the action). Piaget could demonstrate these concepts by detailed accounts of infant behavior. When infants changed the conformation of their lips to fit a nipple, this provided one of many examples of accommodation. And when infants tried to suck upon every object that brushed their lips, this was but one of many examples of assimilation.

Other important theoretical concepts were also introduced. One of these was the *schema*. A schema is essentially a structurized system of assimilations and accommodations—a behavior pattern. Sucking, for example, as it becomes elaborated, involves both assimilation and accommodation and the pattern gets extended and generalized as well as coordinated with other action patterns. When infants begin to look at what they suck and to suck at what they see, there is a coordination of the looking and the sucking schemata. Objects are constructed by the labo-

rious coordination of many different schemata.

In *Origins*, Piaget thus emphasized description and concepts that, at every point, could be tied to behavioral observations. They are extremely careful and detailed and reflect Piaget's early biological training. I once had the opportunity to see his notebooks, and they were filled, page after page, with very neat notations written in a very small hand. Here is an example of one of Piaget's observations:

Laurent lifts a cushion in order to look for a cigar case. When the object is entirely hidden the child lifts the screen with hesitation, but when one end of the case appears Laurent removes the cushion with one hand and with the other tries to extricate the objective. The act of lifting the screen is, therefore, entirely separate from that of grasping the desired object and constitutes an autonomous "means" no doubt derived from earlier and analogous acts.

In *The Construction of Reality in the Child*, Piaget concerned himself more with the content of infants' thought than with the mental processes. He employed many of the same observations but from the perspective of the child's-eye view of the world. These inferences were, however, always tied to concrete observations and were checked in a variety of different ways. In this book, Piaget talked about infants' sense of space, of time and of causality, but at each point buttressed the discussion with many illustrative examples and little experiments such as the following:

At 0:3 (13) Laurent, already accustomed for several hours to shake a hanging rattle by pulling the chain attached to it . . . is attracted by the sound of the rattle (which I have just shaken) and looks simultaneously at the rattle and at the hanging chain. Then while staring at the rattle (R) he drops from his right hand a sheet he was sucking, in order to reach

with the same hand for the lower end of the hanging chain (C). As soon as he touches the chain, he grasps it and pulls it, thus reconstructing the series C-R.

Piaget used this example to demonstrate the infant's construction of a notion of practical time.

One of Piaget's important conclusions from the work presented in *Reality* is that for young infants (less than three months), objects are not regarded as permanent, as existing outside the infants' immediate experience. If, for example, one is playing with a young infant who is smiling and laughing up at the friendly adult, the child will not cease to laugh if the adult moves swiftly out of sight. To the young infant, out of sight is quite literally out of mind. By the end of the first year, however, infants cry under the same circumstances. One-year-olds have constructed, via the coordination of looking and touching, schemata, a world of objects that they regard as existing outside their immediate experience and that they can respond to in their absence.

Piaget's *Play, Dreams and Imitation in Childhood* is the third work in the infant trilogy and argues that the symbols with which we represent reality are as much constructions as the reality itself. Piaget found that symbols derive from both imitation (a child opens its mouth in imitation of a match box opening) and play (a child holds up a potato chip and says, "Look, a butterfly.") In Piaget's view, therefore, symbolic activities derive from the same developmental processes that underlie the rest of mental growth and are not separate from, but are part of, intellectual development. Piaget also found that the development of symbolic processes does not usually appear before the age of two. This coincides with the everyday observation that children do not usually report dreams of "night terrors" until after the second year. It is not until that age that most children have the mental ability necessary to create dream symbols.

Piaget's studies on infants were conducted during the 1930s, at which time he was also teaching, following new lines of research and writing theoretical articles on logic and epistemology. His fame attracted many gifted students to Geneva. One of these was Gertrude Szeminska, a Polish mathematician who did some fine work on mathematics and geometry. *The Child's Conception of Number* was one fruit of their collaboration. Another gifted graduate student was Bärbel Inhelder, whose thesis on the conservation and the intellectual assessment of retarded children was a landmark in the extension of Piagetian conceptions to practical problems of assessment and evaluation. Bärbel Inhelder became Piaget's permanent collaborator, and when Piaget retired, his university chair was given to Inhelder—a significant fact in a country where women still do not have the right to vote.

During the '30s, Piaget's lifelong academic affiliations and work patterns became fully established and solidified. Although he had a university appointment from the start of his career, the J. J. Rousseau Institute did not become an official part of the university until the 1940s. Piaget worked hard to insure that it was an interdisciplinary institute so that it would not be saddled with the stigma usually associated with schools of education at universities. Largely because of Piaget's influence, teacher training is heavily weighted in the direction of child-development theory and research. In addition to the courses on child development offered by Piaget and his staff, students must participate in child-development research. With the aid of his student population, it was possible for Piaget and his graduate students to examine large numbers of children of all ages when they were conducting a particular research investigation. The assertion, which is sometimes made, that Piaget's studies were based on very few subjects, is true only for his infancy investigations. In all of his other explorations, Piaget employed hundreds of subjects.

Piaget's general mode of working is to set up a problem for a year or for several years and then to pursue it intensely and without distraction. Indeed, when Piaget is working, say on "causality," he does not want to talk about or deal with other research problems from the past. Once he has completed a body of work, he loses interest in it and all of his energies are devoted to the task at hand. Generally, Piaget meets with his colleagues and graduate students once a week, at which time the possible ways of exploring the problem are discussed and data from ongoing studies are presented. These are lively, exciting sessions in which new insights and ideas constantly emerge and serve as stimuli for still further innovation.

I have a rather vivid memory of one particular seminar meeting. It is usually the visiting scholars who are the most vocal while the Genevan graduate students tend to be rather quiet, although they are quite animated in their own meetings. In any case, Piaget had been talking about some of the research and I interjected, saying that I was playing devil's advocate, but why did he insist upon using the words *assimilation* and *accommodation*? After all, would not the American terms *stimulus* and *response* serve equally well? The question brought instant silence from the group, most of whom were aghast and waiting for lightning to strike me where I sat. Piaget, however, was most amused and a lively twinkle came into his eye. "Well, Elkeend," he said, "you can use *stimulus* and *response* if you choose, but if you want to understand anything, I suggest that you use *assimilation* and *accommodation*."

At the end of the year, Piaget gathers up all the data that has been collected and moves to a secret hideaway in the mountains. There he takes long walks, cooks loose omelets, thinks about the work that has been done and integrates it into one or several books that he writes in longhand on square pieces of paper. Piaget has a habit of writing at least four publishable pages every day, usually very early in the morning. The remainder of his mornings are spent teaching, meeting with students and staff or with a continuation of his early morning writing. In the afternoons, Piaget routinely takes a walk. It is then that he sorts out the ideas he is working on and thus prepares for the next day's writing. To this day, Piaget keeps to this routine as his health permits. It has been estimated that he has written the equivalent of more than 50, 500-page books.

Perhaps the major achievement of the 1930s and 1940s was the elaboration of Piaget's theory of intelligence into the four stages as we know them. This theory was articulated in close connection with his conservation experiments that provided the data base. The experiments, which resembled those on the permanence of objects in infants, enabled Piaget to compare children's performance on somewhat comparable tasks at many different age levels.

As a result of numerous investigations of children's conceptions of space, time, number, quantity, speed, causality, geometry and so on, Piaget arrived at a general conception of intellectual growth. He argues that intelligence, adaptive thinking and action develop in a series of stages that are related to age. Although there is considerable variability among individual children as to when these stages appear, Piaget does argue that the sequence in which the stages appear is a necessary one. This is true because each succeeding stage grows out of and builds upon the work of the preceding stage. At each level of development, children are again confronted with constructing or reconstructing reality out of their experiences with the world constructed during the previous stage. In addition, they must not only construct new notions of space, time, number and so on, they must also either discard or integrate their previous concepts with the new ones. From a Piagetian standpoint, constructing reality never starts entirely from scratch and always involves dealing with old ideas as well as with acquiring new ones.

In the last few decades, Piaget has extended his researches into new areas, such as memory, imagery, consciousness and causality. He has refined and consolidated his theoretical conceptions and has related them to different disciplines. While it is not really possible to review all of this work here, some aspects of it are significant for education.

One of the major research contributions during this period was the study of memory from the standpoint of Piaget's developmental stages. The research was published in a book under the joint authorship of Piaget and Inhelder.

As did Frederic C. Bartlett's book

"What he has provided is much more valuable than tightly controlled experiments: challenging ideas that open whole new research areas."

Remembering, this 1972 work by Piaget and Inhelder, *Memory and Intelligence,* has a good chance of becoming a classic in its field. As in the case of Bartlett's book, the Piaget and Inhelder work presents new data, new conceptualizations and fresh and innovative research approaches. While *Memory and Intelligence* provides no final answers to questions about memory, it offers a richness of hypotheses, and of experimental techniques, that will stimulate other researchers for years to come. Considering that this truly innovative book was written during Piaget's 70th year, one can only marvel at his unabated creativity and productivity.

The argument of the book is straightforward enough. What is the nature of memory? Is it passive storage and retrieval or does it involve intelligence at the outset and all along the way? Piaget's answer is that memory, in the broadest sense, is a way of knowing which is concerned with discovering the past. Although symbols and images are involved in memory, they do not constitute its essence. Rather, intelligence has to be brought to bear to retrieve the past. Hence, all "memories" bear the imprint of the intellectual schemata used to reconstruct them. Intelligence leaves its mark not only on the memory itself, but even upon the original registration that can only be coded within the limits of children's existing schemata.

All of this is not particularly new and could be derived from the work of Bartlett and other writers. What is new and what gives this book its special promise of becoming a classic is the repeated demonstration that children's memory of a given past experience changes with their level of intellectual development. A child, for example, who is shown a series of size-graded sticks before he or she can understand the relations involved, and who draws it poorly, may reproduce it correctly from memory six months later. The child's intellectual understanding of the series modified the memory of it in ways that are predictable from cognitive developmental theory.

To be sure, there are many questions one can raise about the "experiments" themselves. Often the number of children involved is not very large and not all the children show the expected results. The procedures are not always clearly described and the results are presented in tables of percentage passing and without the imprimatur of significance tests. This is simply Piaget's style. There is no point in being annoyed by it or in demanding that he become more rigorous. What he has provided, in the end, is much more valuable than tightly controlled experiments: namely, ideas that challenge the mind and open up whole new areas for experimental research.

The work on memory is only one of a series of areas to which Piaget and his colleagues are applying this theory of intellectual development. In addition, work on imagery, learning, consciousness and causality have all been completed or are under way. Considering that much of this "creative" intellectual work has come during Piaget's eighth decade, one has to acknowledge that creative scientific work is not necessarily the province of the young.

Piaget has also published a number of books that serve to summarize and integrate much of the work that he has done over the past half-century. These books include a general text on child development that introduces the Piagetian work for a general audience. Then there is Piaget's book on biology and knowledge that relates the developmental findings regarding intelligence to more traditional biological conceptions and shows their underlying unity. A little gem of a book, *Structuralism,* outlines in a few brief chapters the central thrust of this movement, which unites many contemporary workers, including Piaget, Chomsky, Levi-Strauss' and Erving Goffman. Piaget makes clear that structuralism is a method of analysis and not a discipline or content area.

Of particular relevance to education is Piaget's *Science of Education and the Psychology of the Child,* which is essentially a critique of traditional education. The argument is that education is too concerned with the technology of teaching and too little concerned with understanding children. In Piaget's view, the overemphasis on the science of educating, rather than upon the science of the children being educated, leads to a sterile pedagogy wherein children learn by rote what adults have decided is valuable for them to learn. Basically, Piaget feels that teacher training and educational practice must have child development as their basic discipline. The psychology of the child should be the primary science of education.

These are but a few of the achievements of the last few decades of Piaget's work. And his energy and enthusiasm are unabated as he continues his work on physical and biological causality. Early this summer, he is participating in two conferences, an educational conference in New York and the annual Piaget conference in Philadelphia. At this writing, I am very much looking forward to seeing him again and hearing the latest ideas and research coming from Geneva. I have encouraged as many of my students who can attend to be present as well, since Piaget, to my mind, exemplifies more than genius. At least equally important is the example he presents of a man who, despite his early success, maintained an unwavering commitment to research, to intellectual independence and to the welfare of children all over the world.   HB

14

The Roots of Prosocial Behavior in Children

Paul Mussen

I admit to being an imposter at a meeting on Piagetian theory, but since this was known when I was invited, I do not feel that I have to apologize. I am not now, nor have I ever been a Piagetian in my own research or in theoretical orientation. Of course, no serious developmental psychologist is uninfluenced by Piaget and I am no exception. I have read a great deal of Piagetian theory and research and have no question about its immense value for the understanding of the development of cognitive functions such as thinking, reasoning, judging, and problem-solving. I also have a long-time friendship with Barbel Inhelder, Piaget's right arm in his work, and my family and I made innumerable social points when, on a visit to Berkeley, Piaget was our houseguest for several days. We have, in fact, considered putting up a plaque announcing that "Piaget slept here," but we got enough social mileage from the visit to hold us for a long while.

But in my major area of research interest, development of prosocial *behavior* (*overt* behavior and *actions*) —generosity, altruism, helping, and sharing—I find Piaget's work of some, but only minor, help. The matters with which Piaget was concerned in his early work —particularly in *The Moral Judgment of the Child* (1948)—are highly relevant in this area. It is not realistic to try to understand phenomena like prosocial actions without explicitly recognizing that they are inherently, naturally complex; that is, that there are many, many determinants of prosocial actions, and each of them has some influence and each interacts with every other influential factor. So of course cognitive factors are important and Piaget's major notions of heteronomous and autonomous morality do give us some insight into what kinds of considerations and motivations must underlie the moral conduct of young children.

You will recall that Piaget postulated three stages in the development of moral reasoning. *Heteronomous morality* or *moral realism* is characteristic of children who have not yet reached the stage of concrete operations. During this stage, the child is *morally realistic;* he regards duty as "self subsistent and independent of the mind, as imposing itself regardless of the circumstances in which the individual may find himself." Rules, obligations, and commands are regarded as "givens," external to the mind, inflexible, and unchangeable. Justice is whatever authority (adults) or the law commands; whatever rewards or punishment authorities give. The good is obedience and wrongdoing is judged according to the letter, not the spirit, of the law. The child's moral reasoning is governed by egocentrism and concepts of immanent justice. Circumstances are not taken into account in making moral judgments.

The next stage is an intermediate one and then in the third stage the child's moral thinking becomes more *autonomous*. The most mature stage, called *autonomous morality, moral relativism* or *morality of cooperation,* generally emerges at about 11 or 12 years of age. Equity dominates in the child's thinking about justice; extenuating circumstances, motivations, and intentions weigh heavily in making moral judgments. Equalitarian concepts of justice prevail; arbitrary punishments, imminent justice, moral absolutism and blind obedience to authority are rejected. Rules are considered to be products of social interaction and, therefore, changeable.

The achievement of mature, autonomous concepts of justice is, to a large extent, the product of cooperation, reciprocity and role-taking among peers. In Piaget's view, there are no absolute authority figures in the peer group, and children therefore develop ideas of equality, cooperation, and group solidarity. The child is required to assume others' views—to take roles—and, at the same time, discussion and criticism among equals prevails. Thus, the child's egocentrism is diminished and concern for the welfare and rights of others increases.

I want to make the point here, though, that the empirical data suggest that these stages have relatively limited predictive power. Even Kohlberg's stages which follow, but expand, Piaget's schema are not strongly related to moral behavior. Much more important are socialization variables and that's what I want to focus on.

From *Piagetian Theory and its Implications for the Helping Professions,* edited by R. Weizman, R. Brown, P. J. Levinson, and P. A. Taylor, U.S.C. Press, 1978. Proceedings Seventh Interdisciplinary Conference (Volume I): Cosponsored by University Affiliated Program, Childrens Hospital of Los Angeles and the University of Southern California Schools of Social Work and Education.

But first let me give you a somewhat formal definition of prosocial behavior: Prosocial behavior refers to voluntary actions that aid or benefit another person or group of people (referred to as the targets) motivated by the actor's concern with the welfare of the other(s) and without anticipation of external rewards. Such actions often entail some self-sacrifice or risk of sacrifice on the part of the actor. A wide variety of behaviors is encompassed by this rubric, including generosity, altruism, sympathy, helping people in distress by giving material or psychological assistance, sharing possessions, donating to charity, and participating in activities designed to improve the general welfare by reducing social injustices, inequalities, and brutality.

MORAL JUDGMENT AND PROSOCIAL BEHAVIOR

In considering the factors influencing these kinds of responses, we certainly cannot dismiss moral reasoning and judgment completely. However, we have all known individuals capable of the highest levels of moral reasoning and mature concepts of morality who do not always *behave* in highly moral or prosocial ways. There are positive correlations between the measures of the cognitive aspects of morality and various forms of prosocial behavior, but these are not high. Low levels of moral judgments, assessed by means of the Kohlberg test, have been found to predict delinquency and cheating in experimental situations. Of more importance for the present discussion is the finding that individuals who are relatively mature in their judgments are more likely to act prosocially than those who are at lower levels of moral reasoning. Significant and positive, though moderate, correlations are typical. Compared with high school boys at a low or immature level of reasoning about prosocial issues, those at more advanced levels were more liberal politically and more likely to volunteer to help an experimenter with a dull task and, among boys and girls between the ages of 7 and 13, scores on a test based on Piaget's stages of moral judgment were found to be significantly related to their generosity (amount of charitability, giving donations). Other data show that level of moral judgment among 5 to 8 year olds, assessed by a test adapted from Piagetian stories, is also positively related to sharing candy with a friend or with strangers.

Finally, Kohlberg moral maturity measures of boys in the fifth grade (approximately 10½ years of age) were significantly positively correlated with sociometric assessments (peer nominations) of altruism and other related behaviors, specifically, cooperation, helping, consideration of others, sharing, and defending victims of injustice. The moral maturity measure was most highly correlated with reputation for being dependable in offering help to others.

All these findings demonstrate that the stage of moral judgment is in fact a significant, although not very powerful, regulator of the individual's propensity to behave prosocially. High levels of maturity in moral reasoning are associated with greater likelihood of manifesting prosocial actions, but the correlations discovered are not strong enough to permit accurate predictions of any particular individual's behavior.

SOCIALIZATION AND PROSOCIAL BEHAVIOR

Having briefly surveyed some studies on the relationships between moral reasoning and behavior, we can turn our attention to our major topic, the impacts of socialization variables, or how prosocial behavior is acquired at home.

Family members, particularly parents, are ordinarily the earliest and most significant agents of socialization. It is therefore to be expected that they contribute most to the child's socialization, and that behavioral predispositions acquired in the family setting will be enduring and resistant to change.

Any or all child-rearing practices and disciplinary techniques may potentially influence children's behavior: demonstration or modeling (performing behaviors that the child can emulate); material rewards; nurturance (caring for the child with warmth, support, and affection); praise and approval; giving or withholding love; explanation and example of rules; lecturing, and giving "lessons"; corporal and psychological punishment. All of these, and many others, are used by parents in the process of socialization.

The impacts of all of these on prosocial behavior should be investigated systematically, and, as we shall see, many of them have been. But no single investigator, or investigation, can examine all of them. Consequently, each study is centered on one variable, or a few variables, that the investigator regards as critical. In implementing their research, investigators use diverse methods. Parent-child relations or child-rearing practices may be assessed by systematic observations in the home, in experimental settings, or in specially devised "situational tests"; by interviewing parents and/or children about critical matters; or by asking parents and/or children to respond to Q-sort items dealing with parental behavior.

EFFECTS OF MODELING PROSOCIAL BEHAVIOR

Once in a while, an ingenious investigator manages to duplicate real-life home situations realistically in an experimental setting and then studies the effects of varied experimental treatments on children's prosocial responses. For example, in one excellent recent experiment on the effects of modeling, the model was well known to the nursery school children who participated in the study. She took care of them five days a week for two weeks and established meaningful relationships with them. In addition, she modeled altruistic behavior several times in two sessions separated by two days.

The investigators assessed the children's original propensities for helping by observing their reactions to pictures of people or animals in distress—for example, a child with a bleeding knee falling off a bike—and to four actual behavioral instances of distress, such as a kitten tangled in yarn struggling toward its mother.

After the original assessments were completed, the children observed the caretaker-model acting in helpful ways in different situations. Some children were exposed only to "symbolic altruism," modeled in dioramas (miniature reproductions) of scenes of distress involving children, families, or animals. There were duplicates of each diorama set; the model had one and the child had the other. The adult's modeling always included her

. . . (a) verbalized awareness of the distress, (b) her sympathy and help for the victim, (c) her pleasure or relief at the comfort or well-being that resulted, and (d) her use of the word 'help' to summarize what had been done. For example, she turned to the first diorama, the monkey trying to reach the banana, and said, 'Oh, Mr. Monkey, you must be hungry. You can't reach your food. I'll help you. Here's your banana. Now you won't be hungry.' She then uncovered the paired diorama and told the child that it was his or her turn. If the child retrieved the banana for the monkey, the adult said, 'I think the monkey feels better because you gave him his food. He isn't hungry now.' If the child did not help, the adult went on to the next set of diaramas, repeating the procedures.

Another group of children observed another kind of modeling; the adult actually modeled altruism to another individual under realistic distress conditions as well as in pictures and dioramas. For example, at one point during training an adult confederate came into the room, tried to retrieve some of the children's supplies, and banged her head against the table. She winced and held her head. The model responded warmly, putting her hand on the confederate's shoulder and saying, "I hope you aren't hurt. Do you want to sit down a minute?" The victim responded appreciatively.

With half the children in each training condition, the model was nurturant, initiating friendly interactions, offering help and support freely, sympathizing and protecting, expressing confidence in the children's abilities and praising them frequently. With the other half of the children, the model was nonnurturant; she was aloof, ignored their requests, gave only minimum help, and generally disregarded the children's achievements or was critical of them.

Two days after the last training session, the altruistic responses of the children were tested again, this time with a new series of pictures and dioramas and two actual behavioral incidents involving distress. Then, two weeks after that, there was an additional testing session outside the nursery school, to appraise the durability and generalization of the effects of training. In this session, the children were taken individually to a neighboring house to visit a mother and her baby, and while there, could help the mother by picking up a basket of spools or buttons that had spilled or by retrieving toys the baby had dropped out of her crib.

The two types of modeling were found to have vastly different effects on children's prosocial behavior. Modeling with dioramas, but unrelated to real experiences with others, produced less increment in altruistic responses than training involving dioramas, pictures, *and* modeling of helping in actual, "live" interactions. On the tests given two days after the end of the training, those trained exclusively with dioramas showed increased altruism *only* in diorama situations; their altruism did not extend or generalize to pictured situations or to behavioral incidents. The critical differential effects of the two kinds of modeling were most apparent on the follow-up test two weeks later. Those who had observed extended modeling, including aid to another individual, by a nurturant adult were more likely to express sympathy and to help the mother or baby in the home setting, than children in any other group. Eighty-four percent of these children spontaneously gave help in this situation, although only 24% of them had helped in the original, pretraining behavioral incidents.

Extrapolating from the results of their study, the investigators make some practical suggestions about socialization by parents:

The parent who conveys his values to the child didactically as tidy principles, and no more, accomplishes only that learning in the child. Generalized altruism would appear to be best learned from parents who do not only try to inculcate the principles of altruism, but who also manifest altruism in everyday interactions. . . . Emphasis on the role of nurturance in the rearing environment does not suggest that it is sufficient. The data demonstrate its importance along with the specific modeling, accompanied by the model's verbal communications. (Yarrow et al., 1973, p. 256)

IDENTIFICATION AND GENEROSITY

More clinical, correlational studies confirm the findings of this experimental study, demonstrating that repeated adult modeling, particularly by a nurturant model, is likely to have powerful, generalized effects. In one study, the generosity of nursery school boys was measured in terms of the amount of candy (won in a game) they were willing to share with friends, a measure significantly correlated with independent ratings of generosity by the nursery school teachers. The most generous and the stingiest boys were then observed in a projective, semi-structured doll play situation in which they expressed their views of their parents, of themselves, and of their interactions with their parents. Compared with the others, the generous boys much more frequently portrayed their fathers as models of generosity, sympathy, and compassion and as nurturant and warm parents. It may be inferred that the father of a generous boy was warm and nurturant. This fostered strong identification with him and, consequently, imitation of his patterns of generosity and sympathy.

STUDIES OF ADULT ALTRUISTS

In addition to studies of children, a number of fascinating investigations of the developmental histories of unusually altruistic adults are highly relevant to the present discussion because of their implications for the development of prosocial conduct. They provide further confirmation that early parental modeling and nurturance are strong determinants of later altruism and predispositions to prosocial behavior.

Christians Who Saved Jews from the Nazis

One dramatic study, primarily the work of Professor Perry London of the University of Southern California and Professor David Rosenhan of Stanford University, was focused on 27 Christians who during World War II risked their lives in efforts to rescue Jews from the Nazis. Because of lack of funds the study was never completed, but pilot work gave the researchers some firm impressions about the characteristics that predisposed these people to such unusual, humane and altruistic acts. Three qualities were predominant: a spirit of adventurousness; a sense of being socially marginal; and, most relevant for this discussion, intense identification with a parent, not necessarily of the same sex, who was a model of moral orientation and conduct. Some of the parents were religious moralists, others were ideological moralists. Having a highly moral parent as a model for identification proved to be a powerful determinant of later self-sacrifice and altruism.

A Study of Freedom Riders

These findings, tentative and preliminary at best, led Professor Rosenhan to another highly relevant study, a study of Freedom Riders, workers who were active in the Civil Rights Movement of the late 1950s and 1960s. They marched in parades, sometimes for hundreds of miles, protested, picketed and gave speeches on behalf of improved socioeconomic status, and equal rights and opportunities for blacks. These activities entailed tremendous expenditures of effort and energy as well as considerable self-sacrifice of money and comfort; in addition, they were carried out at the cost of encountering a great deal of hostility and even assault from opposing forces. Some civil rights workers were murdered and many were cruelly insulted, humiliated, and beaten.

Rosenhan differentiated between two types of Freedom Riders. The *fully committed,* guided by what the investigator called internalized or autonomous altruism, were active for a year or longer, often giving up their homes, occupations, and educations to engage in the civil rights movement. The *partially committed* limited their activities to one or two freedom rides or marches without making such great sacrifices. The two groups did *not* differ in attitudes; they were equally strong believers in the equality of whites and blacks.

What then accounts for the differences in their level of activism or active altruism, in their willingness and ability to devote time and energy to this work and to sacrifice for the welfare of others? Extensive interviews with the participants indicated that modeling, identification, and nurturance were of critical importance. The parents of the fully committed were excellent models of prosocial behavior and concern with the welfare of others. When the Freedom Riders were children, their parents had worked vigorously for altruistic causes, protesting against Nazi atrocities, religious restrictions, and other injustices. Their children, the future Freedom Riders, had witnessed their parents' commitment and efforts and had shared their emotions. By contrast, the parents of the partially committed were "at best, mere verbal supporters of prosocial morality and at worst, critical about those moralities. It was common for our partially committed to report that their parents preached one thing and practiced another." In short, many of these parents provided symbolic but not behavioral modeling of prosocial behavior, and, as a result, their children became only partially committed, less thoroughly altruistic, than the others.

In addition, parental nurturance reinforced the effects of modeling. The fully committed stated that they had always had warm, respecting, and loving relationships with their parents, continuously from childhood through early adulthood. These interactions undoubtedly promoted identification with their parents and, consequently the adoption of parental standards, values, and patterns of behavior. In contrast, the partially committed frequently described their relationships with their parents as avoidant, cool, negative, or ambivalent; many reported that their chief reactions to their parents were discomfort, anxiety, hostility, and guilt.

These findings again indicate that strong predispositions to prosocial actions, reflected in altruism and commitments to justice and equality, are the consequents of observation of strong and consistent models (including parents) who show their own profound prosocial dispositions in both word and deed. In addition, these parents are nurturant and loving, thus strengthening their children's tendency to identify with and imitate the model (parent).

PARENTAL NURTURANCE

Parental nurturance (or a model's nurturance) often serves to reinforce and intensify the positive effects of direct modeling and identification, resulting in increased consideration of others, helpfulness, and generosity. Is parental nurturance *per se* likely to further the development of prosocial dispositions? It does not seem unreasonable to hypothesize that it could indeed produce such effects, for parental nurturance may be viewed as a kind of modeling of prosocial behavior; by being nurturant, parents act as models of consideration, kindness, and sympathy.

There is some limited support for this hypothesis. According to some investigators, parental nurturance fosters the development of generosity. Parental nurturance and affection also have significant positive impacts on preadolescents' consideration of others. This was established in a study in which seventh grade pupils' scores or standings in consideration of others were determined by sociometric methods, specifically the number of nominations by classmates. The children's perspective of their parents' nurturance or affection was assessed by means of a report form administered to lower- and middle-class children. These report forms contained a list of eight reactions—e.g., giving affection, approval, qualified approval, material reward—to the child's "doing something good." The respondents indicated along the 4-point scale how often each of these parental reactions occurred.

Among the middle-class boys and girls, consideration for others was found to be directly related to the mother's affection, but not to the father's. Among the lower class, both maternal and paternal affection were related to boys', but not to girls', consideration of others. In general, then, these findings may be interpreted as being partially consistent with the hypothesis that nurturance, particularly maternal nurturance, enhances the development of prosocial behavior. But the general relationship between parental nurturance itself and children's prosocial actions is not clear-cut. For unknown reasons, the relationship does not obtain in the case of lower-class girls.

Other relevant studies have also yielded equivocal results. Thus, in one study, generosity in middle-class 6- and 8-year-old boys, assessed by two different tests, was found to be significantly correlated with paternal affec-

tion and with maternal child-centeredness and affectionate acceptance of the child, and negatively related to paternal rejection and dissatisfaction with the child. But girls' generosity was *not* related to measures of either parental affection or nurturance.

With this kind of evidence, we cannot draw any definitive conclusions about the impact of parental nurturance *per se* on children's prosocial behavior. Perhaps the simplest and most straightforward conclusion is that simply giving a child warmth, support, and affection—even in large doses—will not ensure that the child will become altruistic, kind, considerate, or generous. Nurturance appears to be most effective in producing or strengthening propensities to prosocial behavior when it is part of a pattern of child-rearing and training that includes modeling of prosocial acts.

THE USE OF POWER ASSERTION AND INDUCTION AS DISCIPLINARY TECHNIQUES

The ways parents discipline their children are likely to affect the children's attitudes toward themselves and toward others. These orientations, in turn, may be expected to play a role in shaping children's prosocial inclinations and behavior. For example, in disciplining a child, the parent effectively models certain kinds of behavior. Parental use of physical force or threat shows the child that aggression achieves some goals, but probably makes the child hostile. If parents reason with their actions, they inevitably model consideration for others, and, at the same time, point out the implications of their children's behavior for others, thus stressing empathy as an important component of social interactions.

Empirical data offer at least partial support for these speculations. The specific disciplinary techniques used by parents or other caretakers do, in fact, have an appreciable effect on children's behavior. Some techniques appear to intensify children's predispositions toward prosocial behavior while others tend to hinder their development.

Extensive pioneering research on these issues has been conducted by Professor Martin Hoffman of the University of Michigan and his colleagues. In one of their most influential studies, a study of seventh grade pupils in Detroit, attention was centered on consideration of others, the degree of consideration being operationally defined by the number of peer nominations for the positions of the classmate "most likely to care about other children's feelings" and "most likely to defend a child being made fun of by the group." Disciplinary techniques were assessed by asking parents to imagine four situations—for example, the child delaying in complying with the parental request to do something or the child being careless and destroying something of value that belonged to another child—and designating their three most likely reactions to each of these, choosing these reactions from a list of 14 possibilities (for example, spanking the child, explaining how the other child would feel about the destruction of a toy). The disciplinary practices listed fell into three main categories or types. The first, *power assertion,* refers to control by physical power or material resources, exemplified by physical punishment, deprivation of material objects or privileges, force, or the threat of these. *Love withdrawal,* the second type of discipline investigated, includes ignoring or isolating the child, refusing to speak to him or her; parental statements of dislike of the child. In the third technique, *induction,* the parent reasons with the child, pointing out the painful consequences of the child's act for himself, for others, or for the parent. Examples of this are telling the child that his or her actions hurt the parent, saying the object damaged was highly valued by the parent, or making reference to concern for another child.

Frequent use of power assertion by the mother was generally associated with *low* levels of consideration for others, while repeated use of induction was positively associated with this type of prosocial behavior. The use of *love withdrawal* techniques was not consistently related to consideration. In short, it is a pattern of infrequent use of power assertion and frequent use of induction by middle-class mothers which generally appears to facilitate the development of girl's prosocial behavior.

The investigators concluded that the use of induction techniques fosters the development of prosocial behavior. This is largely attributable, the investigators believe, to the fact that induction is "most capable of eliciting the child's natural proclivities for empathy." Power assertive techniques, on the other hand, are least effective in stimulating the development of consideration for others because in using this technique, the parent communicates that external power and authority, the parent's in this case, rather than appraisal of the consequences of one's actions for others, are the appropriate bases for deciding what action to take. In addition, the use of power assertion is not conducive to the

. . . internalization of control because it elicits intense hostility in the child and simultaneously provides him with a model for expressing that hostility outward . . . furthermore, [power assertion] makes the child's need for love less salient and functions as an obstacle to the arousal of empathy. Finally, it sensitizes the child to the punitive responses of adult authorities, thus contributing to an externally focused moral orientation. (Hoffman & Saltzstein, 1967, p. 558)

These conclusions about the powerful influences of induction on prosocial behavior have also been substantiated by results of other studies that employed different criteria of prosocial behavior and participants of different ages. For example, Hoffman found that fre-

quent use of induction by mothers, accompanied by low frequency of power assertion, was a significant precursor of high levels of sensitivity to others' needs and of direct helpfulness to peers among preschool children.

The participants in another study were fifth and eighth grade students at a Catholic school. They answered questionnaires about their perceptions of maternal disciplinary techniques, nominated the boys and girls in their classes who were kindest and most considerate, and were given opportunities to donate money to a charitable organization (UNICEF). In addition, the children responded to a self-report scale on values, ranking in order of personal importance 12 statements such as "having a beautiful home and car" "getting a job that helps other people." From these rankings the investigators derived measures of each child's standing on self-centered values (material possessions, self-importance) or other-centered values (concern for others).

Maternal use of inductive techniques was found to be a good predictor of children's prosocial tendencies. At each age level studied, boys and girls who reported that their mothers frequently used induction in discipline were regarded as more considerate by their classmates, attached more importance to other-centered than to self-centered values, and donated more of their earnings to charity. In contrast, use of power assertion by the mother was associated with self-centered values and stinginess in donations.

The findings from these varied studies lead consistently to the same conclusions: Frequent use of induction techniques by parents is conducive to the development of a prosocial orientation while extensive use of power assertive techniques tends to diminish the level of children's prosocial behavior. There is no evidence that sparing the rod will spoil the child.

MATURITY DEMANDS AND ASSIGNMENTS OF RESPONSIBILITY

The effects of another prevalent child-rearing practice have been explored in a thorough, in-depth study by Diana Baumrind of the Institute of Human Development of the University of California. She assessed a family variable which she labeled *maturity demands,* by which she means maintenance of high standards for the child, together with parental control and pressures on the child to behave in mature ways, that is, to perform and achieve in accordance with his or her ability, and to assume responsibilities consistent with his or her level of maturity. High maturity demands proved to be effective determinants of nursery school boys' and girls' manifestations of advanced levels of social responsibility, specifically their altruism and nurturance toward others. The latter were assessed by means of intensive, objective, naturalistic observations by trained observers.

The assumption of responsibility is an integral part of maturity demands that enhances the prosocial behavior of children. This finding is entirely congruent with the results of a highly relevant study comparing several cultures, by Whiting and Whiting. These anthropologists found that children reared in cultures in which there is early assignment of responsibility manifest more altruistic, helping, and supportive behavior than children in cultures that do not follow this practice. Interestingly, in the Soviet Union, part of the elementary school curriculum consists of assuming responsibility for younger children. The purpose of assigning school responsibility is the enhancement of predispositions toward helping and sharing among the pupils. The data from the studies just reviewed here suggest that this goal can be achieved by this means.

To summarize, it seems to me that there are a number of substantial truths about child-rearing practices and prosocial behavior that can be distilled from the findings of these studies. They are not surprising or sensational; in fact, perhaps one of the most interesting general conclusions is that techniques that many sensible people have used for millennia are conducive to the development of prosocial behavior: modeling prosocial behavior, especially by a nurturant model, and identification with a prosocial parent; induction—that is, reasoning and explanation—rather than power assertion in disciplining the child; making reasonable maturity demands. It is comforting to find that scientific findings confirm that much of what is advocated in "folk wisdom" actually works.

A note of caution is necessary. We are very far from a complete understanding of the problem of the origins and development of prosocial conduct. We have more questions than answers. The interactions among determinants—for example, the conditions under which individuals who have achieved high levels of moral reasoning behave prosocially and the conditions associated with their failure to behave in these ways—must be investigated. So must the underlying motivations for prosocial action. There are urgent needs for more naturalistic studies that preserve the inherent complexity of the determinants while investigating their effects. Such studies can yield information about how these determinants operate together in advancing or inhibiting the development of prosocial behavior.

15

DIANA BAUMRIND

Socialization and Instrumental Competence in Young Children

Reviewed in this article are the relationships found in the research literature, and particularly the author's own work, between patterns of parental authority or mechanisms by which adults may influence children, and the development of instrumental competence in young children. By instrumental competence is meant behavior which is socially responsible and independent. Particular attention is paid to the means by which girls are socialized for instrumental incompetence and what can be done by socializing agents to counteract this effect.

For the past 10 years I have been studying parent-child relations, focusing upon the effects of parental authority on the behavior of pre-school children. In three separate but related studies, data on children were obtained from three months of observation in the nursery school and in a special testing situation; data on parents were obtained during two home observations, followed by an interview with each parent.

In the first study, three groups of nursery school children were identified in order that the childrearing practices of their parents could be contrasted. The findings of that study (Baumrind, 1967) can be summarized as follows:

1. Parents of the children who were the most self-reliant, self-controlled, explorative and content were themselves controlling and demanding; but they were also warm, rational and receptive to the child's communication. This unique combination of high control and positive encouragement of the child's autonomous and independent strivings can be called *authoritative* parental behavior.

2. Parents of children who, relative to the others, were discontent, withdrawn and distrustful, were themselves detached and controlling, and somewhat less warm than other parents. These may be called *authoritarian* parents.

3. Parents of the least self-reliant, explorative and self-controlled children were themselves noncontrolling, nondemanding, and relatively warm. These can be called *permissive* parents.

A second study, of an additional 95 nursery school children and their

[1] The research by the author reported in this paper was supported in part by research grant HD 02228 from the National Institute of Child Health and Development, U.S. Public Health Service.

parents also supported the position that "authoritative control can achieve responsible conformity with group standards without loss of individual autonomy or self-assertiveness (Baumrind, 1966, p. 905)." In a third investigation (Baumrind, 1971, in press), patterns of parental authority were defined so that they would differ from each other as did the authoritarian, authoritative, and permissive combinations which emerged from the first study.

Patterns of Parental Authority

Each of these three authority patterns is described in detail below, followed by the subpatterns that have emerged empirically from my most recent study. The capitalized items refer to specific clusters obtained in the analysis of the parent behavior ratings.

The *authoritarian* parent[2] attempts:

to shape, control and evaluate the behavior and attitudes of the child in accordance with a set standard of conduct, usually an absolute standard, theologically motivated and formulated by a higher authority. She values obedience as a virtue and favors punitive, forceful measures to curb self-will at points where the child's actions or beliefs conflict with what she thinks is right conduct. She believes in inculcating such instrumental values as respect for authority, respect for work, and respect for the preservation of order and traditional structure. She does not encourage verbal give and take, believing that the child should accept her word for what is right (Baumrind, 1968, p. 261).

Two subpatterns in our newest study correspond to this description; they differ only in the degree of acceptance shown the child. One subpattern identifies

[2] In order to avoid confusion, when I speak of the parent I will use the pronoun "she," and when I speak of the child, I will use the pronoun "he," although, unless otherwise specified, the statement applies to both sexes equally.

families who were Authoritarian but Not Rejecting. They were high in Firm Enforcement, low in Encourages Independence and Individuality, low in Passive-Acceptance, and low in Promotes Nonconformity. The second subpattern contained families who met all the criteria for the first subpattern except that they scored high on the cluster called Rejecting.

The *authoritative* parent, by contrast with the above, attempts:

to direct the child's activities but in a rational, issue-oriented manner. She encourages verbal give and take, and shares with the child the reasoning behind her policy. She values both expressive and instrumental attributes, both autonomous self-will and disciplined conformity. Therefore, she exerts firm control at points of parent-child divergence, but does not hem the child in with restrictions. She recognizes her own special rights as an adult, but also the child's individual interests and special ways. The authoritative parent affirms the child's present qualities, but also sets standards for future conduct. She uses reason as well as power to achieve her objectives. She does not base her decisions on group consensus or the individual child's desires; but also, does not regard herself as infallible or divinely inspired (Baumrind, 1968, p. 261).

Two subpatterns corresponded to this description, differing only in the parents' attitudes towards normative values. One subpattern contained families who were Authoritative and Conforming. Like the Authoritarian parents described above, these parents had high scores in Firm Enforcement and low scores in Passive-Acceptance. However, they also had high scores in Encourages Independence and Individuality. The second subpattern contained parents who met the criteria for the first subpattern, but who also scored high in Promotes Nonconformity.

The *permissive* parent attempts:

to behave in a nonpunitive, acceptant and affirmative manner towards the child's impulses, desires, and actions. She consults with him about policy decisions and gives explanations for family rules. She makes few demands for household responsibility and orderly behavior. She presents herself to the child as a resource for him to use as he wishes, not as an active agent responsible for shaping or altering his ongoing or future behavior. She allows the child to regulate his own activities as much as possible, avoids the exercise of control, and does not encourage him to obey externally-defined standards. She attempts to use reason but not overt power to accomplish her ends (Baumrind, 1968, p. 256).

We were able to locate three subpatterns reflecting different facets of this prototypic permissiveness. One subpattern, called Nonconforming, typified families who were nonconforming but who were not extremely lax in discipline and who did demand high performance in some areas. The second subpattern, called Permissive, contained families who were characterized by lax discipline and few demands, but who did not stress nonconformity. The third subpattern contained families who were both nonconforming and lax in their discipline and demands; hence, they are referred to as Permissive-Nonconforming.

Instrumental Competence

Instrumental Competence refers to behavior which is socially responsible and independent. Behavior which is friendly rather than hostile to peers, cooperative

Diana Baumrind, Ph.D., is director of the Parental Authority Research Project, a National Institute of Child Health and Development project for the study of child-rearing attitudes and practices at the University of California, Berkeley. She has authored numerous articles on parent-child relations and has begun work on a book on authoritative childrearing.

rather than resistive with adults, achievement, rather than nonachievement-oriented, dominant rather than submissive, and purposive rather than aimless, is here defined as instrumentally competent. Middle-class parents clearly value instrumentally competent behavior. When such parents were asked to rank those attributes that they valued and devalued in children, the most valued ones were assertiveness, friendliness, independence and obedience, and those least valued were aggression, avoidance and dependency (Emmerich & Smoller, 1964). Note that the positively valued attributes promote successful achievement in United States society and, in fact, probably have survival value for the individual in any subculture or society.

There are people who feel that, even in the United States, those qualities which define instrumental competence are losing their survival value in favor of qualities which may be called *Expressive Competence*. The author does not agree. Proponents of competence defined in terms of expressive, rather than instrumental, attributes value feelings more than reason, good thoughts more than effective actions, "being" more than "doing" or "becoming," spontaneity more than planfulness, and relating intimately to others more than working effectively with others. At present, however, there is no evidence that emphasis on expressive competence, at the expense of instrumental competence, fits people to function effectively over the long run as members of any community. This is not to say that expressive competence is not essential for effective functioning in work as well as in love, and for both men and women. Man, like other animals, experiences and gains valid information about reality by means of both noncognitive and cognitive processes. Affectivity deepens man's knowledge of his environment; tenderness and receptivity enhance the character and effectiveness of any human being. But instrumental competence is and will continue to be an essential component of self-esteem and self-fulfillment.

One subdimension of instrumental competence, here designated *Responsible vs. Irresponsible,* pertains to the following three facets of behavior, each of which is related to the others:

a) *Achievement-oriented vs. Not Achievement-oriented.* This attribute refers to the willingness to persevere when frustration is encountered, to set one's own goals high, and to meet the demands of others in a cognitive situation versus withdrawal when faced with frustration and unwillingness to comply with the teaching or testing instructions of an examiner or teacher. Among older children, achievement-orientation becomes subject to autogenic motivation and is more closely related to measures of independence than to measures of social responsibility. But in the young child, measures of cognitive motivation are highly correlated with willingness to cooperate with adults, especially for boys. Thus, in my study, resistiveness towards adults was highly negatively correlated with achievement-oriented behavior for boys, but not for girls. Other investigators (Crandall, Orleans, Preston & Rabson, 1958; Haggard, 1969) have also found that compliance with adult values and demands characterize young children who display high achievement efforts.

b) *Friendly vs. Hostile Behavior Towards Peers.* This refers to nurturant, kind, altruistic behavior displayed toward agemates as opposed to bullying, insulting, selfish behavior.

c) *Cooperative vs. Resistive Behavior Towards Adults.* This refers to trustworthy, responsible, facilitative behavior as opposed to devious, impetuous obstructive actions.

A second dimension of child social behavior can be designated *Independent vs. Suggestible.* It pertains to the following three related facets of behavior:

a) *Domineering vs. Tractable Behavior.* This attribute consists of bold, aggressive, demanding behavior as opposed to timid, nonintrusive, undemanding behavior.

b) *Dominant vs. Submissive Behavior.* This category refers to individual initiative and leadership in contrast to suggestible, following behavior.

c) *Purposive vs. Aimless Behavior.* This refers to confident, charismatic, self-propelled activity versus disoriented, normative, goalless behavior.

The present review is limited to a discussion of instrumental competence and associated antecedent parental practices and is most applicable to the behavior of young children rather than adolescents. Several ancillary topics will be mentioned, but not discussed in depth, including:

The relation of IQ to instrumental competence. My own work and that of others indicate that, in our present society, children with high IQs are most likely to be achievement-oriented and self-motivated. The correlations between IQ and measures of purposiveness, dominance, achievement-orientation and independence are very high even by ages three and four.

The relation of moral development and conscience to instrumental competence. This area of research, exemplified by some of the work of Aronfreed, Kohlberg, Mussen, and Piaget, is of special importance with older age groups and will be covered tangentially when the antecedents of social responsibility are explored.

The relation of will to instrumental competence. This topic, which overlaps with the previous one, has received very little direct attention during the past 30 years. In the present review, this area is discussed to some extent along with antecedents of independence.

The antecedents of creative or scientific genius. Socialization practices which lead to competence are not the same as those associated with the development of high creativity or scientific genius. Most studies, such as those by Roe (1952) and Eiduson (1962), suggest that men of genius are frequently reared differently from other superior individuals. It has been found, for example, that as children men of genius often had little contact with their fathers, or their fathers died when they were young; they often led lonely, although cognitively enriched, existences. Such rearing cannot be recommended, however, since it is unlikely that the effects on most children, even those with superior ability, will be to produce genius or highly effective functioning.

The development of instrumental competence in disadvantaged families. The assumption cannot be made that the same factors relate to competence in disadvantaged families as in advantaged families. The effect of a single parental characteristic is altered substantially by the pattern of variables of which it is a part. Similarly, the effect of a given pattern of parental variables may be altered by the larger social context in which the family operates. The relations discussed here are most relevant for white middle-class families and may not always hold for disadvantaged families.

Development of Instrumental Incompetence in Girls

Rapid social changes are taking place in the United States which are providing equal opportunity for socially disadvantaged groups. If a socially disadvantaged group is one whose members are discouraged from fully developing their potentialities for achieving status and leadership in economic, academic and political affairs, women qualify as such a group.

There is little evidence that women are biologically inferior to men in intellectual endowment, academic potential, social responsibility or capacity for independence. Constitutional differences in certain areas may exist, but they do not directly generate sex differences in areas such as those mentioned. The only cognitive functions in which females have been shown consistently to perform less well than males are spatial relations and visualization. We really do not know to what extent the clearly inferior position women occupy in United States society today should be attributed to constitutional factors. The evidence, however, is overwhelming that socialization experiences contribute greatly to a condition of instrumental *incompetence* among women. It follows that if these conditions were altered, women could more nearly fulfill their occupational and intellectual potential. The interested reader should refer to Maccoby's excellent "Classified Summary of Research in Sex Differences" (1966, pp. 323-351).

Few women enter scientific fields and very few of these achieve eminence. According to the President's Commission on the Status of Women in 1963, the proportion of women to men obtaining advanced degrees is actually dropping. Yet there is little convincing evidence that females are constitutionally incapable of contributing significantly to science. Girls obtain better grades in elementary school than boys, and perform equally to boys on standard achievement tests, including tests of mathematical reasoning. By the high school years, however, boys score considerably higher than girls on the mathematical portion of the Scholastic Aptitude Test (Rossi, 1969). It is interesting to note that a high positive relation between IQ and later occupational levels holds for males, but does not hold for females (Terman & Oden, 1947). According to one study of physics students, girls have more scholastic aptitude and understanding of science and scientific processes than boys (Walberg, 1969). As Rossi has argued:

If we want more women to enter science, not only as teachers of science but as scientists, some quite basic changes must take place in the way girls are reared. If girls are to develop the analytic and mathematical abilities science requires, parents and teachers must encourage them in independence and self-reliance instead of pleasing feminine submission; stimulate and reward girls' efforts to satisfy their curiosity about the world as they do those of boys; encourage in girls not unthinking conformity but alert intelligence that asks why and rejects the easy answers (Rossi, 1969, p. 483).

Femininity and being female is socially devalued. Both sexes rate men as more worthwhile than women (e.g., McKee & Sherriffs, 1957). While boys of all ages show a strong preference for masculine roles, girls do not show a similar preference for feminine roles, and indeed, at certain ages, many girls as well as boys show a strong preference for masculine roles (Brown, 1958). In general, both men and women express a preference for having male children (Dinitz, Dynes, & Clarke, 1954). Masculine status is so to be preferred to feminine status that girls

may adopt tomboy attributes and be admired for doing so, but boys who adopt feminine attributes are despised as sissies. Feminine identification in males (excluding feminine qualities such as tenderness, expressiveness and playfulness) is clearly related to maladjustment. But even in females, intense feminine identification may more strongly characterize maladjusted than adjusted women (Heilbrun, 1965). Concern about population control will only further accelerate the devaluation of household activities performed by women, and decrease the self-esteem of women solely engaged in such activities.

Intellectual achievement and self-assertive independent strivings in women are equated with loss of femininity by men and women alike. Women, as well as men, oppose the idea of placing women in high-status jobs (Keniston & Keniston, 1964). One researcher (Horner, 1969) thinks that women's higher test anxiety reflects the conflict between women's motivation to achieve and their motivation to fail. She feels that women and girls who are motivated to fail feel ambivalent about success because intellectual achievement is equated with loss of femininity by socializing agents and eventually by the female herself.

Generally, parents have higher achievement expectations for boys than they do for girls. Boys are more frequently expected to go to college and to have careers (Aberle & Naegele, 1952). The pressure towards responsibility, obedience and nurturance for girls, and towards achievement and independence for boys which characterizes United States society also characterizes other societies, thus further reinforcing the effect of differential expectations for boys and girls (Barry, Bacon, & Child, 1957). In the United States, girls of nursery school age are not less achievement-oriented or independent than boys. By adolescence, however, most girls are highly aware of, and concerned about, social disapproval for so-called masculine pursuits. They move toward conformity with societal expectations that. relative to males, they should be nonachievement-oriented and dependent.

Girls and women consistently show a greater need for affiliation than do boys and men. The greater nurturance toward peers and cooperation with adults shown by girls is demonstrable as early as the preschool years. In general, females are more suggestible, conforming and likely to rely on others for guidance and support. Thus, females are particularly susceptible to social influences, and these influences generally define femininity to include such attributes as social responsibility, supportiveness, submissiveness and low achievement striving.

There are complex and subtle differences in the behavior of boys and girls from birth onward, and in the treatment of boys and girls by their caretaking adults. These differential treatments are sometimes difficult to identify because, when the observer knows the sex of the parent or child, an automatic adjustment is made which tends to standardize judgments about the two sexes. By the time boys enter nursery school, they are more resistant to adult authority and aggressive with peers. Thus, a major socialization task for preschool boys consists of developing social responsibility. While preschool girls (in my investigations) are neither lacking in achievement-orientation nor in independence, the focal socialization task for them seems to consist of maintaining purposive, dominant and independent behavior. Without active intervention by socializing agents,

the cultural stereotype is likely to augment girls' already well-developed sense of cooperation with authority and eventually discourage their independent strivings towards achievement and eminence. As will be noted later, there is reason to believe that the socialization practices which facilitate the development of instrumental competence in *both* girls and boys have the following attributes: a) they place a premium on self-assertiveness but not on anticonformity, b) they emphasize high achievement and self-control but not social conformity, c) they occur within a context of firm discipline and rationality with neither excessive restrictiveness nor overacceptance.

Socialization Practices Related to Responsible vs. Irresponsible Behavior

The reader will recall that I have defined Responsible vs. Irresponsible Behavior in terms of: a) Friendliness vs. Hostility Towards Peers, b) Cooperation vs. Resistance Towards Adults, and c) High vs. Low Achievement Orientation. Socialization seems to have a clearer impact upon the development of social responsibility in boys than in girls, probably because girls vary less in this particular attribute. In my own work, parents who were authoritative and relatively conforming, as compared with parents who were permissive or authoritarian, tended to have children who were more friendly, cooperative and achievement-oriented. This was especially true for boys. Nonconformity in parents was not necessarily associated with resistant and hostile behavior in children. Neither did firm control and high maturity-demands produce rebelliousness. In fact, it has generally been found that close supervision, high demands for obedience and personal neatness, and pressure upon the child to share in household responsibilities are associated with responsible behavior rather than with chronic rebelliousness. The condition most conducive to antisocial aggression, because it most effectively rewards such behavior, is probably one in which the parent is punitive and arbitrary in his demands, but inconsistent in responding to the child's disobedience.

Findings from several studies suggest that parental demands provoke rebelliousness only when the parent both restricts autonomy of action and does not use rational methods of control. For example, Pikas (1961), in a survey of 656 Swedish adolescents, showed that differences in the child's acceptance of parental authority depended upon the reason for the parental directive. Authority based on rational concern for the child's welfare was accepted well by the child, but arbitrary, domineering or exploitative authority was rejected. Pikas' results are supported by Middleton and Snell (1963) who found that discipline regarded by the child as either very strict or very permissive was associated with rebellion against the parent's political views. Finally, Elder (1963), working with adolescents' reports concerning their parents, found that conformity to parental rules typified subjects who saw their parents as having ultimate control (but who gave the child leeway in making decisions) and who also provided explanations for rules.

Several generalizations and hypotheses can be drawn from this literature and from the results of my own work concerning the relations of specific parental practices to the development of social responsibility in young children. The following list is based on the assumption that it is more meaningful to talk about the effects of *patterns* of parental authority than to talk about the effects of single parental variables.

1. *The modelling of socially responsible behavior facilitates the development of social responsibility in young children, and more so if the model is seen by the child as having control over desired resources and as being concerned with the child's welfare.*

The adult who subordinates his impulses enough to conform with social regulations and is himself charitable and generous will have his example followed by the child. The adult who is self-indulgent and lacking in charity will have his example followed even if he should preach generous, cooperative behavior. Studies by Mischel and Liebert (1966) and by Rosenhan, Frederick, and Burrowes (1968) suggest that models who behave self-indulgently produce similar behavior in children and these effects are even more extensive than direct reward for self-indulgent behavior. Further, when the adult preaches what he does not practice, the child is more likely to do what the adult practices. This is true even when the model preaches unfriendly or uncooperative behavior but behaves towards the child in an opposite manner. To the extent that the model for socially responsible behavior is perceived as having high social status (Bandura, Ross & Ross, 1963), the model will be most effective in inducing responsible behavior.

In our studies, both authoritative and authoritarian parents demanded socially responsible behavior and also differentially rewarded it. As compared to authoritative parents, however, authoritarian parents permitted their own needs to take precedence over those of the child, became inaccessible when displeased, assumed a stance of personal infallibility, and in other ways showed themselves often to be more concerned with their own ideas than with the child's welfare. Thus, they did not exemplify prosocial behavior, although they did preach it. Authoritative parents, on the other hand, both preached and practiced prosocial behavior and their children were significantly more responsible than the children of authoritarian parents. In this regard, it is interesting that nonconforming parents who were highly individualistic and professed anticonforming ideas had children who were more socially responsible than otherwise. The boys were achievement-oriented and the girls were notably cooperative. These parents were themselves rather pacific, gentle people who were highly responsive to the child's needs even at the cost of their own; thus, they modelled but did not preach prosocial behavior.

2. *Firm enforcement policies, in which desired behavior is positively reinforced and deviant behavior is negatively reinforced, facilitate the development of socially responsible behavior, provided that the parent desires that the child behave in a responsible manner.*

The use of reinforcement techniques serves to establish the potency of the reinforcing agent and, in the mind of the young child, to legitimate his authority. The use of negative sanctions can be a clear statement to the child that rules are there to be followed and that to disobey is to break a known rule. Among other things, punishment provides the child with information. As Spence (1966) found, nonreaction by adults is sometimes interpreted by children as signifying a correct response. Siegel and Kohn (1959) found that nonreaction by an adult when the child was behaving ag-

gressively resulted in an increased incidence of such acts. By virtue of his or her role as an authority, the sheer presence of parents when the child misbehaves cannot help but affect the future occurrence of such behavior. Disapproval should reduce such actions, while approval or nonreaction to such behavior should increase them.

In our studies, permissive parents avoided the use of negative sanctions, did not demand mannerly behavior or reward self-help, did not enforce their directives by exerting force or influence, avoided confrontation when the child disobeyed, and did not choose to or did not know how to use reinforcement techniques. Their sons, by comparison with the sons of authoritative parents, were clearly lacking in prosocial and achievement-oriented behavior.

3. *Nonrejecting parents are more potent models and reinforcing agents than rejecting parents; thus, nonrejection should be associated with socially responsible behavior in children, provided that the parents value and reinforce such behavior.*

It should be noted that this hypothesis refers to nonrejecting parents and is not stated in terms of passive-acceptance. Thus, it is expected that nonrejecting parental behavior, but not unconditionally acceptant behavior, is associated with socially responsible behavior in children. As Bronfenbrenner pointed out about adolescents, "It is the presence of rejection rather than the lack of a high degree of warmth which is inimical to the development of responsibility in both sexes (1961, p. 254)." As already indicated, in our study authoritarian parents were more rejecting and punitive, and less devoted to the child's welfare than were authoritative parents; their sons were also less socially responsible.

4. *Parents who are fair, and who use reason to legitimate their directives are more potent models and reinforcing agents than parents who do not encourage independence or verbal exchange.*

Let us consider the interacting effects of punishment and the use of reasoning on the behavior of children. From research it appears than an accompanying verbal rationale nullifies the special effectiveness of immediate punishment, and also of relatively intense punishment (Parke, 1969). Thus, by symbolically reinstating the deviant act, explaining the reason for punishment, and telling the child exactly what he should do, the parent obviates the need for intense or instantaneous punishment. Immediate, intense punishment may have undesirable side effects, in that the child is conditioned through fear to avoid deviant behavior, and is not helped to control himself consciously and willfully. Also, instantaneous, intense punishment produces high anxiety which may interfere with performance, and in addition may increase the likelihood that the child will avoid the noxious agent. This reduces that agent's future effectiveness as a model or reinforcing agent. Finally, achieving behavioral conformity by conditioning fails to provide the child with information about cause and effect relations which he can then transfer to similar situations. This is not to say that use of reasoning alone, without negative sanctions, is as effective as the use of both. Negative sanctions give operational meaning to the consequences signified by reasons, and to rules themselves.

Authoritarian parents, as compared to authoritative parents, are relatively unsuccessful in producing socially responsible behavior. According to this hypothesis, the reason is that authoritarian parents fail to encourage verbal exchange and infrequently accompany punishment with reasons rather than that they use negative sanctions and are firm disciplinarians.

Socialization Practices Related to Independent vs. Suggestible Behavior

The reader will recall that Independent vs. Suggestible Behavior was defined with reference to: a) Domineering vs. Tractable Behavior, b) Dominance vs. Submission, c) Purposive vs. Aimless Activity, and d) Independence vs. Suggestibility. Parent behavior seems to have a clearer effect upon the development of independence in girls than in boys, probably because preschool boys vary less in independence.

In my own work, independence in girls was clearly associated with authoritative upbringing (whether conforming or nonconforming). For boys, nonconforming parent behavior and, to a lesser extent, authoritative upbringing were associated with independence. By independence we do not mean anticonformity. "Pure anticonformity, like pure conformity, is pure dependence behavior (Willis, 1968, p. 263)." Anticonforming behavior, like negativistic behavior, consists of doing anything but what is prescribed by social norms. Independence is the ability to disregard known standards of conduct or normative expectations in making decisions. Nonconformity in parents may not be associated in my study with independence in girls (although it was in boys) because females are especially susceptible to normative expectations. One can hypothesize that girls must be trained to act independently of these expectations, rather than to conform or to anticonform to them.

It was once assumed that firm control and high maturity demands lead to passivity and dependence in young children. The preponderance of evidence contradicts this. Rather, it would appear that many children react to parental power by resisting, rather than by being cowed. The same parent variables which increase the probability that the child will use the parent as a model should increase the likelihood that firm control will result in assertive behavior. For example, the controlling parent who is warm, understanding and supportive of autonomy should generate less passivity (as well as less rebelliousness) than the controlling parent who is cold and restrictive. This should be the case because of the kinds of behavior reinforced, the traits modelled and the relative effectiveness of the parent as a model.

Several generalizations and hypotheses can be offered concerning the relations between parental practices and the development of independence in young children:

1. *Early environmental stimulation facilitates the development of independence in young children.*

It took the knowledge gained from compensatory programs for culturally disadvantaged children to counteract the erroneous counsel from some experts to avoid too much stimulation of the young child. Those Head Start programs which succeed best (Hunt, 1968) are those characterized by stress on the development of cognitive skills, linguistic ability, motivational concern for achievement, and rudimentary numerical skills. There is reason to believe that middle-class children also profit from such early stimulation and enrichment of the environment. Fowler (1962) pointed out, even prior to the development of compensatory programs,

that concern about the dangers of premature cognitive training and an overemphasis on personality development had delayed inordinately the recognition that the ability to talk, read and compute increases the child's self-respect and independent functioning.

Avoidance of anxiety and self-assertion are reciprocally inhibiting responses to threat or frustration. Girls, in particular, are shielded from stress and overstimulation, which probably serves to increase preferences for avoidant rather than offensive responses to aggression or threat. By exposing a child to stress or to physical, social and intellectual demands, he or she becomes more resistant to stress and learns that offensive reactions to aggression and frustration are frequently rewarding. In our studies, as the hypothesis would predict, parents who provided the most enriched environment, namely the nonconforming and the authoritative parents, had the most dominant and purposive children. These parents, by comparison with the others studied, set high standards of excellence, invoked cognitive insight, provided an intellectually stimulating atmosphere, were themselves rated as being differentiated and individualistic, and made high educational demands upon the child.

2. *Parental passive-acceptance and overprotection inhibits the development of independence.*

Passive-acceptant and overprotective parents shield children from stress and, for the reasons discussed above, inhibit the development of assertiveness and frustration tolerance. Also, parental anxiety about stress to which the child is exposed may serve to increase the child's anxiety. Further, willingness to rescue the child offers him an easy alternative to self-mastery. Demanding and nonprotective parents, by contrast, permit the child to extricate himself from stressful situations and place a high value on tolerance of frustration and courage.

According to many investigators (e.g., McClelland, Atkinson, Clark, & Lowell, 1953), healthy infants are by inclination explorative, curious and stress-seeking. Infantile feelings of pleasure, originally experienced after mild changes in sensory stimulation, become associated with these early efforts at independent mastery. The child anticipates pleasure upon achieving a higher level of skill, and the pleasure derived from successfully performing a somewhat risky task encourages him to seek out such tasks.

Rosen and D'Andrade (1959) found that high achievement motivation, a motivation akin to stress-seeking, was facilitated both by high maternal warmth when the child pleased the parent and high maternal hostility and rejection when the child was displeasing. Hoffman, et al., (1960), found that mothers of achieving boys were more coercive than those who performed poorly, and it has also been found (Crandall, Dewey, Katkovsky, & Preston, 1964) that mothers of achieving girls were relatively nonnurturant. Kagan and Moss (1962) reported that achieving adult women had mothers who in early childhood were unaffectionate, "pushy," and not protective. Also, Baumrind and Black (1967) found paternal punitiveness to be associated positively with independence in girls. Finally, in my most recent study, there were indications for girls that parental nonacceptance was positively related to independence. That is, the most independent girls had parents who were either not passive-acceptant or who were rejecting.

Authoritarian control and permissive noncontrol both may shield the child from the opportunity to engage in vigorous interaction with people. Demands which cannot be met, refusals to help, and unrealistically high standards may curb commerce with the environment. Placing few demands on the child, suppression of conflict, and low standards may understimulate him. In either case, he fails to achieve the knowledge and experience required to desensitize him to the anxiety associated with nonconformity.

3. *Self-assertiveness and self-confidence in the parent, expressed by an individual style and by the moderate use of power-oriented techniques of discipline, will be associated with independence in the young child.*

The self-assertive, self-confident parent provides a model of similar behavior for the child. Also, the parent who uses power-oriented rather than love-oriented techniques of discipline achieves compliance through means other than guilt. Power-oriented techniques can achieve behavioral conformity without premature internalization by the child of parental standards. It may be that the child is, in fact, more free to formulate his own standards of conduct if techniques of discipline are used which stimulate ressistiveness or anger rather than fear or guilt. The use of techniques which do not stimulate conformity through guilt may be especially important for girls. The belief in one's own power and the assumption of responsibility for one's own intellectual successes and failures are important predictors of independent effort and intellectual achievement (Crandall, Katkovsky, & Crandall, 1965). This sense of self-responsibility in children seems to be associated with power-oriented techniques of discpline and with critical attitudes on the part of the adult towards the child, provided that the parent is also concerned with developing the child's autonomy and encourages independent and individual behavior.

In my study, both the authoritative and the nonconforming parents were self-confident, clear as well as flexible in their childrearing attitudes, and willing to express angry feelings openly. Together with relatively firm enforcement and nonrejection, these indices signified patterns of parental authority in which guilt-producing techniques of discipline were avoided. The sons of nonconforming parents and the daughters of authoritative parents were both extremely independent.

4. *Firm control can be associated with independence in the child, provided that the control is not restrictive of the child's opportunities to experiment and to make decisions within the limits defined.*

There is no logical reason why parents' enforcing directives and making demands cannot be accompanied by regard for the child's opinions, willingness to gratify his wishes, and instruction in the effective use of power. A policy of firm enforcement may be used as a means by which the child can achieve a high level of instrumental competence and eventual independence. The controlling, demanding parent can train the child to tolerate increasingly intense and prolonged frustration; to broaden his base of adult support to include neighbors, teachers and others; to assess critically his own successes and failures and to take responsibility for both; to develop standards of moral conduct; and to relinquish the special privileges of childhood in return for the rights of adolescence.

It is important to distinguish between the effects on the child of restrictive control and of firm control. *Restrictive control* refers to the use of extensive proscriptions and prescriptions, covering many areas of the child's life; they limit his autonomy to try out his skills in these areas. By *firm control* is meant firm enforcement of rules, effective resistance against the child's demands, and guidance of the child by regime and intervention. Firm control does not imply large numbers of rules or intrusive direction of the child's activities.

Becker (1964) has summarized the effects on child behavior of restrictiveness vs. permissiveness and warmth vs. hostility. He reported that warm-*restrictive* parents tended to have passive, well-socialized children. This author (Baumrind, 1967) found, however, that warm-*controlling* (by contrast with warm-*restrictive*) parents were not paired with passive children, but rather with responsible, assertive, self-reliant children. Parents of these children enforced directives and resisted the child's demands, but were not restrictive. Early control, unlike restrictiveness, apparently does not lead to "fearful, dependent and submissive behaviors, a dulling of intellectual striving, and inhibited hostility," as Becker indicated was true of restrictive parents (1964, p. 197).

5. *Substantial reliance upon reinforcement techniques to obtain behavioral conformity, unaccompanied by use of reason, should lead to dependent behavior.*

To the extent that the parent uses verbal cues judiciously, she increases the child's ability to discriminate, differentiate, and generalize. According to Luria (1960) and Vygotsky (1962), the child's ability to "order" his own behavior is based upon verbal instruction from the adult which, when heeded and obeyed, permits eventual *cognitive* control by the child of his own behavior. Thus, when the adult legitimizes power, labels actions clearly as praiseworthy or changeworthy, explains her rules and encourages vigorous verbal give and take, obedience is not likely to be achieved at the cost of passive dependence. Otherwise, it may well be.

It is self-defeating to attempt to shape, by extrinsic reinforcement, behavior which by its nature is autogenic. As already mentioned, the healthy infant is explorative and curious, and seems to enjoy mild stress. Although independent mastery can be accelerated if the parent broadens the child's experiences and makes certain reasonable demands upon him, the parent must take care not to substitute extrinsic reward and social approval for the intrinsic pleasure associated with mastery of the environment. Perhaps the unwillingness of the authoritative parents in my study to rely solely upon reinforcement techniques contributed substantially to the relatively purposive, dominant behavior shown by their children, especially by their daughters.

6. *Parental values which stress individuality, self-expression, initiative, divergent thinking and aggressiveness will facilitate the development of independence in the child, provided that these qualities in the parent are not accompanied by lax and inconsistent discipline and unwillingness to make demands upon the child.*

It is important that adults use their power in a functional rather than an interpersonal context. The emphasis should be on the task to be done and the rule to be followed rather than upon the special status of the powerful adult. By focusing upon the task to be accomplished, the adult's actions can serve as an example for the child rather than as a suppressor of his independence. Firm discipline for both boys and girls must be in the service of training for achievement and independence, if such discipline is not to facilitate the development of an overconforming, passive life style.

In our study, independence was clearly a function of nonconforming but nonindulgent parental attitudes and behaviors, for boys. For girls, however, nonconforming parental patterns were associated with independence only when the parents were also authoritative. The parents in these groups tended to encourage their children to ask for, even to demand, what they desired. They themselves acquiesced in the face of such demands provided that the demands were not at variance with parental policy. Thus, the children of these parents were positively reinforced for autonomous self-expression. In contrast to these results, the authoritarian parents did not value willfulness in the child, and the permissive parents were clearly ambivalent about rewarding such behavior. Further, the permissive parents did not differentiate between mature or praiseworthy demands by the child and regressive or deviant demands. These permissive parents instead would accede to the child's demands until patience was exhausted; punishment, sometimes very harsh, would then ensue.

Summary

Girls in western society are in many ways systematically socialized for instrumental incompetence. The affiliative and cooperative orientation of girls increases their receptivity to the influence of socializing agents. This influence, in turn, is often used by socializing agents to inculcate passivity, dependence, conformity and sociability in the young females at the expense of independent pursuit of success and scholarship. In my studies, parents designated as authoritative had the most achievement-oriented and independent daughters. However, permissive parents whose control was lax, who did not inhibit tomboy behavior, and who did not seek to produce sex-role conformity in girls had daughters who were nearly as achievement-oriented and independent.

The following adult practices and attitudes seem to facilitate the development of socially responsible and independent behavior in both boys and girls.

1. Modelling by the adult of behavior which is both socially responsible and self-assertive, especially if the adult is seen as powerful by the child and as eager to use the material and interpersonal resources over which he has control on the child's behalf.

2. Firm enforcement policies in which the adult makes effective use of reinforcement principles in order to reward socially responsible behavior and to punish deviant behavior, but in which demands are accompanied by explanations, and sanctions are accompanied by reasons consistent with a set of principles followed in practice as well as preached by the parent.

3. Nonrejecting but not overprotective or passive-acceptant parental attitudes in which the parent's interest in the child is abiding, and, in the preschool years, intense; but where approval is conditional upon the child's behavior.

4. High demands for achievement, and for conformity with parental policy, accompanied by receptivity to the child's rational demands and willingness to offer the child wide latitude for independent judgment.

5. Providing the child with a complex and stimulating environment offering challenge and excitement as well as security and rest, where divergent as well as convergent thinking is encouraged.

These practices and attitudes do not reflect a happy compromise between authoritarian and permissive practices. Rather, they reflect a synthesis and balancing of strongly opposing forces of tradition and innovation, divergence and convergence, accommodation and assimilation, cooperation and autonomous expression, tolerance and principled intractability.

References

Aberle, D. F. & Naegele, K. D. Middle-class fathers' occupational role and attitudes toward children. *American J. Orthopsychiatry.* 1952, 22, 366-378.

Bandura, A., Ross, D. & Ross, S. A. A comparative test of the status envy, social power, and the secondary-reinforcement theories of identificatory learning. *J. abnorm. soc. psychol.*, 1963, 67, 527-534.

Barry, H., Bacon, M. K. & Child, E. L. A cross-cultural survey of some sex differences in socialization. *J. abnorm. soc. psychol.*, 1957,55,327-332.

Baumrind, D. Effects of authoritative parental control on child behavior. *Child Develpm.*, 1966, 37, 887-907.

————. Child care practices anteceding three patterns of preschool behavior. *Genetic psychol. Monogr.*, 1967, 75, 43-88.

————. Authoritarian vs. authoritative parental control. *Adolescence*, 1968, 3, 255-272.

————. Current patterns of parental authority. *Developmental psychol. Monogr.*, 1971, 4(1), in press.

————, & Black, A. E. Socialization practices associated with dimensions of competence in preschool boys and girls. *Child Develpm.* 1967, 38, 291-327.

Becker, W. C. Consequences of different kinds of parental discipline. In M. L. Hoffman & L. W. Hoffman (eds.), *Review of Child Development Research*. Vol. 1. New York: Russell Sage Foundation, 1964, 169-208.

Bronfenbrenner, U. Some familiar antecedents of responsibility and leadership in adolescents. In L. Petrullo & B. M. Bass (eds.), *Leadership and interpersonal behavior.* New York: Holt, Rinehart & Winston, 1961, 239-271.

Brown, D. Sex role development in a changing culture. *Psychol. Bull.,* 1958, 55, 232-242.

Crandall, V., Dewey, R., Katkovsky, W. & Preston, A. Parents' attitudes and behaviors and grade school children's academic achievements. *J. genet. psychol.,* 1964, 104, 53-66.

————, Katkovsky, W. & Crandall, V. J. Children's beliefs in their own control of reinforcements in intellectual-academic achievement situations. *Child Develpm.,* 1965, 36, 91-109.

————, Orleans, S., Preston, A. & Rabson, A. The development of social compliance in young children. *Child Develpm.,* 1958, 29, 429-443.

Dinitz, S., Dynes, R. R. & Clarke, A. C. Preference for male or female children: Traditional or affectional. *Marriage and Family Living,* 1954, 16, 128-130.

Eiduson, B. T. *Scientists, their psychological world.* New York: Basic Books, 1962.

Elder, G. H. Parental power legitimation and its effect on the adolescent. *Sociometry,* 1963, 26, 50-65.

Emmerich, W. & Smoller, F. The role patterning of parental norms. *Sociometry,* 1964, 27, 382-390.

Fowler, W. Cognitive learning in infancy and early childhood. *Psychol. Bull.,* 1962, 59, 116-152.

Haggard, E. A. Socialization, personality, and academic achievement in gifted children. In B. C. Rosen, H. J. Crockett & C. Z. Nunn (eds.), *Achievement in American society.* Cambridge, Mass.: Schenkman Publishing, 1969, 85-94.

Heilbrun, A. B. Sex differences in identification learning. *J. genet. psychol.,* 1965, 106, 185-193.

Hoffman, L., Rosen, S. & Lippit, R. Parental coerciveness, child autonomy, and child's role at school. *Sociometry,* 1960, 23, 15-22.

Horner, M. Fail: Bright women. *Psychology Today,* 1969, 3 (6).

Hunt, J. McV. Toward the prevention of incompetence. In J. W. Carter, Jr. (ed.), *Research Contributions from Psychology to Community Mental Health.* New York: Behavioral Publications, 1968.

Kagan, J. & Moss, H. A. *Birth to Maturity: A Study in Psychological Development.* New York: John Wiley, 1962.

Keniston, E. & Keniston, K. An American anachronism: the image of women and work. *Am. Scholar,* 1964, 33, 355-375.

Luria, A. R. Experimental analysis of the development of voluntary action in children. In *The Central Nervous System and Behavior.* Bethesda,

Md.: U.S. Department of Health, Education, & Welfare, National Institutes of Health, 1960, 529-535.

Maccoby, E. E. (ed.). *The Development of Sex Differences.* Stanford, Calif.: Stanford University Press, 1966.

McClelland, D., Atkinson, J., Clark, R. & Lowell, E. *The Achievement Motive.* New York: Appleton-Century-Crofts, 1953.

McKee, J. P. & Sherriffs, A. C. The differential evaluation of males and females. *J. Pers.,* 1957, 25, 356-371.

Middleton, R. & Snell, P. Political expression of adolescent rebellion. *Am. J. Sociol.,* 1963, 68, 527-535.

Mischel, W. & Liebert, R. M. Effects of discrepancies between observed and imposed reward criteria on their acquisition and transmission. *J. Pers. & soc. Psychol.,* 1966, 3, 45-53.

Parke, R. D. Some effects of punishment on children's behavior. *Young Children,* 1969, 24, 225-240.

Pikas, A. Children's attitudes toward rational versus inhibiting parental authority. *J. abnorm. soc. Psychol.,* 1961, 62, 315-321.

Roe, A. *The Making of a Scientist.* New York: Dodd, Mead, 1952.

Rosen, B. C. & D'Andrade, R. The psychological origins of achievement motivation. *Sociometry,* 1959, 22, 185-218.

Rosenhan, D. L., Frederick, F. & Burrowes, A. Preaching and Practicing: effects of channel discrepancy on norm internalization. *Child Develpm.,* 1968, 39, 291-302.

Rossi, A. Women in science: why so few? In B. C. Rosen, H. J. Crockett, & C. Z. Nunn (eds.), *Achievement in American Society.* Cambridge, Mass.: Schenkman Publishing, 1969, 470-486.

Siegel, A. E. & Kohn, L. G. Permissiveness, permission, and aggression: the effects of adult presence or absence on aggression in children's play. *Child Develpm.,* 1959, 36, 131-141.

Spence, J. T. Verbal-discrimination performance as a function of instruction and verbal reinforcement combination in normal and retarded children. *Child Develpm.,* 1966, 37, 269-281.

Terman, L. M. & Oden, H. H. *The Gifted Child Grows Up.* Stanford, Calif.: Stanford University Press, 1947.

Vygotsky, L. S. *Thought and Language.* Cambridge, Mass.: M.I.T. Press, 1962.

Walberg, H. J. Physics, femininity, and creativity. *Develpml. Psychol.,* 1969, 1, 47-54.

Willis, R. H. Conformity, independence, and anti-conformity. In L. S. Wrightsman, Jr. (ed.), *Contemporary Issues in Social Psychology.* Belmont, Calif.: Brooks/Cole Publishing, 1968, 258-272.

16

Children's Fears

You know there isn't a fire-breathing dragon in the hall closet. Then why does your bright, well-adjusted youngster insist that there is? And how on earth are you going to convince him otherwise?

By Cynthia Lang

A friend of mine, visiting friends in Indiana, brought their children a new picture book—wonderfully illustrated—that told about animals. Later on, when he stopped by the children's room, he saw the six-year-old boy holding the book and reading it to his four-year-old brother.

"This one's a lamb; see his curly coat? And this one..." Together, the boys turned to the next picture, but as the four-year-old flattened out the page with a pudgy hand, his older brother froze. Quickly, he snatched the book away and slammed it shut. Then, with a shudder, he explained, "Lions! Don't even *think* about lions!"

Within a short time, the child's warning had worked its way into our lexicon. Maybe a job was going to end, a love vanish, a project fail? "Don't even *think* about lions!" we would say to one another. Of course we were joking. We knew the difference between our capacity as adults to face what we had to and the concrete fear in the six-year-old's voice. Still, under our grown-up laughter I thought I heard an echo of an ancient rule: do not mention that which you most greatly fear.

Fears and phobias: crucial differences.

I began to think about fears—the children's and our own. Children's fears are different from adults', and for many of the reasons that children are different. They are not just short people, after all; developmentally, they are something else. And yet, their fears and how they handle them can never be divorced from ours. The situation raises questions about the nature of children's fears and what parents can do about them.

Cynthia Lang is a free-lance writer who writes frequently on child-related topics.

Children's fears are normal, at least up to a point. Dr. Dean Parmelee, a psychiatrist at Hall-Mercer Children's Center at McLean Hospital, a psychiatric facility and teaching hospital for the Harvard Medical School in Belmont, emphasizes that it is important to distinguish between normal childhood fears, and phobias, which are characterized not so much by what the child fears as by the manner of feeling.

"Clinically, it's a question of intensity and fixedness: Is this a fear that persists over time, shows up every night, reaches panic proportions? Then we think about calling it a phobia. Otherwise, no. If a child is afraid of horses, it's okay if she doesn't want to go to the circus. But if she doesn't even want to go for a drive in the country because she might see a horse, or, in the extreme, won't go out of the house because a horse might be wandering down the street—then we worry."

As adults, we have a pretty good idea of what children fear: separations; new situations; other people as potential enemies; asking the wrong questions (especially on subjects they aren't supposed to ask about, such as sex, death, household fights, or serious illness); punishment, deserved or undeserved (though they usually think it must have been deserved). But what form do the fears take? Often, children don't ask directly about things that scare them or puzzle them, but instead make up games that act them out. They play doctor, cowboys and Indians, and pursuit scenes from *Star Wars*.

Children are not keen to talk about their fears. Asked directly what they are afraid of, they are likely to answer, "Nothing." Often, however, they add, "Not even the witch or the monster in my closet," an acknowledged litany of scary beings breaking through the determined and brave front. At bedtime, however, children's fears may stop their elusive game of hide-and-seek. Dr. Parmelee says, "Two

factors force fears up to the surface at bedtime. There's the fear of going to bed in the dark, perhaps because we are day animals, because we aren't naturally nocturnal. On top of that, there's the fear of falling asleep—the child knows he or she loses control over the world and may even dream. Who can tell what terrible images will come up on the screen at night?"

In spite of their reticence in talking about them, it appears that children do share common fears. Several studies have categorized the reported fears of large groups of children and it turns out that distinct patterns emerge.

The six-year-old in Indiana is not alone in being afraid of animals—many children are. But monsters are an even bigger threat. In a study of 400 children aged five to twelve, Arthur Jersild found that the largest single class—one-fifth of all fears mentioned—consisted of fears of the occult, the supernatural, and mysterious beings: "Dracula" and "the bogeyman" got high billing. Next came fear of animals, and children cited just about the whole taxonomy of the animal kingdom: alligators, foxes, gorillas, rats, sharks, vultures, pigs, cats, tigers, giraffes, bees. A middle group (in terms of numbers) consisted of fears of nightmares and apparitions, "bad people" like kidnappers and robbers, bodily injury, and gestures, noises, or expressions deliberately made by others to frighten. The smallest group (2 percent or less) consisted of fears of scolding, teasing, failure, guilt, loss of possessions, and relatives' becoming sick or dying.

It's striking that children deal more with fancied dangers than with real ones; they are more likely to have fears that are irrational than to fear events that can actually happen. Jersild's study was made before television took over; interestingly, though, his findings were corroborated by a study conducted by David Bauer, a professor of psychology at California State University, just a few years ago.

Television's scary "mean world."

Despite the similarities in these reports' findings, it would be an exaggeration to say that TV has no impact on children's fears. The Los Angeles County Psychological Association recently issued a comment that in its experience children react to violence on television with "increased anxiety, such as showing restlessness, increased tension, nightmares, fears of going outside the house, and sleep disturbances." Other researchers into the effects of TV speak about a "mean world" syndrome and, in at least one study, document that heavy viewers believe violence is more common in our society than do light viewers: it seems that their social reality is derived from the social reality of TV—not from the reality of their own city streets or suburban neighborhoods.

Nevertheless, Jersild's and Bauer's studies of children's fears strongly suggest that patterns of fears and changes in fears over time primarily reflect childhood development: a succession of changes in the child's perception of reality.

In that context, we can think of fears not only as normal, but inevitable; they reflect personal growth and new undertakings. An infant doesn't cry just because his mother leaves the room; separation still has no meaning for him. But in a few months it will. He'll be more "fearful" because he's "smarter"— that is, more aware, and more thinking. We talk about thoughts and feelings as if they were in separate packages, but, in fact, how children interpret what they notice depends on how they think and what they know. As well as having more experience under their belts, older children have better-developed cognitive equipment; therefore, they are better able to distinguish between what is real and what is imaginary. They know monsters aren't really real, so they are less frightened of TV shows that feature bizarre creatures and, at the same time, more cautious about the dangers of traffic. Younger children, on the other hand, are less certain about the line between fantasy and reality.

Why monsters?

Why do children appear to go through a "monster" phase? Come to think of it, why did the human mind invent monsters at all? What we know about human behavior offers some clues. Psychologically, odd links exist between fears and aggression. Anger that goes unvoiced, or is unacceptable, has a funny way of becoming transformed. Instead of saying, "I hate you!" to his father, a child's mind turns the feeling around: perhaps something out there hates him and is out to get him! Anthropologists have noticed this. In different parts of the world, cultures with strict rules about aggression raise children who are not allowed to show much anger; and, at the same time, adults in the group have greater fears of omnipotent creatures and godlike strangers from over the next hill than do adults in groups that have an easier time letting their children show anger. Psychiatrists notice a similar pattern among individuals. Dr. Parmelee points out that it is impossible to make flat generalizations about all individuals: "But we can talk about fears and their links to conflicts in the child, especially anger. Often fears *are* projections—the child is uncomfortable about his anger and it gets placed outside of him so that he thinks monsters will get him.

"The years from two to six, roughly, are years when children are dealing most directly with aggression. That's just when *(Continued)*

I'd expect to hear the most about monsters. And you have to ask why parents are so uncomfortable with aggression in their kids—tantrums in two-year-olds and icy hostility in teenagers. For most of us, it's because we've never figured out quite how to deal with our own aggression. *The Incredible Hulk* interests me—it's the story of a man whose body turns into a monster's when he is enraged. Now that's something kids can get into because they so often can feel like monsters with their own rage and here's a character doing what they feel like doing when they get really mad."

Among young children, monsters may be most useful precisely because they are unreal—the child doesn't have to handle ambiguities of good and bad in familiar figures like parents or even himself. Instead, he can consolidate any "bad" feelings and attribute them to a being far outside the family.

The satisfying dark side of fairy tales.

Television is such a uniquely insistent part of children's lives that it is easy to forget that children's fears—and dramatic presentations that played on, confronted, or sought to allay them—existed long before the tube. Fairy tales constituted the central body of entertainment for children for centuries. For some children, they still do. Fairy tales are so much a part of our heritage that we overlook their bloodthirsty moments. But some of these mythical tales, full of improbable happenings, are violent indeed. They are also full of simplified human psychology, woven into the stories, of course, long before a professor of psychology was ever appointed to a chair. Perhaps our unexamined instincts as parents were right all along and fairy tales were the best entertainment possible for children.

Bruno Bettelheim would say that they were. In *The Uses of Enchantment* he says, "Many parents believe that only conscious reality or pleasant and wish-fulfilling images should be presented to the child — that he should be exposed only to the sunny side of things. But such one-sided fare nourishes the mind only in a one-sided way, and real life is not all sunny. ... Children know that *they* are not always good; and often, even when they are, they would prefer not to be.

This contradicts what they are told by their parents, and...makes the child a monster in his own eyes."

The fairy tale's central appeal, Bettelheim suggests, has been its willingness to air both sides of reality. Those deep inner conflicts that originate in our primitive drives and our violent emotions are denied in much of modern children's literature, and the child is not helped to cope with them.

So the fairy tale, says Bettelheim, does what parents cannot easily do—it takes these archetypal anxieties seriously and addresses the real fears of children. By directly presenting good and evil, characterized as princes and princesses, nasty witches and ugly dragons, murderous parents and starving children, they give the child a chance to struggle with issues of good versus evil as he identifies with the actors in the story. Or, as Dr. Parmelee puts it, "They allow the child to hop in and be part of the story."

Naturally, parents need to be a little selective about which stories their children hop into, making choices after thinking about the child's age and personality and the nature of the story. For young children, they may be wise to screen out stories — as they would television programs—that appear too violent, where the children in the story come to a bad end, or where evil is embodied in a character too close to home. The stepmother in "Cinderella" works so well because she isn't a real mother, and a child momentarily angry at her own mother can say, "I knew it. She must be my stepmother. My real mother wouldn't treat me like that!"

In the past, parents have usually made these choices. As they've read out loud, they've screened and, even more important, they have been there with their children. TV, which affords no such intimacy between parent and child, is quite another matter. Ironically, television's worst effect may not be in what it presents but in what it prevents. Today, parents don't spend as much time with their children in the evening, they read together less, there are fewer chances to talk over a story or the worries it triggers in a child's mind.

Taming the bogeyman.

Not that confronting a child's fear in the hope of easing it will always help. "If you have a child who is afraid of a green monster," says Dr. Parmelee, "it really won't help to address that, because the most you can say is, 'There really isn't any green monster, so you don't have to worry'—and what good does that do the child when she believes there is a monster? But if the child is afraid of strange dogs, that's different. Instead of talking about why he should or shouldn't *be* afraid, you can help him learn some dog management, teach him what to do when a strange dog comes up to him. Actually, that's teaching him something about managing the environment, which gives him more control and reduces his sense that strange dogs have all the power and he has none."

Ultimately, helping children manage their fears means helping them to see that they are not powerless victims, helpless in the face of new situations, unfamiliar and ominous beings or people, and the sudden storms of their own anger. But that takes time—and more than ten minutes spent now and then: it takes a long-term investment over a course of years. Moreover, children's fears can be seen as developmentally useful, not only to the children as they move from one stage of consciousness and achievement to another, but also to parents. Children's fears present a special challenge to parents because they often embody conflicts that the parents have not resolved. In trying to help their children, parents can take the opportunity to take another look at themselves and ask, "Why is it so troubling to me when my child is frightened this way?" And the fears of children offer an opportunity for parents and children to come face to face with a special facet of their relationship: the parents' capacity to offer protection and help. Beyond momentary reassurance ("there isn't any green monster") parents can help their children modulate feelings of fear and experience the world as a less terrifying place. It can be a constructive, gratifying phase for everyone. ◉

17

Autism: A Defeatable Horror

How Parents Can Treat Their Troubled Children

One theory of this rare but crushing condition blames parents, but the proof is thin. Here is a treatment—not a theory—that teaches parents to be effective therapists and lets them join the struggle to civilize their children, autistic or normal.

by Laura Schreibman and Robert L. Koegel

A. Problems in Childhood and Adolescence

BECAUSE IT STRIKES ONLY ONE CHILD out of 2,500, autism does not seem to be an alarming problem, at least statistically. But then, few children get hit by cars either. When autism does strike, the effects are dramatic and, until recently, tragically untreatable. In the past few years, however, we and other researchers have developed a successful new method of treating autistic children, using their own parents as therapists.

Without special training, parents of autistic children face a particularly depressing task (see "A Christmas Tree for Kristin," page 67). These children often throw violent, screaming tantrums. They may bite themselves or bang their heads against the furniture. Some must be physically restrained to prevent permanent injury. Autistic children may spend most of the day engaged in self-stimulatory behavior such as rocking back and forth, flapping their arms or waving their fingers in front of their eyes. Many are mute, and those who are not parrot meaninglessly whatever sounds they hear.

One characteristic of autistic children that depresses parents and puzzles therapists is their unresponsiveness to their social environment. They do not play with toys, or interact with other children. In fact they show no need for affection or any other form of contact with anybody. They don't even seem to know or care who their parents are. For a loving parent trying to help, this can be crushing. Even severely retarded children often give their parents the satisfaction of love and affection.

Life With a Wild Animal. Those who have never lived with an autistic child might blame parents who give up on them and decide to put them in institutions. But even the kindest, most loving and patient parent finds it difficult or impossible to live with what one has called "a wild animal, a living terror."

Many parents find themselves chained to their home, forced to adjust their lives to their children. They don't invite friends over because they fear embarrassment. When you enter some homes you are struck by the barrenness: no draperies, no delicate furniture, no plants, ashtrays or other throwable objects.

Taking an autistic child to any public place means gambling against the odds of disruption or embarrassment. At a restaurant, the child may start screaming for no reason, throwing food or spoons. At a friend's house, the child may rock incessantly back and forth against the seat cushion. Simply taking the child for a drive risks a dangerous tantrum. Getting away alone can also be difficult. Most baby sitters are incapable of looking after an autistic child; and those potentially able are usually reluctant to take on the responsibility.

To add to the parents' dilemma, few public schools offer much support. Autistic children cannot function in normal classrooms, not only because of their disruptive behavior, but also because of their serious behavioral limitations. They do not use language, understand instruction, pay attention, or interact with others. Few schools have personnel trained to deal with such problems. Even the staffs of schools for the mentally retarded, where many autistic children are placed, usually lack the training necessary for dealing with them.

Condemned for Life. Although a number of techniques for treating autistic children have been developed in recent years, they are not yet generally available. With no help from schools or specialists, and unable to handle their children themselves, most parents do give up eventually. Their children end up in mental institutions, condemned for life because they have nowhere else to go.

The desperate decision on institutionalization usually comes after several unsuccessful trials with available programs, especially as the child grows older and harder to handle. One California child, for example, now 13 years old, has attended 16 schools and clinics so far. Eight rejected her because of her disruptive behavior; her parents withdrew her from the others because they saw no improvement. The father of another child who had bounced around various clinics and schools grew demoralized over the prospect of the boy's life in a mental hospital. One night he shot and killed his son while he slept.

Until recently, the most common theory of autism blamed it on the parents, suggesting that their own emotional problems somehow cause their children's tragic withdrawal. Therapists who adhere to this theory often counsel parents to seek psychotherapy themselves. No one has ever proven, however, that parents cause autism, or that treating the parents will help cure their children. In the absence of proof, blaming parents uselessly and cruelly reinforces the guilt they mistakenly feel, thus adding to their already heavy burden. One bit of evidence that complicates the parental-blame theory is the fact that autism strikes four times as many boys as girls.

A more current theory, also unproven, describes autism as an organic disorder, caused by some biochemical problem in the brain. This theory also offers little hope to parents. Since they can do nothing about an organic problem, they are simply told to learn to live with it.

But even if the disorder is organic in nature, should that discourage parents from seeking further treatment? If a child breaks his leg, we do not sentence him to life in a hospital. Why should we do so for an autistic child?

Parents As Therapists. The few professionals who treat autistic children generally exclude parents from the treatment process. But since parents are the most important agents of change in any child's life, excluding them wastes a valuable and necessary resource. In our research, we have proved not only that parents and teachers can learn to become effective therapists, but that their participation in the treatment process is essential.

By systematically rewarding appropriate behavior while ignoring or punishing inappropriate behavior, our parent and teacher therapists have produced dramatic improvement in previously untreatable autistic children. Using similar behavior-modification techniques, pioneers in the field such as Montrose Wolf, Todd Risley, Frank Hewett, and particularly Ivar Lovaas, have been able to control the disruptive behavior of these children, and teach them to talk, to play, and to deal with other people [see "A Conversation with Ivar Lovaas," PT, January 1974].

Compared to other methods of treating autism, the behavior-mod approach has several major advantages: it is based on principles of learning that can easily be taught to nonprofessionals; its effectiveness can be measured by objective data rather than subjective impressions; it does not blame the parents; and it does not require any knowledge about the cause of autism.

With this approach, autistic children could achieve considerable improvement in a clinical setting. But after leaving the clinic, those discharged to hospitals, foster homes, or parents who had not received training began to deteriorate rapidly, losing most of their treatment gains. In contrast, children discharged to parents who had received training maintained all of their treatment gains, and often continued to improve.

To test the importance of behavior-mod training, we asked a group of 26 untrained parents, teachers and college students to try to teach an autistic child some particular skill, such as tying shoes, or distinguishing colors. We provided each adult with a supply of food to use in rewarding the child.

In more than 50 15-minute teaching sessions, only one of the adults produced any measurable improvement in the child's response. In fact, in 28 sessions, the child made fewer correct responses at the end of the session than in the beginning. Many of the adults had great difficulty simply controlling the children, let alone teaching them. The children were confused and frustrated; they frequently screamed, threw objects, and attempted to kick or bite their teachers. Although they tried hard, the untrained adults were clearly ineffective therapists.

We next experimented with letting the parents and teachers watch a trained therapist teach a particular task, to see if that would improve their own approach. We found that such observation helped the adults in teaching the *same* task to their children, but only that particular one. For example, if a parent had observed a therapist teaching a child to tie his shoes the parent could then teach his own child how to tie his shoes, but not how to brush his teeth, or how to say "mama."

Five Essential Steps. Since autistic children have numerous behavioral problems, an effective training program must teach parents and teachers to deal with a large variety of behavior. In collaboration with our colleagues, Dennis Russo and Arnold Rincover, we therefore identified a set of five general procedures that apply to all situations:

1
Identifying The Target Behavior

Untrained parents and teachers tend to pick global goals, such as happiness or self-confidence. While there is nothing wrong with trying to make a child happy, a therapist can only achieve this goal if he first defines the particular behavior a child would need to learn to become happy. For example, if the therapist defines a happy child as one who laughs, talks, and plays with toys and other children, he can teach the child these specific behaviors and, it is to be hoped, end up with a happy child.

2
Presenting Proper Instructions

The therapist must first get the child's attention, and then make sure the child can easily understand the instructions. Our research has shown that autistic children often fail to respond correctly when presented with multiple instructions. For example, when teaching the child to discriminate colors, the untrained teacher might say: "Now we are going to work on colors. I'm going to teach you to touch a red square when I say 'red,' and to touch a green square when I say 'green.' But don't touch any of the other colors unless I say their name. Ok, now get ready to touch the red square, but don't touch any of the other colors. Ok, now do it." Such instructions don't work with autistic children.

In an efficient presentation, the therapist must first wait until any inattentive or disruptive behavior has stopped, then establish eye contact with the child. Then the teacher should present a simple instruction such as "touch red."

3
Prompting Correct Responses

Sometimes, even when the therapist presents an instruction correctly, the child will not respond because the response is simply not part of his repertoire. For example, if the therapist asks the child to say

The children
were confused and frustrated; they frequently
screamed, threw objects, and attempted
to kick or bite their teachers. Although
they tried hard, the untrained adults were
clearly ineffective therapists.

1 Andy's father rests as Andy, an energetic powerhouse, bounces on a chair. Autistic children often have boundless energy, wearing their parents down.
2 A therapist works with Andy, while his father watches through a one-way screen. Systematic observation helps therapists chart the child's progress, while providing parents an opportunity to watch professionals work.
3 Like many autistic children, Andy stares at lights, moving objects and other seemingly ordinary things.
4 Andy and author Schreibman share a moment of joy, showing therapy can be fun.

"b," a mute child might try, but his noise would in no way resemble the sound "b." Under such conditions the therapist can prompt or guide the child's response. He might hold the child's lip together to help form the sound. The prompt must work, however. It must produce the correct response. If not, no matter how good the intentions, or how many times it has worked, it should be abandoned for a better prompt. One should also minimize the number of extra cues.

4
Shaping and Chaining Behavior

Both of these procedures break the target behavior down into a sequence of very small steps. The therapist rewards successive approximations of the target behavior until the child finally responds correctly and completely. To earn a reward, each response must be at least as good an approximation as the previously rewarded response. In shaping, for example, if the therapist tries to get the child to say "ball," and the child's first two attempts come out "ba" and "baaal," then both responses should be rewarded because they represent progress. If, on the other hand, the child first says "ba," then "baaal" and then "ba" again, the last sound should not be rewarded because it is not as good as the previous response.

5
Providing Effective Consequences

After a child makes a correct response, the therapist should provide an appropriate consequence. The child must receive a reward when he responds correctly, and no reward when he does not. One must not reward an incorrect response because the child was "trying hard," or fail to reward a correct response because it is something every child "ought to know." The consequences must also be unambiguous. The therapist should not smile while saying "no," or frown while saying "good."

After explaining and demonstrating these five procedures to the adults in our program, we then observed while they practiced them on their own children. All of them reached an acceptable level of effectiveness, usually within one to five hours. This range possibly depends on such factors as their education, intelligence, and desire to succeed.

Once they had mastered the five-part technique, we asked the adults to teach their child some new behavior. This time, every one of them produced marked increases in the child's correct responses, re-

The successful adults did not think of the children as "ill"; instead of pitying and excusing bizarre behavior, they concentrated on increasing normal behavior. They showed a willingness to commit a major personal effort to helping their child.

The Fruits of Therapy: Learning to perform complex tasks, such as using a record player, represents great progress for an autistic child. Kristin's success liberates her so that she can entertain herself with the joy of music.

gardless of what behavior they were working on. Their success seems especially impressive to us in that although amateurs, they learned to become effective therapists in a matter of hours, in sharp contrast to the years of extensive training usually prescribed for professional therapists.

The Successful Parent-Therapist. Comparing the results of all the adults in the experiments, the more successful ones could be distinguished by certain general characteristics. They cared a great deal about succeeding, showing happiness when the children improved, and anger when the children disrupted the sessions. The successful adults did not think of the children as "ill"; instead of pitying and excusing bizarre behavior, they concentrated on increasing normal behavior. They showed a willingness to commit a major personal effort to helping their child; instead of relying on professional help.

Ideally, both parents and teachers should work together to produce lasting changes in the behavior of autistic children. Once properly trained, they can provide continuous treatment for the child throughout the day. Literally every activity at home and at school becomes a learning experience. The child learns to dress and feed himself, to go to the bathroom alone, to play with toys and other children. At school he learns not only reading, writing and speaking, but also how to play with groups of supervised and unsupervised children, and how to behave in a classroom.

It is difficult to say just how much progress the children will make under this treatment, since the school programs developed through our training studies are quite new. They are at the Pachappa School, in Riverside, California, the Orcutt Autistic Class in Orcutt, California, and the Princeton Child Development Institute in Princeton, New Jersey. We can say that the children's appropriate behavior is steadily increasing, and that both parents and teachers are extremely pleased.

We can make some systematic report on 16 children who participated in our first experimental classroom during the years 1971 to 1973. All of them had been diagnosed as autistic by agencies not associated

with our research. All were severely psychotic. Six were completely mute, and the rest displayed minimal if any intelligible verbal behavior. All engaged in a great deal of self-stimulatory behavior. Most were too disruptive to be tested on standardized intelligence tests. Although their average age was seven, their average social development ranged from two to four years. All had been expelled from or denied admission to regular public schools or special education classes. Four had been placed unsuccessfully in programs for retarded children.

Using the behavior-mod procedures described above, one teacher, two aides, and two parttime speech therapists began to teach these children to respond to commands, to imitate, and to use an elementary vocabulary as well as some reading and arithmetic skills. Ten of the 16 children were discharged within 18 months, and went on to regular or special education classes in the public schools. The other six still attend special schools for autistic children, developed from our model. While

their progress has been slow, we expect them to be able to attend regular classes one day.

We do not claim to be able to cure autism; and some autistic children may never be completely normal. But we have found that all can achieve significant progress. Regardless of the degree of difficulty, we have not yet seen an autistic child who could not improve enough to be educated in a school program if his parents and teachers receive proper training.

All of the parents who have received our behavior-mod training report that it helps them not only with their autistic children, but also with their other, normal children. This raises an interesting point: perhaps the rearing of children is too important to be left to intuition. Society has provided training programs for most other important professions, yet offers prospective parents nothing but Dr. Spock, mothers-in-law, and tradition. Instead of letting everyone simply bumble on with the traditional trial-and-error method, perhaps it is time for research-based programs for training parents.

18

IMPAIRED CHILDREN:

by Judith Bloch

Photos: Jeff Sanderoff

During a break in classroom activity, a teacher comforts children. Insert: A youngster works on language development.

For a long time, through the 1950s and 1960s, there was an inadvertent silent conspiracy between parents and professionals to resist early identification of the young, impaired child who presented no clear or gross organic abnormalities. High-risk children between the ages of 18 months and 5 years, and even those with serious problems in learning, language or behavior, all too frequently were not identified or evaluated. Preschool programs for these children, who were not considered eligible for a regular nursery school, were not available.

Professional reluctance to identify atypical children under 3 years of age may be partially attributed to the difficulty in diagnosing the emotionally disturbed, and to the limitations of formal testing procedures. The lack of suitable programs for children and the discomfort of professionals as well as parents in dealing with this problem also delayed identification of the children.

The traditional professional assumption that a behaviorally disordered child has been psychogenically produced by the parents, especially the mother, tended to make mothers the targets of examination and therapy. Parents—shamed, anxiety-ridden and burdened with child care—did not press for services for their children. As a result, there were decades

Reprinted from *Children Today* Magazine. November/December 1978. U.S. Department of Health, Education and Welfare.

Helping Families Through The Critical Period of First Identification

of obsessive professional preoccupation with diagnosis and etiology, and a dearth of programs for the impaired child.

Today, however, there is increasing community concern about early identification of children with developmental lags or deviant behavior. Professional and parental denial is less frequent. The new federal legislation, PL 94-142 which mandates a public school education for all handicapped 3-year-olds, recognizes the importance of education for developmentally disabled and handicapped young children. The increasing number of applicants for this kind of service reflects certain attitudinal changes: the growing acceptance of the value of early identification and its potential for remediation and a readiness to reconsider the assumptions of psychogenic causality. Today more clinicians agree that behavior is complex and multi-determined. As a result, many more methods for working with children and their families have been established.

However, the initial tasks for all professionals remain the evaluation and assessment of a child's difficulties and a beginning recommendation regarding remediation. All this must be accomplished without alienating or undermining the confidence of the family, since a working partnership with the parents will be necessary in order to have the greatest influence on the child's behavior. If we understand why so many couples choose to assume the obligations of parenthood, we will be better prepared to work with them and their children.

The wish to become a parent is prompted by a variety of needs and expectations, among which is the desire to expand one's circle of loved ones—to love and be loved. Virginia Satir discusses this eloquently in her book *Conjoint Family Therapy*.[1] For fathers, parenting may mean an assertion of manhood, for mothers, a fulfillment of their biological destiny. We choose parenthood for many different reasons, but the hope is always

that this will be a time of emotional enhancement. With conception and parenthood come aspirations for the family, dreams of love, security and achievement. The plan is for a healthy, happy child. The expectation is that the child will be an asset, although the specific form of this fulfillment depends on individual parental needs and fantasies. For many this is a critical way to satisfy a need for purpose and responsibility. Some see parenthood as a second opportunity to satisfy their own unfulfilled childhood needs or to realize thwarted adult ambitions. Still others may hope that parenthood will be a means of providing protection and care for themselves in their old age.

Parental expectations and fantasies are threatened by acknowledgement of a child's impairment. Parental denial serves to protect the family's self-esteem and image, while professional confirmation of pathology in a child challenges those dreams. The family then feels set apart.

Denial of a child's impairment offers parents additional time to become accustomed to the pain and disappointment these changes in family expectations and self-concept bring. Thus, we can see that the family, at the point of first early identification of impairment, is a family in crisis. Even as parents bring their child for diagnosis and evaluation, their questions focus on prognosis and outcome. At the same time that a parent acknowledges some impairment, he or she seeks reassurance that the child will be all right, that is, will be ready for a regular kindergarten in two years. The worry is not only about today, but tomorrow as well.

The Pre-Schooler's Workshop

Our Pre-Schooler's Workshop, a voluntary agency, was established in 1966 as a community-based alternative to state hospital care for the seriously impaired child and as a facility for early identifica-

tion, evaluation and education of the young child who is delayed or deviant in development.[2] At present, the agency serves families with children between the ages of two and seven who have learning, language or behavior problems.

Diagnoses of children served include childhood schizophrenia, infantile autism, hyperkinesis, behavior and emotional disorders and developmental lags. The school provides the kind of experiences and environment which can influence children's behavior in ways that may not be possible later.

The program is implemented in a therapeutic nursery/kindergarten where the emphasis is on social, emotional and intellectual development and acquisition of basic skills and language. The objective is to maximize each child's potential, enabling some to move on to attendance at a public school facility or, when an impairment is more severe, to develop enough self-care and communicative skills to avoid institutionalization.

The atypical child we serve places the nuclear family at risk. Research indicates that marital problems, divorce, suicide and alcoholism are more prevalent in families of handicapped children. Therefore we strive to provide services that will protect and support the basic family unit. Our experience demonstrates that a parent-professional team partnership is one way to provide this support.

The intent in our work with the family is to develop a system of support and intervention that will encourage and enable parents to participate in their child's program, one that will embrace agreed-upon priorities and objectives. The first stage of this process is the one I will discuss in this article. It begins with the parent's initial contact with the agency—the very first telephone call to the school—which is the first of many

Judith Bloch, ACSW, is director of the Pre-Schooler's Workshop in Syosset, New York.

steps taken in establishing a therapeutic alliance which usually continues for two or three years.

The school social worker is the first professional the parent usually has contact with and he or she remains available throughout the screening and admission procedures, providing information about our school or dealing with immediate and pressing parental concerns of child management during any of the initial "waiting" periods, which are kept as brief as possible. In serving as a liaison agent between school and home, this worker can help parents understand our concept of a coordinated system.

Later, the professional staff and parents will work together to evaluate the family resources, coping skills and priorities that will be crucial determinants in the family's plan for participating in their child's program. But at this stage the primary hope is simply to establish a link with the social worker that will facilitate the development of the therapeutic alliance between school and home. The quality of this first parent-professional dialogue, during a time of heightened anxiety and tension as parents seek a diagnosis and program, will influence the pattern to follow. Unfortunately, too many case records indicate that hospitals, agencies and clinicians are often inaccessible during this important period when parents seem most vulnerable, open and ready to collaborate. Typically, some school professionals become available, following their own timetables, after a semester begins, often too late for parents who have already been compelled to arrive at their own resolution in the absence of professional help. Under such circumstances, negotiating an agency system serves only to further tax a family's emotional and coping resources.

During this period of early identification of impairment, even strong, intact families may appear disorganized and chaotic, so much so that professionals may falsely assume that there has been a good deal of long-standing parental pathology or serious marital problems, and that these have been responsible for creating or aggravating the child's difficulties. The formerly widespread acceptance of the concept of inadequate mothering may have been based on too many such clinical impressions.

In *A Child Called Noah* Josh Greenfeld shares a harrowing account of his reactions as the father of an autistic child.[3] This painfully honest diary chronicles daily family living that is filled with more stress and pain than any family should have to bear. In the beginning phase of dawning awareness that his beautiful son is impaired, Mr. Greenfeld and his wife experience dramatic fluctuations in mood. They alternate between fear, tears and guilty preoccupations that lead to marital quarrels and accusations, and then wild hope, despite their recognition of the severity of Noah's impairment.

In our experience at Pre-Schooler's Workshop, parental response appears to follow a similar pattern, a developmental sequence not unlike that of terminally ill patients who have been given information regarding their diagnosis. Elizabeth Kubler-Ross describes this at length in *On Death and Dying.*[4] At first, the tendency of those patients and our parents is to deny either the problem (totally or partially) or the implications of the pathology. Following this, parents of children at our school may have extended periods of mourning or social isolation as the family struggles to maintain its emotional balance. Denial can be seen as a means of keeping affect within bearable limits. It serves to help parents cope with the guilt that follows a wish that the child had not been born, had been born different, or had not been born into their family.

The professional literature describes mothers of these children as perplexed and anxious. While we too have seen uncertainty and confusion in many mothers, it seems a normal reaction to the unpredictable, chaotic behavior of their atypical child and the uncertainty of the course to follow. A parent or mothers group established at this beginning phase can impact upon each family's overwhelming sense of isolation. Parents can provide one another with a mutual support system that will emerge as a result of sharing a common experience. One mother, who participated in such a parent group at our school, spoke of the enormous relief she felt in meeting other families with similar difficulties. Despite the vast differences in education, social status, income and interests among the families in the group, she experienced a sense of community and understanding that eased some of her gnawing anxiety and chronic stress. The group meeting, she told us, marked the first time that she could talk comfortably about her child, without apology or shame, and the first place where she and her child were accepted without embarrassing questions.

Her comments support our observations that such a group is helpful in facilitating parents' movement from one stage to another. In this instance, many of the parents moved in just a few weeks from a stage marked by feelings of isolation, fear, uncertainty and helplessness to one of group participation, mutual support and problem-solving. A non-judgmental group setting permitted these parents to share and spontaneously unburden themselves of worries and fears common to all parents of impaired children, and thus the group became a vehicle for learning. While each parent responded to and utilized the group in his or her own unique manner, the group experience hastened the adapting process for all.

We recently interviewed a young couple with a severely impaired first-born child. As her daughter approached her third birthday and did not seem to be making any gains, the mother became increasingly immobilized until she was barely able to plan for or care for the child. As a result of the questioning and scrutiny of a traditionally oriented psychiatrist with a psychogenic view of behavior, she had become obsessed with thoughts and questions related to her very clearly ambivalent maternal responses. She began to compare her "failure" with her only child with her mother's success in rearing a large family of 10 children.

She and her husband withdrew from their active social and business life. She was also unable to tell her siblings of her concern regarding her daughter. In the parent group at our school, where they had come to seek a diagnosis, the couple found that they were not alone in their pain, confusion and rage. The group experience was critical in freeing the mother to begin to become more active in her own and her child's behalf.

For some parents, there is an intensification of grief as their denial diminishes and they come to a greater realization that their child's difficulties may be long-lasting, that all the pathology may not be reversible, and that there may be limitations to their child's potential capacity to learn and to function. Mourning sets in for the death of those dreams and expectations for their children that many parents so tenaciously hold onto. This period of sadness can be long and painful as the family begins to understand it must relinquish some of its expectations of emotional gratification from parenthood. Awareness of their child's special problems compels parents to reorder their dreams. This mourning process and its impact on the family has been described by Albert J. Solnit.[5]

The resentment and anger demonstrated by many of our parents again parallels the sequence described by Kubler-Ross. It seems to accompany or follow the denial process, although there is no rigid schedule. Many of our parents have expressed rage at the injustice of being singled out to carry a special burden, of being deprived of their anticipated joy in parenthood. They are angry because they feel impotent and they are afraid they will not be able to help their child. This anger may sometimes complicate parental dialogue with the professional community or interfere with the necessary planning for the child. Unfortunately, in their grief, parents may misdirect this anger towards their spouse or child. Josh Greenfeld was speaking not only for himself but for many other parents when he wrote:

"I also notice that I have become more distrustful of Foumi [his wife], have lost some of my faith in her, so necessary for our marriage, for any marriage, because she has borne me Noah. Even though genetically, I suspect, it is I who am the cause. But worse than cheating or mutual suspicion when it comes to unfixing the mystique that glues a marriage, I guess, is to have a disturbed kid. At first I thought it would draw us closer together, necessarily cement our relationship. Now Foumi and I have to be wary that it doesn't draw us apart. We have to be intelligent enough to realize there is a strain on any marriage whenever a baby is sick. And we always have a sick baby."[6]

Given an understanding of these feelings—the parents' wish to deny the problem because of the pain it brings and the need to acknowledge the problem in order to begin a program of remediation—what should the professional do? Clearly one cannot be a party to the denial. On the other hand, a confrontation of the parental pattern of denial with a premature focus on the child's prognosis may push the family to an even deeper level of sorrow. The basic family unit must be protected so that coping capabilities and problem-solving behaviors, now and in the years to come, will be enhanced. The professional must understand that he or she is dealing with a family in crisis and at risk.

Establishing A Therapeutic Alliance

Because at first the family is most likely to perceive their child's problems as paramount and other family needs as subordinate, the initial phase lends itself to the establishment of a therapeutic alliance with parents through a focus on the evaluation of the child's functioning. The task in the initial stage of professional dialogue is to identify the problem, the child's current level of functioning and the most suitable program for remediation. This must and can be a joint effort. In our experience, most parents have been reliable informants and should participate in the assessment process. This gives them a meaningful task to perform, one which contributes to the remedial program that follows and which helps to counteract the parents' feelings of impotence.

At the Pre-Schooler's Workshop (PSW), we have developed a comprehensive evaluation instrument and systematized the assessment procedure. Now, both professionals and parents use the same instrument, at the same time, as they independently observe and record the child's behavior in order to arrive jointly at a baseline for behavior assessment. The *PSW Assessment Instrument* is designed to record the child's current level of functioning with self-help, language, social, affective, cognitive and motor skills. Most of the items surveyed do not require a formal testing session but are the products of observations made in school by the teacher, speech pathologist and psychologist and in the home by the parents.

The assessment instrument provides valuable information about the child's performance and specific developmental skills, as well as his or her deficiencies. It is administered at regular intervals and serves to facilitate the development of each child's individualized education program. Parental participation in this assessment is required and vividly demonstrates to family members the essential role they can play in planning for their child.

A small excerpt from the *PSW Assessment Instrument* is shown in the accompanying chart. The behaviors listed in column I are typical of normal stages of development; those listed in column II are deviant or interfering behaviors, or behaviors appropriate only to a very young toddler.

For the family, the task of observation, with its focus on doing, rather than introspecting, provides immediate relief from tension and confusion. It also gives the family a better understanding of their child's current level of functioning, and specific information regarding realistic, short-term expectations.

We believe that the traditional practice of extensive history-taking in the first

Photo: Rita Bernstein

A moment of closeness at the Pre-Schooler's Workshop.

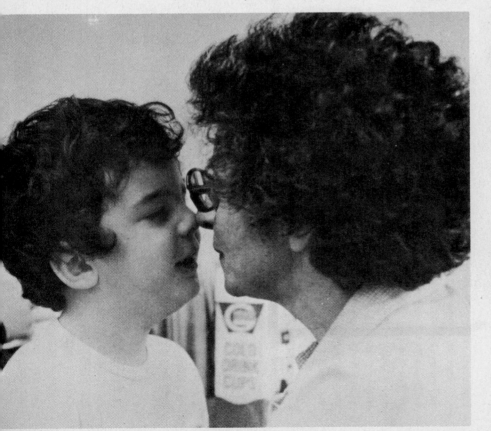

interview, with its focus on the mother's feelings and attitudes before, during and after pregnancy, should be discontinued. This type of investigation serves only to heighten a mother's anxiety and uncertainty and interferes with the need to mobilize her strength for the tasks ahead. In this first stage, we do not confront parents with their denial or anger or seek to elicit their feelings about their child's handicap, although we do not avoid opportunities to enable both mother and father to make contact with and express their painful inner feelings. The intent of our contacts during this first stage is to support parents, to begin the process of problem-solving, and to reduce unproductive parental preoccupations with guilt and etiology.

From the onset, it is important to indicate one's professional attitude and stance. At our school we are open about our biases regarding the etiology of impairment. We state our assumption that there are biological as well as environmental and psychological determinants of behavior and in our initial interviews we tell parents they are not considered responsible for creating their child's disorder. On the other hand, parents are told that they, like all parents, can have great influence on their child's behavior. We also explain that since atypical children are more fragile and vulnerable, their parents must be more consistent and "perfect" than parents of other children—a most difficult task.

We indicate our interest and readiness to work with them now on assessment of their children, and later on amelioration, in a manner that is compatible with their lifestyle and our professional diagnosis. While a better understanding of the family's reaction patterns does lead to generalizations, no family should be so categorized that there is no allowance for the individualization which must become the cornerstone of all our work with parents. There will always be too many variables which will affect the parental adaptive response. We have found that with time family needs and priorities are likely to change. This first collaboration around assessment, if successfully achieved, sets the stage for future parent-team alliances.

Our staff has had the experience of observing gains in functioning in seriously impaired youngsters and is confident that a parent-professional team can enhance a child's development. A cautiously optimistic approach toward the likelihood of an improvement in the child's functioning as a result of this alliance is stated at the beginning of our work with a family.

Parents are also told that they will be given written copies, at regular intervals, of the professional staff reports detailing their child's functioning in self-help, social and cognitive skills and in motor and language development. Such permanent written records serve to counteract any parental tendency to persistent denial of the implications of the child's pathology. The records focus on the next anticipated skill to be mastered and the remediations necessary. This results in an implicit expectation of achievement. At the same time, parents have on hand reports to which they may repeatedly refer, in the more anxiety-free setting of their home, rather than hurriedly in a professional's office. This enables them to review and integrate the findings, at their own pace and as often as they find necessary, and to have a file documenting their child's development.

I have discussed the beginnings of the mourning/grieving process for the family. Its subsequent course will be affected by the nature of parental expectations, their resources and vulnerabilities, and their child's progress. The quality of encounter the family has with the professionals can significantly ease this painful process. The initial parent/professional exchange should set the stage for the long-term therapeutic alliance that the family must form with the professional community in order to protect the family and enhance the child's development. ∎

Excerpt from *Pre-Schooler's Workshop Assessment Instrument*
Relationship to Other Children

Column I

- Demonstrates leadership ability.
- Engages in cooperative organized play without close adult supervision.
- Demonstrates attachment to particular child or children.
- Enjoys attention of other children.
- Initiates play with other children.
- Shares play objects.
- Takes turns in play.
- Understands and shares emotions of other children.
- Plays simple group games with adult help.
- Chooses to play alongside other children rather than alone.
- Watches and may imitate play of other children.

Column II

- Ignores or is unaware of other children.
- Avoids interaction even when approached by other children.
- Aggressive with other children (e.g., bites, hits, kicks, teases, provokes, bosses, criticizes, etc.).
- Unable to participate in group activities unless closely supervised by teacher/adult.
- Unable to participate in group activities at all.

[1] Virginia Satir, *Conjoint Family Therapy*, 2nd Revised Ed., Palo Alto, Science and Behavior Books, 1967.

[2] See Judith Bloch, "A Preschool Workshop for Emotionally Disturbed Children," *Children*, Jan.-Feb. 1970.

[3] Josh Greenfeld, *A Child Called Noah*, New York, Holt, Rinehart and Winston, 1972.

[4] Elisabeth Kubler-Ross, *On Death and Dying*, New York, Macmillan Publishing Co., Inc., 1970.

[5] Albert J. Solnit and Mary H. Stark, "Mourning and the Birth of a Defective Child," *The Psychoanalytic Study of the Child*, Vol. XVI, 1961.

[6] Greenfeld, op. cit.

19

The Stresses of Treating Child Abuse

by Stuart Copans, Helen Krell, John H. Gundy, Janet Rogan and Frances Field

Child maltreatment is a serious and widespread problem. It is estimated that in the United States alone more than one million children are victims of physical abuse or neglect each year and at least 2,000 children die annually from circumstances associated with abuse or neglect.

With heightened public and professional awareness of this problem, there has been a tremendous increase in the number of cases reported and in the attention focused on the care given to families in which child abuse or neglect has occurred or seems likely to occur.

Traditionally, a wide range of community workers and agencies have provided basic human services to these high risk families: private physicians, public health nurses, visiting nurses, school health personnel, child health clinics, neighborhood health centers, physician's assistants, hospital emergency room personnel, welfare departments and mental health clinics. As increased knowledge of the etiology and treatment of child abuse is gained, these community personnel are asked to provide specific psychological treatments along with medical follow-up and social support.

Work with these high risk families is difficult, and often it does not help the family's problem. In some cases this is because resources are too limited or intervention begins too late but in many cases it is the lack of adequate training and support for workers that hampers the delivery of care. Work with high risk families is particularly difficult because of the highly charged feelings aroused by such work. These feelings often prevent workers from making proper decisions and mitigate against good management of cases, even when the cases are adequately understood. A crucial part of a worker's training involves learning to recognize, examine and work with these feelings. However, the process does not stop with training, and ongoing support for such self-examination should accompany any job involving work with high risk families.

In this article we will describe an experimental child abuse training program developed for a wide range of community workers involved in the care of high risk

"Feeling Totally Responsible For Assigned Families"

Drawings: Stuart Copans

Reprinted from *Children Today* Magazine, January/February 1979. U.S. Department of Health, Education and Welfare.

families and examine the factors that frequently interfere with the delivery of effective care. The program was designed by a pediatrician, a social worker, a public health nurse and two child psychiatrists. It included a study group which met weekly for six months in order to focus on the feelings and conflicts aroused during the course of working with abusing or potentially abusing families.[1]

The Training Group

The training group grew out of a monthly pediatric conference initiated in 1975 at a rural medical center—the Dartmouth-Hitchcock Medical Center, Hanover, New Hampshire—by an interdisciplinary regional "Children-At-Risk" program. The task of this monthly pediatric conference is to coordinate the care given to the high risk families seen in the hospital or at its out-patient clinics with the care offered by neighboring community agencies. During these conferences it had become apparent that although the many professionals and para-professionals working with these families were familiar with the literature related to child abuse, they often felt that they lacked sufficient emotional support for their efforts and that they needed help in learning how to deal with the feelings their work aroused in them. As a result, they were uncomfortable working with the families and often made inappropriate decisions about how to manage their cases.

For example, after one conference, a physician who was an authority on child abuse casually mentioned a case that had recently come through the emergency room of his hospital. The emergency room nurse and the pediatric social worker had consulted him about a child with a laceration, which the mother stated she had inflicted. The physician reported that he was ambivalent about making a child abuse report—even though he knew that there was a significant risk to the child of serious future injury and he recognized the parents' need for child behavior counseling—because he was a friend of the family and considered reporting the incident to be a punitive act.

Another case presented at one of the conferences involved a child who had been brought into the emergency room eight times because of injuries, including one instance when the parents reported that the child had received his injuries by falling on an ice pick. Both the father's cardiologist and his psychotherapist, who had been asked to attend the high risk conference, said that they would not recommend that the pediatrician involved report the case to Protective Services because doing so would be harmful to the father. Another worker present at the conference suggested that the fact that the child's mother worked in the hospital was another reason for not reporting the case to Protective Services.

In a third case, a diagnosis of child abuse had been made and the protective services agency notified. Since the protective services worker had too large a caseload to see the family as often as necessary, the reporting physician had arranged to have a public health nurse also work closely with the family. The nurse was moralistic and judgmental and the protective services worker could see that her approach to the family was inappropriate and ineffective. However, she was unable to discuss this observation with either the nurse or the reporting physician.

A fourth case involved an adolescent girl brought to the mental health center by her mother, who was angry because the girl had complained of neglect by her mother. During the evaluation, the psychiatrist learned that the mother's boyfriend, who was living with the family, had engaged in serious sexual play with the girl, once directly in front of the mother, who claimed she was "too tired" to protest. A protective services worker subsequently visited the family, at which time the incident was admitted to but minimized, and the worker decided that no additional involvement was necessary. Although the psychiatrist thought this decision was inappropriate, he did not follow up the case himself.

In all four cases, it was not lack of knowledge that prevented the provision of adequate care for high risk families but rather an inability to translate knowledge into action because the professionals involved lacked training and/or support in dealing with their feelings. It was for these reasons that a group training program was planned for community workers.

The group consisted of two co-leaders and 11 participants, including four social workers, two case aide workers, five registered nurses and one outreach worker. The agencies represented included three home health agencies from two states, a day care center, a community mental health center, a medical school outreach project and a federally funded Children and Youth Project.

The training began with a one-day seminar to present

Stuart Copans, M.D., is Director, Child-Adolescent Mental Health Center, Brattleboro Retreat, Brattleboro, Vt., and Assistant Clinical Professor of Psychiatry, Dartmouth Medical School, Hanover, N.H. Helen Krell, M.D., is Assistant Professor of Psychiatry; John H. Gundy, M.D., is Associate Professor of Clinical Pediatrics; and Frances Field, M.N., is Assistant Professor of Maternal and Child Health, all at Dartmouth Medical School. Janet Rogan, ACSW, is a pediatric social worker at Mary Hitchcock Memorial Hospital, Hanover, N.H. Their article is based on a paper selected as best of nearly 100 submitted to the 1978 National Child Abuse and Neglect Conference.

basic knowledge about child abuse and continued with 1½-hour group meetings once a week for six months. The task of the group was to examine the feelings aroused in workers by their work and to discuss how these feelings aided or interfered with effective delivery of care.

Factors That Interfere With Delivery Of Care

It is clear that knowledge about child abuse does not always lead to effective management of cases. What makes it so difficult for workers with adequate knowledge to function as competent professionals when dealing with high risk families?

Through group discussions 11 major sets of feelings and processes that frequently interfere with effective delivery of care by workers were identified. These were:

- Anxieties about being physically harmed by angry parents and about the effects of a decision.
- Denial and inhibition of anger.
- Need for emotional gratification from clients.
- Lack of professional support.
- Feelings of incompetence.
- Denial and projection of responsibility.
- The feeling that one is totally responsible for families assigned to a worker.
- The difficulty in separating personal from professional responsibility.
- Feelings of being victimized.
- Ambivalent feelings toward clients and about one's professional role.
- The need to be in control.

Each of these sets of feelings warrants more detailed discussion.

Anxiety About Physical Harm

Anxieties about physical harm are common in work with high risk families. In many cases there is a history of violence and it is appropriate and realistic to be frightened and to ask for assistance. However, very often the anxiety is irrational and unconsciously determined.

For example, one worker visited a mother in a family with a history of abuse. She told the mother that it would be necessary to involve Protective Services and that she would return the next day to discuss this when both the father and mother would be at home. The mother predicted that the father, who had beaten her in the past, would surely "beat up" the worker when she returned.

Initially the worker became quite fearful and panicky and felt totally unable to return to the home, although she realized that wives in abusive families often suggest that a worker will be harmed by the man in the house, as a way of telling the worker not to come back. After a discussion with her supervisor, she arranged to have another worker accompany her on her visit with the

father and mother. In the group she was able to describe her initial anxiety and inability to proceed with the case as being related to her own childhood experiences and fears of her father. As a result of the group discussion, she was able to return to the family without fear. In fact, once she stopped reacting to the father as if he were her own father, she found him to be in great distress about the family situation and willing to have her help.

Anxiety About The Effects of A Decision

An example of this form of anxiety was given by a nurse who had been working with an alcoholic mother for over a year. It had become clear that the children were being mistreated; yet the mother kept promising to do better and threatened to kill herself if the children were taken away. The nurse was reluctant to report the case because of the mother's threat. After the group discussed the case, the nurse filed a report, the children were removed from the home, and the mother sought help from a local Alcoholics Anonymous group for the first time. The nurse was able to see that her fear that

"Anxieties About Being Physically Harmed By Angry Parents"

she would be responsible for the mother's suicide had led her to act inappropriately, exposing the children to unnecessary risk.

Need For Emotional Gratification From Clients

Most workers wanted to be liked by their clients and to feel professionally competent. High risk families typically do not gratify these needs, causing much frustration for the worker. One worker from an outreach project recognized her need for gratification through discussion of the following case.

The worker had been seeing a family at home several times a week. Each time she had visited the family she had been asked to do a favor for one of the members. Soon the favors occupied the whole visiting period and longer, as she was asked to do such things as drive the mother to an art show and borrow money for the family from a local priest. The worker began to feel that she was being "used" but hated herself for having that feeling. The family liked her but she was becoming angry with them, and she also recognized that the family was not making any progress. As she discussed this case in the group, it became obvious to her that she did these favors for the family because she needed them to like her and to be grateful to her. By satisfying her own need to be liked, she was fostering excessive dependency. Once the group helped her to identify her need to be gratified by her clients, she was able to set limits on their demands on her, and they began to solve their own problems more effectively.

This same worker began to question her motives relating to other aspects of her behavior on this case. Through introspection in the group and through insights obtained from other members, she realized that she had been avoiding the mother's boyfriend and knowledge of his continued bruising of a child because she was afraid of him. As a result of working through her feelings in the group, she was able to approach the boyfriend's behavior therapeutically. She found him to be sad, lonely and jealous of the attention the mother had gotten from her and very responsive to help. Subsequently, complaints from the neighbors that the boyfriend was beating the child ceased. Other group members also discovered that they acted inappropriately at times out of fear or to make their clients like them. Almost every group member also said that one of the most difficult things about his or her work was the clients' lack of appreciation.

Lack Of Professional Support

Lack of support from their professional "family" of co-workers seemed a common problem among group members. This lack of ability to support one another was closely linked to the need for support mentioned earlier. As one worker put it, "I've got so much to deal with, I don't feel like having anybody else unload their problems on me."

One worker offered an example from her own agency. A new worker was having severe emotional difficulties. The other agency workers refused to recognize the man's symptoms and he was allowed to continue to work. The group member who was attempting to deal with the situation alone had become so angry and agitated that she was unable to do her own work effectively. Finally, she came to the group in tears, asking for support. She had held back such a request earlier out of fear of "breaking down" in front of the group. Apparent in this case was a reluctance to admit "weakness" in self or others. Such reluctance is common and leads to difficulty in asking for, or giving, professional support.

After group discussion of this difficult problem the worker returned to her agency and, by dealing directly with the head of the program, was able to obtain professional help for the disturbed worker and to have him temporarily relieved of his clinical responsibilities.

Workers frequently came to the group with difficult cases they had not been able to discuss with their fellow workers or supervisors. Prior to the formation of the group, they had rarely discussed the uncomfortable feelings aroused in their work. As the group progressed,

"Denial And Inhibition Of Anger"

members were able to bring their feelings and conflicts into open discussion and, later, to resolution in their own agencies.

Denial And Inhibition Of Anger

One worker described an instance when she had waited outside a house in the rain for hours knowing that the mother whom she had come to visit was inside, although no one answered when she rang the doorbell. When asked how she had felt about the situation, the worker said, "Oh no, I wasn't angry with her." After further discussion in the group, however, she discovered that she did have angry feelings toward that family. Other members of the group said that they usually avoided this kind of child abuse case and had become aware that their avoidance was one way of expressing anger that they did not consciously recognize. As one worker put it, "The nice thing about having a large caseload is that when a case gets too difficult or frustrating, you can ignore it for a while because you always have too much else to do."

Feelings Of Incompetence

Feelings of incompetence seemed universal among our group members. These feelings are hardly surprising given the difficulties inherent in their work and their inability to support one another.

One very competent worker said that she felt professionally inadequate most of the time. Since she rarely received comments on her work, she assumed it was not good. It was a great relief to her to discover that others shared these feelings of failure. As a result of recogniz-

ing this problem in the group, many workers returned to their agencies and asked for critical feedback on their work. Most of them also felt much less incompetent, as they could see from case discussions that there is generally no "best way" or "right answer" in such work.

Denial And Projection Of Responsibility

An outreach worker in the group told how she had been working with a family for several months and suspected that one of the children had been abused. She reported this and discussed the case briefly with the protective services worker, who agreed to see the family very soon. The outreach worker ceased to work with the family, assuming that the other worker had taken over. Two months later she checked on the family and discovered that they had never been seen by the protective services worker. The outreach worker was furious. After "stewing" about it for several days, she called the worker and "gave him hell" for not seeing the family. He became defensive and angry. He said that since he had such an overwhelming caseload he attended first to cases in which no other agency was involved, and that the outreach worker should have been following the family. In this case, each worker had denied his or her own responsibility and assigned it to the other. Meanwhile, the family had been attended by no one. In the group these two people were able to resolve their differences and to devise a treatment plan by which the family obtained necessary services.

Feeling Totally Responsible For Assigned Families

Workers frequently described feeling that they were totally responsible for the families assigned to them. This was generally much more of a problem than their refusal to assume responsibility.

One protective services worker in the group was following the case of an infant being cared for by his 86-year-old grandfather and his mentally retarded mother. The worker knew removal of the child would be very painful for the grandfather, who was quite attached to the child, and felt that if he removed the child, he would be personally responsible for the grandfather's suffering. After much discussion in the group, the worker was able to see that he had taken on too much responsibility in this case. Once he realized this, and some of the reasons for his behavior were worked through, he was able to see his responsibility more realistically. As a result, he went to court and asked for removal of the child who, a year later, showed dramatic developmental improvement in his foster home.

"Denial and Projection Of Responsibility"

Difficulty In Separating Personal From Professional Responsibility

One worker in the group explained that she had been a public health nurse in her native small town for several years. She had been hard-working, diligent and competent, and had worked with many high risk families. One family began calling her at any hour of the night for minor complaints and she had responded by going out to the home each time. She had become exhausted and was unable to carry out her duties and care for her own family. However, she considered it wrong to refuse to come when called; she felt it was her personal, professional responsibility to meet a client's need at any time. After much discussion in the group, she was able to set limits on clients' excessive demands. Furthermore, she was able to decide to take a day off to celebrate her daughter's birthday—something she would never have done before.

A second manifestation of the difficulty in separating personal emotional involvement from professional responsibilities was illustrated when a group member was asked to testify as an expert witness in a case of child abuse in which the state petitioned the court for termination of parental rights. After a thorough investigaion, the worker had considered it best to terminate parental rights and had so testified in court. The mother was in the courtroom at the time. During the hearing the worker began to feel guilty about her testimony. She avoided looking at the mother and had to keep telling herself to remember

"*Difficulty Separating Personal From Professional Responsibility*"

that she had been asked to make a recommendation regarding the children, not the mother. Nevertheless, the worker felt remorseful afterwards. She considered herself a failure as a professional and a "bad" person for having recommended that a mother be deprived of her children. It was only after discussing her feelings and frustrations in detail that she was able to see that she had acted properly.

Feelings Of Being Victimized

Repeatedly, the workers in the group blamed case failures and frustrations on families who "just weren't motivated," on "other agencies which weren't cooperating," or on the state government which was "full of bureaucrats who wanted to glorify themselves." This enabled the workers to avoid facing their own limitations and failures, as well as the disturbing fact that for certain families there is nothing one can do.

Often a hopeless attitude towards the system kept workers from advocating change within it. A worker from one protective services office explained, "We'll never get any more workers in our office, so why try?" Nevertheless, shortly after they had discussed this in the group a new director was able to hire two more workers for that same office.

Other participants observed that members from that office were unrealistically pessimistic. This engendered group discussion about how expecting too much from families can leave workers feeling depressed and demoralized. Case discussions among group members enabled each of them to be more realistic about their families and, as a result, members felt less "burnt out."

Ambivalent Feelings Towards Clients

Ambivalent feelings frequently interfered with effective client care. For example, one worker had been visiting a home for months. One day she gently suggested that the mother might dress her children in warmer clothes for the winter. The mother became extremely angry and shouted at the worker for over 20 minutes. The worker felt great concern for the mother and children but she also disliked the mother for becoming so angry. At first she handled this by denying both her feelings and the problem. She avoided visiting the home for weeks, using the rationale that the family's problem "wasn't that bad" and that she would do more harm going where she was not wanted. Her gnawing conscience had led her to bring the problem to the group and, as a result of the discussions about it, she became more aware of her own feelings and conflicts and was able to become involved in home visits again. Initially the mother was cool towards her but the worker persisted and slowly reestablished their trusting relationship.

"*Feelings Of Being Victimized*"

Let me down Mrs. Smith, I'm here to help you.

Other members in the group also discovered that they had acted inappropriately at times out of ambivalent feeling toward their clients.

Ambivalent Feelings About One's Professional Role

One worker talked about quitting his job because of his ambivalent feelings about it. He often worked 12-hour days, seven days a week, but then complained bitterly about the long hours. He was unable to reach a balance between feeling responsible and liking his job and feeling overworked and hating it. Sometimes when a case truly demanded after-hours care he would become resentful of that particular family. Many other group members admitted feeling the same way. Partly as a result of the group discussions, the first worker resigned from his agency, to work as a cabinetmaker for over a year. Later, he again sought work in the area of child abuse and he now sets limits on what he can do and feels much more satisfied and less ambivalent about his professional responsibilities.

The Need To Be In Control

Most workers mentioned that they had at some time felt a need to control their situation with clients or to control the clients themselves. Some had insisted on a certain degree of motivation in the parents before they would work with a family, despite their knowledge that abusing parents are difficult to work with because of their poor motivation and that it is necessary to reach out to them to establish a working relationship.

Discussion

Many persons who work with high risk families experience their own feelings, actions and doubts as evidence of their personal and professional unfitness. The members of our group felt this way even though they were, in fact, highly competent workers. Careful selection of persons hired to work with abusing families will *not* eliminate these feelings.

It is well-known that patients reestablish with their

therapists the relationships they have had with the significant people in their lives. Similarly, therapists receiving supervision of their work with such patients may try to establish this same kind of relationship with their supervisors. In the same way, problems that characterize high risk families seemed to be recapitulated in the relationship of workers to group leaders. There was a remarkable similarity between the problems and issues raised by the workers in our group and those noted in high risk families.[2]

One method of dealing with the difficulties encountered in this kind of work is to develop a continuing support group of individuals who work together. In rural areas where the families are far apart and workers often work alone, this is not feasible. Therefore, it is necessary to develop methods of training and sources of support for these workers. The group described in this paper seemed to provide an effective method for exploration and resolution of feelings and conflicts.

Training methods in psychiatry, pediatrics, nursing or social work do not prepare workers for the feelings and reactions triggered by work with families at risk for child abuse. If not recognized and examined, these feelings often interfere with the provision of good care. Workers assigned to high risk families must be given the training and support necessary to recognize and deal with these feelings and conflicts in ways helpful in the care of clients.[3] ∎

---

[1] The work described in this paper was supported by funds from the New England Resource Center for Protective Services, The Richard King Mellon Foundation and Title XX of the States of New Hampshire and Vermont.
[2] Richard Galdston, "Child Abuse and the Epidemiology of Violence," in the *Proceedings,* Second Annual Children's Advocacy Conference, Durham, N.H., April 1976.
[3] Wyman R. Sanders, "Resistance to Dealing with Parents of Battered Children," *Pediatrics,* Vol. 50, No. 6, 1972.

IV. Middle Childhood

Photograph courtesy of Phillip Whitten

The child's intellectual and social horizon expands tremendously during the middle childhood years. Meanwhile, physical growth continues, but at a slower rate than in the earlier period; at this age, the child's body proportions are already very similar to the adult's. On the average, boys are slightly taller and heavier than girls up until the age of 10, but from then until age 15, girls, on the average, surpass boys in both height and weight.

Cognitive abilities change dramatically during the school years, becoming more complex, better differentiated, and more like the adult's. As a consequence of important neurological developments that occur between five and seven, the age when formal schooling begins in most Western cultures, a number of cognitive capacities become apparent. The child is now able to remember complicated instructions, shows increased ability to inhibit inappropriate responses, and seems aware of his or her own problem-solving processes. At approximately age seven, children enter what Piaget calls the *concrete operational* stage. They develop an appreciation of transformations and can discriminate unimportant from important changes—they have achieved *conservation,* the understanding that properties of objects remain the same, even though they may appear to change. For example, the amount of water does not change when it is poured from a low, wide glass to a tall, thin one. At this stage children are able to think in terms of more than one dimension at a time; thus, in the previous example, they realize that the second glass is both taller *and* narrower than the first.

Children of this age are able to classify or understand the defining properties of classes and to decide which objects to include and which to exclude. By eight or nine they appreciate that certain classes are related to each other in a hierarchical manner—for example, that all apples belong to the class "fruit" and all fruit belongs to the class "foods." All of these abilities represent great advances over the cognitive thought processes of the preschool child.

From the point of view of socialization, attendance at school and playing outside the home provide opportunities for more sustained and closer relationships with peers and adults other than parents. The amount of time the child spends at school and other activities outside the home increases steadily from kindergarten to high school. Hence the child has many opportunities for learning new responses and imitating new and different models.

Children of this age are searching for their own places in the social world and strongly want to fit into the structure of society. Yet they seem to live in two worlds, that of their parents and other adults and that of their peers. These worlds exist side by side, but the peer group has its own culture, its own history, and its own social organizations. As agents of socialization, peers provide each other with information about kinds of behaviors that are appropriate in various situations, rewarding acceptable responses and punishing unacceptable ones. In addition, children are likely to emulate what they observe their peers doing, including both maladaptive responses (such as aggressive outbursts) and prosocial behaviors (such as donating to charity, expressing sympathy, or helping someone in distress).

Teachers may also influence the child's socialization in significant ways. Through their application of rewards and punishments, they can modify the child's behavior and, in addition, can also serve as models that children readily imitate.

The media also contribute to the process of socialization. By the time the average American child reaches adolescence he or she has spent a total of over 15,000 hours viewing television. It hardly seems possible that television viewing does not have an effect on many children's behavior. Furthermore, violence in various forms is a prevalent theme in television programs, and recent studies indicate that television violence does, in fact, instigate aggressive behavior. Nevertheless, we must be cautious about interpretation and overgeneralization, because most of the studies are conducted in contrived settings, quite different from those in which children ordinarily watch television. Although the question of the effects of this medium on children's behavior is still unresolved, it seems safe to conclude that television is in general not uplifting or beneficial to child viewers.

Psychologists have traditionally espoused the theory that parents have an overwhelming influence in shaping the child's personality and that early child-rearing practices have highly significant, enduring effects. Recently, however, some psychologists have begun to question these theories because children also differ so sharply from one another in temperamental characteristics (presumably genetically determined) and because they are socialized by many agents outside the family (for example, peers, teachers, and the media). Specifically, these psychologists maintain that broad social and historical forces, as well as other agents of socialization, play as large a role as the family in molding the child's behavior and development. The argument is well presented in Skolnick's article "The Myth of the Vulnerable Child" in this section. Although many would challenge the author's conclusions, her article cautions us not to neglect the fact that the family and its functions are strongly influenced by social, cultural, and historical contexts. As Clausen states in the article

"American Research on the Family and Socialization," the family "is responsive to the conditions of life in the society, to economic conditions, wars, and to natural catastrophies that from time to time afflict all society."

Changes in Western society occur rapidly and have strong and lasting impacts on family life. Recently, the rate of marriage has declined and the rate of divorce has increased markedly in all social classes. The number of single-parent families has doubled in a decade. Yet, until recently, there was little research on the effects of divorce on children's adjustment and development and/or on the special problems of the single parent. As these problems have become more widespread, they are now the topics of more systematic research, as the last three articles in this section demonstrate.

20

THE MYTH OF THE VULNERABLE CHILD

Anxious parents should relax. Despite what some psychologists have been telling them for years, they do not have make-or-break power over a child's development. / By Arlene Skolnick

AMERICANS HAVE LONG been considered the most child-centered people in the world. In the 20th century, this traditional American obsession with children has generated new kinds of child-rearing experts—psychologists and psychiatrists, clothed in the authority of modern science, who issue prescriptions for child-rearing. Most child-care advice assumes that if the parents administer the proper prescriptions, the child will develop as planned. It places exaggerated faith not only in the perfectibility of the children and their parents, but in the infallibility of the particular child-rearing technique as well. But increasing evidence suggests that parents simply do not have that much control over their children's development; too many other factors are influencing it.

Popular and professional knowledge does not seem to have made parenting easier. On the contrary, the insights and guidelines provided by the experts seem to have made parents more anxious. Since modern child-rearing literature asserts that parents can do irreparable harm to their children's social and emotional development, modern parents must examine their words and actions for a significance that parents in the past had never imagined. Besides, psychological experts disagree among themselves. Not only have they been divided into competing schools, but they also have repeatedly shifted their emphasis from one developmental goal to another, from one technique to another.

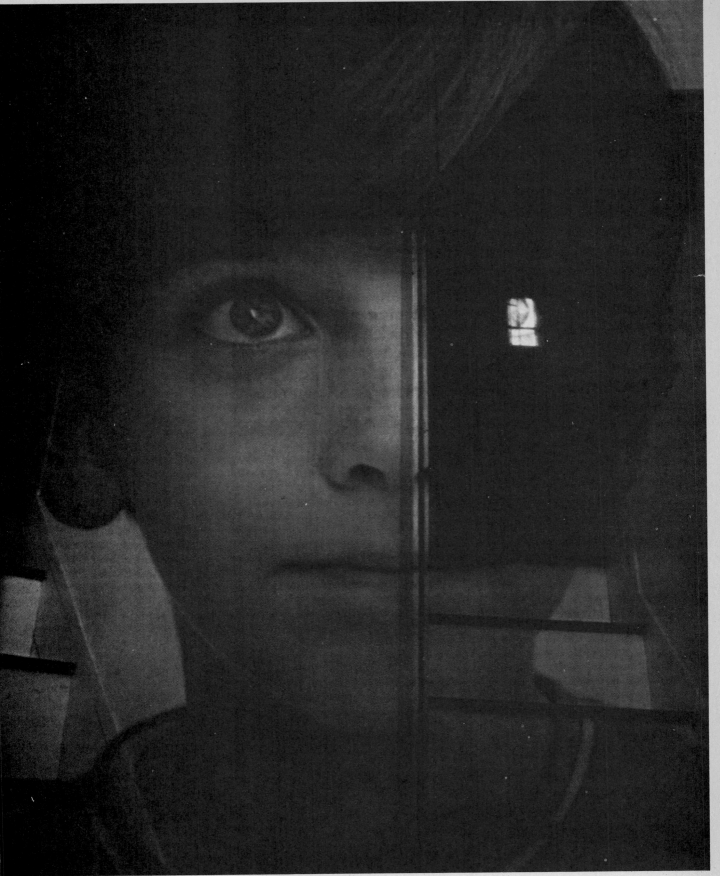

Two Models of Parenting

Two basic models of parental influence emerge from all this competition and variety, however. One, loosely based on Freudian ideas, has presented an image of the vulnerable child: children are sensitive beings, easily damaged not only by traumatic events and emotional stress, but also by overdoses of affection. The second model is that of the behaviorists, whose intellectual ancestors, the empiricist philosophers, described the child's mind as a *tabula rasa*, or blank slate. The behaviorist model of child-rearing is based on the view that the child is malleable, and parents are therefore cast in the role of Pygmalions who can shape their children however they wish. "Give me a dozen healthy infants, well-formed, and my own specified world to bring them up in," wrote J. B. Watson, the father of modern behaviorism, "and I'll guarantee to take any one at random and train him to be any type of specialist I might—doctor, lawyer, artist, merchant, chief, and yes, even beggar man and thief!"

The image of the vulnerable child calls for gentle parents who are sensitive to their child's innermost thoughts and feelings in order to protect him from trauma. The image of the malleable child requires stern parents who coolly follow the dictates of their own explicit training procedures: only the early eradication of bad habits in eating, sleeping, crying, can fend off permanent maladjustments.

Despite their disagreements, both models grant parents an omnipotent role in child development. Both stress that (1) only if parents do the right things at the right time will their children turn out to be happy, successful adults; (2) parents can raise superior beings, free of the mental frailties of previous generations; and (3) if something goes wrong with their child, the parents have only themselves to blame.

Contemporary research increasingly suggests, however, that both models greatly exaggerate the power of the parent and the passivity of the child. In fact, the children's own needs, their developing mental and physical qualities, influence the way they perceive and interpret external events. This is not to say that parents exercise no influence on their children's development. Like all myths, that of parental determinism contains a kernel of truth.

But there is an important difference between influence and control. Finally, both models also fail to consider that parent-child relations do not occur in a social vacuum, but in the complex world of daily life.

Traditionally, child-study researchers have assumed that influence in the parent-child relationship flowed only one way, from active parent to passive child. For example, a large number of studies tested the assumption, derived from Freudian theory, that the decisive events of early childhood centered around feeding, weaning, and toilet-training. It is now generally conceded that such practices in themselves have few demonstrable effects on later development. Such studies may have erred because they assumed that children must experience and react to parental behavior in the same ways.

Even when studies *do* find connections between the behavior of the parents and the child, cause and effect are by no means clear. Psychologist Richard Bell argues that many studies claiming to show the effects of parents on children can just as well be interpreted as showing children's effects on parents. For instance, a study finding a correlation between severe punishment and children's aggressiveness is often taken to show that harsh discipline produces aggressive children; yet it could show instead that aggressive children evoke harsh child-rearing methods in their parents.

> **"Many studies claiming to show parents' effects on children can just as well be interpreted as showing children's effects on parents."**

A Methodological Flaw

The image of a troubled adult scarred for life by an early trauma such as the loss of a parent, lack of love, or family tension has passed from the clinical literature to become a cliché of the popular media. The idea that childhood stress must inevitably result in psycho-logical damage is a conclusion that rests on a methodological flaw inherent in the clinical literature: instead of studying development through time, these studies start with adult problems and trace them back to possible causes.

It's true that when researchers investigate the backgrounds of delinquents, mental patients, or psychiatric referrals from military service, they find that a large number come from "broken" or troubled homes, have overpossessive, domineering, or rejecting mothers, or have inadequate or violent fathers. The usual argument is that these circumstances cause maladjustments in the offspring. But most children who experience disorder and early sorrow grow up to be adequate adults. Further, studies sampling "normal" or "superior" people—college students, business executives, professionals, creative artists, and scientists—find such "pathological" conditions in similar or greater proportions. Thus, many studies trying to document the effects of early pathological and traumatic conditions have failed to demonstrate more than a weak link between them and later development.

The striking differences between retrospective studies that start with adult misfits and look back to childhood conditions, and longitudinal studies that start with children and follow them through time, were shown in a study at the University of California's Institute of Human Development, under the direction of Jean Macfarlane. Approximately 200 children were studied intensively from infancy through adolescence, and then were seen again at age 30. The researchers predicted that children from troubled homes would be troubled adults and, conversely, that those who had had happy, successful childhoods would be happy adults. They were wrong in two-thirds of their predictions. Not only had they overestimated the traumatic effects of stressful family situations, but even more surprisingly, they also had not anticipated that many of those who grew up under the best circumstances would turn out to be unhappy, strained, or immature adults (a pattern that seemed especially strong for boys who had been athletic leaders and girls who had been beautiful and popular in high school).

Psychologist Norman Garmezy's work on "invulnerability" offers more recent evidence that children can thrive in spite of genetic disadvantages and environmental deprivations. Garmezy began by studying adult schizophrenics and trying to trace the sources of their problems. Later, he turned to developmental studies of children who were judged high risks to develop schizophrenia and other disorders at a later age. When such children were studied over time, only 10 or 12 percent of the high-risk group became schizophrenic, while the majority did not.

Other Sources of Love

The term "invulnerables" is misleading. It suggests an imperviousness to pain. Yet, the ability to cope does not mean the child doesn't suffer. One woman, who successfully overcame a childhood marked by the death of her beloved but alcoholic and abusive father, and rejection by her mother and stepmother, put it this way: "We suffer, but we don't let it destroy us."

The term also seems to imply that the ability to cope is a trait, something internal to the child. One often finds in the case histories of those who have coped with their problems successfully that external supports softened the impact of the traumatic event. Often something in the child's environment provides alternative sources of love and gratification—one parent compensating for the inadequacy of the other, a loving sibling or grandparent, an understanding teacher, a hobby or strong interest, a pet, recreational opportunities, and so on.

Indeed, the local community may play an important role in modulating the effects of home environments. Erik Erikson, who worked on the study at the Institute of Human Development, was asked at a seminar, "How is it that so many of the people studied overcame the effects of truly awful homes?" He answered that it might have been the active street life in those days, which enabled children to enjoy the support of peers when parent-child relations got too difficult.

Psychologist Martin Seligman's learned-helplessness theory provides a further clue to what makes a child vulnerable to stress. Summarizing a vast array of data, including animal experiments, clinical studies, and reports from prisoner-of-war camps, Seligman proposes that people give up in despair not because of the actual severity of their situation, but because they feel they can have little or no effect in changing it. The feeling of helplessness

is learned by actually experiencing events we cannot control, or by being led to believe that we have no control.

Seligman's theory helps to explain two puzzling phenomena: the biographies of eminent people that often reveal stressful family relations, and Macfarlane's findings that many children who did come from "ideal" homes failed to live up to their seeming potential. The theory of learned helplessness suggests that controllable stress may be better for a child's ego development than good things that happen without any effort on the child's part. Self-esteem and a sense of competence may not depend on whether we experience good or bad events, but rather on

> ## "Controllable stress may be better for a child's ego development than good things that happen without effort on the child's part."

whether we perceive some control over what happens to us.

Parents Can't Be Pygmalions

Many of the same reasons that limit the effect of events on children also limit the ability of parents to shape their children according to behavioral prescription. The facts of cognition and environmental complexity get in the way of best-laid parental plans. There is no guarantee, for example, that children will interpret parental behavior accurately. Psychologist Jane Loevinger gives the example of a mother trying to discipline her five-year-old son for hitting his younger sister: if she spanks him, she may discourage the hitting, or she may be demonstrating that hitting is okay; if she reasons with the child, he may accept her view of hitting as bad, or he may conclude that hitting is something you can get away with and not be punished for.

Other factors, interacting with the child's cognitive processes and sense of self, limit the parents' ability to shape their children. Perhaps the most basic is that parents have their own temperamental qualities that may modify

the message they convey to their children. One recurrent finding in the research literature, for example, is that parental warmth is important to a child's development. Yet warmth and acceptance cannot be created by following behavioral prescriptions, since they are spontaneous feelings.

Further, the parent-child relationship does not exist apart from other social contexts. A study of child-rearing in six cultures, directed by Harvard anthropologists John Whiting and Beatrice Whiting, found that parents' behavior toward children is based not so much on beliefs and principles as on a "horde of apparently irrelevant considerations": work pressures, the household work load, the availability of other adults to help with household tasks and child care, the design of houses and neighborhoods, the social structure of the community. All these influences, over which parents usually have little control, affect the resources of time, energy, attention, and affection they have for their children.

The effects of social class may also be very hard to overcome, even if the parent tries. Psychiatrist Robert Coles has written about poor and minority children who often come to learn from their families that they are persons of worth—only to have this belief shattered when they encounter the devaluing attitudes of the outside world. Conversely, middle-class children from troubled homes may take psychological nourishment from the social power and esteem that are enjoyed by their families in the community.

Science and the Family: Historical Roots

Given the lack of evidence for the parental-determinism model of child-rearing, why has it been so persistent? Why have we continued to believe that science can provide infallible prescriptions for raising happy, successful people and curing social problems?

As psychologist Sheldon White has recently observed, psychology's existence as a field of scientific research has rested upon "promissory notes" laid down at the turn of the century. The beginnings of modern academic psychology were closely tied to education and the growth of large public expenditures for the socialization of children. The first psychologists moved from philosophy departments to the newly forming education schools, expecting to provide scientific methods of education and child-rearing. The founding fathers of American psychology—J. B. Watson, G. S. Hall, L. M. Terman, and others—accepted the challenge. Thus, learning has always been a central focus of psychologists, even though the rat eventually came to compete with the child as the favored experimental animal.

If the behaviorists' social prescriptions conjure up images of *Brave New World* or *1984*, a more humane promise was implicit in Freudian theory. The earliest generations of Freudians encouraged the belief that if the new knowledge derived from psychoanalysis was applied to the upbringing of children, it would be possible to eliminate anxiety, conflict, and neurosis. The medical miracles achieved in the 19th and early 20th centuries gave the medical experts immense prestige in the eyes of parents. There seemed little reason to doubt that science could have as far-reaching effects on mental health as it had on physical health. Furthermore, as parents were becoming more certain of their children's physical survival, children's social futures were becoming less certain. When the family was no longer an economic unit, it could no longer initiate children directly into work. Middle-class parents had to educate their children to find their way in a complex job market. The coming of urban industrial society also changed women's roles. Women were removed from the world of work, and motherhood came to be defined as a

separate task for women, the primary focus of their lives. Psychological ideas became an intrinsic part of the domestic-science movement that arose around the end of the 19th century; this ideology taught that scientific household management would result in perfected human relationships within the home, as well as in the improvement of the larger society.

The Limits of Perfectibility

As we approach the 1980s, Americans are coming to reject the idea that science and technology can guarantee limitless progress and solve all problems. Just as we have come to accept that there are limits to growth and to our natural resources, it is time we lowered our expectations about the perfectibility of family life. Instead of trying to rear perfectly happy, adjusted, creative, and successful children, we should recognize that few, if any, such people exist, and even if they did, it would be impossible to produce such a person by following a behavioral formula. Far from harming family relations, lowered expectations could greatly benefit them.

What is more, the belief in parental determinism has had an unfortunate influence on social policy. It has encouraged the hope that major social problems can be eradicated without major changes in society and its institutions. For example, we have in the past preferred to view the poor as vic-

tims of faulty child-rearing rather than of unemployment, inadequate income, or miserable housing. Ironically, while we have been obsessed with producing ideal child-rearing environments in our own homes, we have permitted millions of American children to suffer basic deprivations. A seemingly endless series of governmental and private commissions has documented the sorry statistics on infant mortality, child malnutrition, unattended health needs, and so on, but the problems persist. In short, the standards of perfection that have been applied to child-rearing and the family in this century have not only created guilt and anxiety in those who try to live up to them, but have also contributed to the neglect of children on a national scale. ∩

Arlene Skolnick is a research psychologist at the Institute of Human Development, University of California, Berkeley. Skolnick, who received her Ph.D. from Yale, is chiefly interested in marital relationships and changes in self-concepts in later life. She has written *The Intimate Environment*, coauthored *Family in Transition* (both published by Little, Brown), and is now writing a developmental-psychology textbook for Harcourt Brace Jovanovich.

For further information, read:
Clarke, Ann M. and A. D. Clarke, eds. *Early Experience: Myth and Evidence*, Free Press, 1977. $13.95.
Garmezy, Norman. "Vulnerable and Invulnerable Children: Theory, Research and Intervention." American Psychological Association, MS 1337. 1976.
Goertzel, Victor and Mildred G. Goertzel. *Cradles of Eminence*, Little, Brown, 1978, paper, $4.95.
Macfarlane, Jean. "Perspectives on Personality Consistency and Change from the Guidance Study." *Vita Humana*, Vol. 7, No. 2, 1964.

"When I Have A Sixth-Grader"

Carol Feldman and Naomi Krigsman

21

This cartoon by Mark Lewis, which in his book accompanies the first sentence that appears at the head of this article, is one of the drawings in Part I of his book—written and illustrated "in the eyes of a person who never read a Dr. Spock book." Part II refers to one who has and includes drawings of an elephant ("My son can have any pet he wants.") and of a father patiently sitting while his son recites the Gettysburg address ("My son will be able to 'talk' to me.").

"My son will be able to do anything he wants . . . with my permission!

"And my son won't have to ask me for a baby when he really wants a dog."

This excerpt is taken from a book entitled *When I Have a Sixth-Grader* which the author, a sixth-grader, wrote as part of a school project called "Dialogue."

"Dialogue" was a project that involved everybody in the school: children, parents, teachers, administrators, the P.T.A. and pupil personnel staff members. Its goals were educational, psychological and instructional. We two school psychologists were lucky to take part in it,

Carol Feldman and Naomi Krigsman are school psychologists with the New Rochelle Public Schools, New Rochelle, New York.

Reprinted from *Children Today* Magazine, July/August 1977. U.S. Department of Health, Education and Welfare.

especially since the entire project was initiated by the children, and *they* invited *us*.

It all started when a book, *The Grass Pipe* by Robert Coles, was being discussed by some sixth-graders and their teachers in a suburban elementary public school in Westchester County, New York. Two major issues dealt with in the book, peer pressure and communication with parents, evoked personal reactions among the students and they drew many parallels between the difficulties of characters in the book and problems in their own relationships with peers and parents.

During the discussions, the children proposed that the school organize evening meetings for themselves and their parents for the purpose of examining relationships and improving communication within families. Their teachers, Ruth Hirsch and Miriam Lewinger, immediately followed through on the children's request and asked us to work out the details. It was decided that pupil personnel staff members would meet with groups

141

SHE CAN SWIM IN THE WATER
AS LONG AS SHE WANTS EVEN
IN COLD WEATHER.

Jill Castro plans a free, happy life for her sixth-grader. "She can watch the sun set every night and watch it rise every day," is a second picture caption in her book. "She can run around barefooted whenever she wants," says another.

of children, parents and teachers for an evening of "Dialogue." The principal would be the host, and the P.T.A. would serve refreshments. Everyone would have an opportunity to talk.

We first met with the teachers and the invited group leaders to plan the sessions. Each leader (five psychologists, two social workers, a psychiatrist and a guidance counselor) would involve a group of parents and children in a 90-minute discussion. The technique to be used would be up to each leader, but the goal would be the same for all groups: to stimulate open communication between adults and children. To acquaint both children and parents with how others view similar issues, we decided that the groups would be randomly composed, with no two members of a family attending the same group.

The children were then given letters to take home, inviting their parents to attend the meeting—but only if accompanied by their children.

The meeting took place in March. About 80 children, accompanied by either one or both parents, gathered in the auditorium. A welcome by the principal, an introduction by a sixth-grade teacher and an explanation of the evening's format by the school psychologist began the event. Numbers from 1 to 9 (for corresponding groups) were assigned to each member of the audience, and groups met in classrooms (also numbered 1 to 9) with the group leaders. Each teacher also attended a group. After the sessions we returned to the auditorium to hear summaries of each group's discussion.

Similar concerns were expressed by participants in all of the groups. Parents, of course, were interested in their right to parent, believing that since they were more experienced they were, therefore, better judges of what was best for their children. Children, by and large, acknowledged that right but also expected mutual trust and respect.

A common complaint was that parents make decisions —about their child's bedtime, chores, television watching and room maintenance—which often seem arbitrary to the children. When some parents took issue with these complaints, as parents are bound to do, the children conceded that the parents were right at least part of the time. One girl, asked by a parent if she thought that children should have responsibilities at home, said, "Sure, I should have some jobs to do. But why do I always have to take out the garbage?"

It was reported that several children found parents' methods of punishment unlikely to be effective: "They holler too much"; "They nag"; "They ask too many questions." One child suggested the alternative of using "positive punishment" but, when pressed, he could not define what he meant. A new slant on an old theme was offered by one child: adults have too much freedom—

"She can go anywhere in the world," Ellen Steingesser wrote next to this illustration. However, the author also noted at the end of her book: "When I have a sixth-grader I will probably be like my mother now!"

in picking their own friends, messing up their own rooms and letting the cooking slide, for example. One parent shared her impression that all too often parents take their children for granted.

The evening concluded with refreshments, served by P.T.A. members, and informal talks.

In class the next day, the children indicated that they wanted to explore the subject further, and the teachers were ready. Over the next few weeks, each child would write and illustrate a book entitled *When I Have a Sixth-Grader*. In addition to the obvious goals of encouraging their creativity and enhancing their skills in composition and art, this phase of the project would also focus on making case bindings for their books and discussion of copyright law. It was to be a literary and artistic endeavor that would yield a treasure of information to us as psychologists.

The children wanted to have another meeting with parents. We sent home questionnaires, asking parents if they thought the first meeting had been helpful and whether they would like another. Most parents answered yes to both questions. Some indicated that talking with children other than their own, as they had in the first meeting, had helped them to sharpen their listening skills, but most parents wanted to be able to attend a group with their child if they chose to. They also suggested topics for discussion.

The second meeting was held in May. From the suggested topics we selected five for discussion that evening: boy-girl relationships; discipline and setting of limits; areas of responsibilities; communication among family members; and relationships with siblings.

The evening's format followed that of the first meeting, but children and parents could choose which of the five groups they wished to join. Although not as many persons attended the second meeting, the participants expressed a good feeling about the discussions. The children were generally satisfied that fewer people attended because they had an opportunity for "a closer discussion." "I was less embarrassed to talk," one child noted. The children who attended the session on boy-girl relationships had the most to report. A number of boys felt that they had learned new techniques for talking to girls, and to anticipate how a girl might answer. One boy wondered, "When you go steady, do you just talk on the phone, or do you go to a movie?"

The children tried to turn the next day in school into one of continuing discussion. Nobody wanted to do any work. Finally it was agreed that the school psychologist would meet with a group of about 15 interested children to discuss "relationships."

In the meetings, which took place once a week for three weeks, the children's relationships with parents were of secondary concern, while their interaction with peers received the most attention. A new issue, one concerned with children's physical size and development, was raised. Girls felt self-conscious about "going with" boys who were considerably smaller in stature than they, and boys looked for reassurance that height "doesn't really matter." It is notable that when parents were present during a discussion the talk did revolve around parent-child interaction, and that it was not until the group was composed exclusively of children that such concerns receded and child-to-child relationships became the primary topic.

The "Dialogue" project was thus closed, but each child took home a book that was to be saved "until we have sixth grade children."

The "how to" books for themselves as future parents actually turned out to be books on "How I would like to be raised," without ever being acknowledged as such by the authors. In reviewing them, we were able to draw several conclusions about what some of today's 12-year-olds are thinking.

Although writing the books gave the children an opportunity to engage in an infinite degree of wishful thinking, it is remarkable that only seven girls and one boy among the 60 children in the three classes who prepared books made no acknowledgement of the need for supervision by an authority. All of the others made at least one reference to the notion that their activities and fanciful whims require some limitations, and some children apparently saw a need for having strict supervision in every sphere.

The subjects the children wrote about covered an extremely wide range, from pets and ownership of material goods to interpersonal relationships. In classifying the books according to topic categories, we found that relationships among family members—living together—received the most attention. Personal freedom with regard to such matters as restricting access to their room and maintaining it in their own way, determining bedtime, and following their own grooming and eating habits was another major concern. The sixth-graders also wanted freedom to choose friends and to hold "sleepover" parties. Thoughts about possessions, mobil-

ity, future goals, school attendance and allowances were also frequently mentioned.

Of course, implicit and never questioned in any of the books is the assumption of each young author that he or she will one day become a parent. Boys viewed themselves as future fathers of boys and girls as mothers of girls. Other possibilities simply did not occur to any child.

What made "Dialogue" a unique and worthwhile project to us? First, it is not often that all involved in one grade of a school—five classes in our case—including the children and their parents and teachers as well as school support staff, all join together in a combined effort.

Educationally, it was profitable to all involved. For many of the children, "Dialogue" represented a new way to communicate their thoughts and feelings, and a rare opportunity to share as equals in a group interchange with adults, to be listened to and to listen to others.

As they wrote their books, the children were able to engage in creative work while paying attention to grammar, spelling, vocabulary and punctuation—almost without realizing it. And, of course, the project provided lessons in art and several aspects of book production.

Psychologically, the project provided children with the experience of finding out how others—both parents and peers—feel. Many of the children reported that family discussions were now being conducted in ways new to the participants.

As school psychologists, we learned that by working closely with teachers we were able to organize a successful, multifaceted experience that provided something the children had asked for and which, at the same time, furnished a rich instructional resource.

American Research on the Family and Socialization

22

John A. Clausen

Photograph by Virginia Hamilton

The family is a basic unit of social organization in all societies. However, its composition, the functions that it serves, the division of labor within it and the allocation of its resources vary greatly from one society to another. Anthropologists, sociologists, psychologists, educators, psychiatrists, historians and political scientists have all been active in family research in the United States. They seek to answer many questions, but one focal point for almost all is how the family orients a child to the world and how it prepares him or her for full participation in society, what we commonly call *socialization*—the whole process of the child's becoming a competent member of society.

There are several approaches to studying the family as an instrument of socialization. The family is, first of all, a context or matrix for development, set in the larger social environments of the neighborhood, the culture of which it is part and the social structure, including the economic and political systems.

The family has been characterized as a unit of interacting personalities, though it has been peculiarly difficult to conceptualize that unity in operational terms. Studies of the effect of family context on child development tend therefore to focus on structural features—the size and composition of the family, the partial or total absence of a parent (usually the father, since families without mothers tend to be seen as non-families)—or they focus

on salient experiences or conditions such as economic deprivation, conflict between parents or the effects of life crises. In such research the investigator may seek (1) to delineate the ways in which socialization practices are influenced by the family's structural features or conditions of life or (2) to show that outcomes in child behavior are directly responsive to these features or conditions.

Related to the study of general features of the family as they affect the development of the child are those studies that ask how placement of the family in the larger social structure or cultural milieu influences the childrearing orientations and behaviors of parents and other agents of socialization. Social class and religious and ethnic background have been most utilized as indices of placement but features of parents' occupational experiences have also been examined recently.

Another type of investigation examines the ways in which particular orientations toward childrearing and the actual practices of parents impinge upon a child. The majority of psychologists' studies of childrearing are of

---

John A. Clausen, Ph.D., is chairman, Department of Sociology, University of California, Berkeley, and research sociologist at the university's Institute of Human Development. His article is based on an address delivered at the US-USSR Seminar on Preschool Education in Moscow, U.S.S.R.

Reprinted from *Children Today* Magazine, March/April 1978. U.S. Department of Health, Education and Welfare.

this type. They seek to learn how particular modes of parental control, techniques of reward and punishment, communication patterns and the like influence a child and his cognitive, emotional and social development and competence. For the most part, the technique of analysis is correlational, seeking to relate current parental practices to a child's current behaviors. In a few instances, longitudinal studies make it possible to trace relationships between early parental behaviors and later child outcomes.

Each student of the family is influenced by the perspective and preoccupations of his own discipline. I shall comment on a number of trends in American research that seem to me both interesting and significant; as a sociologist I shall stress studies of contextual and structural features more than studies seeking to delineate relationships between specific parental practices and child behavior.

Interest in the history of the family and of childrearing has increased enormously in the past decade, with younger historians playing a leading role. Although historical studies can tell us little about childrearing in the distant past, they have called into question earlier assumptions about the family. For example, they have demonstrated a distinct difference between the household and the family as social units in pre-industrial Europe and North America. They indicate also the greater prevalence of the nuclear family of parents and their unmarried offspring than had previously been suspected. Moreover, studies using materials available in local archives which reflect life in the past century or two do permit reconstruction of the family life course in ways that illuminate the developmental experiences of children.[1]

Another area of family research that has implications for child socialization, though not directly concerned with it, relates to the correlates and consequences of age at marriage (especially the consequences of early marriage and of pregnancies of teenagers) and to decisions about childbearing and the spacing of pregnancies. Early marriages tend to be less stable and a substantial body of research now attests to the undesirable consequences of teenage pregnancy for both mother and child.

Social Change

Social change has continued to impinge sharply on the American family. During the past decade we have witnessed an increase by one-third in the proportion of women who remain single to age 25, along with a marked decrease in the average number of children born in a family.[2] The number of working mothers has more than doubled since the end of World War II—and half of all mothers of school-aged children are now in the labor force.

Working mothers of preschool children turn where they can to a variety of child care arrangements, formal and informal. In 1974, for example, approximately 1.3 million children were in licensed or approved day care centers or in family day care, 1.7 million were in informal out-of-home care and nearly 5 million were in nursery school or pre-kindergarten programs (about three-quarters of them part-time).[3] The care received in full-time day care centers has varied greatly; research on the effects of substitute care in some of the better centers suggests few differences between children reared at home and those raised in group care settings, but many day care centers, especially proprietary centers conducted for profit, give care that can only be rated "fair" or "poor."[4]

As the rate of marriage has declined, the rate of divorce has increased at all class levels. The number of single-parent families (most often a mother and young children) has nearly doubled in a decade, as a consequence both of increasing divorce on the part of parents of young children and a rise in illegitimacy, largely accounted for by adolescent pregnancies. The very strong movement for increased rights and equal treatment for women, both in and out of the home, has undoubtedly played a part in these trends.

Household size has steadily decreased over recent decades, as more housing has become available. Alternate living arrangements as opposed to the traditional family household are on the increase. In the decade of the 1960s there was an eightfold increase in the number of household heads who live apart from relatives but share their living quarters with an adult partner of the opposite sex. Communal living arrangements of groups of adults and children have also increased. In such households children tend to be warmly loved and well cared for in the early years but not to be much supervised as they grow older.[5]

Research on the effects of these changes is still very limited. There have been a number of studies which examined the effects of the presence or absence of a parent on the child's development. Most frequently, of course, it is the father who is absent. A very careful review on the topic of "Children in Fatherless Families" concludes that there is little solid evidence that mere absence of the father produces serious distortion in the child's cognitive and emotional development or gender identity.[6] In general, the way in which a mother functions with her children is far more important than the number of adults in the household. At the same time, there can be no question but that a mother who must cope alone with problems of household and income maintenance faces a much more stressful situation than one who can count on a husband's help. Much depends on the kind of child care arrangements that can be made if the mother works, and on the mother's ability to arrange some time for relaxed enjoyment of her children. Perhaps the most consistent finding relating to the effect of father absence on children's cognitive development is that boys from such families tend to have higher verbal than mathematical skills, a reversal of normal expectation when both parents are present.

More important than his mere presence or absence is the actual role of the father in the socialization of a child. Although fathers were long neglected by students of child development, they are now being studied increasingly. Indeed, several recent books are devoted entirely to the father's role in childrearing, drawing on considerable research evidence.[7] The father is important not only as a role model for the child and a source of emotional support and childrearing partner to the mother but also as a source of orientation to that segment of the culture shared by males. The father also plays an important part in the establishment and maintenance of the set of standards and values that provides the moral climate of a family. This role may be filled by others, as can the emotional support role, but there is increasing evidence that both mothers and children benefit markedly from a father's active participation in child care.

Social Class and Socialization

It is 20 years since Urie Bronfenbrenner published his analysis of "Socialization and Social Class Through Time and Space," showing evidence that in some respects, at least, the social classes were moving closer together in their childrearing practices.[8] Social class has continued to be a major variable in examining not only parental practices but general orientations toward childrearing, contexts of development and transitions such as those to school and work. Two decades ago Daniel Miller and Guy Swanson examined differences among families classified not only on the basis of social class but also on the setting of the father's occupation, whether "entreprenurial" or within a large bureaucratic organization.[9]

More recently, Melvin Kohn, building upon the insights of Marx and Weber, has attempted to analyze how the conditions of occupational life affect the psyche, values and childrearing orientations of American parents.[10] In his early work, Kohn demonstrated that middle-class parents are more likely than working-class parents to want their children to be considerate of others, intellectually curious, responsible and self-controlled, while working-class parents are more likely to want their children to have good manners, to do well in school and to be obedient. Thus the middle-class parent tends to put emphasis upon self-direction for the child, the working-class parent to place a higher value on conformity. But Kohn does not stop at social class. He is able to demonstrate that fathers whose jobs entail self-direction—who are not closely supervised, who work with ideas rather than things, and who face great complexity on the job—value self-direction in their children, while those whose work requires them to conform to close supervision and a highly structured work situation are more likely to want their children to be conforming.

Categorization by social class, as used in American research, rests largely on educational attainment and occupational status. So measured, social class indexes a whole host of differences in life experiences, among them the type of housing occupied and the neighborhood of residence, the role differentiation between the parents, the fluency of language usage in the family, tendencies toward concrete versus abstract verbal expression and thought and the breadth of social participation of the parents. Under these circumstances, to know that various aspects of child development are associated with social class is merely to reiterate that life style and life chances are markedly influenced by a family's place in the social structure. Many efforts are now being directed to delineating the specific mechanisms by which such effects are mediated, since childrearing practices are associated with, but by no means wholly determined by, class position.[11]

Much recent research focuses on the development of competence in the child. In general, the competent child is characterized as self-reliant, self-controlled and uninhibited in his relationships with others but not overly aggressive or demanding. Competence obviously entails the development of cognitive, physical and social skills as well as emotional control. Parental warmth and encourage-

ACYF Family Research

In 1974 the Office of Child Development—now the Administration for Children, Youth and Families—began a 5-part research effort centering on the family as a focal point for research bearing on child development. During the first two phases of the effort, ACYF supported research projects which looked at child development within different types of families—among them, one-parent families, minority families, low-income families and families in which both parents work. Research projects also examined the interaction of families with community services, schools and other institutions. Television was studied both within the family system and as part of the institutional system.

Now, in the third phase, ACYF is supporting pilot studies to test the kinds of changes in services and interventions needed to enhance child development and improve interaction between families and institutions. Full-scale demonstrations of promising programs will be supported in the next phase.

Finally, the knowledge derived from these and other studies will be used to design new programs and policies to meet the needs of children and families and to provide guidance for existing ACYF programs.

ACYF is also funding a series of projects which will look at ways to communicate scientific knowledge about child development to different types of families, examine the kinds of information that families have and need on child development and its impact on childrearing and study ways to make information on supportive services more accessible.

In addition, the Children's Bureau, ACYF, supports demonstration projects that are attempting to prevent foster placement of children by providing comprehensive services to families under stress. The use of social service contracts between agencies and families to improve case planning is being tested in other projects.

Demonstration projects that provide comprehensive services to abused and neglected children and their families, and research projects that are exploring factors contributing to child abuse and neglect and promising prevention and treatment techniques are supported by the National Center on Child Abuse and Neglect in the Children's Bureau.

ment coupled with parental control seem to be essential ingredients in the production of competent children, but it appears that the combinations of parental acceptance and control appropriate for producing competent young children differ for boys and girls. For the induction of competence away from home in children of preschool age, recent research indicates that neither the affectionate and permissive parent nor the cold, authoritarian parent is as effective as the parent who combines affection with strict control and yet encourages joint discussion of family-related issues.[12]

Another topic which has received a great deal of attention in the past decade is the nature and explanation of sex differences in personality and performance. A recent assessment of available research evidence demonstrates that many of the widely held beliefs about sex differences are simply not substantiated. For example, the long-standing belief that girls are more "social," more "suggestible" and have lower achievement motivation than boys, or that girls are better at rote learning and simple repetitive tasks while boys are better at those that require a higher level of cognitive processing—all these have been disproven by systematic research.[13] A few sex differences seem more firmly established: that girls have greater verbal ability than boys, that boys excel in mathematical ability and in visual-spatial ability beyond age 12, and that males are more aggressive.

Differences in parental response to girls and boys seem to increase as children grow older and to be greater in the case of fathers than in that of mothers, but studies bearing directly on sex-differentiated responses of fathers or of either parent toward older children are relatively rare. Recent research on the interactions of biological and social systems suggests that parenting behaviors are more influenced by biology than some celebrants of unisex would like to believe; in particular, hormonally related responsiveness of mothers to infants seems firmly established.[14]

The fact that boys and girls are responded to quite differently by their parents in all known societies cannot be unimportant in leading to typical patternings in the development of the sexes. Since parents are often unaware of the ways in which their behaviors differ, however, observational studies of the actual behaviors of the parents toward boys and girls are needed to supplement interview materials. Such research is now going on, and, indeed, a major development in recent socialization research has been the turn to painstaking observation in place of or as a supplement to interviewing.

Methodological advances include the systematic assessment of bias and unreliability when retrospective data are obtained on early family experiences and childrearing practices; the development of observational techniques and category systems for use in both naturalistic and laboratory settings; and the utilization of short-term longitudinal studies of over-lapping cohorts in order to differentiate cohort effects—that is, the effects of particular historical events or social changes—from the effects of age.[15]

Studies by anthropologists continue to increase our knowledge of the ways in which very different social structural arrangements and cultural themes influence childrearing. Especially influential here has been the work of Beatrice and John Whiting in their studies of six different cultures.[16] Their publications have focused successively on the cultures and their general patterns of childrearing, on mothers and their behaviors (with some examination of fathers' roles as well) and on the children themselves. It should be noted that attempts to delineate modal personality types in various cultures or nations has been largely abandoned. Efforts are rather concentrated on delineating the specific linkages between features of the basic maintenance systems of societies, household composition, parental practices and child behaviors.

The anthropological perspective leads naturally to a consideration of the family as a whole. The family is an organized unit, one that functions through ongoing transactions among members and between the family and the larger community. What attributes of that unit as a whole best index its effects on the development of children? Past research leaves much to be desired, but the following are surely among those important features of families that are associated with favorable child development in the United States: harmony rather than conflict between parents; equality of authority or at most modest differences in parental power and authority; clearly patterned, mutually acceptable procedures for dealing with important problems and decisions; involvement of the child in decisions affecting him or her, as appropriate to the child's age; and accurate labeling of feelings and intentions in communication within the family.

The study of communication processes in the family has been of particular interest to workers in the field of psychiatric disorders. Parents in families with a schizophrenic child, in particular, have been found to "mislabel" their emotions and actions, to have difficulty in achieving a shared focus of attention, to disqualify their own utterances, and to maintain shared fictions about the family as a unit.[17] There is much evidence to suggest a genetic component in schizophrenia, but since fewer than half of identical twins are concordant for schizophrenia, experiential features are probably involved as well.

We are now beginning to get much more systematic research on communication processes in normal families, usually involving the observation of the family in a laboratory situation but occasionally entailing videotaping in the home.[18] It is not yet clear what the major correlates and consequences of communication deviance are, but the field seems a promising one. For example, observational studies of parent-child interaction in the home suggest that very low levels of communication from mother to child are involved in instances of markedly retarded language development.[19]

The ways in which illness or psychopathology of a parent impinge upon the child in other respects, particularly as threatening behaviors or child neglect are entailed, are also under investigation in many places. Mental illness may go unnoted and untreated, often leading to conflict between parents and feelings of abandonment by the child.[20]

Long-term longitudinal studies continue to add to our knowledge of socialization in the family. Two major contributions have come from the Institute of Human Development at Berkeley, which has for more than 40 years followed several hundred study members born in the 1920s. Jack Block and Norma Haan have examined continuities and discontinuities in personality from the pre-adolescent years to the late thirties[21] Parental warmth, acceptance and stability tend to affect the child's development and performance at all age levels, but there is much personality change well beyond childhood. Some study members who had unhappy childhoods and showed serious problems in adolescence nevertheless arrived at age 40 competent and self-accepting. Others who gave early promise have had a more problematic time in middle age.

A recent book by Glen Elder traces the effects of economic deprivation during the depression of the 1930s upon the lives of the then pre-adolescent study members.[22] The boys, in particular, appear to have been challenged by the dismal experiences of their families and many rose to the challenge by taking on part-time jobs to help their parents. Girls, on the other hand, were more largely pushed into help with domestic chores. Not accidentally, the birth cohort to which these women belong has been the most home-oriented of any in recent decades.

In conclusion, the family mediates between the larger community and its demands and the developing child. It is responsive to the conditions of life in the society, to economic conditions, wars, and to natural catastrophes that from time to time afflict all societies. A major thrust in interdisciplinary studies now in process is to seek to trace the effects of such family adaptations upon the child. ∎

[1] See, for example, the papers prepared for a workshop, "The Family Life Course in Historical Perspective," published in Volume 1 of the newly founded *Journal of Family History* (Winter 1977).

[2] See Arthur J. Norton and Paul C. Glick, "Changes in American Family Life," *CHILDREN TODAY*, May-June 1976 and Urie Bronfenbrenner, "The Challenge of Social Change to Public Policy and Developmental Research," paper presented at the President's Symposium, "Child Development and Public Policy," at the Annual Meeting of the Society for Research in Child Development, Denver, April 1975.

[3] See *Toward A National Policy for Children and Families*, Report of the Advisory Committee on Child Development, National Academy of Sciences, Washington, D.C., 1976.

[4] *Ibid*, Appendix: "Research on the Effects of Day Care on Child Development." See also Mary Keyserling, *Windows on Day Care*, National Council of Jewish Women, New York, 1972.

[5] See, for example, Bennett M. Berger and Bruce M. Hackett, "On the Decline of Age Grading in Rural Hippie Communes," *Journal of Social Issues*, Volume 30, No. 2, 1974; also J. Rothchild and S. B. Wolf, *Children of the Counterculture*, New York, Doubleday, 1976.

[6] Elizabeth Herzog and Cecelia E. Sudia, "Children in Fatherless Families," in *Review of Child Development Research*, Volume 3, edited by Bettye M. Caldwell and Henry N. Riccuti, Chicago, University of Chicago Press, 1973.

[7] For example, David B. Lynn, *The Father: His Role in Child Development*, Belmont, California, Wadsworth, 1974; Michael E. Lamb (ed.), *The Role of the Father in Child Development*, New York, Wiley, 1976.

[8] Urie Bronfenbrenner, "Socialization and Social Class Through Time and Space," in *Readings in Social Psychology*, E. E. Maccoby, T. M. Newcomb and E. L. Hartley (eds.), New York, Holt, Rinehart and Winston, 1958.

[9] Daniel R. Miller and Guy E. Swanson, *The Changing American Parent: A Study in the Detroit Area*, New York, Wiley, 1958.

[10] Melvin L. Kohn, *Class and Conformity: A Study in Values*, Second edition, Chicago, University of Chicago Press, 1977.

[11] The evidence is summarized in Alan C. Kerchkoff, *Socialization and Social Class*, Englewood Cliffs, New Jersey, Prentice Hall, 1972.

[12] See Diana Baumrind, "The Development of Instrumental Competence Through Socialization," *Minnesota Symposium on Child Psychology*, Anne Pick (ed.), Minneapolis, University of Minnesota Press, 1973.

[13] Eleanor E. Maccoby and Carol N. Jacklin, *The Psychology of Sex Differences*, Stanford, California, Stanford University Press, 1974. A critical evaluation of the shortcomings of existing evidence is provided by Jeanne Block in "Another Look at Sex Differentiation in the Socialization Behaviors of Mothers and Fathers," to be published in *Psychology of Women: Future Directions for Research*, New York, Psychological Dimensions, Inc., 1978.

[14] See Alice S. Rossi, "A Biosocial Perspective on Parenting," *Daedalus*, Spring 1977.

[15] Marian Radke Yarrow *et al.*, "Recollections of Childhood: A Study of the Retrospective Method," *Monographs of the Society for Research in Child Development*, Volume 35, No. 5, 1970. The work of Baumrind, referred to in note 12, is illustrative of developments in observational methods. Issues of cohort and longitudinal analysis are dealt with in John R. Nesselroade and H. W. Reese, *Life Span Developmental Psychology: Methodological Issues*, New York, Academic Press, 1973.

[16] See Beatrice Whiting (ed.), *Six Cultures: Studies of Child Rearing*, New York, Wiley, 1963; Leigh Minturn and W. W. Lambert, *Mothers of Six Cultures: Antecedents of Child Rearing*, New York, Wiley, 1964; and B. B. and J. M. Whiting, *Children of Six Cultures: A Psychocultural Analysis*, Cambridge, Mass., Harvard University Press, 1975.

[17] Some of the research relating to schizophrenia is reported in David Rosenthal and Seymour Kety (eds.), *The Transmission of Schizophrenia*, London, Pergammon Press, 1968. (See especially Part III, "Social, Cultural and Interpersonal Studies.")

[18] A more general review of studies of communication in the family is given by Theodore Jacob, "Family Interaction in Disturbed and Normal Families: A Methodological and Substantive Review," *Psychological Bulletin*, January 1975.

[19] Margaret Wulbert *et al.*, "Language Delay and Associated Mother-Child Interactions," *Developmental Psychology*, January 1975.

[20] Several studies examining such effects are contained in *The Child in His Family*, edited by E. James Anthony and C. Koupernik, New York, Wiley, 1970. See also J. Clausen and C. Huffine, "The Impact of Parental Mental Illness on the Children," in *Research on Community and Mental Health*, Roberta Simmons (ed.), Greenwich, Conn., JAI Press. (To be published in 1978.)

[21] Jack Block and Norma Haan, *Lives Through Time*, Berkeley, California, Bancroft Press, 1972.

[22] Glen H. Elder, Jr., *Children of the Great Depression*, Chicago, University of Chicago Press, 1974.

CHILDREN

The Electronic Fix

by Ed Kittrell

In order to understand the impact of television on children it isn't necessary to study all the latest reports on behavioral research. As an alternative, you can simply watch a child watching television.

What you will usually observe is an immobile, uncommunicative subject, oblivious to his surroundings, with a face devoid of expression and eyes that stare vacantly into space—in short, a child exhibiting the classic posture of an addict.

Please don't misunderstand the metaphor. I am not comparing Captain Kangaroo with the neighborhood pusher, nor am I suggesting that a morning spent with Bugs Bunny and Magilla Gorilla will lead to a life of depravity and shame.

There are, however, a couple of remarkable similarities in the *experiences* of drug-taking and television watching, especially in the childhood population.

In the first place, both actions serve to remove the child from his environment, to blot out the real world. Television, like drugs, can be used as a means of escape. Secondly, drug-taking and television watching are basically passive states. They require little thought or preparation. The desired effect is achieved without any expenditure of energy or commitment.

Like a drug, television can act as both a sedative and a stimulant, depending on the child and the program he is watching. Many parents prescribe a dose of television to relax a child—just before

Reprinted from *Children Today* Magazine, May/June 1978.
U.S. Department of Health, Education and Welfare.

WOW

dinner, for example. Others have noticed that certain programs can send a child dashing through the house, imitating the combative behavior of a video hero. Whatever the effect, parents are at least subconsciously aware of television's enormous power over a child. And they are unsure about how to deal with it.

It is television's subtle, "narcotic" effect on children which is concerning more and more parents and educators. In the long run, making the television experience an enriching one for children will require creative approaches that address this fundamental question.

Until now, we've barely scratched the surface in this area. Instead, the public pressure concerning television and children has focused on two more obvious issues: violence and advertising.

The violence question predates the TV generation. In the 1930s and 40s, parents worried about the ways in which violence portrayed in movies and comic books might affect their child's behavior. As television itself became more widespread, and as popular programs competed with each other for higher levels of mayhem, the concern mounted. Studies were launched, commissions were created.

It can be argued that all of this activity, culminating in the Surgeon General's report in 1972, produced more heat than light. Studies of the relationship between television viewing and aggressive behavior in children were conducted using a variety of techniques. One 5-year study, commissioned by the American Broadcasting Company, measured a child's tendency toward aggression after exposure to violent programming by the force with which he hit an electronic pounding platform. The conclusion: "Under certain conditions and depending on the types of violence portrayed, exposure to televised violence is capable of producing increased inclination toward aggression in children."

What does that mean? you might ask. Perhaps it is easier to accept the analysis of Dr. Randall P. Harrison, a communications professor who summed up the various studies this way: "If you believe there's a link between cigarette smoking and cancer, then you probably ought to believe there's a link between watching TV violence and human aggression." Many people apparently agree with him, for groups such as the American Medical Association and the National PTA have been able to mount effective campaigns which have, most observers agree, reduced the amount of violence portrayed on network television. The issue is far from resolved, but some progress has been made.

The issue of television advertising aimed at children is just beginning to gain national attention. Led by Action for Children's Television (ACT), a number of organizations are pressuring the Federal Trade Commission to review the propriety of such advertising, beginning with the commercials for heavily-sugared foods and candy.

They are likely to find many parents in their corner. A recent national survey reported that parents consider "the gimmes"— demands by their children for products advertised on television—one of the major problems in raising children. Parents know they would not allow a salesman into their living room to pitch toys or candy to their children. Yet they see television commercials doing just that, dozens of times a day.

The argument in favor of banning television advertising aimed at children would seem to have some logic on its side. It is absurd to suggest that young children are an intellectual or emotional match for sophisticated advertising featuring animation, music, skillful photography and kindly salesmen. A

recent study concluded that many children have only a minimal understanding of what TV commercials are or what they do. Children have difficulty distinguishing between fantasy and reality, between advertising and informational programming. Advertisers know this, and they exploit it.

A ban on children's advertising also has some basis in legal precedent. The oldest known legal system, the Code of Hammurabi, made commercial exploitation of children punishable, in some instances, by death. Our legal code has always protected children against their own lack of judgement, preventing them from signing contracts, drinking alcohol or driving a car. The "attractive nuisance" doctrine of tort law holds that a person who maintains premises that are both enticing and dangerous to small children (a swimming pool, say) is responsible for any injury that the child may suffer. Even if the child knows of the risk, the owner must take steps to protect children against their own inability to withstand temptation.

Banning television advertising for children will not be an easy task. "Kidvid" is big business, with advertisers spending nearly $600 million a year on children's shows, and broadcasters realizing 25 percent of their overall profits from the seven percent of their programming aimed specifically at children. More and more, however, some regulation of children's television advertising seems like an idea whose time is coming— soon.

Limiting violence and advertising on programs for children, though, is only the first step toward making television a useful member of the average American family. To some extent, violence and advertising are issues that can be handled through laws and regulation. Dealing with the more subtle and complex effects of television, on the other hand, will require creative, individual responses from parents and children.

There is so much we don't know

about television's long-term effects on children. But we have suspicions, and many, many questions. What role does television play in developing role models and value systems for children? Does it encourage a passive attitude toward life? Does it blunt a child's own imaginative powers, or his ability to play in a natural, creative way? Do "flashy" educational programs such as "Sesame Street" spoil children for the more regimented, difficult learning that comes in the classroom? By filling so much leisure time, does television inhibit the kind of personal, emotional discoveries that children so often make when they are truly alone with themselves?

Most important, what effect does television have on interaction within the family? Surveys report that a majority of parents and children admit arguing often about which television programs to watch. Other effects, however, could be even more damaging. When the set is on, it discourages communication between brothers and sisters, children and parents. A family watching television is alone with each other. There is no need for the games, questions and even arguments that can help cement the family relationship. As one researcher recently asked after completing a 10-year study of how Americans use their leisure time: "I wonder if we aren't moving toward, or have arrived at, a society in which mass communication is more prevalent than interpersonal communication?"

In many cases, answers to these questions will be more personal than scientific. The most effective solutions for the problems raised by television will also be the personal ones arrived at by individual families.

Some critics of television, and even the broadcasters themselves, have suggested that the way to deal with television is to ignore it. If you don't like it, turn the set off. This can be effective in the short run, but it does not solve the problem. Television is the most pervasive force in American society. More than 95 percent of

"...watch a child watching television...oblivious to his surroundings, with a face devoid of expression and eyes that stare vacantly into space..."

American homes have at least one television set. By the time the average child graduates from high school, he will have spent more time in front of the set than in the classroom. If your child doesn't watch television at your house, he will at his friend's, or he will hear about it from his classmates. It is simply impossible to ignore television and the issues it raises, especially for children.

Besides, television is far from intrinsically evil. Physicians know that there is no such thing as a drug with no beneficial (or harmful) effects. Even the opiates have medicinal value, and many a family doctor has suggested that an occasional drink might benefit a patient. The essence of intelligence is knowing how to use any commodity so that it enhances one's happiness and development.

Families should be encouraged and educated in ways to make television a creative, positive force in a child's life. Newsman John Chancellor once told a reporter that he had his children write a review of the shows they watched. This assignment not only cut down viewing but helped develop critical and language skills. Parents with young children can watch programs *with* their children, instead of succumbing to the temptation to use the tube as a babysitter.

There are other ways to integrate the television experience into the overall environment that shapes children. It takes thought, and commitment, on the part of families. It is not easy. But the alternative is television as the electronic fix, the powerful and potentially dangerous drug available to your child free of charge, every day, in your own home. ∎

Ed Kittrell is Chief, Department of Communications, American Academy of Pediatrics.

24 How Children Influence Children:
The Role of Peers in the Socialization Process

Emmy Elisabeth Werner

UNICEF Photo by David Mangurian (Mexico)

In his review on family structure, socialization and personality, John A. Clausen points out that an older sibling may be caretaker, teacher, pacesetter or confidant for a younger one. Yet such a reference work as the *Handbook of Socialization Theory and Research* by D. B. Goslin includes few references about caretaking of children by agemates. What cross-cultural evidence we can find, however, indicates that caretaking of children by siblings, cousins or other peers is a significant phenomenon in most societies of the developing world.

Sibling and Child Caretaking

Child caretaking is widespread cross-culturally, but relevant material about this topic is scattered throughout many ethnographic studies, which makes comparative analysis difficult. In one cross-cultural survey on the age of assignment of roles and responsibilities to children, based on ethnographies of 50 cultures, pancultural trends in the age of assignment of child care roles were observed.[1] These centered on the 5- to 7-year-old period, when care of siblings, peer play and the understanding of game rules are most frequently initiated. This is the same age when Western societies introduce formal schooling.

The most common worldwide pattern is informal child and sibling care that is

Emmy E. Werner, Ph.D., is a Professor of Human Development and Research and Child Psychologist at the University of California, Davis.

This article appeared in *Children Today* Magazine, March/April 1979. U.S. Department of Health, Education and Welfare. It was adapted from *Cross-Cultural Child Development: A View from the Planet Earth*, by E. E. Werner. Copyright © 1979 by Wadsworth, Inc. Reprinted by permission of the publisher, Brooks/Cole Publishing Company, Monterey, California.

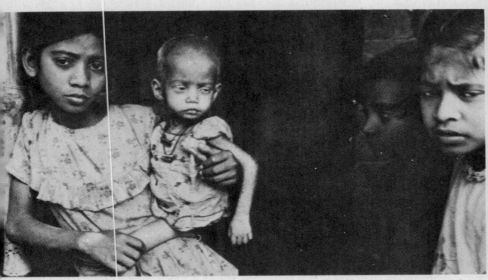

part of the daily routine of children within the family and that is carried out without formalized organizational rules. Under these circumstances, child caretakers frequently operate under two simultaneous sets of pressures: one from their small charges, the other from their parents. In all non-Western societies investigated by the Whitings in their Six-Cultures Study, children were expected to do some child tending.[2] However, there were striking differences in the types of caretaking mothers were willing to delegate, the age at which they considered a child competent, and the amount of supervision considered necessary.

One question on the mothers interview indicates the value placed on the help given by the child nurse. When the mothers were asked who had helped them care for the sample child when he or she was an infant, 69 percent of the mothers from the East African community, 41 percent of the mothers from the Mexican barrio, 25 percent of the Filipino, 21 percent of the North Indian, but only 12 percent of the New England and Okinawan mothers reported having been helped with an infant by a child. The three highest-ranking societies, the East African, the Mexican and the Filipino communities, were also the societies that ranked highest in the nurturant behavior of their children, as observed independently in naturalistic settings.

There is usually a strong contrast between infancy and young childhood in terms of child and adult caretaking

practices. The care of toddlers requires different skills and behaviors on the part of child caretakers than the care of an infant. Observations of the interaction of children with 2- to 4-year-old siblings in the Six-Cultures Study indicate that caretakers of toddlers were comparatively more apt to reprimand, criticize and punish. This is in some contrast to the predominant nurturant and responsive attitude shown toward the infants in these societies. Thus, the role of the child caretaker is a function of at least three factors: the physical maturation of the child; the availability of different caretakers; and the differing cultural conceptions of maturity of a child, which, in turn, leads to different patterns of caretaking by children.

Antecedents of Child Caretaking

The residence and size of a family, as well as the daily routines, subsistence economy and maternal workload, are related to the frequency of child caretaking in the developing world. Sibling caretaking is more common in societies where women have more work to do, where the work takes the mother from home or is difficult to interrupt, and where circumstances of residence, birth order and family size make alternative caretakers available. A domestic group with a large number of kin and cousins present, a mother with many offspring and a daily routine that keeps brothers, sisters and other adults available for caretaking would be the optimal situation for the development of nonparental and sibling caretaking.[3] . . .

Consequences of Child Caretaking

There is a great need for additional data that document the possible effect on a child of either providing or receiving child caretaking. Most of the data available deal with attachment behavior and differences in affiliation versus achievement motivation.

Sibling caretaking seems to be of special importance in cultures that are polygynous. Africa leads the world in polygynous societies. A study of Kikuyu children illustrates the importance of the sibling group in socialization.[4] After the child is raised by the mother for the first one or two years and is given a great deal of maternal care that fosters strong attachment, he or she will move in with the siblings when the mother is pregnant again. The sibling group is mostly responsible for the socialization of the young child and becomes the main source of the child's emotional involvement.

In a short-term longitudinal study of 3-year-old American preschoolers, one researcher found that secure attachment may play a dual role in children's relationships with other children.[5] It may directly promote peer competence by encouraging a positive orientation toward other children, and, insofar as mothers who foster secure attachment also encourage expanded interactions, it may indirectly promote social competence by giving children the opportunity to learn from peers.

Studying urban Japanese families, Caudill and Plath were impressed with

Children in a small, remote hamlet in India (far left), a day care center in Togo (left) and on a sidewalk in Monrovia, Liberia. UNICEF photos by Abigail Heyman (far left) and Bernard Wolff (left and right).

the role of siblings in the instruction and care of the younger babies, and by how this responsibility for parenting appeared to diminish any sibling rivalry and to create close bonding between brothers and sisters.[6] They ascribed the strong affectionate bond in interdependence between different members of the family to the sleeping arrangements. When the baby is new, he or she sleeps with the mother; when another baby comes, the child sleeps with an older brother or sister. Sleeping with another member of the family apparently strengthens family bonds and expresses a strong nurturant family life, at the same time lessening the sexual aspects of sleeping together.

In their Six-Cultures Study, the Whitings found that children who interact with infants were more nurturant and less egotistic than children who did not care for infants. These authors suggest that caretaking of infants appears to affect overall interaction with peers.[7] This becomes quite apparent when we take a look at the consequences of sex differences in child caretaking. B. Whiting and C. P. Edwards compared boys and girls in seven societies, the six cultures mentioned earlier plus the Kikuyu of Kenya, and observed incidences of nurturant and responsible behavior.[8] Older girls, aged 7 to 11, offered help and support to others more often than did boys. There were no such sex differences for children aged 3 to 6. The authors interpret the increased nurturance of older girls as due to the assignment to girls of increased childrearing duties,

particularly infant caretaking. Another researcher observed Luo boys in Kenya who were expected to perform child-caretaking chores usually assigned to girls.[9] Such boys displayed more feminine social behaviors than boys not needed for such tasks.

Thus, it appears that sex differences in nurturance and responsible behavior may only occur at particular ages and are not uniform across all cultures. The critical factor for the development of nurturant behavior seems to be the demand for child care tasks within the home. It would be interesting to see whether similar findings could be replicated in our own culture, as sex-role expectations change in the wake of a more egalitarian type of childrearing.

Several authors, including R. Levy and J. E. Ritchie, have attempted to generalize about the effects of child caretaking on the development of individual differences in children.[10] These authors have dealt with ethnographic accounts of child caretaking in Polynesian societies and have argued that sibling caretaking restricts the development of individual differences in both children and adults. The possible effects of child caretaking were presented by Levy as the development of an easygoing or apathetic "you can't fight City Hall" orientation to life. Weisner and Gallimore suggest that these consequences need to be interpreted in terms of the social context in which the child will live as an adult.[11] The socialization goal of the societies in which these observations were made is the integration of the child

into the social context, rather than fostering individual achievement and independent skills. Thus, it may be that children raised in a sibling-caretaking system develop psychological and behavioral characteristics that are adaptive in some settings and not in others. Systematic differences can be expected in the learning experiences of young children when taught by siblings rather than parents.[12]

From a brief overview of the rather scarce data available on sibling caretaking in the Six-Cultures Study and in Polynesian groups in Hawaii, New Zealand and Tahiti, it appears that sibling caretaking in extended families anywhere in the world may be a functional adaptation of low-income groups that allows economically marginal families flexibility in coping with crises and increases the number of potential resource contributors. A case in point is the American Indian family in the American metropolis society, which differs significantly from the nuclear-family, conjugal pair and single-person types that predominate in White America.[13] The less stable and the lower the amount of income among American Indian families, the larger the household. Brothers or sisters of the husband and wife, and nieces and nephews, all join together to pool their meager resources. This grouping together also characterizes other poverty-stricken households among other ethnic and racial minorities within the industrialized urban West.

It remains to be seen what positive

roles siblings can play in helping the younger child adapt to changes brought about by modernization and industrialization, since older children appear more open and exposed to modern influences than younger ones.

Affiliation Versus Achievement Motivation

Evidence of the effects on motive development of sibling caretaking is either severely limited or indirect . . . In the Polynesian, African, Asian and Latin American societies where child caretaking has been studied, it appears that early parental demand for nondependence serves, in part, to shift independence training to older siblings. Thus, refusal of help by parents redirects the child's overtures to siblings, who provide nurturance and training and, in turn, pressure for independence.

Of critical importance is the fact that this shift from adult to sibling caretaking can occur without the toddler learning self-care skills, which may impose a rather strong burden on the young caretaker that may lessen the child's achievement motivation at the crucial age when it tends to crystallize. Given the mother's behavior, the child has no alternative but to turn to siblings; thus, achievement motivation may be sacrificed for the sake of affiliation.

Reliance on sibling caretakers as a factor in the development of affiliation motivation has been suggested by studies of Hawaiian-Americans.[14] The pattern of being interdependent and affiliating with others is a significant feature of Hawaiian life and may cause problems in the classroom. Accustomed to sibling care, Hawaiian children are inclined to attend to peers rather than teachers and individual work, behavior that is often interpreted by teachers in terms of motivational and attentional deficits.

On the positive side, S. MacDonald and R. Gallimore found in a number of classroom studies that Hawaiian-American students perform at high levels if allowed to interact or affiliate with peers in team work or in the sharing of earned privileges.[15] Whether peer interaction is more motivating for those from families in other cultures where there is a great deal of sibling care of children is a hypothesis that has not been directly tested.

To sum up, child caretaking appears to be an important antecedent to nurturant, responsible behavior and to behavior that leads to affiliation rather than achievement motivation. Though it is presently preponderant in the non-Western world, child caretaking may in the future play an important role as an alternative to maternal caretaking in the West. P.M. Greenfield suggests that day care centers should involve older children and siblings in child care and that schooling or tutoring of primary school children should involve children as well as adults.[16] The Whitings argue that whether a child is told to take care of younger siblings or whether he or she is sent to school instead may have a more profound effect upon the profile of the child's social behavior than the manipulation of reinforcement schedules by the parents. Thus, major attention needs to be paid in future cross-cultural studies to the role of child caretakers as transmitters of new social values and as links between the family and the rapidly changing outside world.

Children's Play Groups and Games

Children's play groups are not necessarily dependent on caretaking patterns, but the two variables are frequently closely related. Child caretaking affects the sex composition of play groups and their physical and social mobility. Where caretaking is not limited to one's own siblings, it shapes contacts with children not in one's immediate family.

In a review article on exploration and play, Weisler and McCall trace the developmental sequence in the nature of children's social play.[17] At first the child plays in isolation, without reference to what other children are doing. The first indication of a social element is the occurrence of parallel playing, in which the nature of the child's behavior is influenced by and may be similar to that of nearby children, but there is no direct social interaction. Subsequently, there may be short interactions between children consisting of socially instigated but not truly interactive play, as when the behavior of another child is imitated. Later, full-scale group play can be observed, in which one child interacts verbally and physically in a prolonged sequence with other children.

UNICEF Photos, left to right: a day care center in Tanzania, by Alastair Matheson; children in China, by Jack Ling; and a boy pursuing his studies in Lahore, Pakistan, by Mallica Vajrathon.

Several theoretical orientations have emphasized the role of play as a means of reducing tension and anxieties. Cross-cultural comparisons might reveal, in addition, different social and cultural values that are infused in the play of young children. . .

Children's games around the world appear to play an important part in resolving conflicts over socialization pressures and teach social values and social skills essential for successful adaptation in a given society, whether through physical skills, taking chances or making rational choices in a deliberate strategy.

A number of ecological and child-training correlates appear associated with assertive, competitive and rivalrous behavior in children. Increasing modernization, as measured by exposure to school and city life, and the opportunity for social mobility and the removal of the inhibiting effects of traditional stress on obedience and control of aggression seem to contribute to an increase in these behaviors, more so among boys than girls and among older than younger children. Extrafamilial socializers can counteract this trend in societies where cooperation is stressed as part of a deliberate philosophy.

Summary

In sum, the influence of peers as mediators of social change cannot be underestimated. The results of studies of child caretaking, of games and of competitive versus cooperative behavior in the classroom seem to indicate that peers, with and without the direct support of teachers and the sociopolitical system of a given society, transmit social values that are important in the process of modernization. The young, as role models for still younger children, become important pacesetters in the developing world and in human cultural evolution. ∎

[1] B. Rogoff, M.J. Sellers, S. Piorrata, N. Fox and S. White, "Age of Assignment of Roles and Responsibilities to Children: A Cross-Cultural Survey," *Human Development*, 1975, 18.

[2] B. Whiting and J.W. Whiting, *Children of Six Cultures*, Cambridge, Mass., Harvard University Press, 1975.

[3] L. A. Minturn, "A Survey of Cultural Differences in Sex-Role Training and Identification," in N. Kretschmer and D. Walcher (eds.), *Environmental Influences on Genetic Expression*, Washington, D.C., U.S. Government Printing Office, 1969.

[4] J. I. Carlebach, "Family Relationships of Deprived and Non-Deprived Kikuyu Children from Polygamous Marriages," *Journal of Tropical Pediatrics*, 1967, 13.

[5] A.F. Lieberman, "Preschoolers Competence with a Peer: Relations with Attachment and Peer Experience, *Child Development*, 1977, 48.

[6] W. Caudill and D.W. Plath, "Who Sleeps By Whom?: Parent-Child Involvement in Urban Japanese Families," *Psychiatry*, 1966, 29.

[7] Whiting and Whiting, 1975, op. cit.

[8] B. Whiting and C.P. Edwards, "A Cross-Cultural Analysis of Sex Differences in the Behavior of Children Aged Three Through Eleven," *Journal of Social Psychology*, 1973, 91.

[9] Carl R. Ember, "Female Task Assignment and Social Behavior of Boys," *Ethos*, 1973, 1.

[10] See, for example, R.I. Levy, "Child Management Structure and Its Implications in a Tahitian Family," in E. Vogel and N. Bell (eds.), *A Modern Introduction To The Family*, New York, Free Press, 1968 and J.E. Ritchie, *Basic Personality in Rakau*, New Zealand, Victoria University, 1956.

[11] T.S. Weisner and R. Gallimore, "My Brother's Keeper: Child and Sibling Caretaking," *Current Anthropology*, 1977, 18(2).

[12] M. Steward and D. Steward, "Parents and Siblings As Teachers," in E.J. Mash, L.C. Handy and L.A. Hamerlynek (eds.), *Behavior Modification Approaches to Parenting*, New York, Brunner/Mazel, 1976.

[13] J. Jorgensen, "Indians and the Metropolis," in J.O. Waddell and O.M. Watson (eds.). *The American Indian in Urban Society*, Boston, Little Brown, 1971.

[14] R. Gallimore, J.W. Boggs and C.E. Jordan, *Culture, Behavior and Education: A Study of Hawaiian-Americans*, Beverly Hills, Calif., Sage, 1974.

[15] S. MacDonald and R. Gallimore, *Battle in the Classroom: Innovations in Classroom Techniques*, Scranton, Intext, 1971.

[16] P.M. Greenfield, *What We Can Learn from Cultural Variation in Child Care*, paper presented at the American Association for the Advancement of Science, San Francisco, 1974.

[17] A. Weisler and R.B. McCall, "Exploration and Play: Resume and Redirection," *American Psychologist*, 1976, 31(7).

Child's Play

For many years psychologists viewed play
as an unquantifiable behavior.

But it is now seen as an important guide
to cultural and intellectual development.

Jerome Bruner

25

Photograph by Virginia Hamilton

Experimental psychology tends to be rather a sober discipline, tough-minded not only in its procedures, but in its choice of topics as well. They must be scientifically manageable. No surprise, then, that when it began extending its investigations into the realm of early human development it steered clear of so antic a phenomenon as play. For even as recently as a decade ago, Harold Schlosberg of Brown University, a highly respected critic, had published a carefully reasoned paper concluding sternly that, since play could not even be properly defined, it could scarcely be a manageable topic for experimental research. His paper was not without merit, for the phenomena of play cannot be impeccably framed

into a single operational definition. How indeed can one encompass so motley a set of entries as childish punning, cowboys-and-Indians, and the construction of a tower of bricks into a single or even a sober dictionary entry?

Fortunately, the progress of research is subject to accidents of opportunity. Once data begin seriously to undermine presuppositions, the course can change very quickly. A decade ago, while Schlosberg's words still reverberated, work on primate ethology began to force a change in direction, raising new and basic questions about the nature and role of play in the evolution of the primate series. On closer inspection, play is not as diverse a phenomenon as had been thought, particularly when looked at in its natural setting. Nor is it all that antic in its structure, if analysed properly. But perhaps

Reprinted from *New Scientist*, April 18, 1974. Copyright ©
1974, New Science Publications.

most important, its role during immaturity appears to be more and more central as one moves up the living primate series from Old World monkeys through Great Apes, to Man—suggesting that in the evolution of primates, marked by an increase in the number of years of immaturity, the selection of a capacity for play during those years may have been crucial. So if play seemed to the methodologically vexed to be an unmanageable laboratory topic, primatologists were pondering its possible centrality in evolution!

A first field finding served to reduce the apparently dizzying variety of forms that play could take. On closer inspection, it turns out that play is universally accompanied in subhuman primates by a recognisable form of metasignaling, a "play face," first carefully studied by the Dutch primatologist van Hooff (see sketch below).

Sketch showing a chimpanzee play face.

It signifies within the species the message, to use Gregory Bateson's phrase, "this is play." It is a powerful signal—redundant in its features, which include a particular kind of open-mouthed gesture, a slack but exaggerated gait, and a marked "galumphing" in movement—and its function is plainly not to be understood simply as "practice of instinctive activities crucial for survival." When, for example, Stephen Miller and I set about analyzing filmed field records of juvenile play behavior made by Irven DeVore while studying savanna baboons in the Amboseli Game Reserve in East Africa, we very quickly discovered that if one young animal did not see the "metasignal" of another who was seeking to play-fight with him, a real fight broke out with no lack of skill. But once the signal was perceived by both parties the fight was transformed into the universally recognizable clownish ballet of monkeys feigning a fight. They obviously know how to do it both ways. What was it for, then, play fighting? And why should the accompanying form of metasignaling have been selected in evolution?

We begin to get a hint of the functional significance of play in higher primates from the pioneering observations of the group led by Jane van Lawick-Goodall studying free-ranging chimpanzees at the Gombe Stream Reserve in Tanzania. Recall first the considerably longer childhood in chimpanzees than in Old World monkeys —the young chimp in close contact with the mother for four or five years during which the mother has no other offspring, whilst in monkeys, the oestrus cycle assures that within a year new young are born, with the rapidly maturing animals of last year's crop relegated to a peer group of juveniles in which play declines rapidly.

SITTING WITH MOTHER

David Hamburg of Stanford, a psychiatrist–primatologist working at Gombe Stream, has noted the extent to which young chimpanzees in the first five years spend time observing adult behavior, incorporating observed patterns of adult behavior into their play. Van Lawick-Goodall has a telling observation to report that relates this early observation-cum-play to adult skilled behavior —an observation that deepens our understanding of the function of early play. Adult chimps develop (when the ecology permits) a very skilled technique of termiting, in which they put mouth-wetted, stripped sticks into the opening of a termite hill, wait a bit for the termites to adhere to the stick, then carefully remove their fishing "instrument" with termites adhering to it which they then eat with relish. One of the young animals, Merlin, lost his mother in his third year. He had not learned to termite by four-and-a-half nearly as well as the others, though raised by older siblings. For the young animals appear to learn the "art of termiting" by sitting by the mother, buffered from pressures, trying out in play and learning the individual constituent acts that make up termiting, and without the usual reinforcement of food from catching: learning to play with sticks, to strip leaves from twigs, and to pick the right length of twig for getting into different holes. These are the constituents that must be combined in the final act, and they are tried out in all manner of antic episodes.

Merlin, compared to his age mates, was inept and unequipped. He had not had the opportunity for such observation and play nor, probably, did he get the buffering from distraction and pressure normally provided by the presence of a mother. This would suggest, then, that play has the effect of providing practice not so much of survival-relevant instinctive behavior but, rather, of making possible the playful practice of subroutines of behavior later to be combined in more useful problem solving. What appears to be at stake in play is the opportunity for assembling and reassembling behavior sequences for skilled action. That, at least, is one function of play.

It suggests a more general feature of play. It is able to reduce or neutralize the pressure of goal-directed action, the "push" to successful completion of an act. There is a well-known rule in the psychology of learning, the Yerkes-Dodson law, that states that the more complex a skill to be learned, the lower the *optimum* motivational level required for fastest learning. Play, then, may provide the means for reducing excessive drive. The distinguished Russian investigator Lev Vygotsky in a long-lost manuscript published a few years ago reports an investigation in which young children could easily be induced not to eat their favorite candy when laid before them when the candy was made part of a game of "Poison." And years before, Wolfgang Köhler had reported that when his chimps were learning to stack boxes to reach fruit suspended from the high tops of their cages, they often lost interest in eating the fruit when they were closing in on the solution. Indeed, Peter Reynolds in a widely acclaimed paper on play in primates given to the American Association for the Advancement of Science in Philadelphia in 1972 remarks that the essence of play is to dissociate goal-directed behavior from its principal drive system and customary reinforcements. It is no surprise, then, to find results indicating that prior play with materials improves children's problem solving with those materials later.

Kathy Sylva of Harvard and I worked with children aged three to five who had the task of fishing a prize from a latched box out of reach. To do so, they had to extend two sticks by clamping them together. The children were given various "training" procedures beforehand, including explaining the principle of clamping sticks together, or practice in fastening clamps on single sticks, or an opportunity to watch the experimenter carry out the task. One group was simply allowed to play with the materials. They did as well in solving the problem as the ones who had been given a demonstration of the principle of clamping sticks together and better than any of the other groups. In fact, what was striking about the play group was their tenacity in sticking with the task so that even when they were poor in their initial approach, they ended by solving the problem. What was particularly striking was their capacity to resist frustration and "giving up." They were playing.

THE YOUNG LEAD THE WAY

There are comparable results on primates below man where the pressure is taken off animals by other means —as by semi-domestication achieved by putting out food in a natural habitat, a technique pioneered by Japanese primatologists. It appears to have the effect of increasing innovation in the animals studied. Japanese macaques at Takasakiyama have taken to washing yams, to separating maize from the sand on which it is spread by dropping a handful of the mix into seawater and letting the sand sink. And once in the water, playing in this new medium to the edge of which they have been transplanted, the young learn to swim, first in play, and then begin swimming off, migrating to near islands. In all of these activities, it is the playful young who are centrally involved in the new enterprises, even if they may not always be the innovators of the new "technologies." But it is the young who are game for a change, and it is this gameness that predisposes the troop to change its ways—with the fully adult males often the most resistant or, at least the most out of touch, for the novelties are being tried out in the groups playing around the mother from which the big males are absent. Jean Claude Fady, the French primatologist, has shown that even ordinarily combative adult males will cooperate with each other in moving heavy rocks under which food is hidden—if the pressure is taken off by the technique of semi-domestication.

Ample early opportunity for play may have a more lasting effect still, as Corinne Hutt has shown. She designed a super-toy for children of three to five years old, consisting of a table with a lever, buzzer, bells and counters, different movements of the lever systematically sounding buzzers, and turning counters, etc. Children first explore its possibilities, then having contented themselves, often proceed to play. She was able to rate how inventive the children were in their play, dividing them into non-explorers, explorers, and inventive explorers, the last group carrying on all the way from initial exploration to full-blown play. Four years later, when the children were aged seven to ten, she tested them again on a creativity test designed by Mike Wallach and Nathan Kogan in the United States, as well as on some personality tests.

The more inventive and exploratory the children had been initially in playing with the super-toy, the higher their originality scores were four years later. The non-exploring boys in general had come to view themselves as unadventurous and inactive and their parents and teachers considered them as lacking curiosity. The non-exploratory and unplayful girls were later rather unforthcoming in social interaction as well and more tense than their originally more playful mates. Early unplayfulness may go with a lack of later originality.

Obviously, more studies of this kind are needed (and are in progress). But the psychiatrist Erik Erikson, reporting in his Godkin Lectures at Harvard in 1973 on a thirty-year follow-up of children earlier studied, has commented that the ones with the most interesting and fulfilling lives were the ones who had managed to keep a sense of playfulness at the center of things.

PLAY HAS RULES

Consider play now from a structural point of view as a form of activity. Rather than being "random" it is usually found to be characterized by a recognizable rule structure.

New studies by the young American psycholinguist Catherine Garvey show how three- to five-year-old children, playing in pairs, manage implicitly even in their simplest games to create and recognize rules and expectancies, managing the while to distinguish sharply between the structure of make-believe or possibility and the real thing. Amusing though Catherine Garvey's protocols may be, they reveal a concise, almost grammatical quality in the interchanges and an extraordinary sensitivity on the part of the children to violations of implicit expectancies and codes.

It is hardly surprising then that different cultures encourage different forms of play as "fitting." Ours tend, in the main, to admire play and games of "zero sum," one wins what the other loses. The anthropologist Kenelm Burridge contrasts our favorite form with a typical ritual food-exchange game of "taketak" among the Tangu in New Guinea, a tribe that practices strict and equal sharing. The object of their game is to achieve equal shares among the players—not to win, not to lose, but to tie. It is reminiscent of a game reported years ago by James Sully. He tells of two sisters, five and seven, who played a game they called "Sisters," a game with one rule: equal shares for each player, no matter what, in their case quite unlike life! We are only at the beginning of studying the functions of play in fitting children to their culture, but there are some classic studies.

If the rule structure of human play and games sensitizes the child to the rules of culture, both generally and in preparation for a particular way of life, then surely play must have some special role in nurturing symbolic activity generally. For culture is symbolism in action. Does play then have some deep connection with the origins of language? One can never know. Yet, we have already noted the extraordinary combinatorial push behind play, its working out of variations. Play is certainly implicated in early language acquisition. Its structured interactions and "rules" precede and are a part of the child's first mastery of language. Our own studies at Oxford on language acquisition suggest that in exchange games, in "peek-bo," and in other structured interactions, young children learn to signal and to recognize signals and expectancies. They delight in primitive rule structures that come to govern their encounters. In these encounters they master the idea of "privileges of occurrence" so central to grammar, as well as other constituents of language that must later be put together.

Indeed, there is a celebrated and highly technical volume by Ruth Weir on language play in a two-and-one-half year old child, *Language in the Crib,* in which she reports on the language of her son Anthony after he had been put to bed with lights out. He pushes combinatorial activity to the limit, phonologically, syntactically, and semantically, often to the point at which he remonstrates himself with an adult "Oh no, no."

Much more is being learned about play than we would have expected a decade ago. We have come a long way since Piaget's brilliant observations on the role of play in assimilating the child's experience to his personal schema of the world, as preparation for later accommodation to it. A new period of research on play is underway. Nick Blurton-Jones has shown that Niko Tinbergen's ethological methods can be applied to children at play as readily as to chimps in the forest. The new work begins to suggest why play is the principal business of childhood, the vehicle of improvisation and combination, the first carrier of rule systems through which a world of cultural restraint is substituted for the operation of impulse.

That such research as that reported raises deep questions about the role of play in our own society is, of course, self-evident. Although we do not yet know how important play is for growing up, we do know that it is serious business. How serious it is can perhaps be condensed by citing the conclusion of a study done on children's laughter by Alan Sroufe and his colleagues at Minnesota. They find that those things most likely to make a child laugh when done by his mother at a year are most likely to make him cry when done by a stranger.

26

The Aftermath of Divorce

E. Mavis Hetherington, Martha Cox, and Roger Cox

The incidence of divorce has increased dramatically over the past decade. If the divorce rate stabilized at its 1974 level, it is estimated that over 40 percent of new marriages would ultimately end in divorce. In addition, although the birthrate in the United States is declining, the number of divorces involving children is rising. While the rate of remarriage has also risen, it has not kept pace with the divorce rate, especially in families where children are involved. Thus, during the past ten years there has been an increase in the proportion of divorced persons, particularly divorced parents, relative to partners in intact marriages (Bronfenbrenner 1975).

In divorces in which children are involved, the mother usually gains custody of the child, except in unusual circumstances. Although the proportion of children living with their divorced fathers is increasing, in the latest yearly population survey by the Census Bureau only 8.4 percent of children of divorced parents were reported as residing with their fathers (Current Population Report Series P-20, 1976). Thus, the most frequently found family condition in the immediate postdivorce situation is that the child lives in a home with the mother and has intermittent or no contact with the father. It may be because of these circumstances that social scientists studying divorce have focused on the impact of divorce on mothers and children, rather than on the entire family system, including the fathers. Even in studies with these restricted perspectives, the approach has been largely descriptive. The characteristics of divorced mothers and their children are described and compared to those of mothers and children in intact homes (Biller 1974; Herzog and Sudia 1973; Hetherington and Deur 1971; Lynn 1974). Attempts to study changes in family interaction and functioning after divorce are rare.

Divorce can be viewed as a critical event that affects the entire family system and the functioning and interactions of members within that system. To get a true picture of the impact of divorce, its effects on the divorced parents and on the children must be examined.

The findings reported here are part of a two-year longitudinal study of the impact of divorce on family functioning and children's development. The first goal of the larger study was to examine family responses to the crisis of divorce and then examine patterns of family reorganization over the two-year period following divorce. It was assumed that the family system would go through a period of disorganization immediately after the divorce, followed by recovery, reorganization, and eventual attainment of a new pattern of equilibrium. The second goal was to examine the characteristics of family members which contributed to variations in family processes. The third goal was to examine the effects of variations in family interactions and structure on children's development.

In this article, we will focus on changes and stresses experienced by family members, and factors related to alterations in parent-child interactions in the two years following divorce.

METHOD

Subjects

The original sample was composed of 72 white, middle-class children (36 boys, 36 girls) and their divorced parents from homes in which custody had been granted to the mother, and the same number of children and parents from intact homes. The mean ages of the divorced mothers and fathers and the mothers and fathers from intact homes were 27.2, 29.6, 27.4, and 30.1, respectively. All parents were high school graduates and the large majority of parents had some college education or advanced training beyond high school. Divorced parents were identified and contacted through court records and lawyers. Only families with a child attending nursery school (who served as the target child) were included in the study. The intact families were selected on the basis of having a child of the same sex, age, and birth order in the same nursery school as the child from a divorced family. In addition, an attempt was made to match parents on age, education, and

From *Mother/Child, Father/Child Relationships* edited by J. H. Steven and M. Mathews. Reprinted with permission from the National Association for the Education of Young Children and the author.

length of marriage. Only first- and second-born children were included in the study.

The final sample consisted of 24 families in each of four groups (intact families with girls, intact families with boys, divorced families with girls, divorced families with boys)—a total of 96 families for which complete data were available. Sample attrition was largely due to remarriage in the divorced families (19 men, 10 women); separation or divorce in the intact sample (5 families); relocation of a family or parent; and lack of cooperation by schools, which made important measures of the children unavailable. Also, 8 families no longer wished to participate in the study. Because one of the interests of the investigation was to determine how mothers and children functioned in father-absent homes and how their functioning might be related to deviant or nondeviant behavior in children, families with stepparents were excluded from this study but remained in a stepparent study. In the analyses presented here, 6 families were randomly dropped from groups to maintain equal sizes of groups.

When a reduction in sample size from 144 families to 96 families occurs, bias in the sample immediately becomes a concern. On demographic characteristics such as age, religion, education, income, occupation, family size, and maternal employment, there were no differences between those subjects who dropped out or were excluded from the sample and those who remained. When a family was no longer included in the study, a comparative analysis was done of its interaction patterns and those of the continuing families. Some differences in these groups will be noted subsequently. In general, there were few differences in parent-child interactions in families who did or did not remain in the study. However, there were some differences in the characteristics of parents who remarried and how they viewed themselves and their lives.

Procedure

The study used a multimethod, multimeasure approach to the investigation of family interaction. The measures used included interviews with, and structured diary records of, the parents, observations of the parents and child interacting in the laboratory and home, behavior checklists of child behavior, parent rating of child behavior, and a battery of personality scales administered to the parents. In addition, observations of the child were conducted in the nursery school. Peer nomination, teacher ratings of the child's behavior, and measures of the child's sex-role typing, cognitive performance, and social development also were obtained. The parents and children were administered these measures two months, one year, and two years after divorce.

Parent Interviews. Parents were interviewed separately on a structured parent interview schedule designed to assess discipline practices and the parent-child relationship; support systems outside the family household system; social, emotional, and heterosexual relationships; quality of the relationship with the spouse; economic stress; family disorganization; satisfaction and happiness; and attitudes toward themselves. The interviews were tape-recorded. Each of the categories listed in Table 1 was rated on scales by two judges. In some cases the category involved the rating of only a single 5- or 7-point scale. In others it represented a composite score of several ratings on a group of subscales. Interjudge reliabilities ranged from .69 to .95, with a mean of .82. The interviews were derived and modified from those of Baumrind (1967, 1971), Martin and Hetherington (1971), Sears, Rau, and Alpert (1965), and others.

TABLE 1.   Categories for Rating Parent Interviews

Control of child	Economic stress
Maturity demands of child	Family disorganization
Communication with child	Problems in running household
Nurturance of child	
Permissiveness-restrictiveness with child	Relationship with spouse
Negative sanctions with child	Emotional support in personal matters
Positive sanctions with child	Immediate support system
Reinforcement of child for sex-typed behaviors	Social life and activities
Paternal availability	Contact with adults
Maternal availability	Intimate relations
Paternal face-to-face interaction with child	Sexuality
Maternal face-to-face interaction with child	Number of dates
Quality of spouse's relationship with child	Happiness and satisfaction
Agreement in treatment of child	Competence as a parent
	Competence as a male/female
Emotional support in child-rearing from spouse	Self-esteem
	Satisfaction with employment
	Conflict preceding divorce
	Tension in divorce

Parent Personality Inventories. The parent personality measures included the Personal Adjustment Scale of the Adjective Checklist (Gough and Heilbrun 1965), the Socialization Scale of the California Personality Inventory (Gough 1969), Rotter's I-E Scale (Rotter 1966), and the Spielberger's State-Trait Anxiety Scale (Spielberger, Gorsuch, and Lushene 1970).

Structured Diary Record. Each parent was asked to complete a structured diary record for three days (one weekday, Saturday, and Sunday). Fathers were asked to include at least one day when they were with their children. The diary record form was divided into half-hour units and contained a checklist of activities, situations, people, and five 7-point bipolar mood rating scales. The dimensions on the mood rating scales included: (1) anxious—relaxed; (2) hostile, angry—friendly, loving; (3) unhappy, depressed—happy; (4)

helpless—competent, in control; and (5) unloved, rejected—loved.

Each 30-minute unit was subdivided into three 10-minute units. If very different events had occurred in a 30-minute period, the subject was encouraged to record these separately and sequentially. For example, if a father had a fight with his boss and a phone call from his girl friend in the same half hour, these were recorded sequentially in separate columns. Parents were instructed to check off what they were doing, where they were located, who they were with, and how they were feeling on the mood scales in each 30-minute unit from the time they rose in the morning until they went to sleep at night. The record sheet also left space for any additional comments parents cared to make.

Although parents were encouraged to record at the end of each 30-minute period, because of the situation in which they found themselves, this was sometimes impossible. Any retrospective recording was noted, and the time the entry was made was also recorded. In the first session, a series of standardized scales dealing with affect, stress, and guilt had been included in the battery of parent measures; however, since the diary mood rating scales were found to be better predictors of behavior than these more time-consuming tests, the standardized scales were subsequently dropped from the study.

Parent-Child Laboratory Interaction. Parents were observed separately interacting with their children in the laboratory in half-hour free play situations and half-hour structured situations involving puzzles, block building, bead stringing, and sorting tasks. The interaction sessions with each parent were scheduled on different days, separated by a period of about a month. One-half of the children interacted with the mother first, and one-half with the father first. All sessions were video-taped to permit multiple coding of behavior. Behavior was coded in the categories presented in Table 2. The coding procedure was similar to that used by Patterson, Ray, Shaw, and Cobb (1969); the observation period was divided into 30-second intervals, and an average of approximately five behavior sequences of interactions between the subject and other family members was coded in the 30-second interval. To improve reliability, a tone sounded every six seconds during the recording interval. Two raters rated all sessions; interjudge agreement on individual responses averaged 83 percent.

Checklist of Child Behavior. Although at least three hours of observations of the parent and child interacting in the home situation were collected at three different times, this was not a sufficient time period to obtain an adequate sample of the child's behavior in which we were interested and which occurred relatively infrequently. Parents were given a behavior checklist and a recording form divided into half-hour units, and

TABLE 2. Parent-Child Laboratory Interaction Coding

Parent behavior	Child behavior
Command (positive)	Opposition
Command (negative)	Aversive opposition
Question (positive)	Compliance
Question (negative)	Dependency
Nonverbal intrusion	Negative demands (whining, complaining, angry tone)
Ignores	
Affiliate (interact)	Aggression (tantrums, destructiveness)
Positive sanctions	Requests
Negative sanctions	Affiliate
Reasoning and explanation	Self-manipulation
Encourages	Sustained play
Dependency	Ignores
Indulgence	Cries
Opposition	
Compliance	
Encourages independence	

were asked to record whether a given child behavior had occurred in a particular half-hour period. Three hours of recording were available for fathers, but twenty-four hours were available for mothers. Given behaviors included both acts regarded by parents as noxious, such as yelling, crying, whining, destructiveness, and noncompliance, and those regarded as desirable, such as helping, sharing, cooperative activities, compliance, sustained play, or independent activities.

Parent Rating Scales of Child Behavior. A parent rating scale of child behavior was constructed and standardized on a group of 100 mothers and fathers. Items used in previous observation questionnaires and rating scales, or items which seemed relevant to the interests of this study, were included in an initial pool of 96 items. Parents were asked to rate their children on these items using a 5-point scale, with 1 being never occurs, occurs less often than in most children, and 5 being frequently occurs, occurs more often than in most children. Items which correlated with each other, seemed conceptually related, or had been found to load on the same factor in previous studies, were clustered in seven scales containing a total of 49 items. Only items which correlated with the total score in the scales were retained. Items were phrased to describe very specific behavior, as many of these items were also used on the Checklist of Child Behavior previously described. The seven scales were aggression, inhibition, distractibility, task orientation, prosocial behavior, habit disturbance, and self-control. Divorced parents were asked to rate each item on the basis of the child's current behavior.

Data Analysis

Repeated measure manovas* involving test session (two months, one year, two years), sex of child, sex

* multiple analysis of variance

of parent, and family composition (divorced versus intact) were performed for each measure, interview, and laboratory interaction task. Repeated measure manovas were also performed on the mood ratings and the amount of time spent in various activities reported in the structured diary records, on the checklist, and in the rating scales. A repeated measure manova excluding the sex of child variable was performed for the parents' personality measures. Correlational analyses of all variables within and across subgroups also were performed. In addition, multiple regression and cross-lagged panel correlations and structural equations were calculated for selected parent and child variables in an attempt to identify functional and causal relationships contributing to changes in the behavior of family members across time.

RESULTS

The results of the study will not be presented separately for each procedure used. Instead, the combined findings of the different procedures will be used to discuss alterations in life-style, stresses, and coping by family members and family relations, and how these factors changed in the two years following divorce.

Change, Stress, and Coping in Divorce

How does the life of a single parent differ from that of married parents? In changing to a new single life-style, what kinds of stresses and satisfactions are experienced by members of a divorced couple? How might these be related to parent-child relations? The main areas in which change and stress were experienced were: (1) those related to practical problems of living; (2) those associated with emotional distress and changes in self-concept and identity; and (3) those related to interpersonal problems in maintaining a social life, developing intimate relationships, and interacting with the ex-spouse and child.

Practical Problems. The main practical problems of living encountered by divorced parents were those related to household maintenance and economic and occupational difficulties. Many divorced men, particularly those from marriages in which conventional sex roles had been maintained and the wife had not been employed, initially experienced considerable difficulty in maintaining a household routine and reported distress associated with what one termed "a chaotic life-style."

One of the sets of interview scales was family disorganization, which dealt with the degree of structure in proscribed household roles, problems in coping with routine household tasks, and the regulating and scheduling of events. On this scale and in the structured diaries, the households of the divorced mothers and fathers were more disorganized than those of intact families, although this disorganization was most marked in the first year after divorce and decreased significantly by the second year. Members of separated households were more likely to eat pickup meals at irregular times. Divorced mothers and their children were less likely to eat dinner together. Bedtimes were more erratic, the children were read to less often at bedtime, and the children were more likely to arrive at school late. Divorced men were less likely to eat at home than married men. They slept less and had more erratic sleep patterns, and had more difficulty with shopping, cooking, laundry, and cleaning. Some relief from stress associated with housework occurred with six of the fathers when female friends or an employed cleaning woman participated in household tasks.

Eleven of the 48 divorced fathers reported little difficulty in household maintenance and said they enjoyed having full responsibility for ordering their lives. Most of these men had participated actively in household tasks and child care during their marriages and, following divorce, were more likely to assist their ex-wives in maintaining their homes than fathers who previously had difficulty in coping with such tasks.

Greater economic stress in divorced couples as opposed to married couples was apparent in our sample. Although the average income of the divorced families was equal to that of the intact families, the economic problems associated with maintaining two households led to more financial concerns and limitations in purchasing practices for divorced couples. Divorced fathers were more likely than married fathers to increase their workload in an attempt to raise incomes. This created some duress in the first year after divorce when many fathers reported feeling immobilized by emotional problems and unable to work effectively. In addition, financial conflicts were one of the main sources of disagreement between divorced couples.

It has been suggested by Herzog and Sudia (1973) that many of the deleterious effects of a father's absence on children could be eliminated if economic stability was provided for the mother with no husband at home. However, in our study the number of significant correlations between income and reported feelings of economic stress, parents' reported or observed interactions with children, and children's behavior in nursery school, was not above chance. This was true whether we used the total income for divorced husbands and wives or the separate income for each of the households of the divorced spouses in the analyses. It may be that in our middle-class sample, with an average combined maternal and paternal income of about $22,000, the range was not great enough to detect the effects of economic stress.

Changes in Self-Concepts and Emotional Adjustment of Parents. Interview findings, diary mood ratings, and parents' personality tests showed many differences between the self-concepts and emotional adjustments of parents in divorced and intact families. Many of these differences diminished over the two-year period after divorce, with a marked drop occurring between one year and two years. In the first year following divorce, divorced mothers and fathers felt more anxious, depressed, angry, rejected, and incompetent. The effects were more sustained for divorced mothers —particularly for divorced mothers of boys, who at the end of two years were still feeling less competent, more anxious, more angry, and more externally controlled, as measured by the I-E Scale, than married mothers or divorced mothers of girls. The diary record indicated that these negative feelings were most likely to occur in episodes involving interactions with sons. This finding should be noted, for a position to be advanced later is that the mother-son relationship is particularly problematic in divorced families.

Divorced parents also scored lower on the socialization scale of the California Personality Inventory and Personality Scale of the Adjective Checklist throughout the three sets of measures. Does this mean that divorced people are less well-adjusted than married couples, or that an adverse response to the stresses associated with a conflictual marriage and divorce endure over the two-year postdivorce period? This question could not be answered from our data. The five couples in the larger intact sample who subsequently separated or divorced scored lower on these scales than the nondivorcing couples, and scored as more external on the I-E Scale only in the period immediately preceding the divorce, which suggests that these scales may be affected by the conflict associated with an unsatisfactory marriage and divorce.

Perhaps because he left the home and suffered the trauma of separation from his children, the divorced father seemed to undergo greater initial changes in self-concept than the mother, although effects were longer lasting in the mother. The continued presence of children and a familiar home setting gave mothers a sense of continuity that fathers lacked. Mothers complained more often of feeling physically unattractive, of having lost the identity and status associated with being married women, of a general feeling of helplessness. Fathers complained of not knowing who they were, of being rootless, of having no structure and no home in their lives. The separation induced great feelings of loss, previously unrecognized dependency needs, guilt, anxiety, and depression.

Changes in self-concept and identity problems were greatest in parents who were older or had been married longest. Two months after divorce, about one-third of the fathers and one-fourth of the mothers reported an ebullient sense of freedom which alternated with apprehension and depression; by one year the elation had been largely replaced by depression, anxiety, or apathy. These negative feelings markedly decreased by two years.

A pervasive concern of the fathers was the sense of loss of their children. For most this feeling declined with time, but for many it remained a continual concern. Eight fathers who initially were highly involved, attached, and affectionate parents reported that they could not endure the pain of seeing their children only intermittently. By two years after the divorce, they coped with this stress by seeing their children infrequently, although they continued to experience a great sense of loss and depression. However, it should not be thought that all divorced fathers felt less satisfied with their fathering roles following divorce. Ten of the fathers reported that their relationships with their children had improved and that they were enjoying their interchanges more. Most of these fathers came from marriages in which there had been a high degree of husband-wife conflict.

One of the most marked changes in divorced parents in the first year following divorce was a decline in feelings of competence. They felt they had failed as parents and spouses, and they expressed doubts about their ability to adjust well in any future marriages. They reported that they functioned less well in social situations and were less competent in heterosexual relationships. Nine of the divorced fathers reported an increased rate of sexual dysfunction. In addition to these feelings specifically related to marriage, 36 of the divorced fathers reported that they felt they were coping less well at work.

The flurry of social activity and self-improvement which occurred during the first year following divorce, particularly in divorced fathers, seemed to be an attempt to resolve some of the problems of identity and loss of self-esteem experenced by divorced parents.

One year after the divorce, the father was in a frenzy of activity. Although at this time contacts with old friends had declined, dating and casual social encounters at bars, clubs, cocktail parties, and other social gatherings had increased. In this period many of the divorced men and women were also involved in programs of self-improvement. Twenty-eight of the divorced fathers, in contrast to 14 married mothers, were engaged in activities such as night school courses in photography, languages, potting, jewelry-making, modern dance, and creative writing; structured physical fitness programs; and tennis, golf, or sailing lessons. However, by two years following the divorce, both the social life of divorced fathers and self-improvement programs for both divorced parents had declined. It should be noted that although these activities kept the parents busy and were associated with more positive emotional ratings, the most important factor in changing the self-concept two years after divorce was the establishment of a satisfying, intimate, heterosexual relationship. Only one father became involved in a homosexual relationship. He happened to have low ratings of self-esteem and happiness, but it is obvious that on the basis of this finding no conclusion can be drawn about the relative satisfaction of homosexual or heterosexual relationships.

Interpersonal Problems, Social Life, and Intimate Relationships. Stresses are experienced by most divorced couples in social life and in establishing meaningful, intimate interpersonal relationships. Almost all the divorced adults in this study complained that socializing in our culture is organized around couples and that being a single adult, particularly a single woman with children, limits recreational opportunities. Both the interview findings and the diary records kept by parents indicated that social life was more restricted for the divorced couples in the two years following divorce, and that this effect initially was most marked for women. Divorced parents reported that two months following divorce married friends were supportive, and diary records indicated that considerable time was spent with them. However, these contacts rapidly declined. The dissociation from married friends was greater for women than for men, who were more often included in social activities and sometimes participated in joint family outings on visitation days. Shared interests and concerns led to more frequent contact with other divorced, separated, or single persons. Divorced mothers reported having significantly less contact with adults than did married parents and often commented on their sense of being locked into a child's world. Several described themselves as prisoners and used terms like being "walled in" or "trapped." This was less true of working than nonworking mothers. Many nonworking mothers complained that most of their social contacts had been made through their husbands' professional associates and that with divorce these associations had terminated. In contrast, the employed mothers had contact with their co-workers, and these relations often extended into after-hour social events. Although the employed women complained of the difficulty of finishing household chores and of their concern about getting adequate care for their children, most felt the gratifications associated with employment outweighed the problems. Social life for our total sample of divorced women increased over the two-year period; however, it always remained lower than the social life for married women.

Divorced men had a restricted social life two months after divorce, followed by a surge of activity at one year, and a decline in activity to the wives' level by two years. In contrast to divorced women who felt trapped, divorced men complained of feeling shut out, rootless, and at loose ends, and of a need to engage in social activities even if they often were not pleasurable. Divorced men and women who had not remarried in the two years following divorce repeatedly spoke of their intense feelings of loneliness.

Heterosexual relations played a particularly important role in the happiness and attitudes toward self of both married and divorced adults. Happiness, self-esteem, and feelings of competence in heterosexual behavior increased steadily over the two-year period for divorced males and females, but such feelings were not as high even in the second year as those for married couples. It should be noted, however, that the subjects who later remarried, and were shifted from this study to a stepparent study, scored as high on happiness, although lower on self-esteem and feelings of competence, as parents in intact families. Frequency of sexual intercourse was lower for divorced parents than married couples at two months, higher at one year for males, and about the same at two years. Divorced males particularly seemed to show a peak of sexual activity and a pattern of dating a variety of women in the first year following divorce. However, the stereotyped image of the happy, swinging single life was not altogether accurate. One of our sets of interview ratings attempted to measure intimacy in relationships. Intimacy referred to love in the sense of valuing the welfare of the other as much as one's own, a deep concern and willingness to make sacrifices for the other, and a strong attachment and desire to be near the other person. It should be understood that this use of the term *intimacy* is not synonymous with sexual intimacy although, of course, the two frequently occur together. Intimacy in relationships showed strong positive correlations with happiness, self-esteem, and feelings of competence in heterosexual relations for both divorced and married men and women. Table 3 shows that if subjects in the divorced sample, but not the married sample, were divided into those above and below the medium in terms of intimacy in relationships, happiness correlated negatively with frequency of intercourse in the low-intimacy group and positively in the high-intimacy group. The same pattern held for self-esteem. This was true for both divorced males and females. The only nonsignificant correlation was for low-intimacy males immediately following divorce. Many males, but few females, were pleased at the increased opportunity for sexual experiences with a variety of partners immediately following divorce. However, by the end of the first year both divorced men and women were expressing a desire for intimacy and a lack of satisfaction in casual sexual encounters. Women expressed particularly intense feelings about frequent casual sex-

TABLE 3. Correlations Between Frequency of Sexual Intercourse and Happiness in High- and Low-Intimacy Divorced Groups

	High intimacy		Low intimacy	
	Male (N = 24)	Female (N = 24)	Male (N = 24)	Female (N = 24)
Two months	+.40*	+.43*	−.09(n.s.)	−.42*
One year	+.40**	+.47**	−.41*	−.46*
Two years	+.54**	+.52**	−.48**	−.57**

* p < .05
** p < .01

ual encounters, often talking of feelings of desperation, overwhelming depression, and low self-esteem following such exchanges. A pervasive desire for intimacy, which was not satisfied by casual encounters, characterized most of our divorced parents, and the formation of an intimate relationship seemed to be a powerful factor in the development of happiness and satisfaction.

Relationships Between Divorced Partners. At two months following divorce, relations with the ex-spouse and children remained the most salient and preoccupying concern for divorced parents. Most (66 percent) of the exchanges between divorced couples in this period involved conflicts. The most common areas of conflict were finances and support, visitation and child-rearing, and intimate relations with others. The relationships between all but four of the divorced couples were characterized by acrimony, anger, feelings of desertion, resentment, and memories of painful conflicts, all tempered by considerable ambivalence. Attachments persisted, and in some cases increased, following the escape from daily confrontations. Six of the 48 couples had sexual intercourse with each other in the two months after divorce. Thirty-four mothers and 29 fathers reported that, in case of a crisis, the ex-spouse would be the first person they would call. Eight of the fathers continued to help the mother with some home maintenance and 4 baby-sat when she went out on dates. With time, both conflict and attachment decreased, although anger and resentment were sustained longer by mothers than by fathers. The establishment of new intimate relationships and remarriage were particularly powerful factors in attenuating the intensity of the divorced couple's relationship.

At one year after divorce—which seemed to be the most stressful period for both parents—29 fathers and 35 mothers reported that they thought the divorce might have been a mistake, that they should have tried harder to resolve their conflicts, and that the alternative life-styles available to them were not satisfying. By the end of the second year, only 9 fathers and 12 mothers felt this way.

In our larger sample, which included parents who

remarried, remarriage by the spouse was accompanied by a reactivation of feelings of depression, helplessness, anger, and anxiety—particularly in mothers. Many reported that their feelings of panic and loss were similar to those experienced at the time of the original separation and divorce. Anger by the mother was almost an invariable concomitant of the ex-husband's remarriage, even if she was the first to remarry. Sometimes this anger took the form of reopening conflicts about finances or visitation; sometimes it was directed at the children and their split loyalties; often it focused on resentment and feelings of competition with the new wife. While 5 of the 10 men whose ex-wives remarried reported approval of the new husband, only 4 of the 19 women whose ex-husbands remarried approved of the new wife. The new wives seemed to exacerbate these feelings by entering into particularly hostile competitive relationships with the ex-wives in which criticism of the children and the ex-wives' childrearing often were used as the combative focus.

Parent-Child Relations

Thus far we have been focusing mainly on changes in the divorced partners in the two years after divorce and have seen that divorced couples encountered and coped with many stresses. We will now look at differences in family functioning and parent-child interactions as measured in both interviews and direct observations in the laboratory situation.

The interaction patterns between divorced parents and children differed significantly from those of intact families on many variables studied in the interview and on many of the parallel measures in the structured interaction situation. On these measures the differences were greatest during the first year; a process of re-equilibration seemed to be taking place by the end of the second year, particularly in mother-child relationships. However, even at the end of the second year, parent-child relations in divorced and intact families still differed on many dimensions. Although there were still many stresses in the parent-child interactions of divorced parents after two years, it is noteworthy that almost one-fourth of the fathers and one-half of the mothers reported that their relationships with their children had improved over those during the marriage when parental conflict and tensions had detrimental effects.

Some of the findings for fathers must be interpreted in view of the fact that divorced fathers became increasingly less available to their children and ex-spouses over the course of the two years. Although at two months divorced fathers were having almost as many face-to-face interactions with their children as fathers in intact homes—who were often highly unavailable to their children (Blanchard and Biller 1971)—these interactions declined rapidly. At two months, about one-fourth of the divorced parents reported that fathers, in their eagerness to maximize visitation rights and maintain contact with their children, were having even more face-to-face contact with their children than they had before the divorce. This contact was motivated by a variety of factors. Sometimes it was based on the father's deep attachment to the child or continuing attachment to the wife; sometimes it was based on feelings of duty or attempts to assuage guilt; often it was an attempt to maintain a sense of continuity in the father's life. Unfortunately, it was often at least partly motivated by a desire to annoy, compete with, or retaliate against the spouse. By two years after the divorce, 19 divorced fathers saw their children once a week or more, 14 fathers saw them every two weeks, 7 every three weeks, and 8 once a month or less.

Results of the diary record, interview findings, and laboratory observations relating to parent-child interactions will be presented in a simplified fashion and, when possible, presented together. The patterns of parent-child interaction showed considerable congruence across these measures.

Divorced parents made fewer maturity demands, communicated less well, tended to be less affectionate, and showed marked inconsistency in discipline and control of their children in comparison to married parents. Poor parenting was most apparent when divorced parents, particularly divorced mothers, interacted with their sons. Divorced parents communicated less, were less consistent, and used more negative sanctions with sons than with daughters. Additionally, in the laboratory situation divorced mothers exhibited fewer positive behaviors (such as positive sanctions and affiliations) and more negative behaviors (such as negative commands, negative sanctions, and opposition to children's requests) with sons than with daughters. Sons of divorced parents seemed to have a difficult time, and this may partly explain why—as we shall see shortly—the adverse effects of divorce are more severe and enduring for boys than for girls.

Fortunately, parents learned to adapt to problem situations, and by two years after divorce the parenting practices of divorced mothers had improved. Poor parenting seemed most marked, particularly for divorced mothers, one year after divorce, which appeared to be a peak of stress in parent-child relations. Two years after divorce mothers were demanding more autonomous, mature behavior of their children, communicated better, and used more explanations and reasoning. They were more nurturant and consistent, and were better able to control their children than before. A similar pattern occurred for divorced fathers in maturity demands, communication, and consistency, but they became less nurturant and more detached from their children with time; in the laboratory and home observations, divorced fathers ignored their children more and showed less affection.

The interviews and observations showed that the lack of control divorced parents had over their children was associated with very different patterns of relating to children by mothers and fathers. The divorced mother tried to control her child by being more restrictive and giving more commands which the child ignored or resisted. The divorced father wanted his contacts with his child to be as happy as possible. He began by being extremely permissive and indulgent with his child and becoming increasingly restrictive over the two-year period, although he was never as restrictive as fathers in intact homes. The divorced mother used more negative sanctions than the divorced father or than parents in intact families. However, by the second year the divorced mother's use of negative sanctions declined as the divorced father's increased. In a parallel fashion, the divorced mother's use of positive sanctions increased after the first year as the divorced father's decreased. The "every day is Christmas" behavior of the divorced father declined with time. The divorced mother decreased her futile attempts at authoritarian control and became more effective in dealing with her child over the two-year period.

The lack of control divorced parents had over their children, particularly one year after divorce, was apparent in both home and laboratory observations. The observed frequency of children's compliance with parents' regulations, commands, or requests could be regarded as a measure of either parental control or resistant child behavior. A clearer understanding of functional relationships in parent-child interaction may be obtained by examining the effectiveness of various types of parental responses in leading to compliance by children and parents' responses to children following compliance or noncompliance. It can be seen in Table 4 that boys are less compliant than girls and that fathers are more effective than mothers in obtaining compliance from children in both divorced and intact families. This may be at least partly based on the fact that mothers gave over twice as many commands as

TABLE 4. Compliance with Positive and Negative Parental Commands and Parental Reasoning and Explanation

	Percentage of compliance with positive parental commands							
	Intact				Divorced			
	Girl		Boy		Girl		Boy	
	Father	Mother	Father	Mother	Father	Mother	Father	Mother
Two months	60.2	54.6	51.3	42.6	51.3	40.6	39.9	29.3
One year	63.4	56.7	54.9	44.8	43.9	31.8	32.6	21.5
Two years	64.5	59.3	57.7	45.3	52.1	44.2	43.7	37.1

	Percentage of compliance with negative parental commands							
	Intact				Divorced			
	Girl		Boy		Girl		Boy	
	Father	Mother	Father	Mother	Father	Mother	Father	Mother
Two months	55.7	49.3	47.5	36.4	47.0	34.8	35.6	23.4
One year	59.2	51.5	50.3	38.8	39.1	27.2	28.3	17.2
Two years	60.5	54.6	53.6	39.0	49.9	39.7	39.7	31.8

	Percentage of compliance with parental reasoning and explanation							
	Intact				Divorced			
	Girl		Boy		Girl		Boy	
	Father	Mother	Father	Mother	Father	Mother	Father	Mother
Two months	49.1	43.3	41.0	31.1	41.3	29.2	29.6	18.4
One year	55.4	48.0	46.2	34.5	26.3	23.1	24.5	14.1
Two years	62.3	58.1	58.1	47.6	50.3	42.5	41.4	36.9

fathers, and divorced mothers gave significantly more commands than divorced fathers or parents in intact families.

The curvilinear effect—with the least effectiveness of any type of parental behavior at one year and a marked increase in control of the child by two years—is again apparent, although divorced mothers and fathers never gained as much control as their married counterparts. Because developmental psychologists have traditionally regarded reasoning and explanation as the font of good discipline from which all virtues flow, the results relating to types of parental demands were unexpected. Negative commands were less effective than positive commands and, somewhat surprisingly, in the two-month and one-year groups, reasoning and explanation were less effective than either positive or negative commands. By the last test session the effectiveness of reasoning and explanation significantly increased over the previous sessions. Two things were noteworthy about the pattern of change in reasoning.

First, it should be remembered that the average age of the subjects was two years older at the final session. The mean age of children at the two-month session was 3.92 years; at the one-year session, 4.79 years; and at the final session, 5.81 years. It may be that as children became more cognitively and linguistically mature, reasoning and explanation were more effective because

children could better understand and had longer attention spans. It may also be that internalization and role-taking were increasing and explanations involving appeals to the rights and feelings of others became more effective. Some support for the position that younger children may not fully comprehend or attend to explanations is found in a point biserial correlational post hoc analysis between the number of words in explanations and children's compliance or noncompliance. After reviewing videotapes of the laboratory situation to see what happens in cases with high use of reasoning and low compliance, we observed that parents often used long-winded, conceptually complicated explanations and the children seemed to become rapidly inattentive, distracted, and bored. Then the children either continued their previous activity or ignored the parents. The average point biserial correlation between noncompliance and number of words across the group was —.58 at two months, —.44 at one year, and —.13 at two years. "Short and sweet" would seem to be an effective maxim for instructing young children. The same type of analysis was performed on the home observations, which had been audiotaped but not videotaped, and the same pattern of results was obtained. Long explanations were associated with noncompliance in younger children.

Second, two years following divorce reasoning was

TABLE 5. Parents' Consequent Behaviors Toward Compliance

Percentage of positive sanctions (affiliate, encourage)

	Intact				Divorced			
	Girl		Boy		Girl		Boy	
	Father	Mother	Father	Mother	Father	Mother	Father	Mother
Two months	39.0	51.1	34.6	49.8	46.6	37.0	44.2	31.8
One year	42.6	49.7	37.2	45.6	47.4	32.5	42.4	28.8
Two years	44.4	49.4	39.8	48.1	36.8	41.6	34.7	37.3

Percentage of ignoring or no response

	Intact				Divorced			
	Girl		Boy		Girl		Boy	
	Father	Mother	Father	Mother	Father	Mother	Father	Mother
Two months	21.4	15.8	18.7	16.3	19.2	28.9	17.6	27.9
One year	23.9	16.2	20.9	17.8	20.4	30.0	17.1	30.3
Two years	22.6	14.9	19.5	16.4	30.2	19.8	25.1	20.0

Percentage of positive commands

	Intact				Divorced			
	Girl		Boy		Girl		Boy	
	Father	Mother	Father	Mother	Father	Mother	Father	Mother
Two months	11.6	16.2	15.1	20.3	6.2	18.8	10.0	20.4
One year	12.3	15.3	14.9	18.6	6.6	20.7	8.3	21.1
Two years	10.9	14.7	15.5	19.9	8.3	17.0	13.5	20.0

Percentage of negative commands or negative sanctions

	Intact				Divorced			
	Girl		Boy		Girl		Boy	
	Father	Mother	Father	Mother	Father	Mother	Father	Mother
Two months	8.6	4.3	10.5	7.6	2.4	8.2	5.0	13.4
One year	6.7	5.1	9.7	6.6	4.2	10.3	8.1	14.9
Two years	6.9	4.8	9.9	6.9	7.6	5.6	9.3	10.5

superior to negative parental commands in obtaining compliance from boys (with the exception of sons interacting with their divorced fathers) but not from girls. Why should reasoning be relatively more effective in gaining compliance from boys? Martin (1974) in his recent review of research on parent-child interactions suggests that coercive parental responses are more likely to be related to oversocialization and inhibition in girls, and to aggression in boys. It may be that the greater aggressiveness frequently observed in preschool boys and the greater assertiveness in the culturally proscribed male role necessitate the use of reasoning and explanation to develop the cognitive mediators necessary for self-control in boys. Some support for this idea was found in the greater number of, significantly larger, and more consistent correlations for boys than for girls between the communication scale of the parent interview, frequency of observed parental reasoning and explanation, and parents' ratings of children's prosocial

behavior, self-control, and aggression. A similar pattern of correlations was obtained between these parental measures and the frequency of negative and positive behavior on the behavior checklist. In contrast, high use of negative commands was positively related to aggression in boys, but not in girls. Although reasoning and explanation are not clearly superior to other commands in gaining short-term compliance, these methods are more effective in the long-term development of self-control, inhibition of aggression, and prosocial behavior in boys.

We can extend our analysis of compliance one step further and examine how parents respond to compliance or noncompliance by children. Developmental psychologists and behavior modifiers have emphasized the role of contingent reinforcement in effective parenting. Parental responses to compliance are presented in Table 5, and parental responses to noncompliance are presented in Table 6; the most frequently occurring

TABLE 6.   Parents' Consequent Behaviors Toward Noncompliance

Percentage of positive commands

	Intact				Divorced			
	Girl		Boy		Girl		Boy	
	Father	Mother	Father	Mother	Father	Mother	Father	Mother
Two months	26.3	27.9	24.2	29.3	23.6	20.6	22.0	23.9
One year	24.8	23.6	25.7	27.5	20.5	16.9	20.0	15.3
Two years	25.1	26.8	26.0	27.9	19.1	23.0	18.0	20.6

Percentage of reasoning, explanation, and encouraging positive questions

	Intact				Divorced			
	Girl		Boy		Girl		Boy	
	Father	Mother	Father	Mother	Father	Mother	Father	Mother
Two months	20.1	25.6	17.9	22.7	18.9	20.1	15.0	16.5
One year	22.7	25.3	20.1	23.2	18.1	16.3	16.9	11.9
Two years	26.8	30.4	24.3	28.5	14.0	27.4	13.2	22.7

Percentage of negative commands, negative sanctions, and negative questions

	Intact				Divorced			
	Girl		Boy		Girl		Boy	
	Father	Mother	Father	Mother	Father	Mother	Father	Mother
Two months	18.5	14.0	20.0	18.3	9.0	24.0	12.0	26.2
One year	20.4	15.7	22.5	17.0	9.9	26.8	13.1	28.1
Two years	22.2	17.5	26.8	17.5	19.8	20.2	22.2	21.7

Percentage of ignoring or no response

	Intact				Divorced			
	Girl		Boy		Girl		Boy	
	Father	Mother	Father	Mother	Father	Mother	Father	Mother
Two months	5.3	8.1	4.1	9.9	13.5	15.8	14.3	16.0
One year	4.8	6.7	3.9	7.3	16.7	17.9	18.1	19.3
Two years	4.0	4.9	3.0	5.8	18.1	11.6	21.6	10.2

Percentage of physical intrusion

	Intact				Divorced			
	Girl		Boy		Girl		Boy	
	Father	Mother	Father	Mother	Father	Mother	Father	Mother
Two months	10.8	6.9	9.5	5.8	11.2	8.3	9.3	8.0
One year	8.6	5.7	8.7	5.4	9.1	8.2	8.4	7.5
Two years	7.2	5.8	6.9	5.0	8.1	6.0	7.3	5.9

responses are included in these tables. Only the most significant effects will be noted.

First, it can be seen that children received positive reinforcement in less than one-half of the times they complied—not a very lavish reinforcement schedule for good behavior. Second, boys who complied received less positive reinforcement; more commands, both positive and negative; and more negative sanctions (such as, "You didn't do that very fast" or "You'd better shape up if you know what's good for you") than girls. Boys were not as appropriately re-

inforced for compliance as girls. This seemed to be the case particularly for divorced mothers and sons across all ages, although divorced mothers became significantly more appropriate in responding to compliance by children from one year to two years after divorce. In contrast, divorced fathers became less reinforcing and attentive to children's positive behaviors in this period.

How did parents respond when children failed to obey their commands? In most cases, they gave another command, sometimes using negative sanctions. Parents in intact families, especially mothers, were also likely to deal with noncompliance by reasoning with children. Sometimes parents, notably fathers, intruded physically by moving the children or surrounding objects. There was much less ignoring of noncompliance than of compliance, especially by fathers in intact families. If parental ignoring responses are examined, it is clear that one way divorced parents coped with noncompliance was by pretending it did not happen. The chains of noncompliance by children, followed by ignoring, were of longer duration in divorced families than in intact families, especially in the interactions of divorced mothers and their sons.

Divorced mothers dramatically increased their use of reasoning and explanation in response to noncompliance in the second year after divorce, while divorced fathers became less communicative and more negative in their responses.

After reviewing the interview and observational findings one might be prone to state that disruptions in children's behavior after divorce are attributable to emotional disturbance in the divorced parents and poor parenting, especially by mothers of boys. However, before we point a condemning finger at these parents, especially the divorced mothers who face the day-to-day problems of childrearing, let us look at the children involved. The findings on the behavior checklist, recording the occurrence of children's positive and negative behaviors in the home in 30-minute units, showed not only that children of divorced parents exhibited more negative behavior than children of intact families, but also that these behaviors were most marked in boys and had largely disappeared in girls two years after divorce. Such behaviors were also significantly declining in boys. Children exhibited more negative behavior with their mothers than with their fathers; this was especially true with sons of divorced parents.

These checklist results were corroborated by the home and laboratory observations, and by parent ratings of children's behavior. Divorced mothers may have given their children a difficult time, but mothers, especially divorced mothers, got rough treatment from their children. As previously remarked, children were more likely to exhibit oppositional behavior to mothers and comply with fathers. The children made negative complaining demands of the mother more frequently. Boys were more oppositional and aggressive; girls were more whining, complaining, and compliant. Children of divorced parents showed an increase in dependency over time, and exhibited less sustained play than children of intact families. The divorced mother was harassed by her children, especially her sons. In comparison with fathers and with mothers in intact families, children of the divorced mother did not obey, affiliate, or attend to her in the first year after divorce. They nagged and

whined, made more dependency demands, and were more likely to ignore her. Aggression of sons of divorced mothers peaked at one year, then dropped significantly, but was still higher at two years than aggression of sons in intact families. Some divorced mothers described their relationships with their children one year after divorce as "declared war," "a struggle for survival," "the old water torture," or "getting bitten to death by ducks." One year following divorce seemed to be the period of maximum negative behaviors for children, as it was for the divorced parents themselves. Great improvement occurred by two years, although negative behaviors were more sustained in boys than in girls. The second year appeared to be a marked recovery and constructive adaptation for divorced mothers and children.

Who is doing what to whom? It has been proposed—most recently by Patterson in a paper entitled "Mothers: The Unacknowledged Victims" (1976)—that the maternal role is not a very rewarding or satisfying one. Patterson demonstrates that the maternal role, particularly with mothers of problem children, demands high rates of responding with very low levels of positive reinforcement for the mothers. He assumes that mothers and their aggressive children get involved in a vicious circle of coercion. The mother's lack of management skills accelerates the child's aversive behavior of which the mother is the main instigator and for which she is the main target. This is reciprocated by increased coercion in the mother's parenting behavior, and feelings of helplessness, depression, anger, and self-doubt. In his study, Patterson shows that decreases in the noxious behaviors of aggressive children through treatment procedures aimed at improving parenting skills are associated with decreases of maternal scores on a number of clinical scales on the Minnesota Multiphasic Personality Inventory (MMPI), with a decrease in anxiety on the Taylor Manifest Anxiety Scale, and with improvement on several other measures of maternal adjustment.

Patterson's model may be particularly applicable to divorced mothers and their children in our study. High synchronous correlations between reported and observed poor parenting in divorced mothers and between reported and observed negative behavior in children occurred at each time period. The greater use of poor maternal parenting practices and higher frequency of undesirable behaviors in children from divorced families, even in the first sessions with mothers and sons, suggests that the coercive cycle was already underway when we first encountered our families two months after divorce. Stresses and conflicts preceding or accompanying divorce might have initiated the cycle. High rates and durations of negative exchanges between divorced mothers and their sons were apparent throughout the study. Sequence analyses of the home and laboratory observations showed that divorced mothers of boys were not only more likely than other parents to trigger noxious behavior, but also that they were less able to control or terminate this behavior once it occurred.

We attempted to use cross-lagged panel correlations between selected parent and child measures at the three time periods to identify causal effects in these interactions. Panel correlations were problematic with our study, which involved a relatively small sample size. Kenney (1975), in his review of cross-lagged panel correlations, stated that it is difficult to obtain significant results with *N*s under 75. In our study, if we analyzed divorced and intact families separately, but pooled boys and girls, we had only 48 families in a group. Because the family dynamics differed somewhat in families with boys and girls, especially for divorced families, it seemed conceptually unsound to combine sexes, but then we were left with a meager 24 families per group. In spite of these difficulties, we did obtain some findings of interest on the panel correlations.

There were many significant synchronous correlations between parent and child behavior. Poor parenting practices and coercive behavior in parents correlated with undesirable and coercive behavior in children; this was particularly true for divorced mothers and their sons. This suggests that the coercive cycle was already underway. Causal direction for poor parenting practices and noxious child behavior could not be identified consistently by the panel correlations. However, the observational measures and child checklist measures—but not the interview and rating measures—indicated that poor parenting by divorced mothers at two months after divorce caused problem behaviors in children at one year. These effects were similar but not significant between one year and two years.

A striking finding was that divorced mothers' self-esteem, feelings of parental competence as measured by the interview, state anxiety as measured by the Spielberger State-Trait Anxiety Scale, and mood ratings of competence, depression, and anxiety on the structured diary record not only showed significant synchronous correlation with ratings of children's aggression and checklist frequency of noxious behaviors, but also yielded significant cross-lagged panel correlations, suggesting that the behavior of the children—particularly of the sons—was causing the emotional responses of the mother. The findings were similar but less consistent for mothers in intact families. Mothers from divorced and intact families showed more state and trait anxiety, feelings of external control and incompetence, and depression than fathers. This suggests that the feminine maternal role is not as gratifying as the masculine paternal role, regardless of whether the family is intact or divorced. The more marked findings in divorced mothers seemed in accord with Patterson's view that mothers of problem children are trapped in a coercive cycle that leads to debilitating attitudes toward themselves, adverse emotional responses, and feelings of helplessness.

In Patterson's study and others comparing parents of problem and nonproblem children, fathers were found to be much less affected by problem children than were mothers. Fathers, particularly divorced fathers, spent less time with their children than did mothers, thereby escaping some of the stresses imposed by coercive children and obtaining more gratification in activities outside the family. Fathers seemed less likely to get involved in a coercive vicious cycle because children exhibited less deviant behavior in their presence; furthermore, fathers were more able to control deviant behavior by children once it occurred, as was shown in fathers' ratings of children's behavior, frequencies of behavior on the checklist, and observations in the home and laboratory.

The cross-lagged panel correlations showed a larger proportion of effects going in the direction of fathers causing children's behavior rather than in children causing fathers' behaviors, relative to the number found in mother-child interactions. Children's behavior showed few effects on the state anxiety, mood ratings, or self-esteem of fathers, especially divorced fathers. In addition, in intact families, negative child behaviors at the one- and two-year periods seemed to be partially caused by poor control, low nurturance, and high use of negative sanctions by fathers at the earlier periods.

The 48 divorced fathers involved in this study probably showed more concern about their children and interacted with them more than most divorced fathers. The fact that they were available for study and willing to participate may reflect a more sustained and greater degree of paternal involvement than is customarily found. However, despite this possible bias, the impact of divorced fathers on children declined with time, and was significantly less than that of fathers in intact families. At two months following divorce, the number of significant correlations between paternal characteristics and behavior and child characteristics was about the same as in intact families. However, two years after divorce the divorced fathers clearly had less influence with their children while divorced mothers had more influence. Divorced mothers became increasingly salient relative to divorced fathers in the social, cognitive, and personality development of their children. This decrease was less marked for divorced fathers who maintained a high rate of contact with their children.

It would seem that in the period leading to and following divorce, parents go through many role changes and encounter many problems, and that they would benefit from support in coping with these problems.

In both divorced and intact families, effectiveness in dealing with the child was related to support from the spouse in childrearing and agreement with the spouse in disciplining the child. When support and agreement occurred between divorced couples, the disruption in family functioning appeared to be less extreme, and the restabilizing of family functioning occurred earlier—by the end of the first year.

When divorced parents agreed about childrearing, had positive attitudes toward each other, and were low in conflict, and when the divorced father was emotionally mature—as measured by the Socialization Scale of the California Personality Inventory (Gough 1969) and the Personal Adjustment Scale of the Adjective Checklist (Gough and Heilbrun 1965)—frequent contact between father and child was associated with positive mother-child interactions and positive adjustment of the child. Where there were disagreements and inconsistencies in attitudes toward the child and conflict between the divorced parents, or when the father was poorly adjusted, frequent visitation by the father was associated with poor mother-child functioning and disruptions in the child's behavior. Emotional maturity in the mother was also found to be related to her adequacy in coping with stresses in her new single life and her relations with the child.

Other support systems, such as parents, siblings, close friends (especially other divorced friends or intimate male friends), or a competent housekeeper, also were related to the mother's effectiveness in interacting with the child in divorced, but not in intact, families. However, none of these support systems was as salient as a continued, positive, mutually-supportive relationship between the divorced couple and continued involvement of the father with the child. For the divorced father, intimate female friends, married friends, and relatives offered the next greatest support in his relationship with the child.

Among our 48 divorced couples, only 6 mothers and 4 fathers sought professional counseling or therapy; the main motivating factor seemed to be having friends who had been in therapy and recommended it. However, in our larger sample of 72 divorced couples, we identified 11 mothers and 6 fathers on whom we had records for one year following entry into therapy. Both the divorced mother and the child demonstrated improved adjustment only in the subgroup of 5 mothers involved in programs to improve parenting skills which made available 24-hour telephone contact with the parent trainer. This was obviously not a large enough group from which to draw firm conclusions about the efficacy of therapy as a support system, but it does suggest that focusing on effective parenting may alleviate some of the problems encountered by the divorced mother and child.

DISCUSSION AND SUMMARY

In this study, divorced mothers and fathers encountered marked stresses in practical problems of living, self-concept and emotional adjustment, and interpersonal relations following divorce. Low self-estem, loneliness, depression, and feelings of helplessness were characteristic of the divorced couple. Although the establisment of new intimate relations helped mitigate these effects, divorced parents were still less satisfied with their lives two years after divorce than parents in intact families.

Disruptions occurred in parent-child relations in many divorced families. Divorced parents infantilized their children and communicated less well with them than parents in intact families. In addition, they tended to be more inconsistent and less affectionate, and to have less control over their children's behavior. Children in divorced families were more dependent, disobedient, aggressive, whining, demanding, and unaffectionate than children in intact families. These effects were most marked in mother-son interactions. A peak of stress in parent-child interactions appeared one year after divorce, and marked improvement, particularly in mother-child relations, occurred thereafter.

Personal and emotional adjustment also deteriorated in the year following divorce. This seemed to be a period in which members of divorced families were testing a variety of coping mechanisms—many of them unsuccessful—in dealing with changes and stresses in their new life situations. However, by the second year after divorce a process of restabilization and adjustment was apparent.

In our current culture, the myth of romantic love and marriage is being replaced by the myth of the romance of divorce. The literature on divorce is replete with titles such as *Creative Divorce, Divorce: Chance of a New Lifetime,* and *Divorce: Gateway to Self Realization.* Many couples initiating divorces are prepared for reduced stress and conflict, the joys of greater interpersonal freedoms, and the delights of self-discovery and self-actualization associated with liberation. Few are prepared for the traumas and stresses they will encounter in attaining these goals after divorce, even if the goals are ultimately reached.

Because this was a longitudinal study, it presented an opportunity to examine how family members responded to and coped with the divorce experience. In the families we studied, there was none in which at least one family member did not report distress or exhibit disrupted behavior, particularly during the first year after divorce. We did not encounter a victimless divorce. Most of the members of divorced families ultimately were able to cope with many of their problems, but the course of adjustment was often unexpectedly painful.

Because this study lasted only two years, it is impossible to state whether the restabilizing process in the divorced family was largely completed at two years, or whether readjustment would continue over a longer period until such adjustment ultimately would resemble more closely that of intact families.

It should be remembered that the results reported in a study like this represent averages and that there are wide variations in coping and parenting within intact and divorced families. There are many inadequate parents and children with problems in intact families. Our study and previous research show that a conflict-ridden intact family is more deleterious to family members than a stable home situation in which parents are divorced. Divorce is often a positive solution to destructive family functioning, and the best statistical prognostications suggest that the rate of divorce is likely to increase. Because this is the case, it is important that parents and children be realistically prepared for the problems associated with divorce that they may encounter. More research and applied programs oriented toward the identification and application of constructive parenting and coping after divorce should be initiated. Divorce is one of the most serious crises in contemporary American life. It is a major social responsibility to develop support systems for the divorced family in coping with changes associated with divorce and in finding means of modifying or eliminating the deleterious aftereffects of divorce.

REFERENCES

Baumrind, D. "Child Care Practices Anteceding Three Patterns of Preschool Behavior." *Genetic Psychology Monographs* 75 (1967): 43–88.

Baumrind, D. "Current Patterns of Parental Authority." *Developmental Psychology Monographs* 4 (1971): 1–102.

Biller, H. B. *Paternal Deprivation.* Lexington, Mass.: Lexington Books, 1974.

Blanchard, R. W., and Biller, H. B. "Father Availability and Academic Performance among Third Grade Boys." *Developmental Psychology* 4 (1971): 301–305.

Bronfenbrenner, U. "The Changing American Family." Paper presented at the Society for Research in Child Development meeting, Denver, April 1975.

Gough, H. G. *Manual for California Personality Inventory.* Palo Alto, Calif.: Consulting Psychologists Press, 1969.

Gough, H. G., and Heilbrun, A. B., Jr. *The Adjective Checklist.* Palo Alto, Calif.: Consulting Psychologists Press, 1965.

Herzog, E., and Sudia, C. E. "Children in Fatherless Families." In *Review of Child Development Research,* edited by B. M. Caldwell and H. N. Ricciuti. Chicago: University of Chicago Press, 1973.

Hetherington, E. M., and Deur, J. "The Effects of Father Absence on Child Development." *Young Children* 26, no. 4 (March 1971): 233–248.

Kenney, D. A. "A Quasi-Experimental Approach to Assessing Treatment Effects in the Nonequivalent Control Group Design." *Psychological Bulletin* 82, no. 3 (1975): 345–362.

Lynn, D. B. *The Father: His Role in Child Development.* Belmont, Calif.: Wadsworth, 1974.

Martin, B. "Parent-Child Relations." In *Review of Child Development Research,* edited by B. M. Caldwell and H. N. Ricciuti. Chicago: University of Chicago Press, 1973.

Martin B., and Hetherington, E. M. "Family Interaction in Withdrawn, Aggressive and Normal Children." Unpublished manuscript, 1971.

Patterson, G. "Mothers: The Unacknowledged Victims." Paper presented at the Society for Research in Child Development meeting, Oakland, Calif., April 1976.

Patterson, G. R.; Ray, R. S.; Shaw, D. A.; and Cobb, J. A. *A Manual for Coding of Family Interaction,* rev. ed. NAPS Document #01234, 1969.

Rotter, J. B. "Generalized Expectancies for Internal Versus External Control of Reinforcement." *Psychological Monographs* 80, no. 1 (1966); whole no. 609.

Sears, R. R.; Rau, L.; and Alpert, R. *Identification and Child Rearing.* Stanford, Calif.: Stanford Press, 1965.

Spielberger, C. D.; Gorsuch, R. L.; and Lushene, R. *State-Trait Anxiety Inventory.* Palo Alto, Calif.: Consulting Psychologists Press, 1970.

27

Single-Parent Fathers:

A Research Review

Benjamin Schlesinger

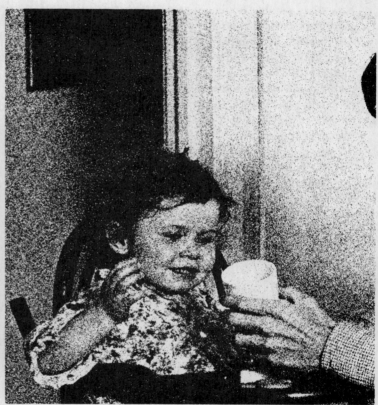

A category of families whose number is increasing steadily each year is the "motherless family." In Canada, it is estimated that 20 percent of all single-parent families (100,680) are headed by men only, and that they are rearing an estimated 182,855 children. The latest American data indicate that there were 450,000 single-parent families headed by men in the United States in 1976.[1] In this article, I will review studies conducted in four English-speaking countries and comment on some of the gaps in knowledge relating to this emerging phenomenon.

Reprinted from *Children Today* Magazine, May/June 1978. U.S. Department of Health, Education and Welfare.

IN AUSTRALIA

Writing in Australia, Chris Bane pointed out some of the needs of single fathers.[2] There are the financial problems incurred. These include "child minding fees during the day for the very young, baby-sitting fees at night, seldom a chance to shop for bargains, seldom able to cook economically, unable to supplement his income with odd jobs, a second job and certainly no second income coming from a working wife." The author also noted that such fathers are restricted in regard

Benjamin Schlesinger, Ph.D., is a professor, Faculty of Social Work, University of Toronto, Ontario, Canada.

to overtime work and business trips and so are unlikely to be promoted.

There are special child-rearing problems too, for apart from finding child-minding facilities—an acute problem during school holidays—the father has to do the housewife's jobs when he comes home from work, spend more time with the children at night and, if he has a daughter, raise her with no mother figure to identify with.

The children may fear that the father will walk out one day as their mother did and there is a danger that they will grow up identifying authority and the source of love with the male sex—certainly having only a male parent prevents a balanced two-sex view of life.

The rush to do housekeeping after work often means that the jobs aren't properly done, that the children don't get enough attention or that they are given tasks to do which may be too much or inappropriate for them. The father's "social life" may be virtually non-existent since he is tied down with the kids and most adult social outings are geared to couples.

Deserted and divorced husbands feel a humiliation which the children may share. There is also the loneliness of missing a spouse to provide companionship and to share responsibility, plus the feeling of the children that they are viewed as "different" by others.

The following recommendations are made by Bain to help single-parent fathers:

· Increased availability of part-time work to assist single parents of both sexes who must combine breadwinning with housekeeping.

· Longer hours at child-minding centers and availability of center care for schoolchildren between the end of the schoolday and the end of the father's workday.

· An organized, registered housekeeper service to ensure good, qualified help and to facilitate the location of housekeepers when needed.

· Increased tax deductions for single fathers, so that expenses for part-time housekeepers could be deductible and full-time housekeepers fully deductible.

· Greater public housing acceptance of lone fathers as tenants.

· School holiday programs for children.

· Counseling services for fathers and children.

· Research on the needs of single parents.

IN BRITAIN

Victor George and Paul Wilding studied 588 motherless families who had been in active contact with various social agencies in England.[3] The families included an average of 3.5 children and had been motherless on an average of 3.7 years.

These authors found that the loss of a mother in a family had serious economic consequences. The incomes of the men decreased in 44 percent of the cases, although the decrease was directly due to the loss of a wife's earnings in only 12 percent. Thus, the economic impact seemed to be largely a result of the loss of the mother's formerly uncomputed economic contribution to the household budget. In addition, responsibility for child care meant that the father's ability to work overtime was now limited. In 35 percent of the families, the father had stopped working for some period of time. Almost 30 percent of the families had received supplementary benefits during their period of motherlessness and 19 percent were receiving them at the time of the study.

The consequences of motherlessness also had a strong impact upon the social and emotional lives of these men. When asked if they felt lonely and depressed, 37 percent said they occasionally felt this way and 30 percent said they felt this way all of the time. The men tended to disengage themselves socially, having little interaction outside the family. Two-thirds of the men found difficulty in sleeping, mainly because they worried a good deal of the time. Some initially reacted to the loss of the mother by drinking more, although this tapered off over time. A large number tended to smoke more or to resume smoking after their wife's death or departure. More serious than these effects in terms of fulfillment of their economic status was the fact that over half reported they were less capable of concentrating on their work. All in all, they were a group undergoing a good deal of stress.

In a more recent study, two researchers included 75 single fathers in a study of 168 single-parent families.[4] Among their major findings regarding employment were the problems of low income and the impact of family breakdown upon the employment situation of the remaining parent, especially in terms of the difficulty of combining work with the day care needs of the children and the vulnerability of one-parent families in the housing market.

None of these problems is confined to the one-parent family. What is particularly characteristic of such families, however, is the way in which these problems tend to interact, and to impinge upon the families concerned at a time when their emotional resources are likely to be at their lowest ebb. A lone father faced with unemployment may be unable to move to another area to seek employment because he is dependent on nearby relatives to look after his children while he is at work, and to offer him much-needed advice and support in his new role as sole parent.

While many parents had found their employers sympathetic and helpful to them in their difficult situation, such help was clearly dependent upon the goodwill of the individuals concerned, rather than upon a system which was adaptable enough to cater to employees with special needs, such as lone parents.

Perhaps the most positive assistance that could be offered to a lone parent would be the provision of a meaningful choice between going out to work or caring full time for their children. Such a choice would require some kind of guaranteed income plan for all lone parents and their families, regardless of whether the parent was a father or mother, and independent of the reason for the family's situation. The income would have to be sufficient to enable the parent to remain at home if he or she felt that this was the family's best interest.

Enabling fathers to work part time or to choose more flexible hours to fit in with family responsibilities would be a radical change, and one which would require a timely reappraisal of society's expectations regarding the role of the father. It is a necessary step, however, if fathers and mothers are to enjoy equality of choice in organizing their lives as lone parents. Children's needs are the same, regardless of their family situation, and fathers and mothers should be given equal opportunity to meet them.

In a social world organized for the participation of couples, a lone parent has no accepted role to play. Far from being supportive, society's attitudes—particularly toward the divorced and separated—are frequently judgmental rather than accommodating, suspicious rather than sympathetic.

The resulting isolation serves to exacerbate lone parents' doubts and anxieties about their total responsibility. With no one to share this burden, worries about their children's health, welfare and behavior can only increase the emotional strain of their lonely position.

The British report points out that the disadvantages facing one-parent families are so wide-ranging, however, that no single agency can hope to provide all the support—material and moral—that is likely to be required. It is clear, though, that more wide-ranging, publicized and easily accessible counseling services are necessary, to offer guidance, advice and reassurance in all aspects of the task of sole parenthood.

The needs of such parents are perhaps best summed up by one widowed father interviewed. He wished for a

place where I could have gone to meet . . . someone who would have listened to me and then suggested how I could have managed with cooking and cleaning and help, a special office for no one else but people who have been left as we are left. I can't stress too much the need for someone you could go to and say: what size dress does my daughter wear? When do you put vegetables on after the meat? How can I stop feeling so sorry for myself? If someone could just come in and tidy up the house for you once a week it would be marvelous, but someone to listen is the main thing.

IN CANADA

In our interviews with motherless families in metropolitan Toronto, we talked with 72 fathers, whose average age was 40.[5] These single fathers were all well educated and almost all were employed at an average income of $11,500. The number of children living with their fathers ranged from one to five, including children as young as a year old and as old as 23.

Most fathers described the breakup of their family as an emotionally charged event and reported noticeable changes in their children's later behavior, including resentment toward their parents. However, many fathers also reported that communications among family members had improved.

The fathers in the study were responsible for preparing breakfasts and suppers during the week. Household chores, such as washing dishes, were usually done by the father or shared with the children, while general housecleaning was mostly the father's responsibility. In almost every instance, fathers and children ate together. Nearly half of the fathers said that when a child was sick they stayed home with him or her. The fathers also took major responsibility in consulting a child's teacher and attending to children's medical problems.

At the time of the study, three-quarters of the fathers were dating, most of them at least once a week, and the majority found their relationships satisfactory. They brought their women friends to their homes, where they met other family members and participated in family activities. Most of the children encouraged their fathers' social activities.

Almost all the fathers knew the whereabouts of the mothers, most of whom were fairly close by, and about half of the fathers said that they sometimes saw them.

About one-third of the fathers indicated that they had needed financial assistance after becoming single parents. Most of those who had applied for bank loans, credit or mortgages had been granted such aid.

Most of the fathers expressed doubt that their children were receiving appropriate parental care and attention, and disciplining the children was a problem for many fathers. Some thought that available social services were geared to women rather than to all single parents, and that it was difficult to locate appropriate services. A small number were dissatisfied with the help they were able to get from social workers or agencies.

IN THE UNITED STATES

Helen Mendes interviewed 32 fathers who were raising their children alone in southern California.[6] Among this sample 15 fathers were black, 14 were white, two were Mexican-American and one was Chinese-American. All but three were employed. Their mean income was $12,500.

Mendes points out that the role of the single father has not yet been institutionalized in American culture. The men in the study who undertook this role did so without clear role prescriptions and the lack of role clarity contributed to the stresses many of them experienced as they adjusted to the need to coordinate employment and child care responsibilities, manage their homes, respond appropriately to their children's emotional needs and rear daughters in motherless homes.

Their experiences indicate that males too should be taught the logistics of homemaking, including budgeting and marketing. However, the study reveals that the most crucial area for the welfare of children growing up in such families seems to be the quality of the emotional relationship between fathers and children. A significant factor in the father's experiences—whether or not they were having difficulties with their children—was their general lack of knowledge about what constitutes normal child development. With one exception, the fathers found books useless in answering the many questions they had about the normalcy of their children's behaviors. Their concern reflects the way in which males are socialized in our society. Males are generally not expected to care for children and so this aspect of their family life education is usually neglected.

The concerns of single fathers also reflected the anxieties they experienced as they performed their atypical paternal roles. Since most did not know other single fathers, they had no one to compare notes with, except married and/or single mothers. Those who did consult with mothers found discussion to be of limited value since the women could not help them with the adjustments they had to make as single male parents.

In another study, 20 single-parent fathers were interviewed in Greensboro, North Carolina.[7] The average age of these fathers was 37 and their average annual income exceeded $18,000. Their racial background was not noted.

In the conclusion to their analysis of the study, the authors said that these fathers felt quite capable and successful regarding their ability to be the primary parent of their children and that the confidence they expressed and the satisfaction they seemed to derive in fatherhood was very difficult to deny. All of the fathers were reported to have experienced some problems, but these were not unlike the difficulties experienced in most families. The sense of pride in being able to cope with the challenge of parenthood and of seeing their children mature under their guidance was a major compensating force.

It appears that these fathers had a cooperative working relationship with their children around household chores, received support from their own parents, had access to proper child care facilities and had a high enough income so that they did not have to depend solely on public assistance. However, one-third of the fathers did receive some sort of public assistance.

Single-parent fathers appear to be taking advantage of the trend toward allowing men to be more nurturing. Some of the men studied received custody of their children because they were felt to be more nurturing than their wives, and others because their wives felt less capable in that respect. Most of the fathers, however, expressed some concern over their ability to be a nurturing parent; they wanted to know if they spent enough time reading and playing with their children, if they were understanding things at their child's level and whether they should get more involved in their children's education. But these concerns are similar to those of most parents and, overall, the single-parent fathers felt quite comfortable in their expressive roles. Recommendations made by the authors of this study include the following:

· Day care facilities should extend services into the evenings. Several fathers found that they sometimes had to work late and the hours of most day care centers put them into uncomfortable dilemmas in their jobs.

· Information on baby-sitting cooperatives is needed. Most fathers do not know how to operate one and many might be interested in its cost-saving advantages.

· Transportation of children to and from day care centers should be available. It is difficult for a working parent to transport children from school to an after-school child care center.

· Classes on single parenthood are needed. Most of the fathers had depended on their wives for childrearing and expressed considerable dismay over their lack of preparation for parenthood.

· A "Big Sisters" counterpart to the "Big Brother" type of organization is needed for those fathers who are rearing daughters. Although it is probably easier for fathers to find adult female companions for their daughters than for mothers to find male companions for their sons, not all fathers find it easy to locate women who really want to help their daughters, rather than find a husband for themselves.

A third study involved interviews with 40 fathers in Columbus, Ohio.[8] These included 15 widowers and 25 divorced fathers. Like other new single-parent fathers, those in this study faced role adjustments when they assumed responsibility for areas of home management for which they had previously had little or only partial responsibility. In households where small children were present, the fathers assumed the major responsibility for their care.

Activities or aspirations previously pursued by fathers during their married years now presented occasional areas of conflict, in light of their additional responsibilities, and their social activities had also been curtailed.

The reason for their state of single parenthood appeared to affect the fathers' perceptions of their adjustment: divorced fathers considered themselves well-adjusted more often than widowed fathers did and divorced fathers were also more anxious to declare their present situation as under control and functioning smoothly.

Social ostracism was experienced by several fathers in the study. Divorced fathers, in particular, tended to avoid the associations they had had as married couples and to gravitate toward activities or relationships involving other single parents.

The majority of the fathers handled the responsibilities of household management alone or with their children. This suggests that much change in former role stereotyping has taken place, a factor that may encourage more divorcing fathers to consider child custody for themselves.

COMMENTARY

In examining the handful of existing studies on motherless families in four English-speaking industrialized countries, some common themes emerge.

Financial Problems

Social class factors play a large part in the lives of the fathers. The middle-class fathers in Canada and America appear to be managing financially, while the British fathers depend to a great extent on welfare assistance. A double standard still exists in most of the countries considered. Fatherless families can obtain government financial assistance while motherless families are not included in official family benefit policies. The underlying assumption is that a man should not stay home but go out to work.

Child Care

Fathers are finding it difficult to obtain child care help (which includes a wide range of needs—from day to after-school care and, in the case of middle-class fathers, housekeepers). The cost of such services are, in some cases, prohibitive and the hours in some caregiving centers may not coincide with the fathers' working hours. None of the existing studies have explored the use of the extended family as caregiver.

Social Life

Taking on the dual roles of father and housekeeper appears to prevent many fathers from attaining a balanced social life, although middle-class fathers can afford a baby-sitter for a night out.

Parenting-Homemaking

Most fathers had had little preparation for parenting and homemaking. Even basic housekeeping duties were a burden and mystery at first, including such simple acts as buying groceries, washing dishes and floors, mending socks, sewing buttons and making beds. This suggests that we should help young men to understand and appreciate the daily activities traditionally assigned to young women. Indeed, home economics may be a must for boys as well as girls, and both need education for parenting.

Personal Problems

Fathers appear to exhibit stress and strain when they become the heads of families in more than the financial sense. Personal problems come to the foreground and require help. If the assumption of headship of a single-parent family is a crisis for many fathers, why not consider "crisis intervention" programs? We know how to intervene in a crisis; let us put to use their knowledge and aid many fatherless families at the onset of single parenthood.

Community Support

In some of the countries under discussion, fathers felt little community support in their dilemma. Most communities are used to fatherless families and probably have not yet accepted as a fact the growing number of motherless families. Would "Big Sister" and "Foster Grandparent" programs be helpful to these fathers? We could consider discussion groups for single fathers which would turn into "self help" groups. Cooperative baby-sitting and shopping arrangements and other joint projects would also help the fathers.

Research

Our knowledge about motherless families now comes from a limited number of studies and a small sampling of selected groups of fathers. We need more research in some of the following areas:

• Cultural, racial, religious and social class differences among motherless families.

• Comparative studies of fathers who rear children in various age groupings—preschool, school-age and adolescent.

• Comparative studies of categories of motherless families—divorced, widowed, separated. Do families in the various categories follow different life-styles, and how does the cause of single-parenthood affect the fathers?

• The effect of the absent mother on motherless families. How, for example, are mothers involved in these families when they are the "absent spouse" or "weekend mothers"?

The phenomenon of motherless families appears to be increasing. Since "motherlessness" seems to have become another viable option for many of our families, we cannot ignore the motherless family but must meet the challenge of how best to help its members adjust to the new situation and to overcome any problems it may bring.

REFERENCES

[1] *Current Population Reports,* Series P-20, No. 311, "Household and Family Characteristics: March 1976," U.S. Bureau of the Census, August 1977.

[2] Chris Bain, "Lone Fathers: An Unnoticed Group," *Australian Social Welfare,* March 1973.

[3] Victor George and Paul Wilding, *Motherless Families,* London, Routledge and Kegan Paul, 1972.

[4] Elsa Ferri and Hilary Robinson, *Coping Alone,* Windsor, England, N.F.E.R. Publishing Co., 1976. (Published by Humanities Press, Fernhill House, Atlantic Highlands, New Jersey, 1977.)

[5] Benjamin Schlesinger and Rubin Todres, "Motherless Families: An Increasing Social Pattern," *Child Welfare,* Sept.-Oct. 1976.

[6] See Helen A. Mendes, "Single Fatherhood," *Social Work,* July 1976.

[7] Dennis K. Orthner, Terry Brown and Dennis Ferguson, "Single-Parent Fatherhood: An Emerging Family Life Style," *The Family Coordinator,* October 1976.

[8] Rita D. Gasser and Claribel M. Taylor, "Role Adjustment of Single Parent Fathers with Dependent Children," *The Family Coordinator,* October 1976.

28

Single-Parent Fathers:

A New Study

by Harry Finkelstein Keshet and Kristine M. Rosenthal

This article is about single-parent fathers who are rearing their young children after marital separation. It discusses what fathers do for and with their children and how being a single parent affects their lifestyles and work responsibilities.

The article is based on interviews, conducted by trained male interviewers, with 49 separated or divorced fathers who live in the Boston area and have formal or informal custody of their children.[1] At the time of the interviews, each father's youngest child was between the ages of three and seven and there were no more than three children in any of the families. Each father had been separated from his wife for at least one year.[2]

Over half of the fathers in the sample (53 percent) were legally divorced; the remainder were separated informally. Most of the men had been married and living with their spouses for a minimum of five years.

The majority of fathers were highly educated; barely a fourth had had less than a full college education and nearly half had either completed or were in the process of completing graduate or professional training. More than half of the fathers were in professional or semi-professional occupations, 20 percent were in business or administration and 20 percent had blue-collar jobs or worked as craftsmen. Another six percent of the sample were students; two percent were unemployed.

Seventy-six percent of the fathers worked full-time or longer at their occupations; the others worked half time or less. A majority of the fathers earned relatively high incomes: 15 percent earned over $25,000, 25 percent earned between $15,000 and $25,000 and 30 percent earned between $10,000 and $15,000.

We felt that residential stability and housing were important factors in childrearing. Therefore, we were interested in the types of housing arrangements the men had made. Over half of the fathers (54 percent) occupied houses which they owned, while the others lived in apartments or rented homes. Most of the men showed a high rate of residential stability—50 percent had lived in the same dwelling for two years or longer and 12 percent had lived in the same place for more than a year.

Half the men lived alone with their children, 35 percent shared housing with other adults and the remaining 15 percent lived with their lovers. Only a few men in the sample lived with extended families.

Almost all of the fathers reported that their children were attending day care centers or schools or were cared for by hired babysitters when the fathers were working.

Until recently, little research on the role of the father in marriage or after marital separation has been reported. Men have been studied as workers and professionals but not as fathers and husbands. For a married man in modern society, the qualities of being a "good husband" have been similar

Reprinted from *Children Today* Magazine, May/June 1978.
U.S. Department of Health, Education and Welfare.

to those of being a "good father." The good father-husband is an economic provider. He forms a relationship and bond with his wife but not necessarily with his child for the relational tie between child and father has not been deemed essential.

There is a very strong cultural bias that women, biologically, psychologically and temperamentally, are best suited for child care and that mothering rather than parenting is the primary ingredient in child development.[3] This reflects the traditional view that male and female roles are based on traits that are essentially different and complementary. Women bear and rear children, and men support and provide for their wives and children. Men are not expected to be active in childrearing in or outside of marriage.

When a marriage ends in divorce, a father not only separates from his wife but is likely to be separated from his children as well. As E. E. LeMasters said: "The father's parental role in the U.S. is particularly tied to the success or failure of the pair bond between himself and his wife."[4]

The failure of his marriage is also likely to mean the loss of child custody for fathers. Most men do not seek custody of their children and those who do may experience sex role bias on the part of the judiciary. In 1971, for example, it was reported that mothers received custody of their children in over 90 percent of the custody decisions in United States Courts.[5]

Information available on the number of single-parent fathers indicates that more men are now being awarded custody of their children and that the men in our study are part of a small but growing number of fathers who are rearing their children after marital separation. Census data show that from 1960 to 1974 the number of male-headed families, with children and no spouse present, increased from 296,000 in 1960[6] to 836,000 in 1974.[7] The number of families headed by males with children under six and no spouse present also increased, from 87,000 in 1960[8] to 188,200 in 1970.[9]

In our study, we were particularly interested in the following four aspects of parenting: entertainment of children outside of the home, homemaking activities, child guidance and nurturance and child- and parent-oriented services. We also asked the fathers if they felt they had been prepared to carry out these activities and whether they received any help from other adults in conducting them.

Entertainment

Our earlier research had shown that fathers of young children in nuclear families and in separated families often entertain their children. In this study, all the fathers reported that they frequently relied on structured recreational activities for their children. A majority of fathers said they took their children swimming and to playgrounds, museums, restaurants and, less frequently, to child-oriented shows and movies. Finding activities for children seemed to be a major part of their roles as recently-separated fathers. One father reported:

"At first, I had to entertain them . . . bowling, movies, swimming, trips to relatives. I often would do reading and roughhousing with them also . . . I thought it was my responsibility to provide some structured activities."

"I went to every park, museum, playground, movie, zoo and what-have-you imaginable . . . I was constantly looking for things to do," another said.

Recreation and entertainment are "doing" activities and as such they are consistent with the parenting activities and male socialization role found within the nuclear family experience. Separated and divorced fathers often played with their children and felt prepared to perform this aspect of the single-parent role. Although most fathers reported that they received little help with their recreational parenting activities, they also said that when they became involved with women their women friends often accompanied them and their children on recreational ventures. It seems that the recreational aspects of parenting served as a comfortable way for them—and other adults—to interact with their children.

Homemaking

Homemaking seemed to us to be an essential part of the single-parent role. We asked the men about meal preparation and general household management.

Over 90 percent of the fathers reported that they frequently performed the homemaking functions of housecleaning, preparing meals and food shopping and, with the exception of housecleaning, most men felt that they had been prepared to perform these homemaking activities when they separated from their spouses. Most of the fathers also said that they did not receive significant help in homemaking, except in food preparation. Here, nearly half the fathers reported getting some assistance from other adults who shared their dwellings.

Child Guidance and Nurturance

The guidance and nurturance aspect of parenting was defined as direct father-child interaction, with the men giving care or direction to their young. We asked questions concerning discipline and the setting of limits; mealtime, bedtime and bathing routines; dealing with children's feelings; and shopping with children for clothing.

The most frequently reported guidance and nurturing activities were discipline, serving meals, bathing children and dealing with children's

Harry Finkelstein Keshet, Ph.D., and Kristine M. Rosenthal, Ed.D., are co-directors of the Parenting Study at Brandeis University. Dr. Keshet, a divorced father with joint custody of his son, is an instructor in the Parenting Program at Wheelock College, Boston, and clinical director of the Divorce Resource and Mediation Center, Inc., Cambridge, Mass. Dr. Rosenthal, a single parent of three children, is an assistant professor at Brandeis University.

feelings and emotional upsets. More than 95 percent of the men reported that they frequently performed these activities on a regular basis. In contrast, less than half of the men said they bought clothing for their children.

The need to provide guidance and nurturance seemed to be more of a problem for the fathers than their entertainment and homemaking roles. Most fathers felt prepared to discipline or bathe their children but were less prepared for dealing with their emotional upsets. As one father explained:

"I felt unprepared for dealing with the children's emotional needs and being open to what they were feeling. I was very inadequate in that I

couldn't deal with my own feelings very well. I was afraid, I didn't know how to listen or respond to them."

"Dealing with feelings openly or expressing them, especially negative feelings, like grief or anger . . . those were the areas where I felt totally handicapped," a second said.

The socialization of males in our society does not prepare them to be nurturant and sex role definitions of childrearing in the nuclear family are likely to emphasize emotional responsiveness as a feminine trait and therefore a part of the mother's role. Boys learn instrumental skills that prepare them to be workers and family providers and they are neither expected nor encouraged to develop emotional skills which may interfere

with their achievement.[10]

The more successfully a man has been socialized in instrumental behavior, the more likely he is to lack effective interpersonal skills. For example, a positive and significant relationship between a father's high achievement motivations and his feelings of inadequacy in the father role, and a negative orientation toward preschool children, has been reported by Veroff and Feld.[11] The authors also suggest that consideration of the emotional needs of young children may be incongruent with what fathers have previously learned about good masculine performance.

Our sample of fathers expressed difficulty in relating to their children's emotional needs, yet they attempted to respond to the requirements of their new roles, sometimes with the help of others. They received the most assistance in those areas where they felt least prepared. For example, 44 percent reported receiving help from others in dealing with children's feelings.

Services for Children and Parents

Being a single parent required acting as the child's sole agent in relationship to agencies and professionals. Nearly 75 percent of the men reported calling for babysitters themselves and over 90 percent were actively involved in all the other common child-oriented activities, such as taking a child to a doctor or dentist and talking with their children's teacher and the parents of their friends. Most of the men (80 percent) felt prepared to perform these functions after separation. The calling of babysitters was performed with a lower level of confidence—nearly half (45 percent) felt unprepared to do this. A majority of the men reported performing these activities with no help from others.

All in all, however, it appears that the fathers in our sample were very active in all the aspects of parenting that we explored. They were most prepared for performing the recreational, homemaking and child-

oriented service aspects of parenting, and least prepared for the child nurturance aspects. They received help from other adults in large measure for nurturant activities and certain homemaking activities, while help was not frequently reported for recreational and child-oriented service activities.

Time as Role Salience

More than half of the fathers (53 percent) reported spending half or more of their time at home interacting with their children. Others spent some time doing so and only four percent said that they spent very little time with their children.

We had expected that at least in the families in which the fathers lived with other people, the children would spend a significant amount of time interacting with other adults. However, we found that only nine percent of the fathers said that their children spent half or more of their time with other adults and 43 percent reported that their children spent very little or no time with other adults.

This finding that the father was the adult in the home with whom the children most frequently spent their time is also supported by data on the kinds of childrearing help fathers received from their lovers or dates. Women lovers rarely took or were permitted to take a major child care role with the father's children. Most frequently they accompanied fathers and children in out-of-home recreational activities.

These findings suggest that the single-parent role was a highly salient one and that fathers even protected their children from the influence of other adults.

Compared to the hours spent with other adults, children spent a much greater part of their time with peers: 45 percent of the fathers reported that their children spent half or more of their time playing with other children; 37 percent reported that they spent some time doing so and only 18 percent reported that they spent very little or no time playing with peers.

In summary, fathers and children's peers were those most involved with the children in terms of time. Other non-related adults, even when they were available, spent less time with the father's children. The new time relationship with their children was described by one father this way:

"Spending time alone with the children came as a change after separation . . . They were alone with me all the time . . . It was the first time I'd been with them alone. I was putting them to bed, getting them dressed, getting their meals . . . I began to see I could do it."

Another explained: "One of the big problems was how being a full-time parent would influence my time. How I could put this whole thing together

in terms of spending a lot of time with them; at the same time, having time to do other things. I didn't know how it would work out."

Role Strains

Three-quarters of the men we talked to said that they felt closer to their children as a result of their change in marital status and new parenting role. Their relationship to the children was more direct, no longer being filtered through the conflicts of an ailing marriage. Yet being a single parent had its own set of difficulties. Many fathers expressed serious concerns with the time strains they experienced after the marital breakdown.

Like most men, the fathers in our sample seemed to fit their time structures into the demands of the workplace, school or other organization in which they participated. As single parents, the needs of their children had priority over the requirements of external organizations, especially when the children were ill or had school vacations. At such times, fathers had to take time off from work or arrange for others to care for their children. Role strain often resulted from conflicts between their child care responsibilities and social needs and work responsibilities.

Work and Child Care

As noted previously, the majority of men in our sample were in demanding professional and semi-professional occupations. In order to ascertain how they perceived the management of child care and work responsibilities, we listed a set of work-related behaviors and asked the men how they felt their child care obligations limited their work activities.

Job mobility was the area cited as being most limited. Fathers reported their work life was hampered in terms of working hours (63 percent), work priorities (62 percent), earnings (55 percent) and job transfer (52 percent). Within the work setting itself, limitations were noted in the areas of type of work (66 percent), promotions (38 percent), relations with co-workers (28 percent) and supervisors (20 percent).

Single parenting clearly limited

earnings, hours and work relations. Work identity, a cornerstone of male self-definition, was challenged by an emerging parenting identity. One father said:

"Taking care of her (his daughter) was a real conflict with work. I was trying to build my business, but had to stop to pick her up at 3:00. It was rough starting something new, not making much money and limiting my working hours . . . Often, what I gave her was given grudgingly because I was feeling terribly limited by the schedule and by the tremendous pressures I was feeling."

In an open-ended question, we asked fathers to indicate the kind of services they felt would help make parenting and work more compatible. Over half (55 percent) said that time flexibility at work would help alleviate the constraints of these often conflicting responsibilities. One father for whom this was already a viable arrangement said:

"The advantages of where I work is that my hours are flexible. There is no problem in going home in the late afternoon to be with the kids . . . I make up the time by coming to work at 7:30 a.m. and every other weekend. Sometimes I bring my kids back to work if there is some great necessity, but I don't want this to happen often."

Fathers were also aware of the need for both long-range and immediate services for themselves and their children. Many felt that their parenting roles had not been accorded social legitimacy. Their employers, co-workers and peers often lacked appreciation or understanding of their needs as single parents and offered them little support. The single-parent father's dilemma has been stated clearly: "Economic efficiency is given so much priority in our society that it is difficult to imagine an American father neglecting his job or refusing a promotion out of deference to the needs of his children . . ."[12]

Social Life and Parenting

Our findings indicated that a major limitation for single-parent fathers

was the decrease in the amount of time spent alone with other adults. Over half of the fathers studied said that they were involved with a woman as a sexual partner. The majority of these women (61 percent) were either divorced or separated and almost half of them had children from a previous marriage. The majority of the fathers reported that their lovers were helpful with the children.

The most frequently reported role for women friends (62 percent) was companionship with fathers and children in recreational activities away from home. A more active and direct child care role at the father's home was not frequently reported. For example, only 31 percent said that their lovers watched their children at home when the father was present and only 15 percent stated that their lovers cared for children alone for substantial periods of time. This suggests that the single-parent fathers in our sample were somewhat reluctant and guarded in allowing their women friends to share substantially in caring for their children.

When questioned about any conflict with lovers concerning a father's relationship to children, over half (56 percent) indicated that this was an issue because of the limitations placed on their social life by child care obligations. Eighty-five percent of the men said that their social life would be different were the children not present. The areas in which fathers felt their lives to be limited by parenting responsibilities were: social life, mentioned by 63 percent of the fathers; sports, noted by 17 percent; and home activities, referred to by 15 percent.

Being a Single Father

Our analysis showed that being a single parent required a major shift in lifestyle and priorities for most men. The bond between parent and child became a new focal point for self-definition and set the criteria for organizing the more traditional spheres of male functioning at work and in social life. The men in our study limited work and social activities to

meet the needs of their children and, in doing so, they felt they had developed a closer relationship with them.

The experience of marital separation had brought the men into the sphere of what is commonly considered the woman's world—of being responsible for children's growth and satisfying children's needs. The men responded by restructuring their daily lives in order to care directly for their dependent children. As a result, fathers felt more positive about themselves as parents and as individuals. A majority of the men reported that being a single parent had helped them to grow emotionally. They felt they had become more responsive to their children and more conscious of their needs, a responsiveness they reported as reaching out to other adults as well. ■

[1]The interviews were part of a larger study, partially supported by a grant from the Rockefeller Foundation.
[2]The criteria used in the selection of the sample of families (the age of the youngest child, the limit on the number of children in each family and the minimum period of separation of parents) circumscribed the range of time of separation experienced among those interviewed. The mean number of years of separation was 2.6. Half (51 percent) of the fathers in the sample had been separated for no more than two years; over a third (36 percent) had been separated for three to four years, and the remainder, for over four years.
[3]John Bowlby, *Maternal Care and Mental Health*, Geneva, World Health Organization, 1951.
[4]E.E. LeMasters, *Parents in Modern America*, Homewood, Illinois, Dorsey Press, 1971.
[5]Robert R. Bell, *Marriage and Family Interaction*, Homewood, Illinois, Dorsey Press, 1971.
[6]U.S. Department of Commerce, Bureau of the Census, *Family Characteristics, 1960 Census.*
[7]U.S. Department of Commerce, Bureau of the Census, *Current Population Reports,* Ser. P-20, no. 271, 1974.
[8]U.S. Department of Commerce, Bureau of the Census, *Family Characteristics, 1960 Census.*
[9]U.S. Department of Commerce, Bureau of the Census, *Family Characteristics, 1970 Census.*
[10]Lenard Benson, *Fathering, A Sociological Perspective*, New York, Random House, 1968.
[11]Joseph Veroff and Sheila Feld, *Marriage and Work in America*, New York, Van Nostrand Reinhold, 1970.
[12]E.E. LeMasters, op. cit.

V. Adolescence

Photograph by Fredrik D. Bodin, Stock, Boston

Even in relatively stable times, adolescence is a challenging and sometimes difficult stage of development. Not since the age of two has the individual undergone as many changes as during the period surrounding puberty. In addition to rapid physical growth and changing bodily dimensions, the young person is faced with the sometimes strange and mysterious impulses and feelings brought on by sexual maturation, as well as by a newfound capability for thinking more abstractly and more self-consciously about himself or herself, the world of the present, and the demands of the future.

Important as they are, all the changes of adolescence do not take place within the adolescent himself or herself. Equally crucial are the changes in society's demands in the few short years between childhood and nominal adulthood. It is during these years that the young person is expected to: achieve independence from parents; establish new kinds of social and working relationships with peers of both sexes and with adults; adjust to increasing sexual maturity and changing sex roles; and decide on personally meaningful educational and vocational goals.

In the process of meeting these challenges, the adolescent must also gradually develop a philosophy of life—a view of the world and a set of guiding moral beliefs and standards that, however simple and basic, are "nonnegotiable." A basic philosophy of some kind is essential to lend order and consistency to the many decisions the young person will have to make and the actions he or she will have to take in a diverse, changing, frequently chaotic world. Finally, the young person must develop a sense of identity, a workable answer to the age-old question, "Who am I, and where am I going?"

None of this is easy, and it is not surprising that many adolescents seem to fluctuate between extremes—between joy and sadness, gregariousness and loneliness, altruism and self-centeredness, curiosity and boredom, confidence and self-doubts.

Furthermore, the rapidity of recent social change has not made the problems of growing up any easier. Geographic mobility and urbanization have tended to erode the stability and interdependence of communities and to weaken the natural support systems—relations, friends, and social institutions such as schools and the church—on which families traditionally were able to rely. Faith in the social institutions of our society generally has been largely replaced by skepticism and mistrust, as these institutions have become ever larger and more impersonal, and—in the eyes of many—ineffective and sometimes corrupt, as our experiences with the Vietnam War and Watergate made all too plain. Even our economic system, for all its material successes, seems unable to cope with the acute problem of youth unemployment, particularly for the poor and the socially disenfranchised. In addition, our nation appears to be facing a crisis of values and a lack of common purpose, reflected most recently in a retreat into an ultimately unsustainable focus on "self-fulfillment" and away from the needs of society—what Christopher Lasch calls "the new narcissism" and what others have referred to as the "me-decade" of the 1970s.

All of this has taken its toll on America's youth. Though most adolescents still accomplish successfully the transition to adulthood, an increasing minority do not. Rates of delinquency and of alcohol and drug use have risen substantially in recent years. The rate of suicide among adolescents has nearly tripled in the past two decades. Ten percent of *all* female adolescents, ages 15 to 19, and 30 percent of female adolescents who are sexually active, become pregnant each year in this country. In addition, hundreds of thousands of unemployed poor and minority youth, particularly in our largest cities, are finding that they are unwanted by society. For such young people, "The American Dream" has become a nightmare, and their response is alienation and despair.

The articles in this section address many of these issues: how adolescents think and feel; the importance of parents and peers in the young person's development; the problems of adolescent sexuality and premature pregnancy; the lure of religious cults; and the use of drugs. Most importantly, perhaps, they also point the way to a better future if only we are willing to commit ourselves —as individuals and as a society—to the optimal development of all our children and adolescents. Whether we have the will to do so in this era of reduced resources and shrinking budgets, remains to be seen. But certainly there can be no more urgent need—for our children and for ourselves.

29

Adolescent Thinking and the Diary of Anne Frank

George Scarlett

The diary of Anne Frank affords one a rare glimpse into the thoughts of an adolescent. And one of the most striking features of Anne's thinking is her tremendous concern for justice and being treated as an equal. Much has been written about the affective development of the adolescent, and more recently the cognitive studies of adolescence have described adolescent egocentrism and the adolescent's task of taking up adult roles. Anne's diary displays the themes and forms common to adolescent thinking, but it is this concern for justice that is perhaps the most striking feature of the book.[1a]

"For in its innermost depths youth is lonelier than old age." I read this saying in some book and I've always remembered, and found it to be true. Is it true then that grownups have a more difficult time here than we do? No. I know it isn't. Older people have formed their opinions about everything, and don't waver before they act. It's twice as hard for us young ones to hold our ground, and maintain our opinions, in a time when all ideas are being shattered and destroyed, when people are showing their worst side, and do not know whether to believe in truth and right and God.

Anne wrote the above passage after two years in hiding and just three weeks before she and her family were discovered by the Grüne Polizie. When, therefore, she speaks of "a time when all ideals are being shattered," she is referring to the condition of war. But her words may also be interpreted as describing the condition of adolescence.

First of all, Anne states that adults have formed their opinions and, by implication, that adolescents are only in the process of doing so. This development of opinions is part of the adolescent's primary task—the formation of an adult role.

Anne received her diary before she and her family were forced to go into hiding because they were Jews. They hid in the back part of an office building, and Anne describes the packing scene prior to their flight:[1b]

The first thing I put in was this diary. . . . I put in the craziest things with the idea that we were going into hiding. But I'm sorry, memories meant more to me than dresses.

Like the first message, we may interpret the above in two ways. One way is to take Anne literally and note that she cherishes the memories of her past more than dresses. The second is that Anne places more value on thoughts than on things. The supremacy of "mind over matter" is directly connected with Anne's major concern for constructing her own role as an adult; it is only because she values thought in itself that she is also concerned with using her powers of thinking to solve the problem of working out an adult role. And the value which is placed upon thought at this time in her life is in turn related to newly acquired abilities to reflect, i.e., to think about one's thoughts and to analyze one's actions.

The situation at the beginning of adolescence is this: the young adolescent, while cherishing thought, at the same time divorces himself from many of the practical concerns that were his as a child. For example, Anne Frank at fourteen describes herself when still in school as a superficial being, meaning that the younger Anne was more concerned with the practical than with reflection. But what we see as distinctly adolescent about Anne's thinking is that she is so centered in the primary problem of constructing an adult role that she is far less concerned with reflection as a means of governing actions than is the adult. That is to say, Anne's thought is far more separated from her activity than it was when she was younger, but it is still tied more to herself than is the thinking of most adults. In commonsense terms, Anne probably thinks a great deal more about herself than do most adults. Paradoxically, this reflecting upon oneself, this egocentric thought, is relatively unreflective, for in reflecting we mean to reproduce in thought what exists in fact.

One of the most striking concerns in Anne's thinking is her concern for justice. We see here not a childlike respect for authority and constraint but a concern for mutual respect between individuals and, most important, a sense of autonomy in the area of morality.

191

She writes: "It isn't the fear of God but the upholding of one's own honor and conscience [that matters]. . . ."[1c] One is reminded of Piaget's statement, "Authority as such cannot be the source of justice, because the development of justice presupposes autonomy."[3]

As an example of Anne's new sense of justice, take Anne's observation of Mrs. Van Daan, a middle-aged woman, who with her husband and sixteen-year-old son, joined the Franks in hiding:[1d]

Mrs. Van Daan is unbearable. I get nothing but "blow-ups" from her for my continuous chatter. . . . This is the latest: she doesn't want to wash up the pans if there is a fragment left. . . . After the next meal Margot [Anne's older sister] sometimes has about seven pans to wash up and Madame says: "Well, Margot, you have got a lot to do!"

No longer does Anne treat adults with the unilateral respect accorded them when she was a child. Anne's new abilities to reflect and her concern for taking up an adult role lead her to insist (at least in thought) upon equality with adults. She judges adults as she would judge her peers except that she is perhaps more sympathetic toward the latter.

Anne's "new morality" is truly a loss of innocence in regard to her relationship to adults. The fact that she no longer regards them as the tree of the knowledge of good and evil stimulates a kind of prophetic rage at the realization that what was once thought to be divine is only the product of human beings, only an idol worshiped by ignorant men. And so, like a great many adolescents, she sometimes judges them more harshly than they probably deserve. For instance,[1e]

Why do grownups quarrel so easily, so much, and over the most idiotic things? . . . I'm simply amazed again and again over their awful manners and especially . . . stupidity. . . .

One other example of Anne's new emphasis on co-operation as the basis for interpersonal relations is found in her record of an argument between herself and a dentist by the name of Dussel who had joined the Franks and Van Daans several months after the Franks first went into hiding. He and Anne shared a room. Anne was fond of reading and asked Mr. Dussel if she might use the desk in their room for a few hours each week. Mr. Dussel very unwisely refused on the grounds that he needed the desk for his work which he felt was more important than the work of a school girl. Anne replied:[1f]

When you first came here we arranged that this room should be for both of us; if we were to divide it fairly, you would have the morning and I all the afternoon! But I don't even ask that much, and I think that my two afternoons are perfectly reasonable.

Anne eventually got her own way.

The subtlety in Anne's morality is nowhere better shown than in her regard for the intentions of people and not just the consequences of their actions. Furthermore, Anne's new powers of thought enable her to concentrate more clearly on the dependence of a person upon his situation. Therefore, Anne's sense of justice is not the childlike concern for the letter of the law but rather for its spirit as manifest in her concern for intentions and for equity. Regarding the suffering of her own family and other Jews, Anne writes, "It is not the Dutch people's fault that we are having such a miserable time."[1g] And later on, towards the end of the war when some of the non-Jewish Dutch were turning against the Jews, Anne writes:[1h]

. . . I can't understand that the Dutch, who are such a good, honest, upright people, should judge us like this, we, the most pitiful of all people of the whole world.

That is to say, it is inequitable to persecute the Jews since they are more handicapped than other groups and deserve pity because of their situation.

Perhaps the most obvious consequence of the adolescent's "new morality" is the temporary rift that it encourages between parent and child. One reason for this is stated by Anne in the following passage:[1i]

My treatment varies so much. One day Anne is so sensible and is allowed to know everything; and the next day I hear that Anne is just a silly little goat who doesn't know anything at all and imagines that she's learned a wonderful lot from books. . . . Oh, so many things bubble up inside me as I lie in bed, having to put up with people I'm fed up with, who always misinterpret my intentions.

Anne is therefore concerned by the inconsistent treatment she gets from adults as well as their not understanding her intentions.

There is a difficult problem facing every parent of a young adolescent that the adolescent cannot appreciate. If we look at the few references Anne makes concerning her own *actions,* we see that they are often impulsive and sometimes indistinguishable from the actions of a child. As she herself puts it, ". . . they haven't given me the name 'little bundle of contradictions' all for nothing!"[1j] The principle contradiction here is between Anne's actions and her thoughts. But this contradiction between childlike actions and an adultlike insistence upon being treated as an equal exists and fosters estrangement only because of Anne's adolescent egocentrism, her inability to see herself as adults see her. Adolescence is perhaps the most morally conscious age group and an age which insists that its intentions be understood. It is therefore ironic that the adolescent is at the same time relatively ignorant of the intentions and perspectives of others.

A parent who does not respect the adolescent's mind is asking for trouble. For example, after Anne and her sister Margot had been quarreling, Anne's father stopped the two and apparently gave a judgment in favor of Margot. Anne wrote afterwards, "It so happened I was neither offended nor cross, just miserable. It wasn't right of Daddy to judge without knowing what the squabble was about. . . ."[1k] Anne was "miserable" not because she thought herself to be totally on the side of justice but because she felt she deserved a fair trial in which she was judged by a peer. Instead she was often treated as follows:[11]

How is it that Daddy was never any support to me in my struggle, why did he completely miss the mark when he wanted to offer me a helping hand? Daddy tried the wrong methods, he always talked to me as a child who was going through difficult phases. . . . I didn't want to hear about "symptoms of your age," or "other girls," or "it wears off by itself."

Anne's concern for justice and being treated as an equal is manifest even more in her relationship with her mother than with her father. Even though both Mr. and Mrs. Frank treated Anne as a child, it is probable that Anne's mother, like most mothers, was more obvious in her treatment. Anne writes, "Mummy sometimes treats me just like a baby, which I can't bear."[1m] And the fact that Anne was a girl increased the chances for more friction between mother and daughter than between father and daughter. Reasons for this have too often been limited to the competition between mother and daughter for the father's love. It seems more feasible, however, to place the major emphasis on the fact that an adolescent girl's real mother often stands in opposition to the ideal mother she hopes herself to be someday. And if (as it seems to be in Anne's case) there are in fact many similarities between mother and daughter, the daughter will become all the more upset and mad at being like her imperfect mother. Anne writes:[1n]

In spite of all my theories, and however much trouble I take, each day I miss having a real mother who understands me. That is why with everything I do and write I think of the "Mumsie" that I want to be for my children later on. . . . To give me the feeling of calling Mummy something which sounds like "Mumsie," I often call her "Mum": the incomplete "Mumsie," as it were, whom I would so love to honor with the extra "ie" and yet who does not realize it.

This passage also reveals Anne's ability to use language in an adult but autistic (i.e., noncommunicable, wish-fulfilling thought) manner. Anne's use of language accomplishes the double task of withholding love without communicating her dissatisfaction to her mother.

It may be a characteristic of adolescent thinking to place particular emphasis on a specific instance of "injustice" occurring near the beginning of adolescence and to cherish the memory of this instance. I have heard too many people relate what to them were crucial experiences of "injustice" around the beginning of adolescence to think this is mere coincidence. Anne writes:[1o]

One thing, which perhaps may seem rather fatuous, I have never forgiven her. It was on a day I had to go to the dentist. Mummy and Margot were going to come with me and agreed that I should take my bicycle. When we had finished at the dentist, and were outside again, Margot and Mummy told me that they were going into town to look at something or buy something, I don't remember exactly what. I wanted to go too, but I was not allowed to, as I had my bicycle with me. Tears of rage sprang into my eyes, and Mummy and Margot began laughing at me. . . . It is queer that the wound that Mummy made then still burns, when I think of how angry I was that afternoon.

What is significant about this incident is that on the surface it does not appear to warrant much attention, but that in reality it was extremely important to Anne because she was being treated as a child at a time when she was beginning to realize she was someone different from a child, someone who deserved to be treated as the equal to an adult.

In general, we may describe Anne's new moral code as a distinction between what is and what ought to be. A child rarely makes this distinction, and if he does, it is for different reasons than those of the adolescent. To make such a distinction is not a child's way of thinking, for it generally signifies thinking in terms of possibilities or hypotheses as opposed to thinking solely in terms of what is at hand. The adolescent's "new morality" is symptomatic of his ability to think that the world does not have to exist the way it does and has existed. Furthermore, the adolescent's concern for what ought to be is part of his concern for what will be.

The future-oriented aspects of adolescent thinking are significant in another respect, for the adolescent's show of altruism and concern for what ought to be is never divorced from his own ambitions. That is to say, appearing at various times in an adolescent's discourses on injustice is the insinuation that the speaker or writer of such discourses may be just the person to actualize the ideals and goals being discussed. This is perhaps no better illustrated than in the motivation of an adolescent to better his predecessors. Anne writes:[1p]

I am becoming still more independent of my parents; young as I am, I face life with more courage than Mummy; my feeling for justice is immovable, and truer than hers. I know what I want, I have a goal, an opinion, I have a religion, and love. Let me be myself and then I am satisfied. I know that I'm a woman, a woman with inward strength and plenty of courage.

If God lets me live, I shall attain more than Mummy ever has done. I shall not remain insignificant, I shall work in the world and for mankind.

Again we note that like so many characteristics of adolescent thinking, the blending of altruism and ambition as shown here is part of Anne's concern for constructing an adult role in society.

Furthermore, the previous example serves as another illustration of adolescent egocentrism and the "new morality." Egocentrism is here manifested by the fact that Mrs. Frank was most likely not the failure Anne depicts her as being. This is suggested by the fact that in all her writings, Anne criticizes her mother for primarily two things: treating Anne as if she were a child and criticizing her. As said before, treating a young adolescent as a child is quite normal for mothers. And as for criticizing Anne, Anne's actions were in all probability often asking for some sort of criticism, for Anne states that Mrs. Frank did not treat Margot in the same manner—indicating that Mrs. Frank was not an indiscriminant criticizer. It was likely the manner in which her mother criticized her rather than the content which Anne most disliked. Therefore, the two things which Anne dislikes about her relationship with her mother are quite interrelated.

The aspect of Anne's thinking which has been described as a blend of altruism and ambition is related in a curious way to another aspect of adolescent thinking and behavior, namely, the occasional discovery of the fragility of personal theories and resulting self-castigation. This always occurs through some kind of social intercourse and differs from an adult's discovering his own mistake in that there is a great deal more self-castigation. The reason for this adolescent reaction has in large part to do with an adolescent's chronic appeal to ideas rather than experiences when presenting an opinion. Furthermore, the "mind over matter" approach to thinking can satisfy some of the ego needs of an individual who is concerned about her being equal to adults. It is a "let's-pretend-I'm-an-adult" world which operates in peace until someone intervenes to point out discrepancies. Anne once wrote a letter to her parents expressing her feelings about how unjustly she was treated and how she felt she deserved to be treated as someone older than they were treating her. Anne's father was saddened by the letter and told Anne that he thought she was being a bit harsh. Anne writes:[1q]

Oh, I have failed miserably; this is certainly the worst thing I've ever done in my life. . . . No, Anne, you still have a tremendous lot to learn, begin by doing that first, instead of looking down on others and accusing them.

Her words reveal that she has a vague notion about the motivation behind many of her moral judgments. Her reaction is not that of an adult who says, "Yes, I was wrong. I hope I won't make the same mistake again." Anne's reaction is, ". . . you still have a tremendous lot to learn. . . ." She therefore seems to be orienting more toward the empirical. In brief, the relative absence of appealing to the concrete is understand-able in the light of her concern for constructing a role in society, and this concern when demonstrated in something like a diary is in part a compensation which allows for the self-assertion and imitation of adult models in thought that prove so difficult for the adolescent to realize in action.

The fact that Anne often chooses to express her wishes and concerns in writing is another characteristic of her behavior which is not childlike. The speech of the very young child serves a relatively minor role in the regulation of his thoughts and actions. Speech in the very young child more often merely accompanies his actions. Around the age of six or seven, a child develops the ability to use inner speech as a means for regulating his activity, but this speech is limited in its being oriented toward the concrete situation the child is in at a given time. Only with the advent of adolescence do we find inner speech playing a greater role in the life of the individual than vocal speech, and by the time of adolescence it is far more difficult to make a distinction between thought and speech than it was in childhood. Although the written word is not identical with inner speech, it is closely allied with it.

Furthermore, we may note that Anne sometimes found it easier to write letters to those living in the same house than to speak with them directly. There seem to be several reasons for this. First, unlike the child, Anne is more concerned with communicating intentions and unsure feelings as opposed to the childish motivation to communicate observations of the activity of the moment or the past. Second, because she lacks the security of either not caring about or not being sure of her place in society, Anne finds it far more difficult to communicate verbally than to communicate in writing. To communicate verbally lays one open to criticism, criticism which a young adolescent is often ill equipped to handle. Furthermore, in writing one can ponder over words whereas speaking often brings out unintended or ill-formed thoughts, thoughts which lead to misinterpretation, one of the things an adolescent most fears. As Anne puts it:[1r]

I'm not a baby or a spoiled darling any more, to be laughed at, whatever she does. I have my own views, plans, and ideas, though I can't put them into words yet. Oh, so many things bubble up inside me as I lie in bed, having to put up with people I'm fed up with, who always misinterpret my intentions.

What we find in adolescent thinking is a realization that there is a gulf between personal understanding and spoken explanation, and it is sometimes easier to retreat into a diary or a letter than to risk failing while attempting to bridge that gulf.

Another aspect of Anne's language which differs from the language of the child is the use of abbreviated language that is quite clear in communicating an intended thought. The child's abbreviated language is unintended and most often difficult to understand. But take the following example of Anne's abbreviated language: "It is drizzly weather, the stove smells, the food lies heavily on everybody's tummy, causing thunderous noises on all sides! The war at a standstill, morale rotten."[1s] The meaning of Anne's account is clear, and furthermore, the omission of the word *is* on two occasions adds a poetic touch to the account. The description has its own rhythm and gives one the feeling of something that was once moving rapidly but is now grinding to a halt. In other words, unlike the child's abbreviated language, Anne's omissions sometimes *add* meaning and facilitate communication.

One way of describing the poetic sense manifest in Anne's abbreviated language is that, unlike the child, Anne is able to appreciate the *form* of something while ignoring its content. In the area of morality we noted that her criticism of elders seemed to be directed as much at the content of the adult's sentences as at the way in which these sentences were said. A child is also sensitive to attitudes hiding behind words, but this sensitivity is only on the intuitive, not the conceptual level. Another example of this ability to appreciate form is brought out in the following criticism Anne made about a book: "I can't drag myself away from a book called *The Knock at the Door* by Ina Boudier-Bahkar. The story of the family is exceptionally well written."[1t] A child might say the book was interesting or very realistic, but it is unlikely he would say "well written." And this interest in form is itself related to the adolescent orientation toward the abstract, toward thinking instead of toward acting.

Adolescent love has received a great deal of attention from many writers concerned with adolescent thinking. And the majority of these writers seem to place considerable emphasis on puberty as the great event marking the beginning of adolescence. But there is more to love than biology, and as Piaget and Inhelder point out, ". . . what distinguishes an adolescent in love from a child in love is that the former generally complicates his feelings by constructing a romance or by referring to social or even literary ideals of all sorts."[2] Furthermore, adolescent love is characteristically a search for extrafamilial relationships which will satisfy the need to be understood and accepted *as an equal*.

The diary is itself taken by Anne to be a friend. She writes:[1u]

I hope I shall be able to confide in you completely, as I have never been able to do in anyone before, and I hope that you will be a great support and comfort to me.

What Anne sees in her diary and what she sees in her peers is the possibility of creating a bond of affection and satisfaction of certain ego needs not being met within her own family. Again, concerning the reason for starting a diary, Anne writes:[1v]

. . . as I don't intend to show this cardboard-covered notebook, bearing the proud name of "diary," to anyone, unless I find a real friend, boy or girl, probably nobody cares. And now I come to the root of the matter, the reason for starting a diary: it is that I have no such real friend.

But even a diary is insufficient in meeting an adolescent's needs. Lucky for Anne, the Van Daans had a son, Peter, to whom she could turn. She writes: "I have longed so much and for so long, I am so lonely, and now I have found consolation [with Peter]."[1w] The intensity of feeling shown here is the factor underlying Anne's claim that she has been lonely for "so long," and it is typical of the adolescent in love to consider even a month or two unbearably long.

Nowhere in the diary is love for love's sake and the construction of a romance brought out more clearly than when she compares Peter Van Daan to her pre-war boyfriend, Peter Wessel. She writes, "Peter Wessel and Peter Van Daan have grown into one Peter, who is beloved and good, and for whom I long desperately."[1x]

Anne's feelings about love are also related to her concern for constructing an adult role. This is especially clear in her concern over sex-appropriate behavior and what it means to be a woman. She writes, ". . . I ponder far more over Peter than Daddy. I know very well that I conquered him instead of he conquering me."[1y] . . . "I like it much better if he explains something to me than when I have to teach him; I would really adore him to be my superior in almost everything."[1z] At another time she is pleased for acting in a way that fits the image of the supportive wife. Concerning a pre-war boy friend, she writes, "I seem to act as a stimulant to keep him awake. You see we all have our uses, and queer ones too at times!"[1aa]

And perhaps the cognitive aspects of adolescent love shed some light on the oft-noted "homosexual" phase many adolescents seem to go through prior to their intense motivation to have relations with the opposite sex. Anne writes:[1bb]

After I came here, when I was just fourteen, I began to think about myself sooner than most girls, and to know that I am a "person." Sometimes, when I lie in bed at night, I have a terrible desire to feel my breasts and to listen to the quiet rhythmic beat of my heart. . . . I already had these kinds of feelings subconsciously before I came here, because I remember that once when I slept with a girl friend I had a strong desire to kiss her, and that I did so. I could not help being terribly inquisitive over her body, for she had always kept it hidden from me. . . . I go into ecstasies every time I see the naked figure of a woman. . . . It strikes me as so wonderful and exquisite that I have difficulty in stopping the tears rolling down my cheeks. If only I had a girl friend!

Can we explain the meaning of this passage by referring only to puberty? Our answer is that if we think of puberty in terms of its relation to the adolescent's concern for constructing an adult role, then it seems puberty serves primarily as a reinforcement of this concern. That is to say, the pride and curiosity in one's own sexual development is based upon the fact that such development means a closer approximation of what it is to be an adult. And likewise, the fear that such development stimulates is in part a fear of how to use and think about what has developed, or in other words, how to be an adult in the realm of action and thought as well as in the realm of the physical.

As a conclusion to this analysis of the cognitive aspects of Anne's diary, I would like to return to the "mind over matter" theme brought out earlier in this discussion. As Piaget has pointed out, adolescent thinking and formal operational thinking in general is not so much a series of specific behaviors, but rather a generalized *orientation*. That is, presented with any problem, it is not unlike the adolescent to *think through* possible solutions. Furthermore, the adolescent is capable of varying (in thought) a single factor (all other things being equal) so as to arrive at solutions systematically rather than by chance. As an example of this ability to think systematically, take the following event that took place while Anne was still in school. Because of her continually talking while in class, Anne was made to write a composition entitled, "A Chatterbox."[1cc]

I thought and thought and then, suddenly having an idea, filled my allotted sides [of paper] and felt completely satisfied. My arguments were that talking is a feminine characteristic and that I would do my best to keep it under control, but I should never be cured, for my mother talked as much as I, probably more, and what can one do about inherited qualities.

In other words, Anne demonstrates her ability to reason formally by structuring relationships and by humorously fabricating a relationship between talking in class and inherited qualities.

As a postscript to this analysis, I think it appropriate to draw some implications from what has been said concerning the nature of adolescent thinking. First of all, this discussion has been limited primarily to the cognitive aspects of adolescent behavior. But where emotional and personality factors have been discussed, it is hoped that these are regarded in the light of the ability to think formally. Furthermore, in regard to the "rift" between adolescent and parents, I think that an awareness that an adolescent is capable of thinking on a more sophisticated level than most adults believe, and an awareness that adolescents are extremely concerned with what it means to be a mature human being, and an awareness that adolescents are extremely concerned with justice, says something to anyone puzzling over how to react to student violence and race relations, topics which are of such importance to us at this time. For the adolescent-parent relationship can serve as a model for understanding the effects of a status differential, where at least one member of the relationship is unhappy over the inequality. Finally, from the two major concerns brought out in Anne's thinking it would seem reasonable to ask ourselves if our society is addressing itself to these concerns enough so as to meet the needs of the adolescent population.

REFERENCES

[1] Frank, A. *The Diary of a Young Girl.* Transl. B. M. Mooyart. New York: Doubleday, Modern Library, 1952, pp. (a) 278; (b) 24; (c) 270; (d) 38; (e) 43; (f) 99; (g) 18; (h) 253; (i) 57; (j) 280; (k) 55; (l) 187; (m) 201; (n) 137; (o) 142; (p) 222; (q) 241; (r) 24; (s) 135; (t) 82; (u) 9; (v) 12; (w) 232; (x) 174; (y) 277; (z) 205; (aa) 19; (bb) 143; (cc) 17.

[2] Piaget, J. and B. Inhelder. *The Growth of Logical Thinking from Childhood to Adolescence.* Transl. A. Parsons and S. Milgram. New York: Basic Books, 1961, p. 336.

[3] Piaget, J. *The Moral Judgment of the Child.* Transl. M. Gabain. New York: Free Press, 1965, p. 319.

Adolescent Friendships

Joseph Adelson and Elizabeth Douvan

In our society, the adolescent period sees the most intense development of friendship. There are a good many reasons for this. Erotic and aggressive drives toward family members become so intense that the youngster must have a neutral arena in which to work them out; he is in process of breaking (or recasting) his ties to the family and desperately needs the support, approval and security, as well as the norms, of a peer group. He is discovering, and trying to interpret and control, a changed body, and with it new and frightening impulses, and so requires both the example and communion of peers. He is about to crystallize an identity, and for this needs others of his generation to act as models, mirrors, helpers, testers, foils.

All in all, it would seem that the adolescent does not choose friendship, but is driven into it. The paradox is that the very needs that drive the child will, if they are not kept in control, imperil the friendship itself. Erotic and aggressive drives, in some degree of sublimation, are the cement of adolescent peer relations. If the sublimations fail (as they often do during this time), the drives spill over into the friendship and spoil it. Adolescent friendships, as we shall see, are based to a considerable extent on narcissism, identifications, and projections. These are tricky processes. If the youngster is too narcissistic, he may be so sensitive to rejection that he cannot abide friendship, or so obtuse to the needs of the other as to be unfit for it. If projection dominates the interaction, it may end in the other being seen as overdangerous. Identifications may become problematic in threatening to blur the all too tentative lineaments of ego identity. These dangers are by no means confined to the adolescent; the adult may avoid close friendships for the same reasons. But the adolescent, generally, will feel these dangers more acutely because of a turbulent intrapsychic situation, and because he has nowhere else to go. If friendship is difficult or dangerous, it is ordinarily less so than isolation, or working these things out in the family. All these circumstances

join to make the adolescent friendship a tempestuous, changable affair. Best friends may change in a moment; strange partnerships may come into being. If we look back to adolescence, we may be stupefied to recall friendships with the unlikeliest, the most alien of partners, to whom we were bonded by a momentary, yet critical mutuality of needs. Even our solid and enduring adolescent friendships may turn out, if we remember them closely enough, not to have been quite so unbroken and harmonious as they first appear in retrospect. They may in fact have blown hot and cold, responsive to all the rise and fall of feeling in self and others.

If some circumstances drive the child to friendship, others give him the opportunity to use and be changed by it. There is the simple fact that he is given, nowadays, the leisure and freedom to explore friendship, free from the responsibilties of work and family which will shortly absorb so much time and energy. Society finds his labor expendable, a circumstance that produces a great many complications; it helps to produce some of the adolescent demoralizations we hear so much about. But ordinarily the adolescent's leisure and freedom from responsibility do not work out so badly. It offers him the occasion for making discoveries about himself and others. The youngster needs time, needs the sense of unlimited time, and usually he will find or make the time. Even in the overorganized segment of the middle class, where the child is likely to be hemmed in by the demands of school and official leisure, he will discover his own slow-down techniques, making sure that there is time left over for the bull session, telephone chatter and all the other (well-publicized) forms of adolescent idleness.

So we have a necessity for friendship and, ordinarily, considerable opportunity for it. Another quality of the adolescent must be noted; he enters friendship with a remarkable eagerness and capacity for change. The contrast with the latency child is an instructive one. Before adolescence the child accepts himself as he is; if he is popular or unpopular, if he has many friends or only one or none—this is the way things are; the child may sorrow over it, but he will not generally feel there is

From Douvan/Adelson, *The Adolescent Experience.* Copyright © 1966, John Wiley & Sons, Inc., Publishers. Reprinted by permission of John Wiley & Sons, Inc.

much he can do about it. He has not yet made the discovery of the tractable self. Sometime near the start of adolescence, the child develops a consciousness of the self as a social stimulus, modifiable by will and intention. He enters the world of self-help, of books and columns on manners, dating, dress, make-up, chit-chat, the world of rituals and resolutions designed to make or remake the self. He enters friendship with an eagerness to make good, and the conviction that the self can be transformed to that end.

Along with this almost conscious, almost deliberate openness to change. we have another level of openness, to which we alluded earlier, the openness to the inner states of experience; with it comes a psychic fluidity, a vulnerability to conflict, an affective lability which together give adolescent intimacies so much of their characteristic flavor. The very fragility of the defenses may at times implicate the youngster in conflict, but on the other hand (and on the whole) they permit a relation to the other which captures the deepest levels of feeling, and so bind the adolescent and friend into an immoderate and unreserved intimacy.

In the explosion of impulses that dominates the early adolescent period, we find that while a goodly share of drive energy is diverted from the family to peers, a considerable amount of it is directed to the self. The adolescent's narcissism is ubiquitous: it expresses itself in a great many obvious ways—in an excruciating self-consciousness, in the concern with clothing and appearance, in shyness, in raucous exhibitionism, in posturing, primping, preening—and in anomalies of emotion and behavior where the origin is less obvious and direct. The narcissistic orientation, as we said earlier, influences the form and function of friendship at this time. There is the well-known adolescent touchiness, a hypersensitivity to rejection which in some cases can assume almost a paranoid intensity, in the conviction that friends are talking about them, or are out to exclude, wound, and humiliate them. The youngster will put himself at the center of the peer universe; the behavior of the other is overinterpreted; casual happenings—the friend's gesture or boredom, or the passing mention of a third person—will be magnified into events of major interpersonal significance.

Even when things do not come to such a pass, the adolescent's narcissism may make his friendships far less interactive than they first appear to be. His tie to the friend may be no more than the need for a forum where, by mutual consent, each participant is allowed equal time to discourse on the self's vicissitudes. In these cases the friend is expected to offer only the mechanical responses of the listener. We also may see the role of narcissism in the choice of friend—the other is someone who is like the self, or more commonly, someone who can represent certain illusory aspects of

the self. In the other, the adolescent can make objective the disavowed or prospective or half-understood qualities of the self. . . . We often find during this period an intolerance and contempt for those of a different bent of character and talent more intense than at any other stage of the life cycle. The need is to define personal identity; to accomplish this, the youngster needs the reassurance and mirroring offered by others of the same disposition.

So a pair, a trio, or larger grouping will establish itself through joint sympathies and mutual identifications. The group tendency is to define itself with considerable exclusiveness (the preoccupation with "cliques" and "snobbishness" is very strong during adolescence), the attempt being to confirm identity by insisting on homogeneity. The outside world, and especially other peers, is excluded, and more, becomes the subject of projection. We find, at this time, a tendency to strengthen ingroup ties and to reduce their inherent tendencies toward ambivalence, through ascribing to others, to the outgroup, those qualities too dangerous to recognize in the self. Of course these projections often cannot be kept outside the group. If the group is large enough, a tendency will develop to exclude temporarily, or to scapegoat, particular members. There is no end to the complexities (and the tedium) of arrangements and rearrangements within the friendship group, particularly among girls: A breaks up a close tie between B and C by retelling to B something she had heard C say about B; so the displaced C will detach D from her intimacy with E and get her to join a vendetta against A and B; it is something like a da Ponte libretto.

Generally, while adolescents choose each other for friends on the basis of likeness, dissimilarity plays a greater role in the functioning of the relation than first meets the eye. Certain general qualities must be alike, social class, interests, taste, morality, but after these likenesses are established, we find that the play of interaction is conducted through differences. Adolescent friendship is based (to some extent) on complementarity (although within a framework of similarity), just as in the case of marital selection as discussed by Winch (1958). Qualities of personality must vary between friends enough to give the relation the zest, tension, and enrichment that comes out of differences.

Finally we come to the art of friendship, the winning of friends—we hesitate at this topic, since it seems to have been pre-empted by the self-help industry. Yet it is clear enough that one of the essential tasks of the adolescent period is learning friendship, learning its demands and responsibilities, its nuances and complexities. Surely, much of what goes into being a friend and being befriended is so much a part of character as to be somewhat removed from learning—warmth, grace, and integrity—these qualities and others like them are too deeply woven into the fabric of personality to be susceptible to change. Although they are not readily lost or acquired, they need to be practiced, tempered, and polished within the framework of personal relations. The child must learn, or sharpen, his discretion, tact, and sensitivity—all that goes into knowing the limits of the other's privacy, acquiring a sense of the implicit. He must learn how to get what he needs from the other, while taking into account (and serving) the other's own needs. He must come to know the tolerable limits of his own aggression, and how much hostility he is prepared to accept without endangering his self-regard; and how to stand up for his rights without guilt and without abusing the rights of the other.

These are just some parts of the interpersonal agenda of adolescence. Of course it could be said, and with some justice, that the child has been learning these things all his life. So he has, but in ways too limited to prepare him for the peculiar exigencies of adolescent friendship. The personal relations between parent and child are intrinsically hierarchical; the relations to siblings are generally ambivalent and competitive; the peer friendships of the preadolescent years are, as we shall soon see, emotionally pallid and not genuinely interactive. The child before adolescence cannot learn, from family and friends, the ego qualities he will need to master the modalities of friendship in adolescence. These relations are the result of personal choice, are interactive, equalitarian, and suffused with the child's deepest emotions. He is only partially prepared by earlier experience; he must now learn the rest himself.

Up to this point we have treated adolescent friendships in a most general fashion, highlighting those processes unique to the period as a whole. Our intention here is to examine the developmental data on girls; through it we hope to understand the forms and functions of the like-sexed friendship as it grows and changes during the adolescent years.

Our data yield clear developmental trends; changes that occur in a simple direct fashion as girls grow older. Beyond this, we find differences among the age groups which are not continuous, but point to distinctive qualities of relationship in the three stages of adolescence.

Generally, we can say the child develops, as she moves through the adolescent era, an increasing emotional investment in friendship, greater sophistication and subtlety in her conceptions about it, a growing capacity for disinterested appreciation of the friend, and greater tolerance of differences within the relationship.

PREADOLESCENCE AND EARLY ADOLESCENCE: GIRLS OF ELEVEN, TWELVE, AND THIRTEEN

It is very possible that our conception of the latency period is something of a fiction. We have fallen into the habit of seeing it as a time of life without passion. The emotions and drives, and all the conflicts they bestir, are held to disappear near age six, to be rearoused at puberty. As our knowledge of the latency period increases, we become aware that it is instinctually placid only in contrast with the Oedipal period before it and adolescence after it. It is psychodynamically more complex than we realized. Nevertheless, the contrast is impressive; we can go only so far in refining our idea of latency. Relative to what precedes and follows it, the preadolescent period is indeed low in drive and conflict; the child is absorbed in the quiet growth of ego capacities. Erikson (1950) calls it a stage of life dominated by "industry." The child begins to develop skills —reading and writing, of course, but also the myriad opportunities of a complex culture—sports and games in an infinite variety, the arts and crafts, collections and hobbies, and riddles and jokes.

It is a busy age, then; and the nature of friendship at this time reflects its busyness, its diligence, and its enriching dilletantism. The friends focus more on activity—on what they are doing together, than they do on themselves. The companion, to be sure, may be used as a point of reference—the child judging herself by the other—but there is little interest in the friend's personality as such. We see this in the fact that girls at this period can tell us so little about friendship. When we ask what a friend ought to be like, and what things make a girl popular with others, the early adolescent mentions fewer qualities than older girls do. More important, the qualities she does mention are fairly superficial ones. For example, she wants a friend to do favors for her. She wants the friend to be amiable, easy to get along with, cooperative, and fair. The friend ought not to be a crab, grouchy, mean, selfish or a showoff.

What we miss in this surfeit of adjectives is the sense that friendship can be emotionally relevant. The girl alludes to those surface qualities of the other that promote or hinder the swift and easy flow of activity. The friendship, we feel, centers on the activity rather than on the interaction itself. In this respect, the friendship is not yet relational. One wants a partner who is neither demanding nor disagreeable, whose personality will not get in the way of activity. The personality of the other is seen as a possible encumbrance to activity; later on it becomes the center of the interaction, as the girl becomes concerned with the friend's qualities in their capacity to disrupt, not the joint activity, but the friendship is still an adjunct to something else, the partnership in work and play.

The preadolescent girl is engaged in the exercise of the ego—the drives and conscience are not yet a source of concern. The child is oriented to the "real" world, to externality, rather than to the inner world. There is little preoccupation with internal qualities, either in the self or the other. The need for friendship arises out of the need to practice and extend the newly won and still growing ego resources. What the child wants is a certain degree and quality of growing room, and if there is any conflict with the family, it will probably be over this issue. The child grown in skills will demand the independence to put them to use; in some cases, the family may be too confined an arena, and a relation to friends may be needed. Most families in our society raise no objection; they may set some limit to the child's demands and the child ordinarily will accept these without fuss. Basically the youngster's emotional commitment is to the family, rather than to friends. Most of our subjects at preadolescence do not believe that they can be as close to a friend as to members of the family. They rarely report conflict with the family about friendship and the choosing of friends. Leisure time is more often spent with the family than with friends.

Boys do not have much importance yet. At least this is what we gather from what our subjects tell us; we may suspect that there is a good deal of anticipation, and no little trepidation, regarding heterosexuality— more than the girl allows herself to think there is, and far more than she will tell an interviewer. Still, as far as overt activity is concerned, friendship means the like-sexed friendship, period. The girl at this age has ordinarily not begun to date. When we put to her a hypothetical question pitting a friendship tie against the possibility of a date, she plumps for the friendship. But if the preadolescent girl does not date boys, she does play sports with them. At this age, the sexes meet on the playground, and judge each other by skill rather than sex. When sex begins to be important, there will be more distinction made between male and female activities than we find at this point. Given this lack of involvement with boys and dating, we are not surprised to find that ethical issues centering on heterosexuality do not play much part in the friendship; soon, however, the girl will be concerned with the ethics of competition for boys, and sexual morality, and the balance to be found between the ties of friendship and the demands of dating.

PUBERTY AND MIDDLE ADOLESCENCE: GIRLS OF FOURTEEN, FIFTEEN, AND SIXTEEN

The processes we discussed earlier now make their appearance. The child is swept into the erotic mysteries; the body changes and the instincts disturb the psychic equilibrium. The doubts, confusions, anxiety, and guilt evoked by the eruption of sexual urges, the incestuous and aggressive dangers in the family—these, and more, as we have said, drive the child from the family and into intimate, intense and sometimes desperate friendships. But the erotic is still too new and frightening: the child does not know enough yet, either about herself or about the opposite sex. The transition to heterosexuality is made through the like-sexed friendship.

These friendships are very different in style and purpose than those of preadolescence. At this age, our findings show, the girls are less tied to the family, spend more time with friends, and are more articulate about the nature and conditions of friendship. The mere sharing of activity diminishes, to be replaced by a relation that is mutual, interactive, emotionally interdependent; the personality of the other, and the other's response to the self become the central themes of the friendship. The girl no longer stresses the concrete and superficial qualities of the friend. It is no longer important for the friend to do favors for one, nor does popularity depend much on good manners as the younger girl is likely to tell us. When girls past puberty report on their friendships they use a vocabulary that is (relatively) abstract, differentiated, and relational. They want a friend they can confide in, someone who can offer emotional support and understanding. When they describe the popular girl, they define her as one who is able to proffer this kind of friendship—someone who is sensitive to the needs of others.

The girls of this age group are unique in some respects, that is, different from both younger and older girls. What stands out in their interviews is the stress placed on security in friendships. They want the friend to be loyal, trustworthy, and a reliable source of support in any emotional crisis. She should not be the sort of person who will abandon you, or who gossips about you behind your back.

Why so much emphasis on loyalty? We imagine that part of the reason is that the friendship is less a mutuality than it appears to be at first. The girl is less interested in the other than she thinks; what she seeks in the other is some response to, and mirroring of, the self. She needs the presence of someone who is undergoing the same trials, discoveries, and despairs. The sexual crisis, in short, is handled through identification. In this way, the girl gains some of the strength she needs to handle impulses; and through the other, she has the opportunity to learn something about her own sexuality. Through the sharing of knowledge and affects, she is relieved, to some extent, of the anxiety and guilt which accompanies the emergence of sexuality.

With so much invested in the friendship, it is no wonder that the girl is so dependent on it. To lose the friend, for the girl at this age, is to lose a part of the self; those qualities of the other that one has incorporated within the self, and those aspects of the self that one has given to the other, and with which one has identified. Intimaces, at this time, are often too symbiotic to be given up without pain. The friend who is disloyal leaves one abandoned to the impulses. Then, too, there is the fact that in leaving she takes away with her the knowledge of the girl's sexual history and fantasies. The girl is likely to feel like the woman analysand in that famous *New Yorker* cartoon, who getting up from the couch, takes a pistol from her purse, and says: "You've done me a world of good, Doctor, but you know too much." It is this sort of feeling, no doubt, which accounts for the anxiety that the friend may gossip behind one's back.

The erotic preoccupations of this period are also reflected in the fact that our data show sexual references to be more common between fourteen and sixteen than either before or after. This group of girls is the most likely to mention sexual immorality as a cause of unpopularity and as a reason why one would not want to be friendly with some girls. In these data we see how the sexual impulses are to some extent handled by projection. Apprehensive about the strength of her own controls, the young girl may become engrossed, fascinated, and repelled by the "bad girl." The advantages of projection are too well known to need extensive treatment here. It is enough to say that by splitting female peerdom into "nice girls" and "bad girls," one is able to deposit unacceptable wishes onto the outgroup, and so reinforce one's defenses against impulse. This device also helps the girl to relieve her guilt for whatever erotic pleasures she permits herself. She will reason that her own behavior is shared by the collectivity of "nice girls," and that, in any case, her own sins pale in contrast with what she imagines are the indulgences of the "bad girl." Perhaps we ought to say here that the "bad girl" is in most cases no simple figment of fancy; in any high school of size, the girl will have the opportunity to know, at a safe distance, a number of girls who wear tight sweaters and too much makeup and who go with the wrong sort of boys. Later, when the girl has come to terms with her own sexuality, she will be able to take the girls of dubious reputation more in stride. At this age, they represent a degree of impulsivity too dangerous to be casual about.

While the erotic seems to touch everything at this age, there are of course other themes present during this most difficult period of adolescence. The girl is not only unsure of her capacity to settle sexuality; she is also confused and uncertain about personal identity and indeed about her worth as a human being. To a considerable extent, she will look to the peer group's appraisal both to define and evaluate her. It is a time when, in order to consolidate identity, confirm status, heighten self-esteem, adolescents form themselves into cliques which are, as we know, more or less exclusionist. Paradoxically, the girl in this age group gives some evidence of democratic sentiment—she tells us that she admires equalitarian manners and dislikes those who are snobbish and status-seeking. Those who live by the ingroup, as the young girl must, will also live in mortal fear of perishing by it. The girl does not view her own ingroup commitments as snobbish, but she fears a possible exclusion from the group, and so makes much of snobbism. Here we find another reason for the emphasis on security and loyalty at this age—the good friend is one who will not abandon her to social isolation.

Another source of insecurity arises from the fact that the girl ordinarily begins to date at this age. We shall discuss dating later in this article. Here we want to say something about its relation to the like-sexed friendship. The friend is needed as a source of guidance, comfort, and support. In the preceding section we discussed the intimate friendship in this function—how the friends share their learning, how, in recounting their experiences to each other, they become able to live vicariously, reinterpret their behavior, relieve guilt, and exercise mutual controls. At this age, too, the girl must begin to come to terms with the ethics of friendship and dating. The girl, needing friendship so desperately, wants to feel that her friend will not abandon her in favor of boys. The dating friendship, at this age, may be seen as competitive with like-sexed friendship. Another form of competition is in the possible rivalry of girls for popularity with boys. The friendship has to recognize and adjust to differential popularity. The girl who is too popular or who flaunts her popularity risks the hostility of her peers. The girl who has won popularity must learn how to accept her good fortune graciously and modestly, so that her friends can learn to temper their envy. We cannot avoid the impression that the adolescent girl is far more concerned about the opinion of girls than of boys. She wants to be popular with boys, for its effects on her appraisal by the peer group of girls.

LATE ADOLESCENCE: GIRLS OF SEVENTEEN AND EIGHTEEN

Our story has a happy ending. The desperate, feverish quality of friendship in the preceding age period now gives way to calmer, more modulated friendships. The girl has become somewhat easier about herself. She has managed to define herself and to find the basis for a personal identity. She has been able to develop fairly secure defenses against impulses and can now allow herself to discharge them in more direct experimentations in sexuality. She has learned how to handle herself with boys, and has acquired the rudiments of social skill. All of these changes relieve the pressure on the like-sexed friendship. Much of the emotional energy that has been invested in girls is now diverted to boys.

As her suspiciousness of boys has dwindled, she is able to turn to them for intimacy. As she has gained skill in the dating relation, she no longer needs the friendship as a retreat, or a source of learning, or a fushion for disappointment. As identity is secure, she has fewer needs for identification-based relations with girls.

The passionate quality of friendship recedes, and it is replaced by a more equable tie to the other. By the time the girl reaches late adolescence she has developed a fairly complex understanding of friendship. This group has more to say than any other about its various functions, and what they tell us is at once more subtle and more abstract. Like early adolescent girls, they stress the confiding and sharing aspects—they want a friend with whom they can share important confidences. Yet we sense a new note in their answers—there is some indication that identifications are less prominent than before. There is now a greater emphasis on the personality and talents of the friend, a stress on what she can bring to the relation in the way of interest and stimulation. The girl becomes aware of and interested in her friend's individuality. There is a greater capacity, we imagine, to tolerate differences, and to value the friend for the ways in which she is unique. This stands in some contrast to the preceding period, where the girl, out of the need to confirm identity, might insist on a homogeneity of character, or where she could tolerate differences only when they allowed her to work out some instinctual dilemma. Now it is possible for the friendship to take on a more disinterested, neutral, playful, and diversified quality. It is no longer an apparatus for the resolution of conflict, and for that alone.

The partial solving of the sexual and identity crises brings with it a reduction of the emphases characteristic of the earlier age period. The girls make fewer references to loyalty, security, and trust when they talk about the qualities a friend should have. Needing friendship less, they are less haunted by fears of being abandoned and betrayed. There is also less of a preoccupation with sexual immorality. There seems to be a diminished use of projection, less tendency to divide girls into the good and the bad, and less concern with sexual reputation as a basis for judging, choosing, and excluding friends. Now that she can manage her sexuality, she is less fascinated by it, no longer so sensitive to it in others.

One other finding may be of some interest. When we ask younger girls what age group they prefer to be with in a social situation, they express a marked preference for older girls. We get the impression of a rush to maturity, a desire to know and grow, and a desire to share the sophistication (and the sexual secrets) of older girls. At seventeen and eighteen, this pattern ends, and we now find that girls prefer age groups which put them at the upper end of the age range. Our older girls have the advantage of greater experience and status without the burden of adult responsibility. So they seem to pause momentarily, and slow down, before they begin the transition to adulthood.

The reader may be weary of hearing that, for our knowledge of developmental processes we have had to rely on the study of girls; to those who have just joined us, let us repeat that the data on boys are limited to the 14 to 16 age group, while our interviews with girls extend from eleven to eighteen. So we cannot provide a complete comparison of male and female friendship patterns during the course of adolescence. We do, however, have enough information to know that the differences are considerable.

Before we look at our data, let us note some general differences which influence the contrasting forms of friendship for the sexes. There is the obvious fact that the girl is socialized so as to place great importance on personal relations; her life task, as wife and mother, requires her to cultivate such traits as sensitivity, warmth, tact, and empathy. The boy, to put matters oversimply, is trained toward activity and achievement; he needs to cultivate assertiveness and independence. (Of course we can easily make too much of these differences, and construct a caricature of the sexes, stressing these contrasting traits to the exclusion of all else.) Furthermore, the fear of homosexuality runs so strong among men in this country as to inhibit any display of "womanly" qualities; it also serves to frighten the man away from close ties to other men. Men fear more often than women a breakthrough of the homoerotic if they allow themselves too great a degree of intimacy with their own sex.

There are some less obvious reasons for the different forms adolescent friendship may take in the sexes. Helene Deutsch (1944, 1945) and other psychoanalytic writers have distinguished the differing psychosexual tasks of adolescent boys and girls. The boy's problem is to sever old object ties and form new ones. The development of adult sexual impulses makes it imperative to withdraw drive cathexes from the family and divert them to new and more appropriate objects. This is, of course, the girl's problem too. The difference between them is that the boy has little trouble in understanding his own sexuality. He experiences the erotic as direct, discrete, immediate, and uncomplicated. His sexual impulses are unambiguous; the organ of sexuality is familiar. There remains much to learn, about controlling and gratifying the erotic, about heterosexuality in general, but he is not long confused about the nature of his sexuality.

The girl's sexuality is not known to her quite so simply. For the girl the erotic is diffuse, remote, ambiguous, and complex. She also has the task of controlling and gratifying impulses, but at the same time she must learn their nature. As we have indicated, she does so through intimate friendship, and through complex identifications with her own kind. Not only is the girl attuned to the interpersonal, but also she is driven to make use of it for self-understanding. The intimate friendship, then, is a resource more necessary to the girl than to the boy.

Let us try putting this another way. For the girl we can image a reticulate triad: identity, the erotic and the interpersonal. The erotic and the interpersonal are much more closely linked in women than in men. Women in our society are object-dependent; they are compliant, passive, and responsive to the fear of losing love, that is, losing the esteem of the other. The woman cannot easily separate, as many men can, her erotic feelings from her ties to another. The achievement of personal identity requires a synthesis of the erotic and the interpersonal. Each of these terms is linked to the others: to define one's identity means to know the erotic, which in turn means to know the relation between the erotic and the interpersonal.

For the boy, the definition of identity is more likely to depend on such qualities as assertiveness, autonomy, and achievement. If we imagine a triad for the boy it would be something like: identity, the erotic, and autonomy (including in the last term a number of other characteristics, such as those given above). For the boy one problem is to come to terms with authority, neither submitting to it, nor identifying with it, nor fighting it obsessively; another (and related) problem is to come to terms with assertiveness, which means that it must not be degraded into cruelty or crushed into timidity, but must be controlled, refined, and adapted into purposeful activity. The boy's sense of the erotic will reflect and be reflected by, influence and be influenced by the development of activity and autonomy. Whether sexuality is, for example, brutal, or passive, or impotent is reciprocally connected with the boy's resolution of the relation to authority. In turn, both the erotic and autonomy (again, in a broad sense) will interact with identity.

So we may say that the adolescent girl, bred to the interpersonal, must solve problems of the interpersonal, and uses interpersonal methods to do so. (In a moment, we shall present some data which indicate how important interpersonal competence is to the girl's integration and effectiveness.) For the boy, the problem at adolescence is, as we have said, the relation to authority, and all that follows from that. The boy, to some extent socialized against intimacy, is also less dependent upon intimate relations during this period. He needs to assert and maintain his independence against control by parents and by parent-surrogates. To this end he needs the gang, the band of brothers, in alliance with whom he can confirm himself as autonomous and maintain a wall of resistance to authority. Even when the boys' close friendship group is small in number, they are apt to give it a ganglike definition, for example, calling themselves "The Three Musketeers" or "The Four Horsemen." Girls, on the other hand, even when they are part of a large group of friends, tend to form into centers of intimate two- and three-somes.

While girls ordinarily show few signs of the true gang spirit, boys do have intimate friendships, based on identification, much as girls do. We have defined ideal types, rather than differences which exist invariably. Our assumption is not that the intimate friendship cannot be found among boys, but rather that it is less common, and that it does not usually achieve the depth of intimacy usual among girls.

But limitations in our data prevent us from testing this hypothesis. As we shall see in a moment the interviews show that 14- to 16-year-old boys are less involved in close friendship than girls are at the same age. Since our sample of boys does not extend into the later stages of adolescence, we have no way of knowing whether we are dealing only with a slower rate of social development (this is generally true of adolescent boys) or whether, as we believe, there is, among American males, an absolute inhibition of friendship which continues not only into late adolescence but also into adulthood as well. The slow pace of development in itself does not tell us much about the ultimate limits of friendship development.

What we do know, what the interview data make quite clear, is that boys in early adolescence are less sophisticated about friendship and less eager for intimacy than girls of the same age. The findings also suggest that the peer group collectively, the gang, is more important to the boy than to the girl, that it serves to orient and support him.

To begin with, boys are less articulate than girls about the nature and meaning of friendship. To all questions in this area, concerning the qualities a friend ought to have, and the bases for popularity and unpopularity, they give fewer answers than do girls. Neither do they count close friendship as important as the girls do. They will more often assert that a friendship can never be as close as a family relationship: 42 percent of the boys feel this way, compared to 61 percent of the girls the same age.

When we ask boys the criteria they use for choosing a friend, and about the sources of a boy's popularity, they name rather concrete qualities. Their answers bear a striking resemblance to those given by the preadolescent girl. They believe a friend ought to be amiable and cooperative, and in general demand little in the way of genuine interaction. They want the friend to be able to control impulses, and here they particularly have aggression in mind. They also mention excessive hostility ("he's mean, a bully, picks fights") as a major source of unpopularity. Apart from exercising a degree of control, the friend is seen as having few obligations in the relationship. Boys at this age do not emphasize, as the girls do, the affective elements in friendship. They make no demands for closeness, mutual understanding, or emotional support. There is less mention made of security, which is heavily stressed by the girls. Since the boys' friendships do not involve the deeper emotions, they are not quite so threatened by the possibility of losing the friend. The support they do ask from the friend is, again, similar to what we find among the youngest girls. They want specific, concrete supplies, rather than warmth and understanding. Their conception of the roots of popularity again reminds us of the criteria mentioned by preadolescent girls, in being specific, concrete, and fairly superficial—good looks and good manners, athletic ability, an amiable, nonaggressive disposition. There is no value placed on sensitivity or empathy; snobbishness and gossip do not figure in their evaluations of other boys. All in all, the boys show little concern with the relational aspects of friendship. Friendship for them, as for the youngest group of girls, involves a tie to a congenial companion, with whom one shares a common interest in reality oriented activities.

Our findings also give us some sense of the relative importance to boys of "gang" life, and of the role of the peer group in helping him to confront authority. Boys are more likely than girls to adduce as a cause of unpopularity the unwillingness to "go along with the crowd." In their view, the failure to conform to peer standards is a more probable basis for peer rejection than it is for girls.

Another difference is in the kind of help one expects from a friend. We have already seen that boys are nearer to the youngest girls in wanting specific, concrete supports. But we also find in the boys' answers a theme which does not get much play from girls—the expected help from a friend when in trouble or in times of crisis. Remember that our preadolescent girls wanted from their friends positive supplies in the form of favors. But boys are less receptive in orientation, and more concerned about possible conflicts with authority. They seem to anticipate being on the spot, or being in trouble. The friend is one who will support you when trouble comes. We feel sure that the trouble the boys have in mind is trouble with the adult world. Another indication of this is in the difference between the sexes as regards verbal hostility. The girls object, as we have said,

to gossip, to being talked about by other girls. Here the objection is to behavior which will damage or destroy one's relation to peers. Boys however object to "tattling," that is, to the boy who breaks peer ranks to collaborate with the adult enemy. So the adolescent boy's assertive-resistant stance to adults, which we examined earlier, is also evident in his definition of friendship and peer relations. We shall look at this again when we discuss the peer group later in the article.

Finally, we want to consider a finding we deem to be of special importance. We have argued throughout this article that the interpersonal is of peculiar importance in feminine psychology, that it plays a central role in the woman's development and experience, more so than for the man. Throughout her life, she meets developmental crises through permutations of the interpersonal—the major motive is the desire for love, the major source of anxiety is the fear of losing love, the major technique in crisis is the appeal for support and supplies from persons important to her. While the boy develops internal controls and strives to meet internal moral standards, the girl regulates her behavior to a greater degree through a sensitivity to signals from key figures in the environment. The boy, to put matters too simply, responds to guilt, the girl to shame. Just as we hypothesized that the consolidation of internal controls is related to personal integration in boys, so we anticipate that, for girls, the degree of personal integration is related to the maturation of interpersonal skills. The girl's talent in relating to objects, her techniques in attracting and holding affection, would, we felt, hold the key to her success in adaptation. Interpersonal skills, we thought, would not be nearly as critical to the boy's integration.

To test these hypotheses, we devised a measure of interpersonal maturation. Using extreme groups, those who show relatively mature attitudes and skills in the area of friendship, and those who are strikingly immature, we compared their responses in other areas of ego development. For girls there is a clear relation between interpersonal maturation and the following variables: energy level, self-confidence, time-perspective, organization of ideas, and positive feminine identification. For boys, however, the degree of interpersonal maturation is not significantly related to energy level, self-confidence, time perspective, or self-acceptance. In short, we gather that the interpersonal mode is interwoven with the girl's personal integration, while it does not have the same degree of influence in the boy's development.

John Janeway Conger

31

A New Morality: Sexual Attitudes and Behavior of Contemporary Adolescents

It has been apparent for some years now that the sexual attitudes and values of adolescents have been changing significantly, that a "new morality" has been developing in the United States and other Western countries (**3, 16, 20**). In comparison to their peers of earlier generations, today's adolescents place a greater emphasis on openness and honesty about sex (**4, 16, 29**). In a number of recent surveys (**8, 9, 10, 33, 34**), the majority (85% or more) of American adolescents expressed the view that young people need more and better sex education and that information about sex should be given in the schools—under most circumstances, in coeducational classes.

In one national survey of the confidential opinions of 1500 middle-class adolescent girls aged 13 to 19, 98 percent said they wanted sex taught in school (**10**). When

asked what was currently being taught and what *should* be taught, most girls responded that such topics as the anatomy and physiology of the female reproductive system and the menstrual cycle not only *should* be taught, but that they were being covered. Most girls also felt strongly that sex education classes should deal with such philosophical or scientific issues as premarital ethics, abortion, birth control and contraception, male and female sex drives, masturbation, homosexuality, loss of virginity, impotence and frigidity, fertility, and the nature of the orgasm. In *all* of these important areas, however, less than half of the sample reported having had school instruction.

In addition, there is a growing tendency among young people to view decisions about individual sexual behavior as more of a private and less of a public con-

Drawing by Stephen Wells is reprinted from *Psychology Today* Magazine. Copyright © 1975, Ziff-Davis Publishing Company

cern (**4, 63**). In part, this appears to reflect a growing sus-piciousness of or disenchantment with established social in-stitutions and their proclaimed values, together with a shift among many young people in the direction of indi-vidual self-discovery and self-expression—of "doing one's thing." But it also reflects a greater emphasis on the im-portance of "meaningful," that is, genuine and sincere, interpersonal relationships in sex as in other areas.

In the view of a majority of contemporary adoles-cents, the acceptability of various forms and degrees of sexual behavior, including premarital intercourse, is highly dependent on the nature of the relationship between the individuals involved (**16, 20, 26, 29**). Eighty percent of adolescent boys and 72 percent of girls in this country agree with the statement, "It's all right for young people to have sex before getting married if they are in love with each other" (**29**). Seventy-five percent of all girls maintain that "I wouldn't want to have sex with a boy unless I loved him" (**29**). While only 47 percent of boys stated this stringent a requirement, 69 percent said, "I would not want to have sex with a girl unless I liked her as a per-son" (**29**). In contrast, most adolescents clearly oppose exploitation, pressure or force in sex, sex solely for the sake of physical enjoyment, and sex between people too young to understand what they are getting into (**16, 20, 29**). Nearly 75 percent of all adolescents concur that "when it comes to morality in sex, the important thing is the way people treat each other, not the things they do to-gether" (**29**).

Despite a growing emphasis among adolescents on openness and honesty, there is little evidence of preoc-cupation with sex, as many parents and other adults seem to think. Indeed, it may well be that the average adoles-cent of today is less preoccupied and concerned with sex than prior generations of young people, including his par-ents when they were the same age. Greater acceptance of sex as a natural part of life may well lead to less preoc-cupation than anxious concern in an atmosphere of se-crecy and suppression. Most contemporary adolescents (87%) agree that "all in all, I think my head is pretty well together as far as sex is concerned" (**29**).

Furthermore, in ranking the relative importance of various goals, younger adolescent boys and girls (13–15) cited as most important: "Preparing myself to earn a good living when I get older," "Having fun," and "Getting along with my parents"; for younger girls, "Learning about myself" was also important. Older adolescents of both sexes (16–19) stressed "Learning about myself" as most important, followed by "Being independent so that I can make it on my own" and "Preparing myself to accom-plish useful things." Among all age groups, "Having sex with a number of different boys (girls)" and "Making out" consistently ranked at or near the top among goals con-sidered *least* important (**29**).

ARE CHANGING ATTITUDES REFLECTED IN BEHAVIOR?

Are the significant and apparently enduring changes in sexual attitudes and values among contemporary ado-lescents reflected in their behavior, and, if so, how? At least until very recently, a number of generally recognized authorities maintained that the overall behavior of today's

Photograph by George W. Gardner

adolescents and youth, though more open and in some respects probably freer, did not differ strikingly from that of their parents at the same age (**20, 24, 28**). Conversely, other observers have asserted that, although attitudinal changes may have been the more dramatic, there have also been marked changes in behavior (**17, 20**). What do the available data reveal? As will become evident, the answer appears to depend on *what* behaviors one is referring to, among *which* adolescents, and *how recently*.

Although current data are admittedly incomplete, the available information indicates that there has been rela-tively little if any change in the past few decades in the incidence of male masturbation (**1, 21, 22, 27, 29**); mas-turbation appears to have remained fairly stable over the years, with an estimated incidence of about 21 percent by age 12, 82 percent by age 15, and 92 percent by age 20 (**13, 27**). However, recent data (**9, 29**) indicate that there has been an increase in masturbation among girls at all age levels, with incidences of *at least* 36 percent by age 15 and 42 percent by age 19. In contrast, only about 17 percent of the mothers of today's adolescent girls had en-gaged in masturbation to orgasm by age 15, and by age 20, only about 30 percent (**12**).

One might be tempted to conclude that masturbation would occur most commonly among adolescents lacking other outlets. Interestingly, however, current masturbation experience among contemporary adolescents occurs about three times as frequently among those engaged in sexual intercourse or petting to orgasm as among the sexually inexperienced (**29**).

Petting does appear to have increased somewhat in the past few decades, and it tends to occur slightly earlier (**12, 13, 16, 20, 23, 24, 29**). The major changes, however, have probably been in the frequency of petting, degree of intimacy of techniques involved, the frequency with which petting leads to erotic arousal or orgasm, and, certainly, frankness about it (**2, 4, 16, 19, 28, 29**).

Premarital Intercourse

Currently, the greatest amount of public discussion (and parental and societal apprehension), as well as the most extensive data, deals with the incidence of sexual intercourse among contemporary youth. A favorite assertion among those who have claimed there have been few *recent* changes in adolescent sexual behavior is that, while there has indeed been a sexual revolution in this century, it took place, not among today's adolescents, but among their parents and grandparents. It does, in fact, appear that significant percentage increases in premarital intercourse occurred during this earlier period. For example, Kinsey's data indicate that only 2 percent of females born before 1900 had premarital intercourse prior to age 16, 8 percent prior to age 20, and only 14 percent prior to age 25 (**12**). In contrast, for the mothers of today's adolescents, the corresponding figures are 4 percent, 21 percent, and 37 percent, respectively (**12, 13**).

This, however, leaves unanswered the question of how the incidence of premarital intimacy among today's parents compares with that of their adolescent sons and daughters. Until very recently, relevant data for such a comparison were lacking, except in the case of college students. However, in a representative national study of adolescents aged 13 to 19, published in 1973, Robert Sorenson (**29**) found that 44 percent of boys and 30 percent of girls have had sexual intercourse prior to age 16. These figures increased to 72 percent of boys and 57 percent of girls by age 19. When compared with females of their mothers' generation in Kinsey's investigation (only 3% of whom had engaged in premarital intercourse by age 16 and less than 20% by age 19), this represents a very large increase, particularly at the younger age level. When compared with males of their fathers' generation (approximately 39% of whom had engaged in premarital intercourse by age 16 and 72% by age 19), contemporary adolescent boys as a whole show a much smaller change, mainly a tendency to have first intercourse at a slightly younger age. However, as will become apparent in the following section, these *overall* findings for boys obscure significant changes taking place among boys of higher socioeconomic and educational levels.

DIVERSITY OF SEXUAL ATTITUDES AND BEHAVIOR

Up to this point, our focus has been on *overall* trends in sexual attitudes and behavior among contemporary youth. Such group trends have meaning and usefulness in their own right, but they should not be allowed to distract our attention from an equally important phenomenon,

namely, the diversity of sexual attitudes and behavior in different sectors of the adolescent and youth population. There is increasing evidence that this diversity is currently marked and probably growing (**5, 16, 20, 29**). Such factors as age, sex, socioeconomic and educational level, race, religion, and even geographical area all appear to be related to sexual attitudes, values, and behavior. For this reason, the results of almost any survey dealing with adolescent sexuality will inevitably seem exaggerated to some young people and adults and minimized to others.

What do we know about some of these variations? As we have already noted, Sorenson's recent survey (**29**), shows that for the first time in such studies, a majority (52%) of American adolescents aged 13–19 reported having engaged in sexual intercourse. As significant as this evidence of a trend toward greater sexual freedom clearly is, it should not be allowed to obscure the complementary finding that a very substantial minority (48%) of adolescents had not as yet had such experience. Furthermore, neither of these broad groups was homogeneous. Thus, adolescents in the nonintercourse group ranged from those with virtually no sexual experience to those with a wide variety of experiences short of intercourse itself, including petting to orgasm.

Among the group with intercourse experience, two major subgroups emerge from the findings of this study: *serial monogamists* and *sexual adventurers*. The former "generally does not have intercourse with another during that relationship. We say 'serial' because one such relationship is often succeeded by another" (**29**, p. 121). The latter, on the other hand, "moves freely from one sex partner to the next and feels no obligation to be faithful to any sex partner" (**29**, p. 121). Among nonvirgins, serial monogamy was more frequent overall; it was also more frequent among girls, older adolescents, those from the northeast and west, and those from larger metropolitan areas. The total number of partners was obviously far higher among sexual adventurers, although it is interesting to note that frequency of intercourse was higher among monogamists.

Not surprisingly, the two groups tended to vary significantly in attitudes, as well as in behavior. Most monogamists believe they love and are loved by their partners, believe in openness and honesty between partners, and deny that sex is the most important thing in a love relationship—although they also expressed greater satisfaction with their sex lives. At the same time their code stresses personal freedom and the absence of commitment to marriage, despite the fact that more than half believe they will or may marry their partner eventually. Sexual adventurers, in contrast, are primarily interested in variety of experience for its own sake, do not believe that love is a necessary part of sexual relationships, and feel no particular personal responsibility for their partners, although neither do they believe in hurting others. For many adventurers, sex itself is viewed as an avenue to communication; as one young adventurer stated, "Having sex together is a good way for two people to become acquainted."

As a group, monogamists tended to be more satisfied with themselves and life in general, to get along better with parents, and to be more conventional in social, political, and religious beliefs. Despite their greater emphasis on sex as a goal in itself, female adventurers report having orgasm during intercourse less frequently than monogamists.

In general, and contrary to recent popular impressions, both the attitudes and behavior of younger adolescents still appear more *conservative* than those of older adolescents (**4, 6, 8, 10, 20**). Younger adolescents may possibly, as some have speculated end up less constrained by social mores than their older brothers and sisters. But the fact remains that for the great majority this is not presently the case.

Girls as a group are consistently more conservative than boys, both in attitudes and values and in behavior. In virtually all population subgroups, the incidence of all forms of intimate sexual behavior is less frequent among girls; girls are also more likely than boys to believe that partners in advanced forms of petting or intercourse should be in love, engaged, or married (**9, 16, 20, 25, 29**). Furthermore, girls are more likely than boys to be influenced by parental wishes and community social standards.

In Sorenson's study, 80 percent of the sexual adventurers were male; in contrast, 64 percent of serial monogamists were female. (The implication here is that a significant percentage of female monogamists were involved with males who were over 19, and hence not included in the study; the other possibility is that in some relationships the girl considered herself a monogamist, while the boy did not.) The greater emphasis among girls on love as a necessary component of sexual relationships is consistent with the stronger interpersonal orientation of girls generally. The extent to which a higher level of sexual activity among boys is a function of physiological differences, cultural influences, or (as seems most likely) both is still an unresolved question (**1, 4, 17**).

College youth emerge as consistently less conservative in their attitudes and values than noncollege peers of the same age. For example, in one study of American youth 17 and older (**35**), college youth were significantly less likely to express the view that premarital sexual relations "were not a moral issue." They were also more likely to believe that "sexual behavior should be bound by mutual feelings, not by formal ties," and they were more likely to express a desire for "more sexual freedom" than their noncollege peers.

Within the college population there appears to be considerable diversity in attitudes and values, both among geographical regions and types of schools attended— particularly in the case of girls. In general students from the east and west coasts emerge as less conservative than those from the Midwest (**16, 20, 25**). In a 1969 study more than two-thirds of midwestern students, but only about 40 percent of eastern students (both male and female), responded affirmatively to the question, "Do you feel that ideally it is still true that a man and a girl who marry should have their first full sexual experience together?" Similarly, three-fourths of girls at midwestern schools, but less than a third of those at eastern schools, agreed that "coitus was reasonable 'only if married' for possible participants who would be in the 21- to 23-year-old age group" (**20**, p. 163). Students at permissive, liberally oriented colleges emerged as less conservative than those at more traditional colleges (**6, 16, 20**). Interest-

ingly, the only apparent exception to the tendency for girls to have more conservative attitudes and values than boys occurs among students in some highly permissive, liberal colleges (**16, 20**).

It is also among college youth that the greatest changes in sexual behavior have occurred since their parents' generation (**4, 16, 20, 30, 31**). This trend appears especially pronounced among some demographically distinguishable groups of female students. In the 1940s Kinsey and others (**12, 13, 23**) found that by the age of 21 the incidence of premarital experience among college-educated persons was 49 percent for males and 27 percent for females. In contrast several recent, broadly representative investigations of American college and university students of comparable ages, conducted between 1967 and 1971 (**9, 16, 20, 30, 31**), indicate a substantial upward shift, particularly among girls. Thus, for males, obtained incidence figures in these investigations ranged from a low of 58 percent to a high of 82 percent; comparable percentages for females ranged from a 43 percent to 56 percent. In both cases the highest percentages were obtained in the most recent samples (**9, 30, 31, 36**).

Interestingly, whereas the percentage of male students engaging in premarital intercourse appeared to have reached a plateau (of about 80%) by 1970, among girls the incidence was apparently still increasing in 1971: Fifty-one percent of female students reported having had intercourse in 1970; 56 percent did so in 1971. Premarital relations are likely to be more frequent among those attending eastern colleges and universities than among those attending midwestern institutions (**20**) and among students attending private, "elite" colleges and universities.

Politically conservative youth are more conservative in sexual attitudes and values than "moderate reformers" and far more conservative than left-oriented "revolutionary" youth (**4, 9, 30, 31, 34**). Thus, among older adolescents *in general* (both college and noncollege), only 18 percent of conservative youth stated they would welcome more sexual freedom, as compared with 43 percent of moderate reformers and 80 percent of revolutionaries (**35**). Similarly, nearly two-thirds of conservative youth viewed premarital sexual relations as a moral issue, compared with one-third of moderate reformers and none of the revolutionaries!

Cultural differences are clearly reflected in the wide variations obtained between nations in various studies (**3, 11, 15, 66, 20**). Canada and the United States consistently rank lowest in incidence of premarital intercourse and England ranks highest, followed by the Scandinavian countries.

Even on the basis of the limited data discussed in this essay, it appears clear that adolescent attitudes and values regarding sex and sexual behavior itself are changing, although the extent of the changes varies widely from one segment of the youth population to another. Indeed, as in other areas of social concern, *the differences between some subgroups of youth appear wider than those between youth in general and adults in general*. There is a real and often ignored danger in generalizing too widely from specialized subgroups (e.g., a particular college campus or a particular urban high school) to youth in general. Furthermore, the greatest *relative* changes in both attitudes and behavior since their parents' generation have occurred among middle- and upper class adolescents, particularly girls. Not surprisingly it is among this socio-economically favored, and probably more socially conflicted, segment of the youth population that the "youth culture" of the 1960s took root and found its sustenance.

DISCUSSION

In brief, these findings, combined with general observation, do indicate an emerging new morality among contemporary adolescents. While this new morality has many positive aspects—a greater emphasis on openness and honesty, mutual respect and lack of dissembling or exploitation, and a more "natural" and better-informed approach to sex—it would be a mistake to conclude that the picture is wholly unclouded. Many experienced adolescents, particularly older adolescents, appear able to handle their sexual involvement and their relationships with themselves without undue stress. (Four out of five nonvirgins report getting "a lot of satisfaction" out of their sex lives; two-thirds of all nonvirgins and four out of five monogamists state that sex makes their lives more meaningful.) However, significant minorities report feelings of conflict and guilt, find themselves exploited or rejected, or discover belatedly that they have gotten in over their heads emotionally. Especially after the first experience of intercourse, girls are far more likely than boys to encounter negative feelings. While boys are most likely to report being excited, satisfied, and happy, girls most frequently report being afraid, guilty, worried, or embarrassed after their initial intercourse experience (**29**).

Obviously there are dangers, particularly for girls, with their generally stronger affiliative needs, in believing that sexual involvement is "okay as long as you're in love." Encouraged by such a philosophy among peers, a girl or boy may become more deeply involved emotionally than she or he can handle at a particular stage of maturity (**1, 4**). "An adolescent may also consciously think that his attitudes are more 'liberal' than they actually are, and involvement may lead to unanticipated feelings of guilt, anxiety or depression" (**18,** p. 643).

There also remain very practical problems, such as the possibility of pregnancy. Many girls today express the opinion that "now that science has given us the (birth control) pill, we no longer have to be frightened about pregnancy. We just have to decide what is right" (**4,** p. 254). Noble as this sentiment may be, the facts indicate that only a small percentage of unmarried girls having intercourse have used the contraceptive pill to prevent pregnancy (**7, 14, 29, 32**); a disturbingly high percentage—between 55 and 75 percent—used no contraceptive device whatever, at least in their first experience, and only a minority consistently use such a device thereafter (**14, 29, 36**). Even among monogamists, only two-thirds reported always using contraceptive devices. Furthermore, despite talk of the pill, less than a third of female nonvirgins have used this method.

Such lack of precaution against pregnancy results partly from ignorance or lack of availability of contraceptive devices. Far more often, however, it results from carelessness, impulsiveness of the moment, a magical conviction that pregnancy cannot really happen, a belief that the spontaneity of sex is impaired ("If the girl uses birth control pills or other forms of contraception, it makes it

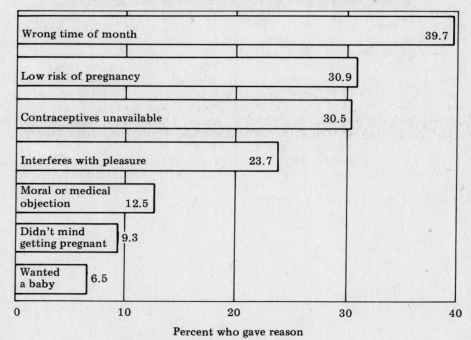

Reasons given by females aged 15–19 for not using contraception.

Reason	Percent
Wrong time of month	39.7
Low risk of pregnancy	30.9
Contraceptives unavailable	30.5
Interferes with pleasure	23.7
Moral or medical objection	12.5
Didn't mind getting pregnant	9.3
Wanted a baby	6.5

Percent who gave reason

seem as if she were *planning* to have sex"), or a belief that the *other* partner has taken precautions. Furthermore, 40 percent of all nonvirgin girls in Sorenson's study agreed that "sometimes I don't really care whether or not I get pregnant." Rather astonishingly, he found that "10 percent of all American female adolescents and 23 percent of all nonvirgin girls report that they have been pregnant at least once" (**29**, p. 324).

It seems unlikely that the trend toward premarital intercourse as an accepted practice, and especially toward serial monogamy as the most frequent and the most socially approved pattern among sexually experienced adolescents, will be reversed. Of all residuals of the youth culture of the 1960s, greater sexual freedom and openness appear to be the most enduring. What one must hope is that adolescents entering sexual relationships can be helped to become mature enough, informed enough, responsible enough, sure enough of their own identities and value systems, and sensitive and concerned enough about the welfare of others so that the inevitable casualties in the "sexual revolution" can be reduced to a minimum. Sexuality as a vital part of human relationships should promote, rather than hinder, growth toward maturity and emotional fulfillment.

REFERENCES

1. Bardwick, J. *Psychology of women: A study of bio-cultural conflicts.* Harper & Row, 1971.
2. Bell, R. R. Parent-child conflict in sexual values. *J. Soc. Issues,* 1966, *22,* 34–44.
3. Christenson, H. T., & Carpenter, G. R. Value-behavior discrepancies regarding premarital coitus in three Western cultures. *Am. Sociol. Rev.,* 1962, *27,* 66–74.
4. Conger, J. J. *Adolescence and youth: Psychological development in a changing world.* New York: Harper & Row, 1973.
5. Conger, J. J. A world they never knew: The family and social change. *Daedalus,* Fall 1971, 1105–1138.
6. Gallup poll, *Denver Post,* May 12, 1970.
7. Grinder, R. E., & Schmitt, S. S. Coeds and contraceptive information. *J. Marriage Fam.* 1966, *28,* 471–479.
8. Harris, L. Change, yes—upheaval, no. *Life,* January 8, 1971, 22–27.
9. Hunt, M. *Sexual behavior in the 1970s.* Chicago: Playboy Press, 1974.
10. Hunt, M. Special sex education survey. *Seventeen,* July 1970, 94 ff.
11. Karlsson, G. Karlsson, S., & Busch, K. Sexual habits and attitudes of Swedish folk high school students. Research Report No. 15. Uppsala, Sweden: Department of Sociology, Uppsala University, 1960.
12. Kinsey, A. C., Pomeroy, W. B., Martin, C. E., & Gebhard, P. H. *Sexual behavior in the human female.* Philadelphia: Saunders 1953.
13. Kinsey, A. C., Pomeroy, W. B., & Martin, C. E. *Sexual behavior in the human male.* Philadelphia: Saunders, 1948.
14. Lake, A. Teenagers and sex: A student report. *Seventeen,* July 1967, 88.
15. Linner, B. *Sex and society in Sweden.* New York: Pantheon. 1967.
16. Luckey, E., & Nass, G. A comparison of sexual attitudes and behavior in an international sample. *J. Marriage Fam.,* 1969, 31, 364–379.
17. Money, J., & Ehrhardt, A. A. *Man and woman, boy and girl: The differentiation and dimorphism of gender identity from conception to maturity.* Baltimore: Johns Hopkins Press, 1972.
18. Mussen, P. H., Conger, J. J., & Kagan, J. *Child development and personality.* New York: Harper & Row, 1969 (3rd ed.).
19. Packard, V. . . . and the sexual behavior reported by 2100 young adults. In V. Packard, *The sexual wilderness: The contemporary upheaval in male-female relationships.* New York: Pocket Books, 1970, pp. 166–184.
20. Packard, V. *The sexual wilderness: The contemporary upheaval in male-female relationships.* New York: Pocket Books, 1970.
21. Pomeroy, W. B. *Boys and sex.* New York: Delacorte, 1969.
22. Pomeroy, W. B. *Girls and sex.* New York: Delacorte, 1969.
23. Reevy, W. R. Adolescent sexuality. In A. Ellis & A. Abarband (Eds.), *The encyclopedia of sexual behavior* (Vol. I). New York: Hawthorn, 1961, pp. 52–68.
24. Reiss, I. L. How and why America's sex standards are changing. In W. Simon and J. H. Gagnon (Eds.), *The sexual scene.* Chicago: Trans-action Books, 1970, pp. 43–57.
25. Reiss, I. L. The sexual renaissance in America. *J. Soc. Issues,* April 1966.
26. Reiss, I. L. The scaling of premarital sexual permissiveness. *J. Marriage Fam.,* 1964, 26, 188–199.
27. Simon, W., & Gagnon, J. H. Psychosexual development. In W. Simon & J. H. Gagnon (Eds.), *The sexual scene.* Chicago: Trans-action Books, 1970, pp. 23–41.
28. Simon, W., & Gagnon, J. H. (Eds.). *The sexual scene.* Chicago: Trans-action Books, 1970.
29. Sorenson, R. C. *Adolescent sexuality in contemporary America: Personal values and sexual behavior ages 13–19.* New York: World Publishing, 1973.
30. Student survey, 1971. *Playboy,* September 1971, 118 ff.
31. Student survey, *Playboy,* September 1970, 182 ff.
32. *The report of the Commission on Obscenity and Pornography.* New York: Bantam Books, 1970.
33. What people think of their high schools. *Life,* 1969, 66, 22–23.
34. Wilson, W. C. et al. *Technical report of the Commission on Obscenity and Pornography, Vol. VI: National survey.* Washington, D.C.: U.S. Government Printing Office, 1971.
35. Yankelovich, D. *Generations apart.* New York: CBS News, 1969.
36. Zelnik, M., & Kantner, J. E. Survey of female adolescent sexual behavior conducted for the Commission on Population, Washington, D.C., 1972.

Adolescent Rebellion in the Kibbutz

Mordecai Kaffman, M.D.

Abstract. The kind of changes that have appeared in adolescent rebellion phenomena in the kibbutz these past 10 years are discussed from the sociocultural viewpoint. The frequency and expressions of the rebellion are conceived as connected closely with the interpersonal, family, social, and cultural context in which the adolescent exists. The increase of adolescent rebellion in the kibbutz seems to have occurred concurrently with the changes that have taken place in the surrounding environment making the system of values and norms in the life of the commune less clear and less valid. These changes have turned the adult society into a more ambiguous identification model than it was prior to the early 1960s.

Investigators who have concerned themselves with the characteristics of kibbutz adolescents agree on one central point: the comparative rarity of signs of youth rebellion ("storm and stress"), which are often regarded as part and parcel of the adolescent process in modern society (Spiro, 1958; Rabin, 1965, 1968; Bettelheim, 1969; Alon, 1975). Instead, a gradual and quiet evolution to the point where the responsibility of adulthood is assumed is described as the trademark of growing up in the kibbutz.

Theoreticians who assume that turbulence and rebellion are essential and healthy components of the adolescent's development have pointed with concern to the failure of the kibbutz to produce a second and third generation that rebels against the values of the commune. The founder generation, on the other hand, took their sons' identification with their own way of life as evidence of the kibbutz education system's validity, if only for the simple reason that otherwise there would be no way of assuring the continuity and expansion of the kibbutz enterprise.

As to the causes of this lack of intergenerational conflict, the investigators' opinions differ and at times are contradictory. The spectrum of interpretations reflects the variety of the authors' creeds and their psychological or sociological points of view. Bettelheim (1969) hypothesizes that it is a continuous process starting from infancy in which the child's individual desires are repressed in order to build "a collective, not a personal ego." Thus, according to Bettelheim, the commune assures the adolescent's full identification with the kibbutz values through the use of subtle repression to subordinate personal interest to the group.

This is an extreme view. Most investigators from the kibbutz itself give the simple explanation that the adolescent in the kibbutz fights the surrounding adult world less because he has fewer objec-

Dr. Kaffman is the Medical Director of the Kibbutz Child and Family Clinic (Tel Aviv-Oranim).
This paper is based on a special lecture delivered at the International Forum on Adolescence, Jerusalem, Israel, July 4–7, 1976.
Reprints may be requested from the author at the Kibbutz Child and Family Clinic, 1 Bnei Ephraim St., Tel Aviv, Israel.

Reprinted with permission from *Journal of the American Academy of Child Psychiatry* and the author.

tive reasons for fighting. Everything in the kibbutz context is directed toward shortening the adolescent moratorium on achieving full autonomy and all the rights of the adult society in the spheres of work, performing responsible functions, and sexual freedom. In addition, one must not forget the fact that the provision of material commodities as well as diverse child care and socialization functions have been transferred from the parents to the educators and the community. Expressions of adolescent rebelliousness and the generation conflict appear mitigated in a culture where the child care functions are shared by a wide range of socializing agents and factors.

The investigators who noted the uneventful transition of the kibbutz adolescent from childhood to adulthood used simple chronological cross-sectional observations. When one traces characteristics of adolescence in the kibbutz from a perspective of 20 years or more, one discerns considerable shifts in the intensity and form in which the process of the adolescent's psychological, ideological, and sociological emancipation expresses itself. The placidity of the 50s modulates in the 60s into moderate signs of youth rebelliousness, which exacerbate rather suddenly and culminate in the quinquennium 1970–75, when signs of "storm and stress" become quite obvious among "normal" kibbutz adolescents without any evidence of psychological imbalance. And while today (1977) there are first indications that this may be simmering down again, the general picture is still very different from the one presented in the past.

ADOLESCENCE IN AN AMBIGUOUS ADULT VALUE SYSTEM

The changing attitudes and values of the kibbutz adolescent group over the past 10 years took place concurrently with changes in the value system of the adult society. I shall confine myself here to noting several factors in the social environment which seem to have had a meaningful effect on the nature of the adolescent response. It is not my intention to point out influences related to the world at large and changes among the youth of Western civilization in general, which undoubtedly have also made their mark on the kibbutz adolescent, but to restrict myself to factors connected solely with the kibbutz itself.

Today's average kibbutz is no longer the intimate, united community of past years, consisting of a handful of idealistic members, all of the same age group and with a solid, homogeneous value system. In today's big kibbutz with its heterogeneous population, inevitable gaps have developed between the pure ideology of the original little commune and the facts of day-to-day life. Not everything goes according to the principles and expectations that were laid down at the beginning of the road. The ideal of absolute equality between members has become slightly dented. Differences have developed in grades of specialization and in individual job satisfaction—mainly to the disadvantage of the women, who have gone back to the traditional occupations of child care, kitchen, and other services. In some cases, critical manpower shortages in the large industrial enterprises that had become part of the kibbutz led to what to the kibbutz was a serious ideological deviation: the employment of hired labor.

The value crisis deepened as a result of the disillusionment of the founding generation when it realized in the 50s that hopes of the early spread of the kibbutz idea in Israel and the expansion of the international infrastructure for a society based on "humanist, democratic socialism" were doomed to disappointment. Frustrated political hopes and ideological isolation were among the causes which made the founding generation turn inward and devote its energies to the kibbutz's internal system and its economic consolidation while abandoning the original aim of serving as an instrument for changing the surrounding society.

The kibbutz adolescent now lives in a world with a more ambiguous value system, which has replaced the former structured social and political beliefs. Twenty-five years ago, the ideological platform of the leftist wing of the kibbutz movement, "Hakibbutz Haartzi," contained clear, binding definitions of its identification—except on the subject of Zionism—with the international socialist camp; and the younger generation, though less enthusiastically and less doctrinairely, accepted its socialist political identity without argument (Spiro, 1958). While the general concept of socialism still remains the guiding ideological principle for the large majority of the founders, they now lack the clear confidence of the past as to the ideological and practical meaning of that concept. This confusion is clearly reflected among the adolescents. A recent survey of a sample of 17- and 18-year-olds from the Kibbutz Artzi (Alon, 1975) shows that more than half of the youngsters were not prepared to define their Weltanschauung as socialistic.

The ideological gap which has emerged between the two generations pains and shocks the founders. Meir Yaari, the acknowledged leader of Hakibbutz Haartzi since its foundation, recently (1976) expressed his feelings as follows:

> I ask myself in astonishment and with a great deal of sadness where we have gone wrong, where we have sinned, that one generation no longer speaks out to the other in the measure for which we had hoped. I know how great the burden is that our sons have to bear: they are outstanding in the work of the kibbutz, in their families and as soldiers. But I ask myself: why have a large part of the younger generation chosen to wash their hands of a Labor-Zionist-Socialist policy in its translation into ordinary everyday life?

The adult generation has tried to handle the questions and doubts as they arose by amending and adjusting those ideological elements which had satisfied its needs in the past. As a result, past beliefs sometimes turned into slogans that lacked the clearness and consistency which were so characteristic of the world of yesterday. The second generation revolted, abandoned the principles that seemed outdated mumbo-jumbo to them. In a multilogue between young members of all trends in the kibbutz movement that took place in the wake of the Six Day War, many said they felt that "the absolute beliefs have disappeared and now there are more doubts than certainties" (Tzur et al., 1969).

The kibbutz experience, therefore, appears to confirm the postulate that whenever the adult value system is in a stage of transition and becomes an ambiguous model of identification, antiestablishment youth movements are prone to emerge (Opler, 1967, 1971). The value and behavior gaps between adults and adolescents, which have steadily widened in the kibbutz in the last ten years, are evident mainly in three spheres:

1. The search for an autonomous youth style, differing from the accepted one of the adult world;

2. A struggle for recognition of the individual's rights and aspirations, with a concurrent lessening of the bond with the group and of consideration for its needs;

3. A meaningful increase in the number of adolescents who decide to leave the kibbutz and adopt another social framework.

ADOLESCENT PEER CULTURE

Only a few years ago, most kibbutz adolescents used to view the kibbutz culture as clearly superior to other cultures (Spiro, 1958; Rabin, 1968). They spoke in critical terms of the decadent values, tastes, and fashions of the youth outside. This attitude faithfully reflected that of the world of their parents, who had founded the kibbutz as a revolutionary cell which was opposed to the style and content of other social contexts. But as the original monolithic ideological attitude weakened, the criticism gradually lessened and the influence of the outside world increased. A considerable part of the kibbutz adolescents adopted characteristic elements of the style and fads of the outside youth generation with which they came into contact in the kibbutz or through the mass media—a youth generation which they had not long ago regarded as the absolute opposite of the way of life of the commune.

A visitor to the kibbutz can now see boys and girls on its sidewalks in intentionally neglected clothes full of patches, walking in the rain in bare feet, or with torn, muddy slippers. The boys let their hair grow to far beyond what was usual; the youngsters have invented a slang of their own in a distorted Hebrew. Instead of the melodious music to which the parents were accustomed, the children play a new, discordant kind of music at top volume. Youngsters from the age of 13 have taken to modern dancing in couples rather than to the traditional folk dances of the pioneers. At first, all this took place in secret hideouts where the youngsters met to hear their favorite music and perhaps to eat their fill of food that was pilfered from the communal larder. In the early 70s, "underground newspapers" appeared in some kibbutz schools, urging the kibbutz youth to show their dissent and rebellion against adult constraints and demanding personal freedom to experiment with ideologies, sex, and drugs. Among other things, the rebellious youngsters also challenged the accepted educational methods and demanded recognition of the right to learn only according to individual wishes and interests, while rejecting compulsory standard curricula. They protested against educators who handed down ideological values in black-and-white absolutes. Against indoctrination with social values they set their right to doubt and nonconformity.

A group of the secondary school students expressed their defiance openly by questioning their teachers' authority and the rules of the school system. This rebelliousness was displayed in provocative ways such as coming late, interrupting and disturbing in the classroom, and irregular attendance. Although the informality and lax discipline of the kibbutz classrooms have always been a recognized pedagogical fact and were part of the informal democratic-educational method, the disturbances are considered to have reached unprecedented levels.

The adult society's reaction to these signs of "revolt" was embarrassment, then anger. However, as long as the adult reaction assumed the form of frontal counterstruggle, the conflict escalated and spread to further youth groups. The failure of the attempts to reestablish the state of quiet coexistence led to a reevaluation of the situation. The adults began to reconcile themselves to the changes in the adolescent world and at times even justified their demands implicitly or overtly. As a result, the adolescents' right to achieve basic changes in ideological indoctrination and in the kibbutz school system became recognized and legalized. In many kibbutz schools the study system was reformed, with the accent on a wider range of free choice of subjects, and respect for individual talents, wishes, and inclinations.

On another plane, the "establishment" gave its approval to the opening of official "nightclubs" on kibbutz premises, where the "kids" could meet, dance, and play music according to their own preferences. The only absolute ban retained was on the use of drugs. The agreed policy of the majority of the kibbutz movement asserts strongly and clearly that "drugs and kibbutz do not go together." The nature and aim of the kibbutz are incompatible with any philosophy that extols or seeks an artificial paradise of oblivion and escape from life. The adult attitude is forgiving only in cases of the use of hashish by youngsters who have obviously taken it only a few isolated times out of adolescent curiosity and a desire to explore new experiences. The clear and uncompromising ideological position of the adults on banning drugs in the kibbutz may be one reason why the drug problem among kibbutz-born youth has not spread beyond a few, very limited circles of youngsters with obvious psychological disturbances. For the present, there are no signs of epidemic spread, and in the few cases of repeated use it is a matter of hashish. The use of other, more dangerous drugs among kibbutz-born youth in the kibbutz environment is exceedingly rare.

Generally speaking, the adult world's technique of tending to seek compromises and avoiding open war against expressions of youth rebellion has borne fruit. The signs of rebellion seem to be somewhat on the decline. Lately (1975–77), one notices an improvement in discipline and in the learning effort; there is more activity in the kibbutz youth movement and a more evident willingness to take part in propagating kibbutz values among urban youth and in helping to organize and operate youth activities among the deprived youth of the "second Israel." There are also indications of restraint in the outward expression of an idiosyncratic youth style.

It should be noted that the adolescent value system has played a dynamic role of some importance in determining changes in the attitudes and behavior of the adult society. Until now, I have mainly concentrated on the problem of the close connection that exists between the social values and attitudes of the adolescent and the respective influences of the paternal and other adult models, but the influence works both ways: the adolescent has an enormous impact on the value system of the adults. It impels the adult world toward changes that include the acceptance and incorporation of the youth set of values, which become a legitimate part of the prevailing adult culture. Not only do the adults eventually acquire and imitate youth styles and fashions; the youth influence goes much further and makes itself felt in ideological values. For instance, the structural changes that have occurred in the kibbutz school are not only the result of the educators' efforts to plan a new type of free school to replace the partly outmoded school organization of some of the kibbutz secondary schools. The growing sense of dissatisfaction of a considerable part of the students, the signs of revolt demanding freedom to learn in one's own way, the resistance to cooperation with the teachers, and the fact that a large part of the pupils left the school without learning much of anything have all played a part in stimulating the search for solutions in the direction of a change of the kibbutz educational system.

A further expression of adolescent rebellion may be discerned in the fight and pressure for more freedom and new privileges in sexual behavior. Until the early 60s, the adolescents unquestioningly accepted the adults' ideological attitude that it was worthwhile to refrain from sexual intercourse during the learning years. By now, the sexual standards set by the adolescents are quite permissive on the subject of early sexual intercourse, though sexual relations are accepted only if they are integrated in the emotional life of both partners. The puritanical attitude to sexual relations in middle adolescence has been abandoned in theory and practice. Instead, permissive sexual attitudes and behavior have become the dominant norm for both male and female kibbutz adolescents.

Individual v. Communal Interests. Today, there has been a clear turn, particularly among the younger generation, in the direction of an increased demand for recognition of the individual's right to realize his personal aspirations and plans, even if they run counter to the aim of the collective (Talmon, 1972; Cohen, 1974). For instance, there has been a marked decline in the influence and power of the weekly members' meeting when it comes to making the adolescent give up his personal plans and accept another essential assignment for the benefit of the community. The weakening of the collective identification seems to have occurred at the same time as an increase in family unity. Contacts and emotional ties with the parents have become progressively more intensive than they used to be. The changes of balance in the youngster's relations with his family and his peers worked in the direction of weakening the influence of the group.

One sign of the change which has occurred in the collective's influence on the individual adolescent is the natural and spontaneous disappearance of a practice which was common only a few years ago and has been described as corresponding to initiation or "purification" group rituals in other cultures (Neubauer, 1965). In many kibbutzim, it was the custom for boys and girls at the age of 17 to 18 to meet together for a marathon group discussion of their individual feelings, doubts, and failures. The participants talked at length about their present-past behavior and their endeavors for the sake of the group. Each personal self-disclosure was checked and challenged by the whole group, which sat in judgment and gave its final verdict on whether the individual was mature enough to assume adult status and fit to continue his life in the kibbutz.

This fateful meeting was a solemn occasion on which the power of the group and the adolescent's loyalty to the kibbutz values were demonstrated. Today, this custom has ceased as the natural consequence of the fact that the peer group has lost a considerable part of its importance as an instrument of social control and its power to make the individual comply with the cultural norms.

Youth Leaving the Kibbutz

Further evidence of increasing intergenerational problems is provided by the significant increase in the proportion of kibbutz children who leave the kibbutz when they become adults. Spiro (1958), in field work carried out during 1951–52, found that almost the entire kibbutz-born generation over the age of 16 viewed the kibbutz as "the best form of societal living not only for them, but for others as well." Other observations and surveys have repeatedly confirmed this strong allegiance of the younger generation to the kibbutz. Rabin (1968) found in the early 60s that only less than 10 percent of the 17- to 18-year-old adolescents were uncertain about remaining in the kibbutz. A kibbutz population census of 1967 showed that out of 3,000 youngsters covered, about 15 percent had left the kibbutz in the course of the year. Until a few years ago, this fallout rate was regarded as a normal and acceptable average.

While we have no statistical data on the present situation, it is generally agreed that today's fallout rate is considerably higher and lies between 30 to 40 percent of kibbutz-born youngsters after completion of military service. Most youngsters now struggle for the right to have some experience of a different way of life and an opportunity to explore the world and test their own abilities in a nonkibbutz setting. The proportion of those who return to the kibbutz after staying outside is still twice that of those who leave, but it is evident that the ratio of those who stay to those who leave shrinks over the years.

The youngster's decision whether to stay in the kibbutz or to leave is by now regarded as part of his legitimate right to self-expression. In the not so distant past, the kibbutz founders regarded leaving the kibbutz as something corresponding to desertion from the frontline in wartime. Most of those who left the kibbutz in the past did so with heavy guilt feelings. Today, such reactions are a matter of the past. Mostly, stayers and leavers alike are sorry to part, but the final decision is accepted out of respect for the individual's right to choose his own way of life.

Conclusions

The prevailing view that adolescence in the kibbutz is characterized by the absence of signs of rebelliousness, puritanical behavior, ascetic sexual codes, and value system shared by parents and children is due to the use of cross-sectional methods of data collection. Follow-up and observations over a long period of years show that there is considerable change in the way in which kibbutz youth expresses its identification with, or rebellion against, the adult society. The generation gap in the kibbutz has its ups and downs. Undoubtedly, the general conditions of the kibbutz structure reduce the adolescence moratorium in the assumption of adult roles and economic responsibility. The specific sociocultural conditions of the kibbutz create fewer areas of conflict between the adolescent on the one hand, and his parents and the adult society on the other. Generally speaking, the adolescent in the kibbutz has less to rebel against. Still, that does not permit the conclusion that an uneventful adolescence is a permanent and necessary fact of kibbutz life.

There are no static patterns in the kibbutz society. On the contrary, it is the scene of incessant social and cultural change which sets its imprint on the course of adolescence. Thus in the last decade, there were clear signs of adolescent rebellion in a considerable part of kibbutz youth. During these 10 years, there have been increasing demands for recognition of the individual's right to achieve his personal wishes and aspirations, even if they were contrary to the needs of the commune. There is a noticeable decline of the influence of the kibbutz as collective and of the peer group on the individual. The number of adolescents who decide not to join the kibbutz and prefer to switch to a different social environment has increased. We witness the emergence of an idiosyncratic "youth style" that differs greatly from the one accepted among adults. The rebellion has also included the educational system, which has become the center of critical attacks and lack of cooperation on the part of the adolescent generation. In the sexual sphere there has been a veritable revolution; youth attitudes and behavior patterns have changed diametrically, from scrupulously puritanical codes in the recent past to a highly permissive approach in the present.

These changes, which are the concrete expression of adolescent rebellion in the kibbutz, represent a trend, which appears as a well-defined, clear pattern only among part of the youth. In the kibbutz, as in any other society, there is room for variations of developmental expression in different subgroups. The stereotype of the typical adolescent exists only as a theoretical artifact (Offer and Offer, 1975; Kaffman and Elizur, 1976).

It would be a mistake to think that the second and third kibbutz-born generation is homogeneous in its attitudes and values. Every few years there are prominent changes of trend in the adolescents' style of life and value system. Today, it is customarily assumed that the kibbutz produces a new, different "generation" every five years. As a matter of fact, there is a gap not only between the adolescents and the adult society, but also between adolescents themselves who are only a few years apart.

It would be something of an oversimplification to present adolescent rebelliousness, the generation gap, and the signs of a peer counterculture as the result of the unilateral struggle of the younger generation against the values and beliefs of the adults. What we have is a two-way, dialectic process, in which the changes that have occurred in the adult world play a parallel and highly important part.

Today's kibbutz shows signs of a general change and partial overthrow of the original set of ideological values. The strict, solid homogeneity that characterized the kibbutz in the past exists no more. The values of the adult society have become more flexible but also more ambiguous. The kibbutz is in a state of transition in determining its specific aims and delineating the spheres of mutual influence of the community, the family, and the individual.

It seems that the experience of the kibbutz proves once more that the level of clarity of the definition and realization of the basic values of the adult society is an important factor in determining the quality and intensity of the adolescent rebellion. The adolescent who seeks to consolidate his own identity and to choose his way at the crossroads where he stands finds his journey more difficult when the adult world around him is confused and does not posit a clear and well-defined system of values and expectations. In this fog, the adolescent sets up roadsigns and traffic lights of his own to help him feel his way. At first, those roadsigns appear to the adults to be weeds that must be uprooted. Later, part of the signs of adolescent rebellion are eventually and gradually accepted, strike root, and in effect become, particularly in times of crisis, powerful propellants in changing the entire society.

REFERENCES

ALON, M. (1975) *Adolescence in the Kibbutz* [Hebrew]. Tel Aviv: Sifriat Hapoalim.

BETTELHEIM, B. (1969), *The Children of the Dream.* New York: Macmillan.

COHEN, N. (1974), *The Kibbutz in the Eyes of Two Generations* [Hebrew]. Rehovot: Research Institute on Rural and Urban Settlements.

KAFFMAN, M. & ELIZUR, E. (1976), Kibbutz adolescents today. *Israel Ann. Psychiat.,* 14:145–154.

NEUBAUER, P. B., ed., (1965), *Children in Collectives.* Springfield: Thomas.

OFFER, D. & OFFER, B. J. (1975), *From Teenage to Young Manhood.* New York: Basic Books.

OPLER, M. K. (1967), *Culture and Social Psychiatry.* New York: Atherton Press.

——— (1971), Adolescence in Cross-Cultural Perspective. In: *Modern Perspectives in Adolescent Psychiatry,* ed. J. G. Howells. New York: Brunner/Mazel, pp. 152–179.

RABIN, A. I. (1965), *Growing Up in the Kibbutz.* New York: Springer.

——— (1968), Some sex differences in the attitudes of kibbutz adolescents. *Israel Ann. Psychiat.,* 6:62–69.

SPIRO, M. E. (1958), *Children of the Kibbutz.* Cambridge, Mass.: Harvard University Press.

TALMON, Y. (1972), *Family and Community in the Kibbutz.* Cambridge, Mass.: Harvard University Press.

TZUR, M., BEN AHARON, I., & GROSSMAN, A., eds. (1969), *Among Young People: Talks in the Kibbutz* [Hebrew]. Tel Aviv: Am Oved.

YAARI, M. (1976), Radicalism and realism [Hebrew]. *Al Hamishmar* (April 23).

33

Parent-Child Relationships, Social Change and Adolescent Vulnerability

John Janeway Conger
University of Colorado School of Medicine, Denver

Photograph by Virginia Hamilton

Contrary to the views of some early writers, adolescence need not be a time of great stress and conflict with parents and society. In fact, even at the height of the 1960s, the "generation gap" was not as large as it was reported to be in the press. A review is presented of factors, particularly within the family, which are predictive of good adolescent adjustment. An analogy is made between the qualities needed for effective parenting of adolescents and those needed for effective psychotherapy with adolescents.

There can be little doubt that adolescence, and particularly early adolescence, is likely to be a challenging and sometimes trying time for young people and their parents. It could hardly be otherwise. A central problem of the adolescent period is the development of a sense of identity, of who one is and is going to become as a person. A sense of identity, in turn, requires a perception of the self as *separate* from others (despite similarities to them); and a feeling of wholeness, of *self-consistency*, not only in the sense of internal consistency at a particular moment, but also over time. The adolescent (particularly the younger adolescent) is faced with rapid increases in height, changing bodily dimensions, newfound

From the *Journal of Pediatric Psychology*, Vol. 2, No. 3, pp. 93–97. Copyright © 1977, by the American Psychological Association. Reprinted with permission.

cognitive capabilities, and the objective and subjective changes related to sexual maturation. In addition to these internal changes, the adolescent is also faced with rapid changes in societal demands and expectations during this period, including the development of a greater independence from parents, choice of educational and vocational goals, and new kinds of relationships with same- and opposite-sex peers and adults. Obviously, all of these developments challenge the young person's feeling of self-consistency, and he or she needs time to integrate them into a slowly emerging sense of a positive, self-confident ego identity.

There is, however, considerable reason to question whether such necessary adaptations inevitably lead to a period of clinically significant adolescent turmoil, as many theorists have asserted - from G. Stanley Hall in the early 1900s (with his rather romantic notions of adolescent *Sturm and Drang*) to Anna Freud and others in the present (Freud, 1969; Hall, 1904-05; Hirsch, 1970, Josselyn, 1954). Recent research on representative, non-clinical populations by such investigators as Offer and Offer (Offer, 1969; Offer & Offer, 1975) Douvan and Adelson (1966), Hathaway and Monachesi (1963), and Block (1971) indicate that while significant numbers of adolescents do experience a period of adolescent upheaval or--in Erikson's phrase- of identity confusion, many others do not.

Thus, in Offer's intensive longitudinal study of a representative sample of middle-class adolescent males in the Midwest, he found little evidence of a high degree of "turmoil" or "chaos" in the majority of his subjects. Similarly, Douvan and Adelson (1966), in their extensive national sample of 3,000 adolescents, concluded that the traditional view of adolescence as a period in which the adolescent "responds to the instinctual and psychosocial upheaval of puberty by disorder, by failures of ego-synthesis, and by a tendency to abandon earlier values and object attachments [Douvan & Adelson, 1966, p. 351]" is based largely on the sensitive, articulate, middle- and upper-class adolescent, frequently the object of clinical concern. Indeed, these investigators express some dismay at the relative *absence* of turmoil in the average adolescent- attributing much of it to a "premature identity consolidation, ego and ideological constriction, and a general unwillingness to take psychic risks [Douvan & Adelson, 1966, p. 351]."

Offer, however disagrees:

> Implicitly, these investigators have adopted the position that lack of turmoil is a bad prognostic sign and must necessarily prevent the adolescent from developing into a mature adult. All our data, including the psychological testing, point in the opposite direction. The adolescents not only adjusted well; they were also in touch with their feelings and developed meaningful relationships with significant others [Offer, 1969, p. 184].

This does not mean that these adolescents were without problems or conflicts. For example, Offer reports that rebellion against parental dictates, usually characterized by "bickering," was common, particularly between ages 12 and 14. Similarly, in the affective sphere, there were indications of occasional anxiety, "acting-out" behavior, and depression (the three most commonly encountered "symptoms"), as well as of shame and guilt, and of phobic, obsessive-compulsive, and other defensive behaviors. However, these symptoms tended, with few exceptions, to be mild (Offer, 1969).

THE "GENERATION GAP"

Other normative research has made it clear that the kind of profound "generation gap," widely asserted during the 1960s to characterize the relations of contemporary adolescents and their parents, did not then, and does not now, characterize the relations of a majority of adolescents and their parents. While there has been and is a gap, and while its size and the number of adolescents affected in any significant fashion were undoubtedly increased by the events of the 1960s- rapid social change, societal polarization, increasing age segregation, and the decline of adult authority- it never reached the proportions proclaimed by the mass media's instant sociology (Harris, 1971; Yankelovich, 1969).

Even in the late 1960s, at the height of the so-called "youth culture," the great majority of both parents and adolescents expressed the view that, while a generation gap existed, it had clearly been exaggerated. Only about one-fourth of adolescents and a like number of parents in this country felt that there was a large generation gap. More recent studies suggest that, if anything, this gap has been further reduced (Conger, 1977; Sorensen, 1973; Yankelovich, 1969).

Similarly, the popular view of the time that a state of declared or undeclared war characterized the relations between the average parent and his or her adolescent young, that the average adolescent disapproved of the way he or she was reared, viewed parents as misguided souls who had sold out their basic values to the establishment, and felt uncomfortable in their presence, also received little support (Harris, 1971; Yankelovich, 1969). Even around 1969-70, three fourths of adolescents in this country expressed general agreement with their parents' ideals, and felt that their parents' childrearing methods had been "about right"- neither too authoritarian nor too permissive. While one-third said they had trouble communicating with their parents, only 18 percent stated that it was their parents' fault, and most said it was "both our faults" (Harris, 1971).

Again, studies conducted in the middle 1970s suggest that, if anything, the percentage of adolescents with positive feelings toward parents has continued to increase. For example, in one representative survey of American adolescents, aged 13-19, 88 percent of all adolescents interviewed stated that they had a lot of respect for their parents as people, and 80 percent (75 percent of boys and 85 percent of girls) stated that they had a lot of respect for their parents' ideas and opinions. Fewer that 20 percent of all 1970s adolescents (25 percent of boys and 13 percent of girls) agreed that "I've pretty much given up on ever being able to get along with my parents [Sorensen, 1973, p. 391]."

I have referred briefly to such diverse findings in an effort to provide a more representative, realistic, and balanced perspective regarding adolescent development generally, as well as a more accurate frame of reference within which to view instances of disturbance or deviancy. My aim is not to suggest that modal adolescents and their parents do not encounter any problems in the course of adolescent adaptation, particularly in today's complex, rapidly changing, and frequently divided society. Obviously, as I indicated at the outset, they do- although their extent and significance appear clearly to have been exaggerated. Nor do I wish to obscure the fact that a significant minority of adolescents do encounter serious and sometimes irreversible disturbances in development.

Indeed, my principal purpose in these remarks is to explore the question of what factors increase the likelihood that the young person will get through the adolescent period without excessive turmoil, without highly disruptive parent-child relationships, and with a reasonable degree of immunity to internal psychological difficulties and to destructive external pressures, including deviant peer-group influences.

SOCIAL INFLUENCES ON ADOLESCENT ADJUSTMENT

While it is impossible to explore the matter in detail in the brief space available here, it should be obvious that we cannot look only to individual psychodynamic or intrafamilial factors for answers to this question. Social factors are also clearly of major importance, particularly in periods of confused and rapid social change. The adolescent growing up in a relatively isolated and homogeneous small town, where common values are largely shared and taken for granted by adolescents, their parents, their peers, and the community as a whole, and where generally acceptable and shared models of adult identity are to be found, faces simpler developmental demands in identity formation than the adolescent growing up in a heterogeneous, frequently conflict-ridden, avant-garde, rapidly changing urban complex, such as the Bay area around San Francisco in the latter 1960s or, conversely, in the socially disorganized and deteriorated ethnic ghettos of our largest cities (Conger, 1971, Note 1).

By the same token, an adolescent growing up in the 1950s (or probably even in 1978), as opposed to an adolescent facing all the conflicting pressures and polarizations of the turbulent decade of the 1960s, inevitably faced a simpler, less confusing, and less con-flict-ridden task of personal and social identity formation. It ap-pears clear that many of the adolescents of the 1960s who now as young adults find themselves struggling outside the social order as major drug users, defeated dropouts, or armed revolutionaries on the run, would have found other alternatives had they not grown up in the middle and late 1960s in explosive, unstable, polarized communities (Conger, Note 2, 1977).

THE ROLE OF PARENT—CHILD RELATIONSHIPS

Nevertheless, within a wide variety of social contexts the role of parent-child relationships still emerges as crucial. For example, the results of a recent investigation (Pittel, Note 3; Pittel, Calef, Gryler, Hilles, Hofer, & Kempner, 1971; Pittel & Miller, Note 4) of the subsequent fate of a sample of 154 presumably representative San Francisco hippies begun shortly after the 1967 "summer of love," has demonstrated that the single best predictor of whether or not they eventually re-entered the societal mainstream was their family background. The reentry group scored significantly higher than the non-reentry group (as defined by continuing serious drug use, unstable personal relationships, and lack of any regular job) on prior measures of family cohesiveness and hap-piness, participation in shared family activities in childhood, ex-tent and openness of communication, and most dramatically, on measures dealing with their sense of family belongingness and ac-ceptance (Pittel & Miller, Note 4).

The real question then is not whether the role of parent-child relationships is crucial, but what kind of relationships. The need for basic feelings of trust, and for loving and caring parents is well documented, both clinically and in many more systematic in-vestigations of normal, neurotic, and delinquent children and adolescents. Without strong and unambiguous manifestations of parental love, the child or adolescent has little chance of developing self-esteem, constructive and rewarding relationships with others, and a confident sense of his or her own identity (Becker, 1964; Biller & Davids, 1973; Conger, 1977; Martin, 1975; Walters & Stinnett, 1971; Weiner, 1970). Parental hostility, rejec-tion, or neglect consistently occur more frequently than acceptan-ce, love, and trust in the backgrounds of children with a very wide range of problems, ranging from cognitive and academic dif-ficulties and impaired social relationships with peers and adults, to neurotic disorders, psychophysiological and psychosomatic disturbances, and character problems, such as delinquency. For example, with remarkable consistency investigations of the parent-child relationships of delinquent adolescents indicate that these relationships are far more likely than those of non-delinquents to have been characterized by mutual hostility, lack of family cohesiveness, and parental rejection, indifference, dissen-sion, or apathy (Ahlstrom & Havighurst, 1971; Bachman, 1970; Bandura & Walters, 1959; Conger & Miller, 1966; McCord, Mc-Cord, & Zola, 1959).

Perhaps less obvious, but of equal importance in my view, is the parents' position on the dimension of control versus autonomy. We are living in a turbulent era of rapid social change, where the need for adolescent autonomy and independence are at a premium; where there are few clear-cut social guidelines and responsibility must come largely from within the individual; and where the op-portunities for generational conflict, hostility, and alienation are legion.

Under such circumstances, research by Elder (1962, 1963), Baumrind (1968, 1975), and others (Bachman, 1970; Kandel & Lesser, 1972; Rosenberg, 1963, 1965) has shown that the young person prospers most with democratic parents- parents who in-volve their children in family affairs and decision-making and who provide age-appropriate, graduated experiences in the assumption of independence, but who confidently retain ultimate respon-sibility- parents who are, in Diana Baumrind's words *authoritative* without being *authoritarian* (Baumrind, 1968). In drawing the distinction, she observes, the *authoritarian* (or in more extreme form *autocratic*) parent "attempts to shape, control, and evaluate the behavior and attitudes of the child in accordance with a set standard of conduct, usually an absolute standard... [Baumrind, 1968, p. 261]." Such a parent values obedience per se as an absolute virtue, and "favors punitive, forceful measures to curb self-will at points where the child's actions or beliefs conflict with what [the parent] thinks is right conduct [Baumrind, 1968, p. 261]." Any sort of two-way interaction between parent and child-- any encouragement of verbal give and take--is negatively reinforced in the conviction that the child should accept unquestioningly the parents' word for what is right (Baumrind, 1968).

In contrast, as Baumrind emphasizes, the *authoritative* (democratic, but not permissive) parent assumes ultimate respon-sibility for the child's activities, but in a rational, issue-oriented manner. Such a parent values both autonomous self-will *and* disciplined behavior. Verbal give and take are encouraged, and the parent attempts to provide "legitimacy" in the exercise of paren-tal authority by frequent explanations of the reasons for demands or prohibitions (Elder, 1963; Hoffman, 1970). The distinction bet-ween authoritarian and authoritative parental behaviors is especially important in the case of adolescents because they are capable of assuming increasingly greater responsibility for their own behavior and because they will need to do so if they are to become mature, self-reliant adults (Conger, 1977). A study of Swedish adolescents showed that authority based on rational con-cern for the young person's welfare was accepted well, whereas authority "based on the adult's desire to dominate or exploit" the adolescent was rejected (Pikas, 1961).

As Elder found, democratic, authoritative parents are most likely to be perceived as fair and as valuing their children; fur-thermore they are most likely to have children who as adolescents are self-confident, high in self-esteem, and independent. In con-trast, lack of confidence, dependence, and lowered self-esteem occur more frequently among the children of autocratic or authoritarian parents (who just tell their children what to do).

Similarly, in a recent comprehensive review of research on moral development, Martin Hoffman (Hoffman, 1970) notes that two basic parental disciplinary patterns affecting moral orientation can be distinguished, *power-assertive* and *nonpower-assertive*-- sometimes called "psychological, indirect or love-oriented discipline." Nonpower-assertive discipline, in turn, can be divided into two main subtypes: *love-withdrawal techniques* and *induction* (in which the parent provides explanations or reasons for requiring certain behaviors from the child). It has been found that neither power-assertive techniques (based on punishment or fear of punishment) nor love-withdrawal techniques (based on anxiety) foster a mature moral orientation. In contrast, induction promotes parental identification, self-esteem and striving for maturity, and an internal moral orientation.

While an authoritarian, or autocratic, non-explaining parent im-pedes the adolescent's development toward maturity, the so-called "equalitarian," or permissive parent is not likely to be much help either. Recent studies by Blum (1972), Jessor and Jessor (1974), others indicate that, among middle-class adolescents at least, high risk drug use and other forms of socially deviant behavior occur most frequently among parents who, while out-wardly expressing such values for themselves and their children as individuality, self-understanding, readiness for change, and maximizing one's human potential, and stressing the need for equalitarianism in the family- what Blum calls "pseudo-democracy"- are actually using these proclaimed values to avoid assuming parental responsibility--whether because of uncer-tainties about their own convictions, indecision about how to handle their children, needs to be liked or to feel youthful, or, as often appeared to be the case, their own antagonism, or at least ambivalence, toward authority- parental or social.

Consequently, as Blum notes, these parents:

find it hard to make decisive value judgments that require the exercise of power over their children and prefer to escape from the obligation of being an authority figure- an untenable position if authority is distrusted in general or if there has been no identification in childhood with adult authority [Blum, 1972, p. 53.]

By setting up the family as a "pseudodemocracy," these parents are able to abdicate decision-making powers, reponsibility, and unequal status. But by placing themselves on the footing of peers, they end up leaving their children to drift essentially alone in an uncharted sea, without any dependable models of responsible adult behavior. Ironically, despite their protestations of parent-child togetherness, parents of high risk drug users actually spent less time in family activities with their children, enjoyed their company less, and were less able to handle problems that arose than the more traditional parents of low drug risk adolescents. It appears that parents in contemporary society face the problem of steering a delicate course between the Scylla of authoritarianism, on the one hand, and the Charybdis of permissiveness, equalitarianism, or neglect, on the other. Furthermore, the ease of steering such a course will be significantly influenced by the direction and strength of the prevailing social winds.

IMPLICATIONS FOR ADOLESCENT PSYCHOTHERAPY

It is obvious that psychotherapists of adolescents have- and must retain- a relationship to their youthful charges that differs significantly from that of parents. Indeed, because adolescents, particularly younger adolescents, frequently come to therapy, not on their own initiative, but because they have been referred by parents, school authorities, or other adults, an initial task of the therapist is likely to be that of convincing the young person "that he is not the focus of an adult conspiracy and that his therapist is not in league with his parents to bring him to heel [Anthony, 1974, p. 243]." Nevertheless, much of what we are learning about optimal parent-child relationships, particularly with respect to the delicate balance between autonomy and control, is clearly applicable to adolescent psychotherapy (Conger, 1977).

In order to work successfully with adolescents, the therapist needs to have special knowledge of, and experience with this age group. In addition, however, he or she needs a number of personal qualities, which specialized training may be able to foster, but rarely create--among them, personal warmth, flexibility, openness and honesty, the capacity for candor, confidence in one's self and the ability to set limits without hostility, a relative lack of defensiveness and reliance on professional status, and- simple though it may sound- just liking adolescents for whatever personal psychodynamic reasons, including the nature of one's own experience as an adolescent (Conger, 1977).

Adolescents, even more than children, have a particular talent for spotting phoniness- and exploiting it. However, if the therapist is straightforward, neither minimizing his or her qualifications nor retreating into professional pomposity, the adolescent will usually develop a feeling of trust and respect--though outwardly the patient may still need to make it overly clear that he or she isn't awed by "shrinks." Above all, the effective adolescent psychotherapist must be flexible: prepared to move from listening, to questioning, to reassurance, to clarification of reality, to interpretation- even to arguing and, when necessary, setting limits (Holmes, 1964). Willingness on the part of the therapist to yield to argument may indicate to the adolescent a measure of respect for his or her increasing capacity for self-determination; it

may also produce an opportunity for both patient and therapist to reduce tension in a constructive, rather than a destructive fashion (*argument* is not synonymous with *quarrel*).

Setting Limits

Setting limits on the adolescent's behavior is sometimes necessary in psychotherapy with this age group. The therapist who fears that any imposition of limits will disrupt the relationship with the patient, or cast him or her in the role of "just another patient" is working with the wrong age group. As Irene Josselyn succinctly observes:

Adolescents not only need but often want limits imposed. They need externally imposed limits because, as a result of their confused state, they are not able to set their own limits. Many adolescents become frightened when they feel that limits have not been defined. They seek a fence beyond which they cannot go, within which they can experiment and by trial and error and accidental success find a self-concept with which they can feel satisfied [Josselyn, 1971, p. 146].

Donald Holmes provides an amusing, but significant example of a positive case of limit setting, which clearly went further toward meeting the patient's need at the time than either logical reasoning or anxious compliance on the part of the therapist:

A 16-year-old girl says, "I'm-going-to-get-out-of-here-and-get-an-apartment-and-get-married-and-you-can't-stop me!" Her doctor replies, "No you're not, and yes I can." She acknowledges, quietly enough, "Oh." [Holmes, 1964, p. 110]

Obviously such directness can be successful only where there is basic trust in the therapist and where the therapist has already made it clear that he or she respects the individuality and worth of the patient. But if the therapist sets limits only where they are necessary for the well-being of the patient, the young person will typically value the therapist because of the security that these limits provide.

The limits are then actually not imposed by the therapist, but are self-imposed by the patient as a result of the strengthening of the patient's own vague awareness that the limits are valid. He sees the therapist not as a restricting parent figure but as an ally of that side of himself that strives for satisfactory self-identity [Josselyn, 1971, p. 147].

Conversely, in many instances, failure on the therapist's part to set limits when they are essential is likely to be interpreted by the patient as a lack of either real concern or understanding on the part of the therapist.

The Struggle for Independence

At the same time, however, it must always be kept in mind that the establishment of independence is a critical developmental task of adolescence, and the therapist must be alert to the dangers of allowing a regressive dependence on therapy to become a substitute for the adolescent's necessary struggle toward ultimate independence and self-reliance. Another way of viewing this problem is to recognize that the adolescent's sense of a clear-cut identity is only just beginning to develop and is still tenuous and potentially in danger of being overwhelmed. The adolescent psychotherapist--like the wise parent, only more so- must be on guard against the sometimes seductive tendency to try to substitute his or her identity for that of the patient or to prolong therapy unduly (Conger, 1977).

In brief, although their roles will inevitably differ in a number of important respects, the effective parent and the effective therapist share a number of essential characteristics. Both need to be worthy of the adolescent's trust and respect, and, in turn, both need to demonstrate basic trust in, and respect for, the adolescent as a unique human being. In addition, however, both need to be authoritative without being either authoritarian or autocratic, on the one hand, or laissez-faire, equalitarian, or neglectful, on the other. Both need to be capable when necessary of setting limits with confidence but without hostility, while also recognizing the adolescent's critical need for appropriate age-graded experiences in the development of independence. Neither job is an easy one, but either will be less difficult for those who genuinely like adolescents, which in the last analysis probably means having come to terms with that part of oneself that also was once an adolescent.

REFERENCE NOTES

1. Conger, J. J. A world they never made: Parents and children in the 1970s. Invited address at the meeting of the American Academy of Pediatrics, Denver, April 17, 1975.
2. Conger, J. J. Current issues in adolescent development. Master lectures series at the meeting of the American Psychological Association, Chicago, August 28, 1975.
3. Pittel, S. M. *The etiology of youthful drug involvement* Unpublished monograph, Berkeley Center for Drug Studies, The Wright Institute, Berkeley, California.
4. Pittel, S. M., & Miller, H. *Dropping down: The hippie then and now.* Manuscript in preparation (tentative title), Haight Ashbury Research Project, Wright Institute, Berkeley, California, 1976.

REFERENCES

Ahlstrom, W. M., & Havighurst, R. J. *400 losers.* San Francisco: Jossey-Bass, 1971.

Anthony, E. J. Psychotherapy of adolescence. In G. Caplan (Ed.), *American handbook of psychiatry.* Vol. 2. *Child and adolescent psychiatry, sociocultural and community psychiatry.* New York: Basic Books, 1974.

Bachman, J. G. *Youth in transition.* Vol. 2. *The impact of family background and intelligence on tenth-grade boys.* Ann Arbor, Michigan: Institute for Social Research, University of Michigan, 1970.

Bandura, A., & Walters, R. H. *Adolescent aggression.* New York: Ronald, 1959.

Baumrind, D. Authoritarian vs. authoritative control. *Adolescence,* 1968, *3,* 255-272.

Baumrind, D. Early socialization and adolescent competence. In S. E. Dragastin & G. H. Elder, Jr., *Adolescence in the life cycle: Psychological change and social context.* New York: Wiley, 1975.

Becker, W. C. Consequences of different kinds of parental discipline. In M. L. Hoffman & L. W. Hoffman (Eds.), *Review of child development.* Vol. 1. New York: Russell Sage Foundation, 1964.

Biller, H. B., & Davids, A. Parent-child relations, personality development, and psychopathology. In A. Davids (Ed.),

Issues in abnormal and child psychology. Monterey, California: Brooks/Cole, 1973.

Block, J. *Lives through time.* Berkeley, California: Bancroft Books, 1971.

Blum, R. H., et al. *Horatio Alger's children.* San Francisco: Jossey-Bass, 1972.

Conger, J. J. A world they never knew: The family and social change. *Daedalus,* Fall 1971, 1105-1138.

Conger, J. J. *Adolescence and youth: Psychological development in a changing world.* (2nd ed.) New York: Harper and Row, 1977.

Conger, J. J., & Miller, W. C. *Personality, social class, and delinquency.* New York: Wiley, 1966.

Douvan, E., & Adelson, J. *The adolescent experience.* New York: Wiley, 1966.

Elder, G. H., J. Structural variations in the child-rearing relationship. *Sociometry,* 1962, *25,* 241-262.

Elder, G. H. Jr. Parental power legitimation and its effect on the adolescent. *Sociometry,* 1963, *26,* 50-65.

Freud, A. Adolescence as a developmental distrubance. In G. Caplan & S. Lebovici (Eds.), *Adolescence: Psychosocial perspectives.* New York: Basic Books, 1969.

Hall, G. S. *Adolescence: Its psychology and its relations to physiology, anthropology, sex, crime, religion, and education.* Vol. 1. Englewood Cliffs, New Jersey: Prentice-Hall, 1904, 1905.

Harris, L. Change, yes--upheaval, no. *Life,* January 8, 1971, 22-27.

Hathaway, S. R., & Monachesi, E. D. *Adolescent personality and behavior.* Minneapolis: University of Minnesota Press, 1963.

Hirsch, E. A. *The troubled adolescent as he emerges on psychological tests.* New York: International Universities Press, 1970.

Hoffman, M. L. Moral development. In P. H. Mussen (Ed.), *Carmichael's manual of child psychology.* Vol. 2. New York: Wiley, 1970.

Holmes, D. J. *The adolescent in psychotherapy.* Boston: Little-Brown, 1964.

Jessor, S. L., & Jessor, R. Maternal ideology and adolescent problem behavior. *Developmental Psychology,* 1974, *10,* 246-254.

Josselyn, I. M. The ego in adolescence. *American Journal of Orthopsychiatry,* 1954, *24,* 223-227.

Josselyn, I. M. *Adolescence.* New York: Harper & Row, 1971.

Kandel, D. B., & Lesser, G. S. *Youth in two worlds.* San Francisco: Jossey-Bass, 1972.

Martin, B. Parent-child relations. In F. D. Horowitz (Ed.), *Review of child development research.* Vol. 4. Chicago: University of Chicago Press, 1975.

McCord, W., McCord, J., & Zola, I. K. *Origins of crime.* New York: Columbia University Press, 1959.

Offer, D. *The psychological world of the teen-ager: A study of normal adolescent boys.* New York: Basic Books, 1969.

Offer, D., & Offer, J. B. *From teenage to young manhood.* New York: Basic Books, 1975.

Pikas, A. Children's attitudes toward rational versus inhibiting parental authority. *Journal of Abnormal and Social Psychology,* 1961, *62,* 315-321.

Pittel, S. M., Calef, V., Gryler, R. B., Hilles, L., Hofer, R., & Kempner, P. Developmental factors in adolescent drug use: A study of psychedelic drug users. *Journal of the American Academy of Child Psychiatry,* 1971, *10,* 640-660.

Rosenberg, M. Parental interest and children's self-perceptions. *Sociometry,* 1963, *26,* 35-49.

Rosenberg, M. *Society and the adolescent self-image.* Princeton, New Jersey: Princeton University Press, 1965.

Sorensen, R. C. *Adolescent sexuality in contemporary America.* NewYork: Harry N. Abrams, Inc., 1973.

Walters, J., & Stinnett, N. Parent-child relationships: A decade review of research. *Journal of Marriage and the Family,* 1971, *33,* 70-110.

Weiner, J. B. *Psychological disturbance in adolescence.* New York: Wiley Interscience, 1970.

Yankelovich, D. *Generations apart.* New York: Columbia Broadcasting System, 1969.

John J. Conger, Ph.D., is Professor of Clinical Psychology and Director of Adolescent Psychiatry at the University of Colorado School of Medicine. Prior to returning to his interests in child and adolescent development in 1970, Dr. Conger served for seven years as Vice-President for Medical Affairs and Dean of the Medical School. He is the author of *Adolescence and Youth: Psychological Development in a Changing World* (2nd edition, 1977).

34

Reunification With Our Children

by Urie Bronfenbrenner

The rising rates of youthful drug abuse, delinquency, and violence have been documented in the charts and tables prepared for the 1970 White House Conference on Children. The proportion of youngsters aged 10 to 18 arrested for drug abuse doubled between 1964 and 1969. Juvenile delinquency has been increasing since 1963 at a faster rate than the juvenile population. More than half the crimes involve vandalism, theft, or breaking and entry. If present trends continue, one of every nine youngsters will appear in juvenile court before age 18, and these figures only reflect offenses which are detected and prosecuted. This anti-social behavior — which takes other forms in other age groups — is an obvious manifestation of the deep and growing alienation of the youth of our society.

The Nature of Alienation

At its core, alienation is a subjective state. It is a feeling of *not belonging* and of rejection of and by the people, community, and society in which a person lives. It is accompanied by disinterest in and distaste for association with these groups and involvement in the activities in which they engage.

Alienation finds expression in different forms of behavior. One is *withdrawal.* Alienated people disassociate themselves from community customs, values, and responsibilities, and choose as the phrase goes, to "do their own thing" with others like themselves. Curiously enough, the new activities, which supposedly spring from within the self, are not unrelated to the community from which the person feels apart. More often than not, "doing your own thing" means "undoing their thing." In a culture which values science, technology, business and national prestige, and places a premium at a personal level, on achievement, industry, emotional control, and propriety (the Protestant ethic), "doing your own thing" has taken the forms of "dropping out," rejection of scientific and business careers, a return to nature, sexual freedom, and a preoccupation with mysticism and inner experience as mediated by drugs. In short, the pattern of seemingly subjective choice reflects an element of *hostility* as well as withdrawal. In its most extreme form, this hostility may involve unashamed, though not always witting, destruction of the community and its institutions.

In addition to withdrawal and hostility, alienation can generate other forms of response. American universities are experiencing an unprecedented shift in student preferences and career plans, for example. The decline of interest in science and technology is paralleled by a new concentration in the humanities and social sciences. More and more students, including the most able, are voicing and pursuing a commitment to improve the quality of life through the creative arts, social service, and social change.

What accounts for these different responses to feelings of alienation? Why do some withdraw while others attack, and still others mount an effort to reform? The answers to these questions require an understanding of the conditions that cause a loss of identity. The first step in answering is to probe the roots of alienation.

The Roots of Alienation

Alienation is a feeling of rejection of and *by* the outside world. This suggests that the alienated person's rejection is a retort in kind to a feeling that he has been deserted and denigrated by his society. Is there evidence that this is true?

A partial answer is that alienation does not appear at random throughout American society; it predominates among population groups who are the victims of deprivation, discrimination, and distrust: the poor, non-whites, women, youth. One other group's estrangement is so complete that it is not even noticed or acknowledged, despite the fact

Urie Bronfenbrenner is Professor of Human Development and Family Studies and of Psychology at the New York State College of Human Ecology, Cornell University, Ithaca, New York.

From *Inequality in Education*, July 1972. Reprinted with permission of the author and the Center for Law and Education, Inc.

that its members comprise over one-fourth of our total population: it is the children of this nation. In the words of a report prepared for the 1970 White House Conference on Children by a committee under my chairmanship:

America's families and their children are in trouble, trouble so deep and pervasive as to threaten the future of the nation. The source of the trouble is nothing less than a national neglect of children and those primarily engaged in their care — America's parents. [*Report to the President,* White House Conference on Children, p. 252].[1]

If this statement is correct, it identifies childhood as the period in which the origins of alienation are to be sought and counteracted. The report quoted before suggests the facts:

The neglect begins even before the child is born. America, the richest and most powerful country in the world, stands thirteenth among the nations in combatting infant mortality; even East Germany does better [*Profiles of Children,* p. 61]. Moreover, our ranking has dropped steadily in recent decades.[2] A similar situation obtains with respect to maternal and child health, day care, children's allowances, and other basic services to children and families.

But the figures for the nation as a whole, dismaying as they are, mask even greater inequities. For example, infant mortality for non-Whites in the United States is almost twice that for Whites, and there are a number of Southern states, and Northern metropolitan areas, in which the ratios are considerably higher [*Profiles of Children,* pp. 90-92].

Ironically, of even greater cost to the society than infants who die are the many more who sustain injury but survive with disability. Many of these suffer impaired intellectual function and behavioral disturbance including hyperactivity, distractability, and low

attention span, all factors contributing to school retardation and problem behavior. Again, the destructive impact is greatest on the poorest segments of the population, especially non-Whites. It is all the more tragic that this massive damage and its subsequent cost in reduced productivity, lower income, unemployability, welfare payments, and institutionalization are avoidable if adequate nutrition, prenatal care, and other family and child services are provided, as they are in a number of countries less prosperous than ours [*Report to the President,* pp. 252-53].

It is not only children from disadvantaged families who show signs of progressive neglect. An analysis of child rearing practices in the United States over a twenty-five year period[3] reveals a decrease in all spheres of interaction between parents and children. Cross-cultural studies comparing American and European (East and West) parents reach the same conclusion.[4]

Photo by: Gail Levin

The Peer Group Culture

As parents and other adults have moved out of children's lives, age-segregated peer groups have moved in. Two of my colleagues have completed a study[5] showing that children today, at every age and grade level, show greater dependency on their peers than they did a decade ago. A parallel study[6] indicates that susceptibility to group influence is higher among children from homes in which one or both parents are frequently absent. "Peer oriented" youngsters also describe their parents as less affectionate and less firm in discipline. Attachment to age-mates appears to be influenced more by a lack of attention and concern at home than by any positive attraction of the peer group itself, for these children have a negative view of their friends and of themselves. They are pessimistic about the future, rate lower in responsibility and leadership, and are more likely to engage in such anti-social behavior as lying, teasing other children, "playing hooky," or "doing something illegal."

More recent evidence comes from a dissertation currently being completed by Mr. Michael Siman. Siman did something which, so far as I know, has never been done before. Working with a large sample of teenagers (ages 12 to 17), most from middle and lower middle-class homes in New York City, Siman identified and studied the actual peer groups (41 in all) in which the adolescents spent so much of their time. Trying to determine the relative influence of parents and peers on teenage behavior, Siman studied three classes of behavior:

1. *Socially constructive activities* such as taking part in sports, helping someone who needs help, telling the truth, doing useful work for the neighborhood or community without pay, etc.

2. *Neutral activities* such as listening to records, spending time with the family, etc.

3. *Anti-social activities* such as "playing hooky," "doing something illegal," hurting people, etc.

Siman also obtained information on the extent to which each teenager perceived these activities to be approved or disapproved by his parents and by the members of his peer group. Among boys, peers were substantially more influential than parents in all three classes of behavior. In most cases, after controlling for peer group attitudes, parental attitudes made no difference whatsoever. The only exception was in constructive behavior, where parents had a secondary influence after the peer group. In the neutral, and especially the anti-social spheres, peer groups were all determining. When it comes to behavior such as doing something illegal, smoking, or aggression, parents' disapproval carried no weight.

What accounts for the growing alienation of children and youth in American society? Why do parents have so little influence? Some people blame parents themselves, charging them with willful neglect and inadequate discipline. But this view disregards the social context in which the families live, and does injustice to parents as human beings. Although there is no systematic evidence on the question, there are grounds for believing that parents today, far from not caring about their children, are more worried about them than ever before. The crux of the problem, indicated by Siman's data, is that many parents have become powerless forces in their children's lives. The nature of the problem has been spelled out in the report for the White House Conference:

In today's world parents find themselves at the mercy of a society which imposes pressures and priorities that allow neither time nor place for meaningful activities and relations between children and adults, which downgrade the role of parents and the functions of parenthood, and which prevent the parent from doing things he wants to do as a guide, friend, and companion to his children . . .

The frustrations are greatest for the family of poverty where the capacity for human response is crippled by hunger, cold, filth, sickness, and despair. For families who can get along, the rats are gone, but the rat race remains. The demands of a job, or often two jobs, that claim mealtimes, evenings, and weekends as well as days; the trips and moves necessary to get ahead or simply hold one's own; the ever-increasing time spent in commuting, parties, evenings out, social and community obligations — all the appearance of neighborhoods, zoning ordinances, occupational mobility, child labor laws, the abolishment of the apprentice system, consolidated schools, television, separate patterns of social life for different age groups, the working mother, the delegation of child care to specialists — all these manifestations of progress operate to decrease opportunity and incentive for meaningful contact between children and persons older, or younger, than themselves.

And here we confront a fundamental and disturbing fact: *Children need people in order to become human.* The fact is fundamental because it is firmly grounded both in scientific research and in human experience. It is disturbing because the isolation of things one has to do to meet so-called primary responsibilities — produce a situation in which a child often spends more time with a passive babysitter than a participating parent.

And even when the parent is at home, a compelling force cuts off communication and response among the family members. Although television could, if used creatively, enrich the activities of children and families, it now only undermines them. Like the sorcerer of old, the television set casts its magic spell, freezing speech and action and turning the living into silent statues so long as the enchantment lasts. The primary danger of the television screen lies not so much in the behavior it produces as the behavior it prevents — the talks, the games, the family festivities and arguments through which much of the child's learning takes place and his character is formed. Turning on the television set can turn off the process that transforms children into people.

In our modern way of life, children are deprived not only of parents but of people in general. A host of factors conspire to isolate children from the rest of society. The fragmentation of the extended family, the separation of residential and business areas, the dis-

children from adults simultaneously threatens the growth of the individual and the survival of society. Child rearing is not something children can do for themselves. It is primarily through observing, playing, and working with others older and younger than himself that a child discovers both what he can do and who he can become — that he develops both his ability and his identity. It is primarily through exposure and interaction with adults and children of different ages that a child acquires new interests and skills and learns the meaning of tolerance, cooperation, and compassion. Hence to relegate children to a world of their own is to deprive them of their humanity, and ourselves as well.

Yet, this is what is happening in America today. *We are experiencing a breakdown in the process of making human beings human.* By isolating our children from the rest of society, we abandon them to a world devoid of adults and ruled by the destructive impulses and compelling pressures both of the age-segregated peer group and the aggressive and exploitative television screen, we leave our children bereft of standards and support and our own lives impoverished and corrupted.

This reversal of priorities, which amounts to a betrayal of our children, underlies the growing disillusionment and alienation among young people in all segments of American society. Those who grew up in settings where children, families, still counted are able to react to their frustration in positive ways — through constructive protest, participation, and public service. Those who come from circumstances in which the family could not function, be it in slum or suburb, can only strike out against an environment they have experienced as indifferent, callous, cruel, and unresponsive. This report does not condone the destruction and violence manifested by young people in widely disparate sections of our society; it merely points to the roots of a process which, if not reversed . . . can have only one result: the far more rapid and pervasive growth of alienation, apathy, drugs, delinquency and violence among the young, in all segments of our national life. We face the prospect of a society which resents its own children and fears its youth . . . What is needed is a change in our patterns of living which will once again bring people back into the lives of children and children back into the lives of people.[7]

These passages explain a breakdown in the social process at two levels: a failure in the family, society's primary institution for making human beings human, and a "withering away" of the support systems in the larger society that enable families to function. Thus, the roots of alienation lie in our institutions as they are presently structured and function. The question is whether these institutions can be changed. Can old ones be modified and new ones be introduced to rebuild the social context which families and children require for their effective function and growth?

Support Systems for Children and Families

Countering the forces of alienation in contemporary American society requires the involvement of all social institutions. Those having direct impact on children and families — such as schools, churches, health and welfare services, and recrea-

tion programs — are needed, as well as organizations whose impact on families, children, and youth is often unrecognized but profound. These include businesses and industries, law enforcement agencies, local and regional planning commissions, architectural firms, transportation and sanitation services, among others.

Day Care

Day care is coming to America. The only question is "what kind?" Shall we, in response to pressures to "put people to work," or for personal convenience, allow young children's care to be delegated to specialists, further separating children from their families and reducing the family's and the community's feeling of responsibility for their children? Or shall modern day care be designed to reinvolve and strengthen the family as the primary agent for making human beings human?

The answers to these questions depend on the extent to which day care programs are located and organized to encourage the involvement of parents and other non-professionals at day care centers and in the home. Like Project Head Start, day care programs will have no lasting impact on child development unless they affect both the child and the people who constitute his day-to-day environment. This means that parents must play a prominent part in the planning and administration of day care programs, as well as in the execution of the program, as volunteers and aides. Programs cannot be confined to centers, but must reach out into homes and communities so that the whole neighborhood is involved in activity in its chil-

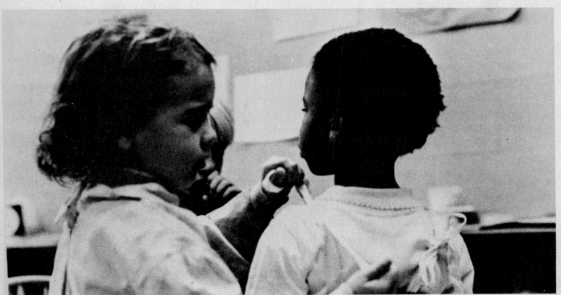

Photo by: Gail Levin

dren's behalf. Day care centers must be located in places that are within reach of the significant people in children's lives. For some families, this means neighborhood centers; for others, centers at the place of work. Variation will be required to find the appropriate solutions for groups in different settings.

Part-time Employment

These solutions all confront a critical obstacle, because effective day care programs require parent participation. How can a mother, let alone a father, participate if she works full time (the main reason the family needs day care in the first place)? The only solution to this problem is increased opportunities for part-time employment. This is why the Report for the White House Conference urged business, industry, and government to increase the number — and status — of part-time positions. The Report also recommended that state legislatures enact a "Fair Part-Time Employment Practices Act," to prohibit discrimination in job opportunities, pay rates, fringe benefits, and status for parents engaged in part-time employment.

The Report also urged employers to modify their policies and practices as they affected family life, especially in these following areas: out of town, weekend, and overnight obligations; frequency and timing of geographical moves; flexibility of work schedule; leave and rest privileges for maternal and child care; and job-related social obligations.

The Role of Women

Setting aside the thorny but important issue of whether women are more gifted and effective than men in the care of young children, the fact remains that in our society today, women, and especially mothers, are primarily responsible for the care of children. With the withdrawal of social supports for the family, the position of women and mothers has become increasingly isolated. With the breakdown of community, neighborhood, and the extended family, an increasingly greater responsibility for the care and upbringing of children has fallen on young mothers. Under these circumstances, it is not surprising that many young women in America are in revolt. While understanding and sharing their rage, I fear the consequences of the solutions they advocate: isolating children still further from the care and

attention they need. As I read the research, the ideal arrangement for the development of the young child is one in which his mother works part-time, so that she can be the full person that being an effective parent requires. A major route to the rehabilitation of children and youth lies in the enhancement of the status and power of women — both on the job and in the home.

Reacquainting Children With Workers

One significant effect of age-segregation has been the isolation of children from the world of work. In the past, children saw their parents at work and often shared substantially in the task; today, many children have only a vague notion of their parents' jobs, and little or no opportunity to observe them, or any other adults, at work. Although there is no systematic evidence, it appears likely that the absence of this exposure contributes significantly to alienation among children and youth. The experiences of other modern urban societies indicate that children's isolation from the adult work world is not inevitable, and may be countered by social innovations. Perhaps the most imaginative and pervasive is the pattern employed in the Soviet Union in which each place of work — each factory, shop, office, institute, or business enterprise — adopts a group of children as their "wards." The children's group is usually a school classroom but may be a nursery, hospital ward or any other collective group of children. The workers visit the children's group and invite the youngsters to their place of work to familiarize them with their activities and with themselves as people. Vocational education is not the aim, it is acquaintance with adults as participants in the world of work.

There is nothing in this approach that is incompatible with the values and aims of our own society, and I have urged its adaptation to the American scene. Acting on this suggestion, Dr. David Goslin of the Russell Sage Foundation persuaded the *Detroit Free Press* to participate in an experiment as a prelude to the White House Conference on Children. Two groups of twelve-year-old children, one from a slum area, the other predominantly middle class, spent six to seven hours a day for three days in virtually every department of the newspaper; they observed and actively participated in the department's activities. There were boys and girls in the press room, the city room, the composing room, the advertising department, and the dispatch department. *Free Press* employees had entered the experiment with serious misgivings: "This is a busy place; we have a newspaper to get out every day. What are those kids going to do, just sit around? And besides, the language that's used around here isn't exactly what you'd want a kid to hear!" What actually happened is recorded in a documentary film.[8] The children were not bored; nor were the adults. And the paper did get out every day. These are some of the spontaneous comments recorded in the film.

"Adults should talk more with children and pay more attention to them instead of leaving them in the dark — because you can't really get to know much about each other unless you talk." — Gian, age 11

"It's sad to see her leaving. In three days she became part of the group up there." — Tony, age 53

"This is a place to meet, a way to understand people." — Megan, age 11

"It's been fun, it really has . . . I talked to him about having him out to our house to meet my sons and visit with us." — Joe, age 36

"If every kid in Detroit and all around the United States got to do this — I don't think there would be as many problems in the world." — Colette, age 11.

The working adults at the *Detroit Free Press* were not the children's own parents. A group of businessmen and industrialists at a Johnson Foundation conference, to follow-up the White House Conference recommendations, came up with a modification which they proposed to try in their own companies: having employees invite their own children to spend an extended period at work with them. The initial thought, that the parents would take time off to be with their children, was rejected when participants pointed out that this would defeat the purpose of the undertaking, which was to enable children to see their parents engaged in responsible and demanding tasks.

If these innovations are to accomplish their objective, they cannot be confined to a single experience, even of three days, but must be continued, at intermittent intervals, over an extended period. The effect of such innovations on the behavior and development of children is not yet established, nor is it known whether American society will find the innovations acceptable and feasible. But there is hope that

experiments of this kind will be tried. The *Detroit Free Press* film has just become available and already the word has come back that a variety of innovations are being initiated. In one community, for example, the city government has decided to "adopt" groups of children to acquaint them with the people and activities involved in that enterprise. In another area, advertisements have been placed in the local newspaper asking many persons (carpenters, insurance salesmen, garage mechanics and social workers, to name a few) whether they would be willing to have one child accompany them as they go through a day's work. As these innovations are introduced, they should be evaluated for their impact on children and also on the adults who, perhaps for the first time, are being asked to relate to a young child in their occupation.

Genuine Responsibilities for Children

If children are to become responsible persons, they must begin to participate in serious tasks from an early age. In cross-cultural research, one of the most salient characteristics of our nation is what Nicholas Hobbs has called "the inutility of childhood" in American society.

Our children are not entrusted with any real responsibilities in their family, neighborhood, or community. Little that they do really matters. When they do participate, it is in some inconsequential undertaking. They are given duties rather than responsibilities; that is, the ends and means have been determined by someone else, and their job is to fulfill an assignment involving little judgment, decision making, or risk. The latter remain within the purvue of supervising adults. Although this policy is deemed to serve the interest of the children themselves by protecting them from burdens beyond their years, there is reason to believe that it has been carried too far in contemporary American society and has contributed to the alienation and alleged incapacity of young people to deal constructively with personal and social problems. The evidence indicates that children acquire the capacity to cope with difficult situations when they have been given opportunity to take on consequential responsibilities in relation to others, *and are held accountable for them.* [Report to the President, p. 247].

The School's Role

While training for responsibility clearly begins in the family, the institution which has probably done the most to keep children insulated from challenging social tasks is the American school system. For reasons rooted in the separation of church and state, this system has been isolated, substantively and spatially, from responsible social concern. The content of American education, viewed from a cross-cultural perspective, seems peculiarly one-sided. It emphasizes subject matter to the exclusion of another molar aspect of the child's development, which is reflected by the absence of any generally accepted term for this second area in our educational vocabulary. What the Germans call *Erziehung,* the Russians *vospitanie,* and the French *education* has no common counterpart in English. Perhaps the best equivalents are "upbringing" or "character education," terms which, to the extent that they have any meaning, sound outmoded and irrelevant. In many countries of Western and Eastern Europe, however, the corresponding terms are not only current, but constitute what is regarded as the core of the educational process — the development of the child's qualities as a person — his values, motives, and patterns of social response. This last category underscores the point that these are matters not only of educational philosophy, as they are sometimes with us, but of concrete educational practice both within the classroom and without — in home, neighborhood, and larger community.

The second insular aspect of the American educational process is that our schools and our children are insulated from the immediate social environment, the life of the community, neighborhood, and families the schools purport to serve, the life for which the schools are supposedly preparing children.

The insularity characterizing the relation of the school to the outside world is repeated within the school system itself. Children are segregated into classrooms that have little social connection to each other or to the school as a common community, for which members might take active responsibility both as individuals and groups.

During the past decade, the trend toward segregation of the school from the rest of society has been rapidly accelerated by the other forces of social disorganization that we have discussed. *As a result, schools have become one of the most potent breeding grounds of alienation in American society.* It is of crucial importance for the development of school age children that schools be reintegrated into community life. Above all, the trend toward the construction and administration of schools as compounds isolated from the rest of the community must be reversed. Many such schools are becoming quasi-penal institutions in which teachers increasingly function as guards, while pupils are treated as prisoners for whom liberty is a special privilege.

Photo by: James Keller

As studies of other contemporary societies show,[9] educational programs do not have to be carried out in isolation from the rest of the society. Russians also apply the pattern of "group adoption" within the school itself, with groups of children doing the "adopting." Each class takes responsibility for a group of children at a lower grade level. A third grade class "adopts" a first grade class in the same school or a kindergarten in the immediate neighborhood. The older children escort the younger ones to the school or center, play with them on the playground, teach them new games, read to them, help them learn. The manner in which they fulfill this responsibility enters into the evaluation of their school performance as a regular part of the curriculum.

Again, there is nothing in this pattern that is incompatible with the values and objectives of our own society. Indeed, some of its elements are present in the tutoring programs which have begun to spring up around the country.[10] In these programs, however, the focus tends to be on the development of skills and subject matter, rather than concern for the total child as a member of the larger community.

One way of making this concept concrete would be to establish in the school, beginning even at the elementary level, what might be called *functional courses in human development.* These would be distinguished from units on "family life," as they are now taught in the junior high school, chiefly for girls who do not plan to go to college, in which the material is presented through reading, discussion, or at most, through role-playing. The approach proposed here would have active concern for the lives of young children and their families at its core. This experience could be facilitated by locating day care centers and Head Start Programs in or near schools, so that they would be an integral part of the curriculum. Older children would be working with younger ones on a regular basis. They could escort the little ones to and from school or center, and spend some time with them out of school. In this way, they could become acquainted with the younger children's families and the circumstances in which they live. This, in turn, would provide a context for the study of services and facilities available to children and families in the community — health care, social services, recreation facilities, and the schools themselves. The scope of responsibility would increase with the child's age, and there would have to be adequate supervision and clear delineation of the limits of the older children's responsibility throughout. The same pattern of responsible involvement could be applied in relation to other groups such as the aged, the sick, the disadvantaged, and those living alone.

Finally, the children should be given an active part in defining the problems in their school and their community, and their responsibility in contributing to a solution. Within the school this implies greater involvement of children in the formulation and enforcement of codes of behavior and in the planning and development of classroom activities. Then the burden of maintaining discipline will not fall solely or even primarily on the shoulders of the teacher, who will be free to perform the primary function of expanding the children's horizon and range of competence.

Neighborhoods and Communities

This article's thesis is that the power of adults to function as constructive forces in the lives of children depends on the degree to which society provides the place, time, example, and encouragement for persons to engage in activities with the young. This implies the existence or establishment of institutions which address themselves primarily to these concerns. At the present time, few such institutions exist. The needs of children are parceled out among a hopeless confusion of agencies with diverse objectives, conflicting jurisdictions, and imperfect channels of communication. The school, the health department, churches, welfare services, youth organizations, the medical pro-

fession, libraries, the police, recreation programs — all see community children and parents at one time or another, but none is concerned with the total pattern of life. If such child and family oriented institutions and activities were to be established, some possibilities of what they might look like include:

(1) *A Commission for Children and Families.* Established at the community or neighborhood level, this commission would have as its initial charge finding out what the community is doing, or not doing, for its children and their families. The Commission would examine the adequacy of existing programs such as maternal and child health services, day care facilities, and recreational opportunities. It would also investigate which places and people were available to children when they were not in school; what opportunities they have for play, challenging activities, or useful work; and to whom children could turn for guidance or assistance. The Commission would also assess the existing and needed resources that provide family opportunities for learning, living, and leisure involving common activity across levels of age, ability, knowledge and skill.

The Commission would include representatives of the major institutions concerned with children and families, as well as other segments of community life such as business, industry and labor. Inclusion of teenagers and older children who can speak directly from their own experiences is especially important. The Commission would be expected to report its findings and recommendations to executive bodies and to the public at large. After completing the initial assessment phase, the Commission would assume responsibility for developing and monitoring programs to implement its recommendations.

(2) *Neighborhood Family Centers.* Families are strengthened through association in common activities and responsibilities. This necessitates places where families can meet to work and play together. The Neighborhood Family Center is such a place. Located in the school, church, or other community building, it provides a focal point for leisure, learning, and community problem solving. The Center offers games and creative activities for persons of all ages — and space for those who merely want to "watch the fun." To eliminate fragmentation of services, the Center can also serve as the local "one door" entry point for obtaining family health, child care, legal aid, and welfare services. The Center differs from the traditional community center in emphasizing cross-age rather than age-segregated activities.

(3) *Community and Neighborhood Projects.* Community organizations should be encouraged to

Photo by: James Keller

provide a variety of activities which enable different generations to have contact and become a significant part of each other's lives. Through community sponsored projects, individuals of all ages can grow in their appreciation of each other as they learn to give to one another through sharing their talents and skills. The growing interest in cleaning up the environment provides an excellent focus for these common endeavors, since it requires a variety of knowledge, skills, and services. Concern for the aged, the sick, and the lonely provide similar challenges. In the organization and execution of such projects, young people should participate not as subordinates, but as active collaborators who can contribute ideas and direction as well as service. In addition to work projects, there is a need for recreational facilities and programs in which cross-age activities can take place (family camps, fairs, games, and picnics, for example).

(4) Youth Participation in Local Policy Bodies. In keeping with the principle that young people become responsible by being given and held accountable for responsibilities that really matter, every community organization having jurisdiction over activities affecting children and youth should include some teenagers and older children as voting members. This would include such organiza-tions as school boards, welfare commissions, recreation commissions, and hospital boards.

(5) Community and Neighborhood Planning. Much of what happens to children and families in a community is determined by the ecology of the neighborhood in which the family lives. The implication of this principle is illustrated in a recent report on the effect of "new towns" on the lives of children. It is perhaps characteristic that the question was raised not within our own society, but in West Germany. The study, con-ducted by the Urban and Planning Institute in Nuremburg in collaboration with the Institute of Psychology at the University of Erlangen-Nuremberg, compared the actions of children living in older German cities. Although copies of the technical report are not yet available in this country, the following excerpts from The *New York Times* (May 9, 1971) tell the story:

In the new towns of West Germany, amid soaring rectangular shapes of apartment houses with shaded walks, big lawns and fenced-in play areas, the children for whom much of this has been designed apparently feel isolated, regimented and bored . . .

The study finds that the children

gauge their freedom not by the extent of open areas around them, but by the liberty they have to be among people and things that excite them and fire their imaginations . . .

Children in the older cities seemed enthusiastic about their surroundings, painting a great amount of detail into a variety of things they found exciting around them, according to those who interpreted their art.

The children in the model communities often painted what were considered despairing pictures of the world the adults had fashioned for them, depicting an uninviting, concrete fortress of cleanliness and order and boredom.

The implications of this research are evident. In the planning and design of new communities, housing projects, and urban renewal, planners, both public and private, need to give explicit consideration to the kind of world being created

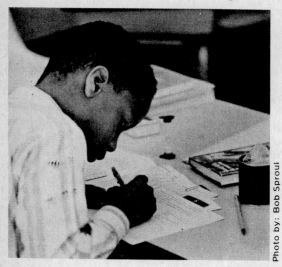

Photo by: Bob Sproul

for the children who will be growing up in these settings. Particular attention should be given to the opportunities which the environment presents for involvement of children with persons older and younger than themselves. Among the specific factors to be considered are the location of shops and businesses where children could have contact with adults at work, recreational and day care facilities readily accessible to parents as well as children, provision for a Family Neighborhood Center and family oriented facilities and services, availability of public transportation, and, perhaps most important of all, places to walk, sit, and talk in common company.

It is perhaps most fitting to end this discussion with a proposal for nothing more radical than providing a setting in which young and old can simply sit and talk. The fact that such settings are disappearing and have to be deliberately recreated points to the roots of the problem as well as its remedy. The evil, and the cure, lie not with the victims of alienation, but in the social institutions which produce it, and their failure to be responsive to the most human needs and values of our democratic society.

FOOTNOTES

1. *Profiles of Children: White House Conference on Children,* pp. 78-79, 108, 179-80. (U.S. Government Printing Office, 1970).

2. Except as otherwise noted, the comparative data cited in this statement are documented in U. Bronfenbrenner, *Two Worlds of Childhood: U.S. and U.S.S.R.,* pp. 95-124 (New York: Russell Sage Foundation, 1970).

3. U. Bronfenbrenner, "Socialization and Social Class Through Time and Space." In E.E. Maccoby, T.M. Newcomb, and E. Hartley (Eds.), *Readings in Social Psychology,* 3rd edition. (New York: Holt, 1958) pp. 400-425.

4. U. Bronfenbrenner, *Two Worlds of Childhood;* E. Devereaux, U. Bronfenbrenner, & R. Rodgers, "Child Rearing in England and the United States: A Cross-National Comparison," *Journal of Marriage and the Family,* May 1969, pp. 257-70; R. Rodgers, "Changes in Parental Behavior Reported by Children in West Germany and the United States," *Human Development* (in press).

5. J. Condry & M. Siman, "An Experimental Study of Adult Versus Peer Orientation" (Unpublished manuscript, Cornell University, 1968).

6. J. Condry & M. Siman, "Characteristics of Peer- and Adult-Oriented Children" (Unpublished manuscript, Cornell University, 1968).

7. *Report to the President: White House Conference on Children,* pp. 241-43 (U.S. Government Printing Office, 1970).

8. "A Place to Meet, a Way to Understand," National Audiovisual Center (G.S.A.), Washington, D.C., 20409.

9. A. A. Jarus, J. Marcus, J. Oren & C. Rapaport, *Children and Families in Israel* (New York: Gordon and Breach, 1970); U. Bronfenbrenner, *Two Worlds of Childhood.*

10. R. Cloward, Studies in Tutoring," *Journal of Experimental Education,* (Fall 1967) pp. 14-25; National Commission on Resources for Youth, *Youth Tutoring Youth — It Worked.* (Final report, January 31, 1969) (36 West 44th St., New York, N.Y. 10036); B. Parke, "Toward a New Rationale for Cross-Age Tutoring" (Unpublished manuscript, Cornell University, November 1969).

Of Youth and the Time of Generations

by Thomas J. Cottle

In the long enslavement of childhood I knelt on hard wood in
cold churches, striking my breast at each mea culpa, and
resolved to confess my sins, do penance, and amend my life; and
so I do; I have forgiven my parents all their care in rearing me.
What I pray for this year is not the remission of my sins, but the
wit to remember them when they come back to me as my
offspring's, and grace to see the luminescence of things lost in
things present. The breath I want now is simpler, only to live,
which is to be hurt, which is to love. . . .
>> William Gibson, *A Mass for the Dead*

The action of the secret passes continually from the hider of
things to the hider of self. A casket is a dungeon for objects. And
here is a dreamer who feels that he shares the dungeon of its
secrets. We should like to open it, and we should also like to
open our hearts.
>> Gaston Bachelard, *The Poetics of Space*

Not too long ago, an attractive college senior gently
asked whether she might speak with me a few minutes. Her manner was marked by that timorous politeness that symbolizes how
ably school systems instruct students to avoid pestering their elders.
The contractual acknowledgment "only a few minutes" always
seems so sad, implying, as it must, an unforgivable presumption
and a taking one away from activities so unalterably more important.

Jenny sat across from me, her hiked up miniskirt, her youth, a
sorrow in her eyes all compelling me to attend to her. She had
come with "no particular problem." She spoke about her courses,
her job, the few hours each week left for schoolwork, and her two
male involvements. One, she explained, was a boy from the mountains of Utah, someone who knows of the poet's world, yet someone at present dreadfully caught in the scary, exhilarating ca-
cophony of the "drug scene." The second, a young man, "straight,"
good head, "my parents like him," "his father is a noble man."

Although Jenny concluded almost every other sentence with the
words "it's funny," nothing she said was ever funny. She had
known sadness; indeed, as she continued I felt as if she were speaking as the burdened parent, herself as her own child. "It's difficult
to stay healthy here . . . I don't know if I can pull my life together. . . . I don't know if I can make it. I hope so . . . I'm not
sure."

We spoke quite a lot more. Periodically she would ask whether
I was sure I had the time. I tried to convince her of my commit-

From *Time's Children*, Little, Brown, 1971. Reprinted with permission from the author.

Photograph by Virginia Hamilton

ment and interest, but somehow her perception of the teacher's role, together with the institutionalization of "office hours," screened a deep concern.

Then, suddenly, Jenny produced the kind of frightened confession I have heard from nearly every young person who has come to me not necessarily for help but for some hoped-for strength in friendship: "When I was thirteen, I became my father's confidante. He was having an affair with a twenty-year-old girl, and I was the only one he could speak to. . . . Later I went to the prep school she had gone to. He thought I'd like it there."

The moments with Jenny resembled so strongly other hours spent with students troubled by their experiences with drugs. Often with these students I found an absence of any fundamental strength; it just seemed as though some last-ditch power to fall back on was gone. Like Jenny, these other young people were not sure they were going to make it.

Months before, in a hospital therapy session, John, a fourteen-year-old boy living with his mother and his four brothers and sisters in a low-income Boston housing project, had spoken of his parents' divorce, a damaging separation that had been preceded by his mother seeking his counsel. Although only eleven at the time, John was, after all, the eldest of her five children. She had been thinking of getting a divorce and wanted his advice. John looked away from me before he spoke. He rubbed his forehead so that I could barely see his eyes. It was difficult to understand him through the nasal sounds, the sniffing, the Boston-scented words which remain for me an accent. "Why did she ask me? Children don't want to know about things like that! Why did she have to ask me?"

Will is a tall, very pale young man, a high school drop-out. He lacks poise but shows honesty along with despair. His very gait is a plea for help. At the time I met him, he was inextricably dependent on Methedrine, pot, LSD, cough syrup, anything that could be popped, dropped, sniffed, smacked, anything that could produce that coveted ecstasy, "the high." My first and only meeting with him lasted for about an hour. No therapeutic or ritualized rules of time had stopped us; however. Will had opened himself, perhaps too quickly. Having plunked down several chapters of his life, he had begun to frighten himself. There had been his questioning of homosexuality; was he wrong not to want to "make it" with girls; his poetic sophistication about the inexorable realities of lower-class life styles and dreams; his lack of anger, his domination by anger, and a missing father: "When my father left, my mother turned to me in a special way. It was as though she wanted my help. It's like she wanted me to take his place. She made me sleep in the same bed." He held his head in his hands and turned toward me with a look some mistakenly call a smirk. But it is not a smirk. Time and the supreme awareness of this "new" youth have transformed both the context and meaning of expression and expressiveness and what sociologist Erving Goffman has called "face work": "I guess I must have an Oedipal thing, huh?"

One last person. Janet, a college student and a friend of a friend of a friend, somehow "found herself," as she said, in my office. She had been "busted," and the court had placed her under the care of one of their psychiatrists. Because the relationship had become perfunctory, Janet now refused to see him for even the prescribed once a month. "He's not interested in me." And soon the blame had shifted inward: "How can he be? I don't spend enough time with him. I'm just another 'monthly.'" Four years before, when she was fourteen, Janet tried to commit suicide. She swallowed all varieties of pills, a total of more than eighty: "I wanted to go to sleep." The precipitating causes were many, but for her the most fearful event occurred three days before the attempt, when her mother took her into the kitchen and closed the door so that her father and brothers would not hear. "'I know you're young,' she said to me, 'but maybe you can help. Your father and I are not having sex. Have you learned anything that might help me?' I swear to you, these were her words." At the sound of her own words she wept.

The theme of young people's involvement with adult authority is an old theme, hammered to life almost daily in studies published on parents of adolescents, hippies, drop-outs, druggies, militants, etcetera. Recently I have noted that some writers "on youth" have openly chastised parents for failing to assume assertive roles with their children. Even some psychiatrists now argue for parental toughness, perhaps as a reaction to an oft-blamed emphasis on permissiveness.

Authority implies an inequality, or what some prefer to call an asymmetry, between the old and the young. The term asymmetry is rather telling as it implies quite unequivocally that there is no even exchange between generations, nor for that matter is there ever a possibility for it. Parents are by definition not peers, and their concern for children does not even imply that "good" families yield loyal colleagues. Yet the asymmetric structure of authority is not all bad, although parents and children are more than a bit ambivalent about it. Longing for the taste of adolescence, parents in many instances overstep the bounds which the asymmetry purports to guard. In some cases, as in those described above, their intrusions turn out to be nothing short of disastrous. For some young people, a quiet inner strength vanishes when their parents trespass on the property of time belonging strictly to youth and destroy the very same asymmetry which they themselves once wished to destroy.

The theme of authority is complicated, therefore, because the young and old alike often wish to tamper with the time defining generational separations but come to realize the potentially devastating results of such an escapade. The asymmetry means restraints on behavior, and the young, being today so profoundly aware of the facts of life, recognize these restraints as well as anyone. Generally, the young seem more open than ever before, or is it that social reality seems more translucent? Perhaps there are fewer secrets today than yesterday, and perhaps too our society presently honors revelation, and the supposed absolution it yields, more than confidential trust.

To a great extent, my concern here is with the breakdown of asymmetric authority and the effects and meaning of parents trespassing upon the property of the young. For there are quite a few highly sensitive young persons, mostly students, not necessarily "disturbed" (that ubiquitous word), who have experienced the rattling of their very souls when a parent chose not to preserve the asymmetry quite possibly required in authority relations. Often I think of the troubled pasts and equivocal futures of these persons living in a society so riddled with thoughts of death and insanity that the spirit of death and the fear of and fascination with insanity pervades their explorations into sex and drugs. But our topic is not *all* young people or the universal causes of mental illness, drug taking or school problems. One cannot generalize about "youth" from a few encounters, nor indeed would one dare generalize about all the hours in another's lifetime on the basis of but a few hours of friendship. Still, from even these few hours, a few pictures, a few concepts however dim, emerge and they seem worth remarking on.

There is little doubt that young people extend, prolong, or simply react to their parents' demands, be they uttered or silently passed on. As Erik Erikson has said, one generation revives the repressions of the generation before it. But equally important, adolescents have become brilliant readers of parental intentions. Or perhaps adults generally — and I include here parents, teachers, ministers, deans and psychotherapists — have too frequently become predictable or transparent in their dealings with young people. High school students now portray with ease the "shrink scene." They anticipate with frightening accuracy the words and moods of churlish school administrators. A fifteen-year-old Negro boy told me that he could not get help from his school guidance counselor: "I wouldn't say this to his face, but he doesn't like Negroes. He may not even know this, but we know it." I spoke to the counselor in question. Not only had the student correctly interpreted the man's attitude; his impersonation of the man's behavior, right down to the speech patterns, was perfect.

All of this suggests to me that the cat of the authority relationship is out of the bag. The young understand and appreciate more of adult motivations and, significantly, the sociological rationalizations for so-called adult action in authority contexts. While they may protest against school principals and programs, the young will also confess a sympathy for their elders' plight of being trapped in the policies of some greater bureaucratic establishment, the "system." Yet they can recognize what they call a "sell-out" or "game player" a mile away, and a heady college freshman, if the matter concerns him at all, can learn to differentiate between the "authentic" liberal and the "institutional" brand from the last row of a lecture hall. Their language simplifications like "smarts," "head," "cool," "cop-out," are illustrations of an almost social-scientific terminology, and, more significantly, they function in reducing complex action patterns to levels succinct and manageable, at least for them. Their language shows, moreover, the swiftness and clarity with which they can first interpret and then act upon personal and institutional demands. (Many students recognize that their parents' social class is still the best predictor of their own school success, and that the poor and particularly the poor blacks cannot hope to compete even with the omnipresent mediocrity found among the "advantaged." Hence, while their understanding of local school competition and the mobility channels school generally offers may be profoundly true or totally incorrect, greater society seems to become more and more disillusioning and uninspiring.)

Perhaps the best illustration of language reflecting social sophistication and the apparent translucency of social reality is the expression "psyche out." A college junior assured me: "It's so easy to know what a teacher wants, or what he'll ask on a test. They never change. Give 'em what they want. You make them happy and you win." Even modest Phi Beta Kappa students claim they have "psyched out" their teachers and their college programs and have emerged superior merely because they were the better game players. The fact remains that to "psyche out" something or someone is to stay one slender step ahead even of expectation. It seems to be the ability to perceive the expression on the face of the future.

While it is progressively more difficult for young people to be duped by authority figures, it is as easy as it always has been to be damaged by them, a result so common when the superordinate, the elder, the parent, the teacher wants to equalize and make perfectly equitable what might better remain as an asymmetric proposition and relationship. Again, asymmetry refers to relationships wherein the commodities exchanged are of unequal and therefore incomparable content; hence the behavior of one person is not a call or demand for the identical behavior in the other. In its most fundamental form, asymmetry describes relationships in which one of the members represents unquestioned authority in a particular context, and thus it refers to interactions engaging parents with children, teachers with students, doctors with patients.

Several years ago, while leading what some of us call a self-analytic group, something not unlike the popular T-group, I was invited to a party given by the members of this group. As it was early in their history, it seemed reasonable to them that an informal evening together might loosen up and simplify all relationships. I was sorely tempted to go, but a wiser man suggested that I not. The asymmetry, he urged, ultimately must be preserved by the person holding authority. I may have lost something by finally declining, but I probably protected a valuable tension in the leader-member relationship, a tension which added to the learning and enhanced the members' chances to attain a sense of autonomy in the group. The symbolic nature of my refusal, moreover, re-affirmed the asymmetry, or inequality, which some of us working in groups feel is essential, and which members in their way often confess is preferred, especially during the early hours of the group's evolution. The leader (or father) must in some sense forever remain the leader, and while this angers many, particularly those in groups, kindness, gentleness and care are in no way automatically precluded by such a philosophy and by the strategy which derives from it.

More recently, members of a self-analytic group observed their leader's participation in a political demonstration. At the following meeting they spoke of him with a newly discovered reverence. How good that he shares the same values and that he exhibits the courage to speak out against administrations, local and national. But they spoke, too, of a disgust for their mothers wearing mini-skirts and for parents generally who act like kids. Anna, a mature young woman, told of a feeling of actual nausea that came over her when her roommate's mother discussed the college courses she, the mother, was attending. Upon returning to her dormitory, Anna made a long-distance phone call home and luxuriated in the relief that her own mother still was pursuing what she called "mother-type" activities: luncheons, museum visits, and food budgeting.

The ambivalence is evident. Young people want to attack authority and I suppose this is probably the way it must be, and always has been. But in matters of human dealings, although not in issues of strict ideology, authority is not to "come down" to the child's level, as parents once so perceptively felt it necessary to kneel down, if only to attain a spatial equality between the generations. Authority is not to give in; it is to remain firm in its commitment to preserve, among other things, that essential asymmetry and the corresponding indelible generational separation, even if this means being seen as a "square" or "straight-arrow." This last statement, however, must not be construed as my suggesting that only authoritarian authority is functional or practical or healthful. This is not what I have in mind.

When a small child orders his parents out of his bedroom, he necessarily fears the enormity of the act. So, in a tearful rage, he can only pray that the parents will go no farther than the living room. Similarly, when members express the intense desire to kick out the leader of self-analytic groups (in symbolic reenactment of the primal horde story, perhaps), invariably they want to know if, should they be successful, he would really go, and if he would return.

There is, then, a primitive core that develops out of interactions with parents, a core that pleads for the overthrow of authority. Yet there is also a hope that one will be unable to do just this. There is a hope, in other words, that the superordinate's strength will resist any attempts to be overthrown. This notion, of course, is paramount in Freud's explication of the Oedipal relationship. Parents simply cannot break down or retreat. They must prevail, and no one wants this more than the child himself. In terms of this infantile core that stays with us, parents are perfect, without problems, immortal. Relationships with them, therefore, preclude both equality and peership. A college student said it this way: "No matter what I do in the face of authority, I end up a child. It happens even when I don't know the authority. Are we forever children to older or more powerful persons?"

When children are born a series of events almost ceremonial in nature takes place, whenever possible, in which the mother's mother lives with her daughter for the first weeks of the newborn's life. Though serving a highly functional purpose, this ceremony tends to reinforce, at more latent levels, the new mother's bond with her own mother. Thus in no way does the arrival of the infant place the mother and grandmother on an equal plane. In a sense, the birth reaffirms the existence and concept of not only generations but history as well, for regardless of one's activities as a parent in one's most recent family, the family one has created, one forever remains a child in that other family, one's first family, the family into which one was born. And this causes more than a few problems.

For example, for children to outachieve their parents, an event not uncommon among college students (and let us not forget, as some would urge us to, that women are confronted with career aspirations and the ensuing competitions as much as men), means that they, the younger, must delicately initiate revisions in parental relationships so that the older generation will not interpret the younger ones' accomplishments as indicators of their own dismal and unprogressing ineptitude. What an incredible task it is for these young and talented students to return during Christmas and summer vacations to the rooms and persons of their childhood; to return where all of us know we cannot again return, then to battle the very essence of what seems to be an unjust but still unstopping passage of time.

Why is it in these times that each of us believes in the development, yes, even in the successes of our surging expectations, but sees only aging in our parents? Perhaps the eternal danger of the immediate future is that while it guarantees reports on the outcome of our most present investments, it brings first our parents and then us closer to some inexplicable end. But for the handful of "right nows" that constitute our involvement with the present, our youthful preoccupations make only our own movement in the life space visible. All the rest, parents and teachers included, remain unchanged, timeless: "It's like they've all stood still. They bring me back to my childhood 'hang-ups.' They know I've grown up, they know I'm at college; but they're used to me as I was when I was last there."

These last expressions and sensations are so clearly not the sensations of regression. Although we all have fought back urges to feel once more, for even a bittersweet interval, the winds of childhood, returning or wishing to return must not be mistaken for regressing. On the contrary, returning is often resuming. This is what is meant by bringing one back to childhood "hang-ups." It seems like regression, for only in our direct involvements with our family does "family time" again move ahead. In our separations from a family, that certain time stops, and the stillness augurs death. But the student returns and the time of the family altogether jolts forward again, alive, just as the family itself becomes vitally alive, although life now becomes a bit more cumbersome. The sensation is precisely the same as seeing someone we haven't seen in years. Almost at once we pick up our conversation exactly as it was at the moment of our separation. Now, because both of us have experienced so much in the interim, we cannot really fill in the spaces, and so we are obliged to disregard the interim and the maturation and change it obviously contains and seek a resumption of those earlier days. Whereas we may feel that we are regressing, in fact we are following reality's dictates right down the line, and doing our level best to resume prior action. And while it is stupendously exhilarating in the first few minutes, or hours, or even days, it sometimes becomes dreadfully cumbersome and, even more, discouraging and unbearable. The time of separations may be that significant, for people once so closely knitted together may find that apart they drift in different directions toward different experiences.

The predicament confronting the child at these times is to help his parents resolve some of the problems that occur when the young outachieve their elders. Variations in accomplishment must be reconciled in ways that legitimately reinforce parents' ultimate authority and special superiority. Irrespective of attainments, son and daughter want to remain in the child's role, at least in this one context and at least in this one home. The parents know the child's task and, like the vaudeville joke, the child knows the parents know, and the parents know the child knows they know.

It is in interpersonal dilemmas and gestures of this sort, gestures made and carried out in such public yet at the same time secretive ways, that families reaffirm health. The gestures imply the mutual recognition and trust of which Erikson has so poetically and firmly spoken. By these gestures, the social and temporal gaps between people, even those who share a treasured intimacy, are preserved, sociologic and psychologic genes are somehow passed from one generation to the next, and one is, in Erikson's words, able "to see one's own life in continuous perspective both in retrospect and in prospect." [1] The division made first by time permits the evolution of the adult and sanctifies the appropriateness and truth of the confirmation and the Bar Mitzvah. For sociological reasons, the gap between the generations stays open. But it is all right because distance need not be construed as distrust, nor separateness as desertion.

There are no such gaps, presumably, in the family histories of those young people presented at the outset of this chapter. In their lives, sociology has been tricked, and time has been placed, as it were, behind itself. By being shoved into unbearable roles, these certain persons were asked to overlook generational intervals which must appear to them to be at least as long as eternity. As the parents despairingly sought to haul in the nets of time in order to make the space between the generations smaller and smaller, they thoughtlessly or impetuously or unwittingly coerced their children into caricatures of marriage counselor, therapist, and, worse, buddy. Jenny *is* the burdened parent; she is as herself, her own child. Her father's confession, the information, the content were all unwanted by her, absolutely and desperately unwanted. In what vessel does one possibly store such information? Time alone should have prevented such utterances, but a "proper sociology" would have guarded against such a "friendship."

In a highly speculative vein, the unquestioned obligation to live sanely through these provocative, seductive and terrifying engagements in which the generations are nakedly slammed together is perhaps the first exposure to what later on becomes the psychology of the drug experience and the basis or content of the drug reaction. The searching for advice, the confessions, and, importantly, the collision with revelations, are without doubt experiences to "blow one's mind." They are the inevitable contact of ageless and recurring dreams and unshakably psychotic moods. They remain almost as a cause of the cerebral explosion pre-LSD and speed. They are "freak-outs" par excellence, and grade school flirtations with insanity.

For two years I saw a girl who is now thirteen in a hospital therapy setting. Kathy's language and psychological test performance indicated a possible psychotic diagnosis. Her recurring dream and one which, truthfully, intrigued us both was of her in a forest being chased by a large bear. Up on its hind legs, it pursued her and quite regularly caught her. The dream had become so terrifying that Kathy had resorted to magical powers invoked through some ritualized bedtime behavior, just to prevent the bear from appearing. How terribly symbolic the content of this is: the personification of impulses at the same time sexual and aggressive. Yet, with more examination, how literal is the content. Kathy's father, an alcoholic for all of Kathy's life, returns home at night from work pitifully drunk and staggers toward her, his shirt off, the hair on his chest, his muscles and his skin exposed, with his smell, with his pants open. Pleading for sex at a locked bedroom door, he is continually rejected by his wife until he promises to "grow up and behave like a man." And so he falls on the sofa, and in the dim light, and with heavy breathing, he masturbates as a little girl watches, bewildered and horrified. Thus the dream evolves, appears and reappears, and never fails to produce an agonizing fright.

Like Kathy, too many children have been "freaked out" by some form or some speech of the family's drama. Now, the strategy of many of these children, although nascent and unconscious, is to get out of their homes, get out of their own lives and out of their minds. What a miracle it is that some do stay, conjuring up reasons for the necessity of their remaining close to suffering parents and a damaged family unit whose mechanism is shattered. But the muffled aggression in their renewed loyalty is unmistakable. The children and their parents are like the envied lovers in the old story who never stopped holding hands until just once, whereupon they beat each other to death. Holding on to a mother's skirt, after all, may be more than a wish to remain near and in touch. It may be playing the boxer who by staying in a clinch prevents himself and his opponent from manning battle stations at arm's length. The act of caring, as gracious and humane as it is, often masks a desire to destroy and cause pain.

When a thoughtless and angry Cambridge mayor's purge on young people led him to chastise "hippies" for having run away from home, I reacted by thinking that on the contrary maybe the parents ran away first, in some fashion, hence the children merely followed suit. Now, after examining life stories like those of Jenny, John and Will, I wonder whether, like the most domesticated of pets, some young people, "pre-hippies," ran away because their parents rushed them, frightened them, and got too close in an uncomfortable way too soon. I wonder whether it was the feeling of being emotionally crowded by their parents that caused them to "split." Or maybe it does in fact have to do with parental and school rejection or derogation, or the constant threat of parents getting a divorce. Maybe the rejection, the running away from children, is more powerful and disruptive than the running toward them. Still, even in unabandoned escape and angered protestation children may be responding to or fulfilling some communicated need or directive of an authority somewhere. Maybe outbursts of anger and "misbehavior" are the only things some parents and some teachers feel comfortable dealing with, as their response to them appears so clear-cut and reasonable. Perhaps they provoke the very outbursts they claim they are seeking to avoid in order to bring about these interactions. How curious the thought, therefore, that protest and escape by the young represent an obeisance of older people turned upside down.

Equally curious is the observation that the familiar need-to-forget-or-escape-from-it-all explanation of alcoholism returns in serious drug taking as a desire to repress. My friend Mickey is a handsome young high school drop-out with an exceptional literary talent. When Mickey was eleven, his parents fought so savagely that he would find his mother lying in pools of blood. Becoming the man of the family, Mickey would have to call for the ambulance, and days later, as it always turned out, after nursing his mother back to health, he would turn his attention to reuniting his parents. This very same pattern was repeated at least six different times in one year.

During one cryptic account of a drug experience, Mickey practically went into a swoon. Then he caught himself, along with the heels of another truth: "But when you come down, man, you come down hard, and that taking each moment one by one dissolves into that rotten other present, the one where you say, I gotta go back to my job. And you ask yourself, why do I do it, and you know, you gotta feel responsible. But it's O.K. because you think about the next high." I suggested to Mickey that coming down means having to think about tomorrow. "Wrong, man," he smiled, for he had one on the shrink. "It's the past; it's on your back like you know what! . . . You say why did it have to happen to me? Fuck tomorrow, baby. It's yesterday I've got to beat!"

In speaking with Mickey and young men like him, one senses an ironical and twisted searching for, most amazingly, what seems to be insanity. While the shocks of childhood were merely flirtations with craziness, by sixteen they have reappeared as an open willingness to consider steady dating with it. At first only a couple of times a week; later on, every day and every night, then all the time. The apparent psychotic quality or "way-out-ness" of the drugs is at once terrifying and exhilarating. The downs hurt but serve to affirm the lingering presence of sanity, or at least the ability to call upon it one more time. Then, if the user is sure it's still there, he goes back up on top all over again. Or so it seemed to me once.

Not ironically, the very same strategy of "blowing one's mind" is sometimes used as a way of keeping out of memory or consciousness the mind-blowing experiences which might have urged persons toward this intimacy with drugs in the first place. But just as drinking fails to induce forgetfulness, drugs seem to be failing many persons in their efforts to "repress" the past and keep it off their backs, or so say many students. If Timothy Leary is right, the next state may just be electronic brain stimulation, hence when pharmaceutical repression fails, attempts may be made to actively engage in a fantasy of total memory ablation. At that time, a metaphysical present will evolve, free of any recollections and expectations; free of all regrets and despair. At least some might wish this as they commence a new era of experimentation.

Failing to understand these complicated and gifted people, I often forget myself and remind them of their futures as adults and as parents. It's not that easy. For one thing, their very sense of future differs from mine. The option to "start again," moreover, as in marriage and career is highly problematic. Many fear they will repeat the desecrating scenes of their childhood: "I'll ruin my kid a helluva lot more than the drugs I take will"; "Are you kidding man, can you see me as a father? You gotta be nuts! And you a shrink!" "A freak kid's gotta better chance than I did!"

If starting again were possible, some, assuredly, would opt for total recommencement. Knowing full well that their parents never wanted them in the first place, some almost cannot go back far enough to reach a time when their own histories might have started off on good footing. Few admit it, however, for this would be to proclaim absolutely one's non-being. It would be to break the slim and delicate threads that now barely hold the generations pridefully together. Kathy told me that her mother was informed by doctors that she could have no more children after the birth of Kathy's nearest older sister. In fact, two more children were born. The mother admitted that she had not wanted either one. Her "not wanting" became the daughter's description of herself as the "unexpected surprise." Kathy and I knew that she understood the conditions of her origins and the facts of her life. Indeed, I felt that her rather tardy inability to comprehend human anatomy and how children are born might have symbolized an even more profound reluctance and self-protection, a very understandable self-protection to be sure.

But there is even more, for, regrettably, the concept of insanity pervades the worlds, however expansive, of many young people. What many want to know is utterly predictable: "Just tell me one thing man, am I crazy? I mean, you know, am I crazy?" The word "crazy" is ubiquitous. It has lost some of its primeval jolt, perhaps, but it holds on to an unmodifiable message. There is so much insanity in television scripts and movies and newspaper accounts. Insanity is even feared when one is witnessing the inexplicable behavior of those around us as they do nothing more than fight aggressively for social and private rights too long in coming. The blacks are called insane, the poor are insane, the "kids" for sure are insane. It it also feared when one is witnessing those well-meaning men who seek to control persons who protest. The cops and the National Guard and soldiers are insane. The young hear the President called mad and the war insane, and they puzzle over insanity's bewildering function in excusing murderers in jury trials. Partly because of this the young may even seek insanity as a way of getting out of the draft. Insanity or a belief in it seems to be able to immobilize some, liberate others. It's a natural resource to be harnessed.

In my day, not so long ago, a "joking" admonition for guaranteed military deferments was simply this: when the army doctor examines you, kiss him. Now it's insanity. Naturally, the worry exists for these young men that they might carry forever the brand of insanity on their sleeves just about where the private stripe might have gone; but still, to be crazy is to avoid military service. Like kissing the doc, it is also the ineluctable avoidance of maleness. An often cruel society rubs this in: a real man fights for his country. Ideologies and spirit react against this of course, but the doubt, however slight, stays. American socialization patterns, normally instituting strict sex role differentiations, take care of that. There will be a lingering doubt, although in much of their questioning and concern, perceptions and anguish the young find older persons who will support them. Many of the "knowing class," they come to learn, now prefer to think of "business as usual" as the real insane course, and jail as an undesirable but still honorable and healthy way out.

Earlier I spoke of a resistance to bearing children and the feeling that one could not successfully assume responsibilities of parenthood. In some cases it seems as though the diffidence some young people display in "going on" masks a wish to start anew. The present urge to keep the cycle from repeating and the intention to keep fresh life from beginning must be considered from the point of view of sexuality. Although the language remains unchanged, actions of "procuring" and "scoring" today refer to drugs. The prophylactic, its slick package dirtied by months in the seams of an old wallet, has been replaced by the nickel bag: "Always be prepared." A funny reversal, furthermore, concerns sex role functions in a new economic market, as girls now solicit funds to pay for their boyfriends' stuff. I was stopped by one of these girls in the street on a beautiful October afternoon: "Excuse me, sir," she began her proposal, "how about a quarter for a cup of God knows what?"

One cannot be certain of the sexual habits of the persons of whom I speak. But anyway, it's no one's business until they mention it. The subject, however, is close to the conversational surface. It is as intimate as it ever was, but seemingly beginning to be freed of its irrational ties to some mysterious and primordial secrecy. As with much of their behavior, many of the young merely make overt what their elders do covertly. In so doing, they seem much more honest and far less foolish. The conspicuous consumption of products and styles by other youngsters, however, is often little more than a mimicry of their parents.

Like Will, many young men on drugs confess their apprehensions about homosexuality. It is not simply that they fear their impulses. This pattern, ironically, seems to be more common among those actually engaged in heterosexual relationships. Instead, they tell of a lack of sexual impulses and a concern that perhaps hard drugs have destroyed the sex drive. Because of their sophistication, they comprehend the possibility that their activities generally could be interpreted as homosexual, but about this they manifest little panic. Some admit that they are able to "make it" with girls only when "high." They confess to fright, but it does not compare to the fear that they may be (going) crazy.

This is the supreme danger, as it suggests again, the complex reversal of not only competence in drug work and sex work but the associated interchange between the organs of sex and the "organ" of drugs, the mind. One almost wants to assert that a phallic phase of development has been temporarily supplanted or postponed by a "cephalic" phase. All life comes to be fixated in the mind, and Leary spoke for the generation at least once when he advertised that each brain cell is capable of brilliant and repeating orgasms. Whether scientific or metaphoric, Leary's words were not forgotten.

Is it then too farfetched to draw parallels, first between the act of getting high and sexual foreplay or the eventual sexual excitement; and next between the actual mind-blowing experience with its visions and thresholds of exhilaration and the orgasm in which the person is exquisitely primed by his own powers; and finally between the depressing down, the returning to time and reality, and the detumescence and resumption of normalcy and normal size? To be sure, the reasoning is dangerous in its analogical foundation, but the symbolic orgasm of the drug state as occult sex seems to have both homosexual and heterosexual aspects.

This then leaves one issue, namely, going mad from a drug experience, the "freak-out," the ultimate reward, the ultimate punishment. It builds to total destruction, at once implosion and explosion. In students' own words, it is brain damage and disintegration. Simultaneously, it is conception, pregnancy, childbirth, castration and death. Some continue to believe that from the womb of the mind a new child, a freak child is born, and it all is supposed to happen in the longest-shortest instant that time ever knew.

By some students' own admission, the freak-out is also a premeditated "cop-out." To take drugs is to willingly step out of the natural flow for a moment or two. In a way, it has much of the quality of living with a sexual partner unmarried, for there is an anticipation of an end coupled with the preparation for some later recourse. Demanding no commitment, or less than common commitment, drug taking is an out permitting the luxury of retiring as undefeated champion. No one can fault the last-minute term paper writer or the patient hospitalized with an overdose or from a bad trip. Both have their excuses and reasons for being remiss and, like little children, excuses for being out of school. Yet both wonder, presumably, about what their competence might be like void of recourse, void of excuse. Both wonder, too, about the lack of preparations for an equivocal future shrieking death, and the minimal confidence already displayed in present endeavor.

Depicted in so many of these notions is the mass communicative society in which we survive. The accomplishments by so many are so great; the knowledge and awareness so swift in arrival and so deep in meaning that in a way we leave the young no excuse for failure other than severe illness and total collapse. Adlai Stevenson once confessed relief that career decisions were behind him. It *is* hard to be young today as so many good people are already so advanced in practically any area that one might choose for himself. And so many new areas have already become crusty. Perhaps this is a reason for so many "dropping out," if only temporarily.

In sexual relations, the excuse that probably maintained the sanity of frightened generations of men no longer exists. Girls have "the pill" or other devices, and aggressive action now swings both ways. Students offer apologies for not smoking pot and agonize over an inability to get excited, much less involved, in political enterprises. To be straight is to be square, and like it or not the straight become defensive and tempted.

Our televised and instant replay society also allows few secrets. We see the war; we see men murdered; and we become frustrated when we cannot discover the exact frame on which is recorded a President's death. And as if that were not enough, our newspapers pry and reveal, our movies reveal, and so too, apparently, do some parents. While many children fantasize that the secrets they safeguard for their parents preserve some mysterious family integrity, others are, in fact, maintaining this very integrity by keeping all family secrets safe and locked away. It is these persons who sometimes bite a quivering lip in fear that exposure of their treasured secrets will cause their families to unravel.

In truth, there *are* young people responsible for the knit of adult involvements, a knit that sometimes fails to include even themselves. In the long run, Jenny's silence helped to keep her parents together, but she has paid a price. It has taken one great effort! For her, living moment to moment is not the medium in which experience fits. Living through the day is both the medium and the experiential essence. Day work matters. One must keep the glue of sanity from softening and walk on, no matter what.

So one keeps in his head or in his diary what he heard Daddy say to that woman, or what he saw Mommy doing in the restaurant, or what he heard Mommy and Daddy say to each other on those nights when their anger exploded so suddenly that no one took the precaution of closing the bedroom door, as if that really made a difference. This is the stuff that stays inside, sealed over until it pops out in a doctor's office, in a creative writing course short story, or in those first poems written for no reason during a Thanksgiving or Christmas vacation.

Then, while all of this goes on, performance demands shriek for attention. One must compete and succeed often enough, make it on one's own, and react to the war and the fact that he or a boy friend will soon be drafted and, not so unlikely, killed! One must be good in school, good at home, good at sports, good at pot and good in bed. Life becomes unmanageably meaningful. It is enough to make one (want to) go insane.

Most make it through, however, even with the knowledge that their culture warns of belligerent Chinese, overkill, communism, and an equivocal future. One cannot know when the next and final war will come, nor when past experience with drugs will suddenly reerupt in the form of a grotesque child or one's own psychotic demise. But most make it through, and ten years later they look in disbelief on their own pasts. "I couldn't do it again," they often will say.

Unmistakably near, death becomes a real reality. Less fuzzy than ever before, its shape and sound hover about self-analytic groups, rap sessions and coffee dates. Damn the future and the inevitable! It was better in the 'Thirties when gravelly throated heroes sang into megaphones. It was better, too, in the last century when men wore frock coats, beards and long hair. It was better and easier because it was the past, and perception of the completed proves the validity of survival, if not of achievement. At very least, the past means having gotten this far. It also means the seat of much of the trouble that many just cannot shake.

Some young people reveal a peculiar attitude about the past. It is not merely that chunk of time that was, but the series of events that once were and yet somehow continue to remain as a lining to the present. Not exactly recalled or retrieved, the past has become the stuff of moment-to-moment encounter and the routine of day work. The past has not yet become past, therefore, in the sense of being over, because its foundation, like a child's body, remains soft and unfinished. There are no completions yet, no triumphs, no guaranteed deferrals or subsistence.

To be sure, youth cries. Sometimes it is out of sadness for its own past, sometimes in reaction to the two societies, the one encountered and the one held as prospect. Some observers insist that more often than not in much of its activities youth cries to be heard, or for help. It is too difficult to know for certain whether this is true, particularly because out of the concern, guilt and solipsism of an older generation grows the presumptuous pride that youth, when it speaks, must always address itself to parents and elders, or that speaking means crying or begging. This simply is not true. Attacks on society are not merely hatreds of parents which have gone productively astray. To the contrary, it often seems as though the questionings of those who *precede* us are simultaneously pleas for recognition and directives intended to justify prior decisions and behavior. Adults want a bit of attention and do a little crying and begging themselves.

No one as yet has studied the notes written by parents to their runaway children in New York's East Village or San Francisco's Haight Ashbury district, a district which seems to have faded. These pitiful missives document so well the lack of generational space and the confession of failure in parenthood and adulthood. They could almost be the letters of children who, wishing to come home, promise never again to misbehave. If they did not cause guilt or confusion in the recipients, the young people who screen them would have little need to prevent them from reaching the runaway children. (Those people, young and old, whose self-appointed life task it is to maintain the separation and lack of communication between parent and child must fear, I would think, the fruits of love's temptation, the very philosophy they often profess or at least once professed. Moreover, they are reminiscent of professional mourners who continually remind the congregation or family of the recent loss by crying and collapsing when others attain momentary composure. It is almost as though reconciliation, equanimity and peace are destructive to their sense of a social order.)

The "Come back home — all is forgiven" notes stand as a testament to what must be seen by the young as a crumbling structure or a tragic reversal of intentionality and interpersonal competence. They reflect adults' pleas for help and forgiveness, and as such they represent a far worse social fact than "hippie" farm colonies or pot parties. The notes only document what the poets know so well: of all rewards, youth is a supreme ideal. The old might wish to be young, but the young seem happy exactly where they are. This, too, is an asymmetry.

Few parents are able to accept the passing of adolescence, especially when their own children dramatize more vibrantly than ever the former gratifications and projected incompleteness of their own lives. It is inconceivable to think that young people have ever been simultaneously idolized and despised, worshiped and envied as they are presently. But without doubt, the problem of age grading is now of paramount significance in the United States. It is one of *the* dimensions: whether it is good or bad, the old are preoccupied with the young, and the young so often seem preoccupied with themselves. Another asymmetry.

The period, moreover, has become so erotic. Previously, when the activities of the young were more secretive, adults were compelled to deal with their own imaginations. Now, when sexuality in particular screams at us from advertisements, fashions, television, movies and magazines, it becomes increasingly difficult to decline youth's unintended invitation and accept the process and reality of aging. We almost forget that many of these invitations in fact do not originate among the young. Nonetheless, adults must work hard to avoid the eternal seductions of the young, for these affairs simply do not work out. Time inevitably chaperones such liaisons, and the primordial strain which comes about through the separation of generations never does permit a successful consummation of these two hearts, the young and the old.

The seduction does not stop with parents, however, for the succulence of youth is dreamed of each day by teachers, counselors, therapists, ministers, etcetera. A most dangerous tack for any of these persons is to be uncritically won over by youth's stated demands and ideologies or interpretations of them. Let me give an example of this point.

We are emerging from an unfortunate era during which time psychotherapy was viewed as either panacea or black magic. Psychotherapists themselves finally have undertaken critical self-examination, and for the most part attacks on theory and procedure have resulted in clarifying statements for the practitioners and their clients. Still, there are some critics who expend a suspiciously great amount of energy communicating to youth the evils of psychotherapy and, even more, the harmfulness of any benign adult interventions. By acting this way, these people purportedly signify their "stand with youth," a stand normally introduced by some phrase which seems an apologia, but which in truth is more of a boastful pledge to be like the young, or even younger.

Frequently these critics demonstrate a striking accuracy in their realignment of youth's goals, ambitions and philosophies. Just as often their arguments are indecorous and evil. Many young people in fact do find illness in themselves and do seek help. They despise the proverbial "shrink scene" and rightly so, but in their quest of a "hip shrink" they wish for a modification or, better, modernization of the psychotherapeutic relationship, but not its annihilation. They know it is no panacea, but in anticipation they feel it has worth and are willing to try. And that's a lot. The best adults may be able to do, therefore, is experiment with the helping apparatus and not discourage the trying.

So those of us who aspire to speak for or understand youth must be aware of the seductive nature of our interests so that we will not reach the point where speaking for youth means no longer needing to listen to it. Genuine representation, after all, does not require reliving; it requires recalling.

One final point regards the heightened sophistication of the young, their eagerness to speak, their facile access to recesses of an experienced childhood, and their poignant observations of adulthood.

While longevity statistics indicate that with each generation human beings may expect to live longer, much of society, as Erikson points out, demands that individuals be allotted less time for youth. Earnest young protoprofessionals, especially, uphold this ethic. Scattered not so infrequently about, however, are those whose parents have denied them even this minuscule tenure. For Jenny, the kid stuff ended at fourteen and was succeeded by what appears to her as an anachronistic awareness. For most, the awareness is simply a function of a precocious curiosity and creative need to experience. For the ones knowingly in trouble, the most immediate and pressing action resembles an attempt to complete some poorly understood mission started long ago by someone else.

That time repeats itself is but a comforting saying. The concept of a family cycle, moreover, is misleading, as it tends to slur over the individual cycles unwinding at various tempi within it. Individual cycles never repeat themselves, for in progressing or carrying on in any guise, "healthy" or "sick," the young, as ingenious as they often are, do little more than obey the wishes of others and the demands that time imposes. Typically, the directions given by those who were here before us are to wait patiently and not walk so fast.

Sociologists have written that a major function of social structures is to direct its members to appropriate goal states, means of attaining them, and attitudes that are best assumed in evaluating goals and means. The desire to become a doctor or lawyer, indeed the need to achieve, does not come from out of the blue. It is learned. So too is the desire to rebel, make love, take drugs, escape and even "freak out." In their way, all of these actions are creative because they develop out of social forms of, as well as private needs for, expression. But they have not "sprung up"; like instincts, they have evolved.

For many today, the evolution is not satisfying, and the internal excursions and elaborations have become (and probably started out as), in David Riesman's terms, "other-directed" movements. Knowing exactly this, many young persons continue, nonetheless, in their other-directed patterns, and thereby show themselves most willing to listen outward and upward. And considering much of our adult behavior, this fact is remarkable.

36

DALE B. HARRIS
Pennsylvania State University
University Park, Penna.

Work and the adolescent transition to maturity

FREEDMAN (5) HAS INSISTED that "the successful transition from school to work is central to the process of coming of age in America." Certainly, the 1950's saw a marked shift from social concern with exploitative child labor to social concern with the developmentally constructive aspects of work experience for youth. Increasing proportions of young people —not merely increasing numbers, but increasing proportions—are at gainful work, except during occasional recessions in the nation's business. The hypothesis here is that part-time, casual work experience can be valuable in the socialization of adolescents. In exploring this contention, we shall not be occupied with the social or educational significance of vocational guidance, vocational training, or the need to make career choices. Rather, we shall focus on the young teenager's introduction to the world of work and its psychological significance.

Attitudes Toward Work

The work of several decennial White House Conferences on children has been well done. We have been thoroughly imbued with the notion that children and youth should not be at work, but should be in school. Even in the past decade, one not infrequently met in welfare and labor circles the notion that work is inherently bad for children and that a signal victory is won when some part-time work opportunity is closed to youth. In discussion after discussion, the emphasis has been on the physical, mental, and social hazards of employment to young people, very seldom (until recently) on the possible socializing, training, or educational features of work experience for them.

This emphasis may only be part of the large assumption that work is dull and debilitating, tolerable only because it is necessary to buy leisure and fun, which are what we really want. As David Riesman (12), William Whyte, Jr. (19), and others have observed, we seem to be reversing the older American ethos with respect to work, the concept of work as intrinsically good, virtuous, and satisfying. There are, of course, other factors involved in eliminating the employment of youth. There is, for example, the wish to eliminate a cheap labor group and to maintain high minimum wages, which have grown steadily as our social awareness has grown.

Yet in recent years we have heard another point of view. We have been warned that idleness in the 'teen years plays directly into the hands of juvenile delinquency. We have heard that the school drop-out problem (which persists in the face of determined efforts to keep all youth in school) indicates that the school and its program are not meeting the needs of a large number of adolescents. Nor will this condition grow less as we return to a more academic empha-

From *Teachers College Record*, November 1961. Reprinted by permission of the author and *Teachers College Record*.

sis in high schools.

The fact is that the proportion of young people enrolled in high school—and in the last few years their absolute numbers as well—has increased for two decades. Yet in spite of this increase, almost half the youth between the ages of 14 and 17 report some paid employment during the year. The *proportion* of this age group who are both enrolled in school and working has been steadily climbing for 15 years. This fact reflects a shift that arose in the necessities of World War II. It has been temporarily checked by short periods of economic recession, but the trend is clear and seems to be here to stay in spite of laws and court decisions increasingly restrictive to the employment of young people under 18. Adolescents *want* work, paid work. But it is well to remember that we are talking about part-time employment. A sizeable proportion of the under-18 youth who are not in school at all are in the ranks of the unemployed. One study (*13*) showed that those who quit school "to find work" actually took twice as long to start looking for it as those who completed school first!

It should be recognized that this discussion refers to the work experiences of all youth, not just the school-leavers. Indeed, school-leavers, as many studies show (*1, 3, 17*), do not have a hopeful future. More are unemployed than their classmates who finished high school. They earn less, hold lower status jobs and have a greater record of irregular employment. The inference in many studies of the early school-leaver is that remaining in school improves prospects for these youth. Those who leave school, however, are a selected group in other ways. They have a lower academic intelligence and earn poorer grades, the latter factor often being directly or indirectly the reason for early school leaving (*11*). Matching a group of early school-leavers with high school graduates in both intelligence and general socioeconomic status, the author (*8*) has shown that as early as the sixth grade, those destined to drop out early do significantly more poorly on a number of personality and social background indices.

While keeping these youth in school may possibly improve their employment prospects, they evidently do not constitute a significant pool of unrealized abilities of a very high order. Furthermore, with high schools tending toward more academic emphasis, this group is not likely to be better served or to diminish in size.

Adolescent Traits

Let us now turn to some characteristics of the adolescent period which seem to be quite characteristic of youth regardless of time and place. In the first place, adolescents are healthy in a physical sense, with a tremendous capacity for marshalling and expending energy. We may be socially concerned about the health of young people, but the fact remains that the years of early adolescence represent just about the healthiest of one's entire life in resistance to infectious disease and onset of various disabilities.

In the second place, normal healthy adolescents are, by adult standards, notably psychopathic, manic, and schizoid in their psychological makeup and behavior (*10*). A less dramatic statement is that in assent to statements of attitudes which notably characterize adults with psychopathic, manic, or schizoid disorders, the *average* American adolescent is surpassed only by 15% of the total adult population. Such findings suggest psychologically that adolescents are excitable, show a high level of activity and drive, have little regard for official social norms, are iconoclastic, and exhibit marked contrasts and inconsistencies in attitudes and behavior. Anyone who has ever lived with a normal teenager needs not be told this! Coupled with the high energy output of the period, this personality structure gives rise to the behavior which distresses adults so much, creates a so-called youth problem, and, indeed, seems to accentuate the delinquency rate, because this rate falls sharply in age groups past 20 years.

In the third place, adolescents seek to establish roles. The word "quest" has always seemed appropriate to characterize their restless, searching behavior. The adolescent needs to find a sense of identity and a sense of personal worth. He needs to clarify his sex role as a developing young man or young woman. He needs to find social skill, a sense of assurance, and a place with his peers. His desire to conform to the peer standard has been so often remarked that we need not mention it. And, finally, he searches for ways to realize his independence socially, emotionally, financially, and intellectually, changing from his childhood dependency on adults.

All these characteristics occur in persons who live in a very rapidly changing social scene. Mature, stable adults are often bewildered by the loss of familiar behavior norms and landmarks. Institutional and ritual supports to the development of roles which existed in the rural village and extended family have disappeared. In mid-century American society, there is a relative lack of restraint on and supervision of youth's behavior. And we must admit in our culture to a considerable exacerbation of two very powerful drives—the drive toward aggression and the drive toward sexual expression.

Given the characteristics of good health and an amazing capacity for energy mobilization; given in the average youth qualities which in adult life are identified as bizarre or deviant; given a driving need to establish mature roles—place these givens in a rapidly changing social context where the clear guide lines of a stable culture seem to be missing, and it is not surprising that we identify youth problems!

It seems probable that serious study and exploration of the significance of work can assist in the solution of some of these problems. This hypothesis cannot be defended directly by data, either observational or experimental. Rather, one must induce from indirect evidence and deduce from the logic of dynamic psychological theory to develop the case. Although the argument rests on no stronger grounds than these, it may serve to provoke thought and investigation.

Responsibility and Role

We may now turn to a discussion of the elements of a theory of adolescent work experience. First of these is the significance of responsibility. Responsibility, by which we mean dependability and accountability as well as the production of high-quality work, is much valued in society. Industry, business, and the professions all want a steady person—a dependable, self-starting, stable functioning, productive individual. Yet a common complaint about adolescents is their irresponsibility. Most of the problems adults have with youth arise in trying to inculcate dependable, conforming behavior to adult norms or from the failure of youth to realize such behavior.

Research on responsibility (*6, 7*) indicates that although its roots seem to be sowed early and crucially in parent attitudes and family relationships, this trait increases with age. The learning process is certainly not completed at adolescence, and it seems clear that the learning of responsibility is rooted in the significant interpersonal relations of a responsible adult with the child and youth. One of the few positive findings of these studies indicated that responsibility in children is associated with certain evidences of social responsibility in their parents. It does not seem to be at all associated with particular training or child-rearing techniques that are often thought to inculcate this quality.

Super's (*14*) study of vocational maturity in ninth grade boys formulated an index of Independence of Work Experience, based on evidence that a boy has obtained paid work on his own initiative, worked for non-family persons, and worked in situations in which he was "on his own," relatively free of supervision. Indications that the work required responsibility for materials, for the satisfaction of persons, and for handling money also enter the index. Super found his measure internally consistent and reliably evaluated, but it did not relate significantly to other measures of vocational maturity, although it did correlate with a measure of Acceptance of Responsibility. Super did not use his index as a *predictor* variable, however, which is the significance the present writer would put upon it. Nor would the variance in the index possible with ninth grade boys be as great as that possible with fifteen- or sixteen-year-olds eligible for working permits. Hence, the index may be more functional above the ninth grade.

The incomplete development of responsibility in the 'teen years suggests, then, that if work experience can be shown to evoke stable and efficient work habits and dependable and accountable attitudes toward work, such experience would be very important. Studies indicate that children more willingly perform around the house those tasks in which they are more nearly equal to adults. They assume readily serious and demanding assignments in contrast to trivial chores which make little demand on ability or interest. Significant work experience should therefore be serious and place performance demands on the person. Super's finding of a correlation between Independence of Work Experience and Acceptance of Responsibility should be followed up in further studies.

A second element of importance is the significance of occupation or work role. Society generally views work role in terms of status or prestige. Jobs are graded along a continuum of "respectability" and give status to the persons holding them. Youth, however, quite generally view occupation in terms of self-development and independence. From the studies of adolescents conducted by both the Boy and Girl Scouts (*15, 16*), it appears that young people regard the post-high-school years in terms of further education, work, or marriage, and interpret all these in relation to self-development and self-realization. Youth, then, perceive the work role in terms of the independence it will give them and the chance to realize abilities and to enhance the self. Hence any work *often* appears desirable and is eagerly sought. Industrial psychologists have noted a pronounced drop in job satisfaction indices as characteristic of workers in their early twenties. It is quite possible that this phenomenon signals a shift from an adolescent to a more mature expectation from the job.

There is a third aspect to the work role in the adolescent years. About half of mid-teenagers work for pay during the school year and about three-fourths work for pay during the summer months. The bulk of this work is done for "strangers," persons outside the immediate family. Indeed, it seems that young people *prefer* to work for pay outside the home. This is not difficult to understand. A child recognizes that though he may be valued by his parents, they *must* support him. Both legally and morally, it is their obligation. To be able to do something someone else will pay for is tangible evidence of worth on a different basis. This realization is by no means unimportant to the adolescent struggling to realize his self-image and a sense of identity while at the same time weaning himself from dependency on his parents.

Moreover, in paying a wage, the employer represents society in its more objective relationships to the teenager. This may be useful in developing a sense of accountability in young people. A child may be expected by family tradition to participate in household chores. Whether they are done well or poorly, willingly or grudgingly, becomes as much a matter of the parents' skill or the amount of irritation they can induce in the child as of the youngster's pride or sense of responsibility. Neither the parent nor the immature child can voluntarily give up the other. In the employer-employee relationship, there is a degree of freedom or option which seems desirable and important for young people to experience and to live with successfully for a time.

Money and Attitudes

There is, of course, also the point that money is important to teenagers. It gives direct access to many social experiences. Studies show that both high school and college students today have much more money for entertainment than similar age groups less than a generation ago. In one study (*18*), this difference is estimated to be in the neighborhood of around 1,000% more cash available for entertainment to post-World War II college students in contrast to pre-World War II students. This is a far greater increase than can be accounted for in terms of a general inflation or a change in general standards of living. It represents a very real change in circumstances for the contemporary adolescent generation. Yet money continues at the head of lists of problems claimed by youth(9)!

The fourth element in a theory of adolescent work experience is the significance of attitudes, both self-attitudes and work attitudes. Erickson (4) has, perhaps more forcefully than any other, emphasized the teen years as the period of achievement of a sense of identity. The sense of self-worth has been held to be the core of all human values. The ego, as a psychological construct, is important in many theories of personality development. If adolescence truly is a time of achievement of this sense of identity, the age is of peculiar importance in the development of personality. We have seen that being able to do work considered payworthy by an unrelated, objective adult can be important in confirming a child's sense of worth, no matter how significant his parental relationships may have been originally in establishing his self-esteem. Simply being aware that one is learning significant "tricks of the trade" can also be an important reinforcer of this attitude. Discovering that he can make suggestions on the job which others accept is a tremendously reinforcing experience.

Much has been made of early work experience as occasioning floundering and failure. Such experiences need not be devastating to the self-image, provided the individual understands them as exploratory and as necessary in developing the best use of his abilities. Too much floundering and too much failure, as clinicians have amply demonstrated, can have a serious, negative effect on the self, despite firmly laid foundations in childhood experiences of acceptance. Fortunate is the young person who is able to get work experience which reveals his developing abilities adequately, thus providing positive rather than negative reinforcement for his sense of identity.

Work attitudes are also important. While much of the adolescent's adjustment to authority is in relation to parents and teachers, the primary authority symbols, we have seen that the employer also is a significant representative of authority. Industrial and personnel psychologists frequently remind us that two important aspects of work adjustment are the adjustment to authority and adjustment to co-workers. More individuals fail on the job for these reasons than for a lack of specific skills. It has been said that industry interprets docility in the worker as "responsibility." However that may be, the young worker must somehow learn to be willing to take directions and to progress slowly toward goals—that is, to serve his apprenticeship or to "win his spurs." Studies show that the younger worker is often more dissatisfied on the job than the older worker. Somehow, the young worker must learn willingness to go through the training program, to bring his skills to the level of the reward he hopes for. This is not easy when work operations are simple, dull, and intrinsically uninteresting.

Finally, in the formation of work attitudes, the young worker's relationship to a responsible adult is of considerable importance. As jobs become more fragmented and specialized and require less craft or skill, it is harder to locate appropriate work experience which reinforces responsible work attitudes. The teenager who can work as a part-time helper to the craftsman is in a much better position to learn attitudes than the youth who pushes a broom or the errand boy in the large office. The boy who helps load cars at the super-market gets much more direct personal reinforcement than the one who fills shelves in the stock room. In every case, contact with adult models seems to be helpful to the formation of the desired attitudes, and such contact is increasingly hard to get. Both business and industry and organized labor often seek to avoid bothering with the teenager. He is an uneconomical producer, on the one hand, and too economical on the other!

Implications

To implement the point of view affirmed by this paper is not easy for a number of reasons, not least of which is the great dearth of research on work experiences of youth, work attitudes of youth, evaluations of training experiences, and the like. But at the present time two or three general patterns of pre-vocational work experience are available to teenage youth. One of these, in some respects the most hopeful in theory and with definite pre-vocational significance, has proved rather disappointing in practice. This is the work-experience program in the high school, where part-time paid employment is offered under the supervision of the school and related to courses in the regular school curriculum. Only a very small number of young people are reached by this type of program, and there has been a general resistance to developing this program both by industry and labor.

Schoolmen find real problems in the adequate administration and supervision of these programs. They are costly. There is some evidence from one study (2) that such programs are more helpful to individuals lower rather than higher in ability and scholarship. Thus, this program may have some potential value for the school dropout. The effort has not caught on widely, however, and one of the significant challenges to educators is to do something about the development of work attitudes in youth who more and more must stay in school.

Another pattern has been to encourage "job-exchanges" for summer employment. Newspapers, PTA, service clubs, and other agencies sometimes sponsor campaigns to list young people seeking work, or to sponsor job-finding campaigns. The National Committee on the Employment of Youth (NCEY), a division of the National Child Labor Committee, has done pioneer work in this field, stimulating local agencies to undertake projects in specific communities. This is a recent and hopeful development, yet too young to appraise adequately.

Volunteer work programs are becoming increasingly popular with youth-serving groups having character-building or international relations goals. The pattern was set early by the American Friends Service Committee and has been adopted rather widely by church groups. And now we hear of a Peace Corps. These enterprises have been and promise to continue to be very highly selective, taking the youth with the greatest early de-velopment of the qualities they seek to foster. On a lesser scale, and perhaps more meaningful to the average youth, are volunteer service jobs in school, civic or citizenship education assignments in the community or projects in settlement houses, summer playgrounds, and the like. Most of these tasks are unpaid, a drawback from the point of view of the objectives urged here as developmentally important.

Outstandingly successful has been a program of paid summer work combined with recreation in the city parks of Berkeley, California, where particular attention is paid to youth needing both money and group experiences.

In summary, we have argued for the significance to youth of part-time job experience, quite apart from vocational guidance or training objectives. We have tried to show that such experiences are actively sought by youth, are often quite difficult to find, and that providing them as a significant part of the transition to adult status constitutes a real challenge to education and the community.

REFERENCES

1. Adams, L. P. When young people leave school. *I.L.R. Research*, 1958, *4*, 9-11.
2. Brown, W. C. Diversified occupations of graduates of 1952. *Univer. of Missouri Bull.* Education Series, No. 60, 1959.
3. Dillon, H. J. *Early school leavers*. New York: National Child Labor Committee, 1949.
4. Erickson, E. H. *Childhood and society*. New York: Norton, 1950.
5. Freedman, Marcia. Work and the adolescent. In *Children and youth in the 1960's*. Washington, D. C.: White House Conference, 1960. Pp. 137-153.
6. Harris, D. B., et al. The measurement of responsibility in children. *Child Developm.*, 1954, *25*, 21-28.
7. Harris, D. B., et al. The relation of children's home duties to an attitude of responsibility. *Child Developm.*, 1954, *25*, 29-33.
8. Harris, D. B. Psychological and social characteristics of a group of school drop-outs, *Child Developm.*, 1960, *31*, 230-233.
9. Harris, D. B. Life problems and interests of adolescents. *School Rev.*, 1959, *67*, 335-343.
10. Hathaway, S. R., & Monachesi, E. D. *Analyzing and predicting juvenile delinquency with the MMPI*. Minneapolis: Univer. Minnesota Press, 1953.
11. Kitch, D. E. Does retardation cause dropouts? *Calif. J. Elem. Educ.*, 1952, *21*, 25-28.

12. Riesman, D., Glazer, N., & Denny, R. *The lonely crowd*. New Haven: Yale Univer. Press, 1953.

13. Riches, Naomi. Education and work of young people in a labor surplus area. *US Month. Labor Rev.*, 1957, *80*, 1457-1463.

14. Super, D. E., & Overstreet, Phoebe L. *The vocational maturity of ninth grade boys*. New York: Bureau of Pub., Teachers College, Columbia University, 1960.

15. Survey Research Center. *Adolescent girls*. New York: Girl Scouts of America, 1957.

16. Survey Research Center. *A study of adolescent boys*. New Brunswick, N. J.: Boy Scouts of America, 1955.

17. U. S. Dept. of Labor. *Hunting a career*. Washington, D. C.: Govt. Print. Off., 1949.

18. Williamson, E. G., Layton, W. L., & Snoke, M. L. *A study of participation in college activities*. Minneapolis: Univer. Minnesota Press, 1954.

19. Whyte, Jr., W. H. *The organization man*. New York: Doubleday, 1956.

37

"The Kids & the Cults"

James S. Gordon

Photograph by Virginia Hamilton

During the past 18 months I have been a participant-observer in meetings of the new religious cults of the 1970s. I have attended a weekend workshop of the Unification Church, visited and eaten in the Ashrams, centers, coffee-houses and communes of the Krishna Consciousness movement, the Divine Light Mission, the Love Family and half a dozen other, smaller groups. I have met with young people in these groups, with parents who are deeply troubled by their children's membership and with parents who are pleased by the changes they have seen in their children—their renewed sense of responsibility and their godliness. I have talked with young people who are very relieved to be out of these groups, and with young people who are puzzled or angered by their parents' attempts to coerce or cajole them into leaving. I have studied the theologies that these cults have constructed or adapted and considered the criticisms that have been leveled at them and at the cults themselves.

HISTORICAL BACKGROUND

Many anthropologists and historians maintain that religious cults have always proliferated in times of social and cultural crisis, and in eras when the possibility of local or global destruction is or seems very real. It seems to me that the hundreds of thousands or, depending on who is estimating their numbers and what groups

Reprinted from *Children Today* Magazine, July/August 1977. U.S. Department of Health, Education and Welfare.

James S. Gordon, M.D., is a research psychiatrist and consultant on alternative forms of service at the Center for Studies of Child and Family Mental Health, National Institute of Mental Health. The opinions expressed in this article are solely those of the author and do not represent those of NIMH.

261

are included, the millions of people who have become involved in the religious cults of the late 1960s and 1970s *have* joined at just such a time.

Five years ago when I set out to understand the effects of the Vietnam War on junior high and high school students I was struck by an unexpected finding: again and again conversations about the war found their way back to the threat of world destruction. The devastation inflicted on Vietnam and the televised images of slaughter—especially the slaughter of children—insistently reminded my young friends of the possibility of their own destruction. It seemed to them that the mighty weapons unleashed on others—and the threat of still more powerful atomic ones—could and just might be turned on themselves.

Over the last 15 years these kinds of fears and the sense of uncertainty they have produced have been continually stimulated. The debacle at the Bay of Pigs began, for the first time since World War II, to raise questions in the minds of America's young people about this country's military invincibility and moral authority. The Vietnam War threw these doubts and our vulnerability into bold relief. Enormous governmental effort could not convince a majority of the young that what seemed so obviously wrong to them was right.

The only movements to which young people could give their allegiance were those of opposition: an anti-war movement which perceived and condemned the United States as an imperialist monster, a counter-culture which turned its back on all of our country's major institutions—schools, families, churches, businesses, professions—and sought to create a social system and world view apart from them.

A much publicized but nonetheless real gap grew between the older and younger generations. The nuclear families from which young people came, and to which they were supposed to look forward, felt tense, inadequate and constraining. The schools—overcrowded and competitive—were experienced as irrelevant and oppressive and the goals for which they prepared the young—a career and social and financial success—seemed hollow.

With the end of the Vietnam War came the end of an era of unprecedented national prosperity. Too focused on one issue, too deracinated to grow beyond it, the anti-war movement evaporated. The counterculture, no longer able to draw nourishment from society's surplus, faded. But no new sense of national purpose or cultural community replaced these movements.

Many young people began to feel as disillusioned with their own collective action as with the society against which it was directed. Owing allegiance to no movement or guiding set of principles they, like their parents, became increasingly privatistic.

When they began to reach out from the isolation of their dormitory rooms and the insufficiency of their jobs to look for something more, for some way to make sense of their own feelings and the world around them, some of them wanted definite answers. Though many young people valued ideals and experiences of the 1960s, as expressed in the civil rights movement and certain social initiatives, they felt a need to inhibit their anarchistic questing with clear guidelines and firm structures. In the religious cults, which seemed to arise almost miraculously to meet their needs, they found both a confirmation of their private longings and a group structure which could help them overcome their isolation. In the web of exotic and highly rationalized theologies they discovered—and have tenaciously held onto—an unerring map, one that could guide them beyond the limitations and uncertainties of secular and political goals.

NEEDS AND ANSWERS

The Search for Transcendent Experience

During the 1960s, psychedelic drugs opened what Aldous Huxley called "the doors of perception" to an unprecedented number of American young people. Aided by LSD, mescaline, peyote, psilocybin and a host of other natural and chemical agents, and guided by such public figures as Timothy Leary, Richard Alpert, Allen Watts, Allen Ginsberg and Carlos Castaneda, they began to discover what William James described 75 years ago as "potential forms of consciousness entirely different" from our normal waking consciousness. With the aid of psychedelic drugs they caught glimpses of a reality gorgeous and terrible beyond the routine of school or work, of a blissfulness which obliterated anxiety and aggression.

Parents, teachers and the mental health establishment tended to dismiss these experiences as aberrant, drug-induced or hallucinatory and in so doing they perpetuated the isolation and mistrust of those who had them. But the religious leaders of the 1970s and the ecstatic and prophetic traditions they drew on confirmed them. The rituals they practiced—prayer, mantras, abstinence—provided means to repeat and deepen these experiences; the organizations they created offered a context in which they could share and, in times of doubt, reinforce these experiences.

The Search for Family

The movements of the 1960s tacitly if not explicitly supplied a new kind of family to their members. The discredited authority of parents was replaced by a sense of brother- and sisterhood. Sometimes, as in the civil rights movement, it was difficult to achieve and hard to sustain; sometimes it seemed as easy to win as the smiles that long-haired youths, passing on the street, exchanged.

The religious cults of the 1970s have drawn on these feelings of fraternity and sorority, amplified them in the context of easily entered communal living situations and reinforced them with emphatic ideological sanctions. The cults offer young people who are confused, troubled, temporarily homeless or permanently drifting a welcome that is both unexpected and, in contemporary America, unprecedented.

If their attentions to potential converts seem synthetic to some observers, it nevertheless feels quite real and unaffected to lonely and searching young people. They are accepted—by saffron-robed, pigtailed Hare Krishnas, by smiling and conservatively dressed Moonies —in all their confusion and uncertainty. They are fed and housed without question or demand. At introductory *satsangs* or discussion groups their questions are patiently answered, their anxieties assuaged by sweet songs and enthusiastic testimony. In the houses they visit—and in which they may elect to live—they are taught to give and to receive solace, to share rather than to compete with one another.

Leadership and Authority

During the last 10 years the failures of national political leadership and its abuses of authority have been mirrored in the absence of a guiding force or purpose in family life and in the shortcomings of religious, social and academic leaders. Young people who were disillusioned with establishment leaders feared and mistrusted their own. The counterculture was suspicious of anyone who became too powerful or well known; the anti-war movement regularly cannibalized and calumniated those whom it had only recently followed; women resented men's dominance and men feared women's.

The young people who are joining the religious movements of the 1970s are in part reacting against this drift and seeking to fill the vacuum it left in its wake. Lacking experience of genuine leadership, increasingly fearful of an anarchy they sense as pointless and threatening, the young are easily attracted to those who manifest absolute conviction and certainty. In the cults, male-female relationships are generally stereotyped and dogmatically defined: women cook, clean and care for children and they follow the men. The shifting uncertainties of relationships among equals are stabilized by patriarchal leaders who provide their followers with a never-ending stream of clear and generally divinely sanctioned directives.

The Need for Community

Contemporary sociologists have amply described the fragmenting effects of advanced industrial capitalism: the decline of the extended family, the radical separation between work and home life, the lack of contact among neighbors and the loneliness in our cities. One of the most obvious attractions of the cults is the sense of community they provide. Outside observers may find these communities to be artificial and jerry-built; they may argue that the price of their formation is too great, that the rules are too arbitrary, the living conditions too harsh, the customs inherently bizarre. However, for cult members these idiosyncrasies and hardships are a cement that binds and distinguishes them from "the outside world."

Cult members know that their personal and work lives form a seamless whole, that all the tasks they perform are at once personal and social. Every talent and chore—from cooking to child care, from poster-making to toilet cleaning and street solicitation—serve the greater good; the satisfaction of successful performance is amplified in the circle of communal appreciation.

In small cults this sense of integration is defined by a tight group of one or several neighboring houses. Members of larger religious cults are, in addition, part of a national or worldwide network: Unification Church members, followers of Krishna or devotees of the Guru Maharaj Ji know that no matter where they may go they will never be alone, that in every large and many small cities they will find an open house and a warm welcome from co-religionists.

An Overriding Sense of Mission

In addition to the feeling of belonging to a family and a community, each group offers its members the opportunity to take part in a uniquely valued, divinely sanctioned mission. This sense of mission dwarfs any disagreements and mutes ideological dispute and doubt. It gives cult members incentive to overcome personal hardship and the will to surmount attacks from the outside. Each obstacle is a challenge, a milestone which glorifies the journey; each attack is a re-confirmation of the group's correctness and of the outside world's lack of comprehension.

Some of the cults—like the tribal "Love Family" in Seattle—believe that their way of life is itself a witness. Members of tiny Christian fundamentalist communities feel that the way they live will bring grace and salvation to them and that it may also stimulate worshipful imitation by those who have "eyes to see and ears to hear." More actively proselytizing groups—the Unification Church is an obvious example although contemporary non-theistic groups such as Erhard Seminars Training (est) and Transcendental Meditation (TM) exhibit some of the same messianic fervor—tend to see themselves as activist vanguards in the evolution of humankind, as divinely appointed healers of all the divisions which plague the earth.

PROBLEMS AND PERSPECTIVES

Many of those who are opposed to the religious cults—parents of cult members, public prosecuters, mental health professionals and leaders of traditional religions—have emphasized the innocence and naivete of the young people who become involved with them, viewing them as victims of seduction and brainwashing by malevolent and acquisitive cult leaders. The parents' obvious concern, the strangeness of cult life and its profound and sometimes disturbing effects on young people all tend to make the critics anxious, arbitrary and myopic. In public and private statements they call these young people "boys and girls" and continually speak of parental rights and responsibilities.

In so doing these critics obscure the fact that the overwhelming majority of young people in cults are past the age of 18 and, thus, in our society, adults old enough to vote and marry and to fight and die in our wars. Even if we are concerned about their membership in cults, I think we must be wary of overemphasizing their youth and dependency and their parents' responsibility for them. Such descriptions lead too easily to a tendency to control all behavior that parents may deem unacceptable, irresponsible or dangerous, and to institutionalization of that control.

Young people who are uncertain about their membership in cults or who want—but do not know how—to leave them, and parents who are concerned about their children, certainly deserve our attention. But if this attention is to be more than reaction, it must be tempered by a deep and respectful understanding of the needs that people have, of the religious experiences they seek, and of the limited alternatives available to them in our society.

Anyone who wants to be helpful to these young people—and their parents—must also understand the family dynamics of which disagreements over cult membership may be but a part. The concerns of parents who want their child out of a cult are real and their opposition to the cult may be well founded, but these concerns and this opposition are also part of an ongoing series of interactions among family members. Removing an unwilling young person from a cult is sometimes a move in a continuing battle for control of that person's life. In the context of working with a family, the young person's choice can be understood as a step toward independence, as a covert expression of resentment against parents or simply as an assertion of

genuine religious commitment—or all of these, or none.

Many psychiatrists tend to focus on the pathological vulnerability of young people who have become involved in religious groups. They use such terms as "ego defects," "narcissism" and "schizophrenia" and hint at profound and generally pernicious neurophysiological changes that young people undergo, as a result of diet, prayer and abstinence, in the course of their indoctrination. I think that emphasizing psychopathology is as much a mistake and is as demeaning to young people as dwelling on their "childishness."

Young people often do come to these religious groups during a period of heightened uncertainty, in a period of life characterized by anxiety about career, sexuality, intimacy and the "meaning of life." But this uncertainty is a product of our society and an integral part of the extended period of youth that we in the industrialized West offer to people in their late teens and twenties. Our young people's search for deeper experience and a more meaningful way of life is one that we should encourage and guide, not diagnose and restrict.

I have met some young people who seemed profoundly, clinically, disturbed before they entered religious cults, as well as during their membership and after their departure. In some cases, membership in these groups has provided the young and a social context in which to resolve or transmute this disturbance. They feel, and to all appearances have become, more loving, productive and happy. In other cases, the belief systems and structures of these groups seem to have exacerbated the rigidity and defensiveness of these young people, to have made them ever more fearful and contemptuous of those with whom they disagree. But even in such instances I think that we must be extremely wary of treating young people as "cases," of insisting that we, whether parents, "deprogrammers," clergymen, lawyers or mental health professionals, know better than they what is good for them. By what right, moral or legal, do we turn people who are content with what they are doing—if they are harming no one else—into prisoners of deprogrammers or patients in mental hospitals?

Critics argue that the cults pursue and proselytize young people who are in a state of heightened vulnerability—lonely people in restaurants, students just entering or leaving college or about to take exams, solitary travelers in bus stations. Cults are accused of not telling prospective members that they are a religious group or that members may eventually have to submit to strict discipline. It is said that their intense indoctrination—long hours of lecture, prayer, meditation, strenuous physical activity and continual group pressure—is a form of "brainwashing" and coercion, that drugs are used to restrict members' freedom, and that a cult's purpose is basically financial or political, not religious.

Some of these characterizations are true of some cults some of the time, but none of them is true of every cult and all of them should be looked into far more thoroughly before our attitudes toward and responses to cults become fixed by pejorative stereotypes. Unorthodox, heretical and anti-establishment religious groups have always been an easy prey to irresponsible inquisitions and persecutions. Too often those who have charged the new religious cults with these abuses—and those who order "legal conservatorship" and mental hospitalization for young people belonging to cults—have no firsthand knowledge or solid evidence about what a particular cult is really like and what its actual practices are.

Legal redress already exists for the most flagrant abuses. A young person held against his or her will can charge a cult with kidnapping; cults which use their tax exempt status to engage in political activities can be investigated; those which drug unwilling members may be prosecuted for assault, and those which solicit funds for non-existent projects for fraud.

Other practices which are condemned in cults have gone unremarked in traditional religious organizations, which, of course, were themselves once cults. Some of these traditional organizations have acquired far more property and influence and they have at times used them for more destructive purposes than today's cults may ever accomplish. The proselytization that even the most intrusive cults do is only a shadow of that which American missionaries abroad have engaged in.

Still other practices presently fall into a borderland between the illegal and the immoral. People should be protected—perhaps by more stringent application of fraud laws—from deceptive and incomplete information about a cult's aims, methods and expectations and its connections to other, non-religious groups. But in making or applying such laws, we have to remember their limitations.

It is hard to see how the indoctrination that prospective cult members voluntarily submit to can be called brainwashing—a term with connotations of imprisonment. And it is harder still to imagine what kind of law can be applied to those who believe that they will receive "knowledge" in a single afternoon with one of the Guru Maharaj Ji's mahatmas or "get it" in two weekends of Erhard Seminars Training. We can hedge the quest of the young, and the not so young, with legal sanctions, but these sanctions will only protect not strengthen or guide them.

I think that if we are really concerned about our young we should devote the greater part of our energy to learning from the choices they are making. We should regard their disagreements and disaffection from us as a critique of the way we—as families, communities and a society—are. If so many young people believe that salvation can be mass produced, merchandised and franchised, then we can only conclude that our society has predisposed them to believe it. If so many join the first group that promises them "a family" then perhaps we ought to re-examine the way we, as family members, live. If the cults they join are dogmatic and Manichaean—splitting the universe into the good cult and the evil world—if they offer rigid and simple solutions to problems that seem complex and subtle, we must ask where our young people have acquired a habit of mind that makes this so attractive.

The larger problem is not with the young people's quest for meaning or transcendence or community or even with the cults that have arisen, for the time being, to satisfy it, but with a society which prepares them so poorly for this quest and which provides so little guidance in it. In a nation which provided a sense of community and purpose to its young, it would hardly be necessary to find a sense of mission elsewhere. In a society that regarded all life as sacred and encouraged the deep inwardness of prayer and meditation that are not simply rote or narcotic, neither young nor old would be so naive about enlightenment nor so slavish to those who promise to bring it to them.

38 Incest Between

by Judith Herman
and Lisa Hirschman

A recent study reveals that it is more prevalent than most of us imagine

The incest taboo is universal in human culture. Anthropologists generally believe it to be the foundation of all kinship structures. Claude Levi-Strauss, the French structuralist, suggests that the taboo is our basic social contract, while Margaret Mead proposes that it is required to preserve human social order. All cultures, including our own, regard violations of the taboo with horror and dread. Nonetheless, in spite of the length of the prohibition, sexual relations between family members occur more frequently than we had earlier imagined. And because of extreme secrecy surrounding the violation of our most basic sexual taboo, we have little clinical literature and no accurate statistics to guide us.

According to the Kinsey report—probably our most reliable source of data on sexual experiences in America—one woman in 75 has had sexual contact with her father during childhood. That is, 1.5 percent of the U.S. female population are incest victims. A number of clinical reports estimate that the figure may be closer to four or five percent.

Mother-son incest, by contrast, is rare. The most comprehensive American survey ever undertaken, S.K. Weinberg's in 1955, found 164 cases of father-daughter incest, compared with only two cases of sexual contact between mother and son. A study of court cases in Germany reported that ninety percent of the cases involved fathers or stepfathers and daughters. Homosexual father-son contact accounted for another five percent. Incest between mothers and sons occurred in only four per-

Judith Herman, a psychiatrist who earned her M.D. at Harvard Medical School, is a member of the Women's Mental Health Collective in Somerville, Massachusetts. Lisa Hirschman received her master's in education from Boston University and is a member of the psychology department faculty at the University of Montreal. This article is based on a talk given at the annual meeting of the American Psychiatric Association in Toronto earlier this year.

Reprinted from The Sciences, November 1977. © 1977 by The New York Academy of Sciences.

cent of these German cases. And according to the American Humane Association (1967), incest appears to follow the prevailing pattern of sexual abuse of children, in which 92 percent of the victims are female and 97 percent of the offenders are male.

The literature fails to account for this striking discrepancy in the behavior of mothers and fathers. It is apparently taken for granted. The failure to question or even speculate on the reasons for the difference reflects the wide acceptance of assumptions about sex roles deeply ingrained in our patriarchal culture.

Because the subject of incest inspires such strong emotional reactions, few experts have even attempted a dispassionate study of its occurrence and effects. Often those who have studied it have been unable to avoid their own defensive reactions.

Freud's Theory

Clearly the most famous instance of denial occurs in Freud's work. In an 1897 letter to his colleague William Fleiss, Freud reveals why he didn't believe the incest reports he heard from so many of his women patients: "Then there was the astonishing thing that in every case blame was laid on perverse acts by the father, and realization of the unexpected frequency of hysteria, in every case of which the same thing applied, though it was hardly credible that perverted acts against children were so general."

Freud concluded that for the most part the sexual act had never occurred. He could not believe that incest was a common event in respectable families. Since mothers rarely sexually approach their sons, Freud concluded—incorrectly—that the same was true for daughters. Freud's followers also assumed that incestual relations occurred only in fantasy and failed to investigate the facts. They focused on the child's desire rather than on the adult's (and the father's capacity for action). Psychoanalytic study, while it places the incest taboo at the center of the child's psychological development, has done little to uncover the secrecy veiling its occurrence.

Those who have investigated incest often tend to judge the child as the instigator of her own seduction. It reveals an attitude similar to the common belief that the victim of rape is responsible for the crime (particularly if she is attractive).

In the course of just a few years in our practice, we encountered what seemed to us to be a surprisingly large number of patients who were incest vic-

Fathers and Daughters

tims. Other therapists, we found, had similar experiences. Out of the first ten therapists we questioned, we learned that four had at least one incest victim in treatment. Within a short time, we had collected fifteen case histories.

In our study, we included only those cases where overt sexual contact had actually occurred between parent and child and only those in which there was no doubt in the daughter's mind that explicit and intentionally sexual contact had occurred and where secrecy was required. Not included were the many women who reported seductive behavior on the part of their fathers.

Remarkably Similar Histories

The incest histories were remarkably similar. Most victims were the eldest or only daughters who had experienced their first sexual approach by their fathers or male guardians between the ages of six and nine. The youngest girl was four years old; the oldest fourteen. Sexual contact usually took place repeatedly and often the relationship lasted three years or more. Physical force was not used, and intercourse was rarely attempted with girls who had not reached puberty. In all but two of these fifteen cases, the relationship remained a secret.

Previous studies, often based on court referrals,

"Silence," by Odilon Redon, 1911. The Museum of Modern Art, Lillie P. Bliss Collection.

give an erroneous impression that incest occurs predominantly in poor families. But this is not so. The fathers' occupations cut across class lines. Several held jobs that required considerable personal competence and commanded social respect—college administrator, army officer, policeman, engineer, physician. Others were skilled workers, foremen, or managers in offices or factories. All the mothers were houseworkers.

Certain common features emerged in the pattern of these victims' family relationships. Most striking was the almost uniform estrangement of mother and daughter, an estrangement which preceded the occurrence of overt incest.

More than half the mothers were partially incapacitated by physical or mental illness or alcoholism, and either assumed an invalid role in the home or were periodically absent because of hospitalization. Their eldest daughters were often obliged to take over the household duties. At best, the mothers were viewed by their daughters as helpless, frail, downtrodden victims, who were unable to take care of themselves, much less to protect their children.

In particular, the daughters felt unable to go to their mothers for help once their fathers had begun to make sexual advances. In many cases, the mothers tolerated a great deal of abuse themselves, and the daughters had learned not to expect any protection. Five of the women said they suspected that their mothers knew about the incest and tacitly condoned it. Two victims who had made attempts to bring up the subject were put off by their mothers' denial or indifference.

At worst, the mother-daughter relations were marked by frank and open hostility. Some of the daughters said they could remember no tenderness or caring from their mothers. In contrast, almost all the victims expressed some warm feelings toward their fathers. Many described them much more favorably than their mothers.

To the outside world, the fathers were often liked and respected members of the community. The daughters responded to their fathers' social status and power and derived satisfaction from being their fathers' favorites. They were "daddy's special girls," but often they were special to no one else.

The victims rarely expressed anger toward their fathers, not even about the incestuous act itself. Most expressed feelings of fear, disgust, and intense shame about the sexual contact, and said that they had endured it because they felt they had no other choice. But though they felt abused by their fathers, they did not feel the same sense of betrayal as they felt towards their mothers. Having abandoned the hope of pleasing their mothers, they seemed relieved to have found some way of pleasing their fathers and gaining their attention.

Power Within the Family

Although the victims reported that they felt helpless and powerless to resist their fathers, the incestuous relationship did give them some semblance of power within the family. Many of the daughters effectively replaced their mothers and became their fathers' surrogate wives. They were also deputy mothers to the younger children, and were generally given some authority over them. Many girls felt an enormous sense of responsibility for holding the family together. They also knew that, as keepers of the incest secret, they had an extraordinary power which could be used to destroy the family. Their sexual contact with their fathers conferred on them a sense of possessing a dangerous, secret power over the lives of others. Keeping up appearances became a necessary, expiating act, at the same time that it increased the daughters' sense of isolation and shame.

What is most striking to us about this family constellation, in which the daughter replaces the mother in the traditional role, is the underlying assumption about that role shared apparently by all the family members. Customarily, a mother and wife in our society is one who nurtures and takes care of children and husband. If, for whatever reasons, the mother is unable to fulfill her ordinary functions, it is apparently assumed that some other female must be found to do it. The eldest daughter is a frequent choice. The father does not assume the wife's maternal role when she is incapacitated. He feels that his first right is to continue to receive the services which his wife formerly provided, sometimes including sexual services.

This view of the father's prerogative to be served is shared not only by the parents and daughters in these incestuous families, but also by the wider society. Fathers who feel abandoned by their wives are not generally expected or taught to assume primary responsibilities as a parent. We should not find it surprising, then, that fathers occasionally turn to their daughters for services (housework and sexual) that they had formerly expected of their wives.

Unable to Love

One of the most frequent complaints of the victims entering therapy was a sense of being different, and distant, from ordinary people. They expressed fear that they were unable to love. Their sense of an absence of feeling was most marked in sexual relationships, although most women were sexually responsive in the narrow sense of the word; that is, capable of having orgasms.

In some cases, the suppression of feeling was clearly a defense which had been employed in the incestuous relationship in childhood. Originally, the isolation of affect seemed an appropriate device to protect against the feelings aroused by their molesting father. Passive resistance and dissociation of feeling appeared to be among the few defenses available in an overwhelming situation. Later, it carried over into their relations with others.

Distance and Isolation

These women made repeated and often desperate attempts later in life to overcome their sense of distance and isolation. Frequently, it resulted in a pattern of many brief, unsatisfactory sexual contacts. Those relationships which became more intense and lasting were fraught with difficulty. While most expressed suspicion of men, they also overvalued them and kept searching for a relationship with an idealized protector and sexual teacher who would take care of them and tell them what to do. Half the women had had affairs during adolescence with older or married men. In these relationships, the sense of importance and power and the secrecy of the incestuous relationship was regained. The men emerged as heroes and saviors.

In many cases, the women became intensely involved with men who were cruel, abusive or neglectful, and tolerated extremes of mistreatment. One remained married for twenty years to a psychotic husband who beat her, terrorized their children, and never supported the family. Several were rape victims.

Why did these women feel they deserved to be beaten, raped, neglected and used? Almost all of the fifteen women described themselves as a "witch," "bitch" or "whore" and saw themselves as socially branded even when no social exposure of their sexual relations with their fathers had occurred or was likely to occur. They experienced themselves as powerful and dangerous to men: their self-image had almost a magical quality. They seemed to believe that they had seduced their fathers, and therefore could seduce any man.

At one level, their sense of malignant power can be understood to have arisen as a defense against the child's feelings of utter helplessness. In addition, however, their self-image was reinforced by the long-standing conspiratorial relationship with their fathers. And, as a matter of fact, as children, they did have the power to destroy the family by exposing the secret.

What's more, most of the victims were aware that they had experienced some pleasure in the incestuous relationship, and together with their fathers they joined in a shared hatred of their mothers. This led to intense feelings of shame, degradation, and worthlessness. Because they had enjoyed their fathers' attention and their mothers' defeat, these women felt responsible for the incestuous relationship. Almost uniformly, they distrusted

their own desires and needs, and did not feel entitled to care and respect. Any relationship that afforded some kind of pleasure seemed to increase their sense of guilt and shame. They constantly sought to expiate their guilt and relieve their shame by serving and giving to others, and by observing the strictest and most rigorous codes of religion and traditional morality. Any lapse from a rigid code of behavior confirmed their innate evil. Some of the women embraced their negative identity with a kind of defiance and pride. "There's *nothing* I haven't done!" one woman boasted.

Those women who were mothers themselves appeared preoccupied with the fear that they would themselves be "bad" mothers to their children, as they felt their mothers had neglected them. Several sought treatment when they became aware of feelings of rage and resentment towards their own children, especially their daughters. Any indulgence in pleasure-seeking or attention to their own personal needs reinforced their sense that they were unfit mothers. In some, the fear of exposure was felt as dread that the authorities would intervene and take their children away. Other mothers worried that they would be unable to protect their daughters from incest in their own families.

Therapy

Very little is known about how to help the incest victim. If the secret is discovered while she is still living with her parents, most often the family is destroyed. Since such an outcome is usually terrifying, even to an exploited child, most victims cooperate with their fathers in maintaining secrecy rather than seeing their fathers jailed or risk being sent away from home themselves.

The Santa Clara County Court offers a model treatment center designed for the rehabilitation of the incestuous family. It involves all members of the incestuous family in both individual and family therapy, and benefits from a close alliance with Daughters United, a self-help support group for victims. Several similar treatment centers are now in the process of development. While it offers a promising model for the treatment of the discovered incestuous family, this model does not help families with undetected incest. The vast majority of incest victims reach adulthood still hiding their secrects. Nor are most therapists equipped to treat those patients who come to them for help.

As with many other ancient women's secrets (abortion, rape), public testimony and consciousness-raising have often provided better therapy for women than professional services. We believe that increased public awareness of the scope of the problem is the first step towards helping incest victims lose their sense of isolation and shame. □

39

Serving Teenage Mothers and Their High-Risk Infants

by Phyllis Levenson, James Hale, Marlene Hollier and Cathy Tirado

About 20 percent of the total number of births in the United States are to teenagers.[1] While this statistic has significant implications for educators, social service program planners and health care providers, it is meaningless to the young mother confronted with the realities of her new baby. Reality for her is represented by constant demands to provide for her baby. Her responses to these demands will determine the future of both mother and baby.

The stresses of providing care are frequently intensified because of the circumstances that often accompany a birth to a teenager. Infants of teenage mothers have an increased susceptibility to mental retardation and developmental delay, as a result of complications in pregnancy or labor, prematurity and/or low birth weight. Other potentially tragic results of pregnancy during the teen years can include repeated, rapid childbearing with negative health repercussions for both mother and child; dropping out of school with no marketable skills; forced early marriages which have a high rate of divorce; and high risk of attempted suicide.[2] Thus, the young mother often lacks the physical, emotional, economic, educational and social resources necessary to help her care for her baby.

Some of the problems encountered

Reprinted from *Children Today* Magazine, July/August 1978.
U.S. Department of Health, Education and Welfare.

by teenage mothers and their children can be seen in the case of Judy, who became pregnant when she was 14 and dropped out of school.

Judy's daughter Tracey was born 10 weeks prematurely and had to remain in the hospital during her early months. After Tracey had been home for several months Judy noticed that she still frequently appeared ill and did not smile or respond when talked to and cuddled. Judy became increasingly worried about her daughter.

At first Judy attributed Tracey's problems to her own inadequacy as a mother. As time went on, however, she knew she should be doing something more to help Tracey, but she didn't know how to identify or obtain local services that might assist them. Judy was also afraid to seek help for fear that she would be held responsible for Tracey's problems, labeled a "bad mother" and have her baby taken away from her.

Judy was further frustrated because she had planned to go back to school after Tracey's birth, but now felt she couldn't leave her. Her mother, with whom they lived, worked all day and said that she was too tired to bother with the baby at night. Since Judy didn't have anyone else to leave Tracey with, she didn't have an opportunity to learn the skills she needed to achieve future independence. Her frustrations and anxieties grew even more intense when she began to suspect she might be pregnant again. At this point, she went to her health clinic and was referred to ITAM.

The ITAM program—the Demon-

Phyllis Levenson, M.P.H., is curriculum specialist, Marlene Hollier, M.A., project director, and Cathy Tirado, R.N., training specialist for The Demonstration and Training Center for High Risk or Mentally Retarded Infants of Teenage Mothers (ITAM), Mental Health and Mental Retardation Authority (MH MRA) in Harris County, Houston, Texas. James Hale, Ph.D., is Deputy Clinical Director of Mental Retardation Services for MHMRA in Harris County.

stration and Training Center for High Risk or Mentally Retarded Infants of Teenage Mothers—of the Mental Health and Mental Retardation Authority in Harris County, Houston, Texas, was established in July 1975 through a triagency grant to address the needs of teenage mothers like Judy and their infants. Participants in the grant are the Mental Health and Mental Retardation Authority, the Houston Independent School District and the Baylor College of Medicine. Primary funding was received from the Bureau of Education for the Handicapped, U.S. Office of Education.

The goals of the program are to provide stimulation to the high-risk infant in order to enhance his or her development, and to offer educational and supportive programs for the teenage mother. Infants who meet the following criteria are eligible for the program: their mother must have been less than 20 years of age at the time of the baby's birth, and the baby must have had a birth weight of 5½ pounds or less, a medical diagnosis of developmental delay or an Apgar score of six or below on the 5-minute examination after birth. Mothers learn about the program through their health clinics, like Judy, or through a multitude of other community referral resources.

A multifaceted program has been designed to serve the infants. When a baby enters ITAM, his or her strengths and needs are assessed, both formally and informally by an assessment team whose members include a physician, nurse, social worker, speech pathologist, physical therapist, behavior management specialist and training specialist. Once assessments are completed and evaluated, individual program plans, which identify specific work areas for mother and infant, are written by the team and supervised by the case manager. These plans are based on a developmentally sequenced curriculum in the areas of motor, language, cognition, self-help and socialization skills.

We felt that a home-based program would be the most effective way of meeting the needs of ITAM program participants. After an individual program plan is developed, the case manager spends approximately 90 minutes weekly working with each infant and mother at their home. Emphasis is placed on training a mother to teach her child, using the techniques demonstrated during home visits.

Consultations by specialists from other disciplines are available to ensure optimal training for the babies. Follow-up evaluations are given every six months and an annual physical examination is performed.

In this manner, the immediate needs of the infants are addressed. However, if a mother fails to assume her role as the primary teacher of her infant, the baby's progress will seldom be maintained. A mother who feels inadequate or anxious most of the time will have little emotional or physical energy left to spend on her baby. This problem is frequently compounded by her ambivalent emotions about her child's limitations or handicap. To help mothers of infants in the program effectively fulfill their parental roles and thus enhance their child's development, a variety of educational and supportive parent programs were designed to supplement the service for infants.

The first task in developing parent programs was to determine a profile of the mothers being served in order to identify their needs.

The 60 mothers enrolled in ITAM range in age from 12 to 20, with an average age of 17. Seventy-eight percent of the mothers are black, 12 percent, white and 10 percent, hispanic. Over half—54 percent—were either pregnant with another child or already had a child in addition to the infant in ITAM at the time of program entry.

Although the median grade the mothers had completed in school was the 9th, many of the mothers were noted to read at very elementary

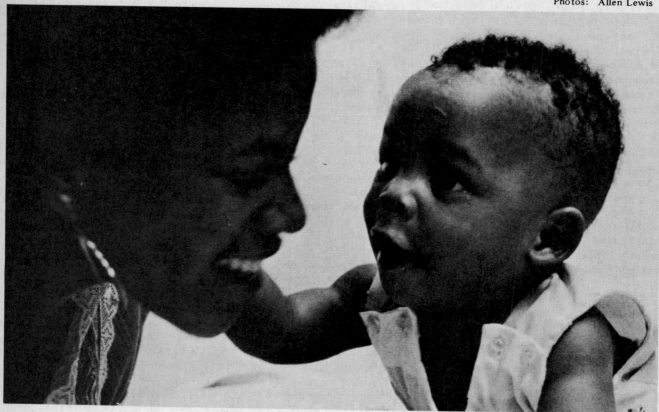

When young mothers are aware of the importance of play activities, they become increasingly comfortable playing with and talking to their babies.

levels and several were unable to read at all. Eighty-five percent of those eligible to continue in school were not enrolled at the time of program entry, and only 12 percent had full- or part-time employment.

Over half were single and dependent on welfare programs or family members (other than their baby's father) for financial support. Sixty-two percent of the mothers entering the program lived with their families and depended on the maternal grandmother for child care. Only a third of the mothers had consistent access to transportation.

This information, together with data obtained at the assessment prior to program entry, observations by case managers and the training specialist and from the mothers themselves, helped us identify the critical, multiple needs which warranted program intervention. The following list includes

those needs which we felt to be most significant and which could be addressed within the scope of our program.

• *Completion of the young mother's own psychological development.* Since the teenage mother is still growing and maturing herself, she may not yet have developed her own identity, a sense of self-worth and independence—all of which directly affect her perceptions of motherhood and the way she functions as a parent. She must have opportunities to complete these specific tasks of adolescence so that she can move toward assuming the responsibilities of parenthood.

• *Separation of the mother's needs from the infant's needs.* Adolescence is predominantly an egocentric time. Thus it is necessary to provide activities for the teenage mother that will help her become more sensitive

to the unique needs of others—specifically her baby.

• *Maternal orientation to the future.* Young mothers must feel that they have a future and are able to exert control over it, so that they will be motivated to plan for themselves and their children. A mother's decision to drop out of school and the inability of many mothers to read limits their prospects for the future. Frequent, repeated pregnancies also drain their physical, emotional and financial resources. The development of realistic, obtainable goals can be fostered by making teenage mothers aware of options to help them overcome such barriers to goal achievement.

• *Information about child development and care.* Knowledge of how to provide appropriate activities and care is essential to effective parenting. Even a mother with the best intentions will become frustrated and angry if her well-meaning but inappropriate efforts to help her baby are seldom met with positive responses. Our assumptions that "everyone knew" certain basic aspects of child care or development were often found to be invalid, and it was necessary to begin at the most elemental level.

• *Strengthening of a mature mother/infant relationship.* We found that many of the mothers had emotional needs that had to be addressed before they would be ready to assume primary responsibility for their infants and be able to relate to them in a mature, nurturing manner. Many of the young women, for example, had ambivalent feelings about becoming a mother. Some mothers had been deprived of their babies after birth because the infants had required prolonged hospitalization and they had not yet formed strong attachments to them. Others depended upon their own mothers to care for the baby.

• *Peer support.* The teenage mother is often isolated from her peers, who are still in school or free from responsibilities. The absence of peer reinforcement often leaves a vast emotional void.

• *Utilization of community resources.* Mothers entering ITAM lacked the skills to identify and use community resources which would facilitate their infants' development.

• *Transportation.* Since the majority of the mothers did not have consistent access to public transportation, or had to rely on family members or friends, provision of transportation services was essential to ITAM's program design.

In response to these needs, several parent program components were designed to complement the home-based infant services and to provide additional opportunities for maternal involvement, enrichment and reinforcement. Since the relative importance of the concerns noted here vary with each individual, program participants use these programs in combination or individually, depending upon their unique requirements.

Parent Programs

Home assignments directly involve the mother in her role as primary teacher. As she works with her baby on weekly assignments and records her infant's progress each day, the mother becomes sensitive to her child's development and learning processes.

These activities and the subsequent feedback received from her case manager help a mother develop realistic expectations for her baby and an understanding of the child's abilities and needs. As her baby progresses through the series of home activities, the mother's feelings of effectiveness are reinforced.

Video tapes of the home training sessions are made every six months to help assess mother/infant interactions. These tapes are viewed by the mother and her case manager in order to reinforce positive maternal behaviors and illustrate those which need to be modified. The tapes are also scored by program staff members to help evaluate mother/infant interactions.

Since the mothers sometimes lacked the motivation to follow through with assigned activities, we began a token system of behavior management called "Be Mod" to give them an added incentive to carry out the recommended procedures. One mother, for example, who failed to keep clinic appointments for her baby, contracted with her teachers to receive a certain number of tokens for each appointment she kept. She could then trade in these tokens at a monthly parent meeting for items like clothes (donated by community groups and individuals) for herself and her baby.

Although this system has only been in effect for a short time, indications are that many of the mothers feel far more motivated to engage in many of the activities if they receive some "personal reward" for their efforts.

Mother/infant group sessions have been initiated as a means of strengthening mother/infant interactions in a group situation utilizing peer support. The emphasis here is on the development of infant socialization skills, although group tasks are oriented toward the needs identified in each child's individual plan. At the beginning of the session, the case managers discuss the tasks of the day and highlight specific points which the mothers should note during that day's session. After trying the activities with their babies, the mothers reconvene to talk about what happened during the session.

In one early session, several of the mothers were hesitant to follow through with the infant stimulation activities assigned and demonstrated by the case managers. They had laughed uneasily when the teacher demonstrated play techniques and were reluctant to try them for fear of being thought "babyish" themselves. Gradually, however, with the support of the teacher and their peers, they became increasingly comfortable talking and playing with their babies. As the importance of babies' play activities were shown and discussed, several mothers reported that they felt more "grown up" because of their participation. The encouragement from friends in the group, and the opportunities to model their actions, had helped these mothers feel comfortable for the first time in "playing" with their babies.

Monthly parent meetings offer mothers opportunities to get together and share experiences and concerns. Care for their children during the meetings is provided.

The programs for these meetings, selected from topics recommended by a volunteer parent advisory committee, have included exercise sessions, toy-making workshops and guest speakers who have discussed such subjects as first aid, make-up and hair styling and career opportunities.

Among the concerns discussed during the meetings is the pressure many mothers feel to assume a more mature role than they feel prepared for. For example, in one meeting, when they were talking about their future hopes and plans for their children, the mothers concluded that it was important to allow children to behave in a manner appropriate to their age since they felt they had been denied this opportunity. One 16-year-old mother explained, "I can't *be* a teenager. In fact, I'm *not* a teenager —I'm a mother."

The meetings have also generated close friendships between many of the mothers—friendships which provide the contact with and feedback from peers so essential to adolescent development.

Classes in parenting skills, another ITAM parent program, are offered three hours a week. The mothers receive school credit for the classes, which are taught by teachers in the Houston Independent School District. The curriculum, which consists of 12 modules, is designed to meet the needs and diversified learning levels of the young mothers enrolled. Particular emphasis is placed throughout on the importance of the mother's feelings and her subsequent actions as they relate to her baby's physical and mental health.

The first two units focus on enhancing the mother's self-esteem and increasing her feelings of effectiveness, while succeeding units address various aspects of child care and development. The last three units are concerned with family planning, prenatal care and the mother's plans for the future.

Included in the curriculum are multiple activities designed to help each mother develop realistic expectations for her child and sensitivity to his or her needs. Activities to promote the mother's psychological development and decision-making ability are also included.

In view of the handicapping conditions common to many of the infants enrolled in ITAM, the development of mothers' realistic expectations and goals for their children is particu-

larly important. Several mothers, who had been told shortly after delivery that their child might not live, reported not having *any* expectations for their children. This outlook influenced not only their attitude toward that child, but toward their other children as well. For example, Terry, the mother of a 14-month-old son and a 2½-year-old daughter who had spinal meningitis at six months, explained that after seeing her daughter's development so severely delayed as a result of the disease she was afraid to allow herself to develop any expectations for either child. "I wanted to have hope, I really did—but it just seemed too hard," she said.

As a result, Terry had virtually ignored her little boy from birth and he was also beginning to show signs of developmental delay. During her evaluation at the end of the course in parenting skills, Terry indicated that she was beginning to accept her daughter's problems and limitations. "Now I can plan for her and my son," she said.

Another theme emphasized in the classes in parenting skills is that mothers are "Very Important People" to themselves and their babies. Many young mothers entering ITAM are dependent upon their own mothers for physical and emotional support and rely on them to care for their infants. As a result, they have not developed an image of themselves as parents, or an understanding of the significance of their parental role.

For example, when Pat first brought David home from the hospital her mother immediately assumed all responsibility for him and Pat found herself relegated to such tasks as laundry, formula preparation and night-time feedings—with only infrequent opportunities to cuddle and play with her baby. Pat never challenged her mother for fear that she would be told to "leave the house." As this pattern continued, Pat became increasingly detached from David. In fact, she said that she often felt jealous of him because she felt that

her mother cared more for him than for her.

As Pat learned to work with her baby, using techniques demonstrated in the home program, and acquired child care skills through participation in the parenting classes, she became more confident of her ability to care for David and assumed more responsibility for him. The self-esteem she gained from her new role was so significant to Pat that when she was asked what she liked best about the course, Pat responded, "My importantness." At a parent meeting several months later, when the mothers were discussing what might happen if they didn't take what they defined as "good care" of their babies, Pat said, "You'd lose your importantness."

In addition to the knowledge gained through the classes in parenting skills, the young women have formed close bonds with their peers. In fact, this peer support has motivated the mothers participating in the classes to become among the most actively involved in other ITAM parent programs. Many have volunteered to serve on the parent advisory committee, which plans the monthly parent meetings, and the mothers have also requested follow-up classes in order to further explore some issues addressed during the course. As a result, additional classes in such areas as meal planning, role definition and disciplining children are now being provided and are being enthusiastically received.

Teenage mothers may also continue their education through home-bound classes, provided by ITAM in conjunction with the Houston Independent School District (HISD) as part of the Special Education Homebound Program. HISD employs three full-time teachers, who help mothers keep up with their regular classes even though obligations to provide care for their babies require them to remain at home.

This one-to-one approach has enabled many young women to experience academic success for the first time, and their heightened self-esteem can be seen in their more positive and hopeful attitudes toward themselves and their babies. As Anita, a 17-year-old mother of three who had dropped out of school in the sixth grade, told us, "I never thought I'd be able to read to my baby. Now I feel maybe I can be an example to my children."

Several mothers have entered vocational training programs, and others are working toward a GED (General Education Development) high school equivalency diploma.

Another problem being addressed by ITAM is the need to increase the mothers' awareness and use of community resources. The curriculum for the classes in parenting skills includes sections identifying local resources available to students and, through role-playing, the mothers learn to use these resources effectively. In one session, for example, the students role-played reporting an illness to a physician and then completed sample medical history forms. During their weekly home visits, case managers offer additional information on resources and often help mothers obtain the additional services required by their babies. ITAM staff members also help the mothers coordinate and apply the recommendations made by local community service agencies and health clinics.

Finally, ITAM provides a van and driver to bring mothers to initial assessments, annual medical reviews, videotaping sessions and all of the parent programs. Since most mothers would not otherwise have access to program activities, the provision of transportation is crucial to the success of the program.

Through program components described here, the Mental Health and Mental Retardation Authority of Harris County is attempting to meet many crucial needs of teenage mothers and their children. We feel that the services offered through ITAM are helping these young mothers to both exert control over their lives and to consider increased options for the future. In choosing among these options, they will be making decisions that will most certainly influence the next two generations. ■

---

[1] Wendy H. Baldwin. "Adolescent Pregnancy and Childbearing—Growing Concerns for Americans," *Population Bulletin*, Vol. 31, No. 2, Washington, D.C., Population Reference Bureau, Inc., 1976.
[2] Jack Zacker and Wayne Brandstalt, *The Teenage Pregnant Girl*, Springfield, Ill., Charles C Thomas, 1975.

40

BOY FATHERS

by LISA CONNOLLY

All eyes are on the unwed mother and her baby, while the other partner stands awkwardly in the background, too often ignored or even forgotten completely.

They sit close together, shyly holding hands. They want to get married but her mother won't let her. Bill and Colette are telling me about themselves.

He is her 16-year-old boyfriend. Tall, slouching and gawky. His face is plain and freckled. His sandy hair is neither short nor long. His low speech sounds like it's been ground through a sluice: jumbled, quick, eagerly saying what needs to be said. The topic is enormously important to him, and he's not used to it yet. The rush of speech over, he pauses, listening to the next question. Hearing the echo of the last.

She is 15 and three months pregnant. Clear, wide green eyes are framed by blonde hair cut bluntly, dutch-boy fashion. She has a freshly scrubbed look that might easily reflect the sheen of prairie wheat in the sun.

He calls her every night at the maternity home where she lives and tells her not to cry. He has quit school and has told his coach he won't be on the baseball team this year. He works instead, nine hours a day at a local hot dog stand and has earned two raises of 10¢ each in two weeks. He buys her maternity blouses and jeans to replace the jeans that are now too small.

When her mother wouldn't permit Colette to see Bill at home, Colette left home, her ninth-grade girlfriends and the swim team and moved to "The Home," a bleak and institutional old Salvation Army facility. In this place she can see Bill on the weekends when he isn't working. In this place her mother can't tell her what to do. In this place they now remember falling in love.

"The first two nights that Colette and me spent together, I'd say that it was more unplanned than anything else. I spent the night and we fell in love—that's how it went. I'll never forget those two nights either, and neither will she. Some of my friends, when they found out that she was pregnant, they said, 'You gotta be crazy to get in trouble!' But I didn't look at it as 'trouble.' Colette and me, we fell in love that way. Did she tell you? I liked her so much. Even now, five months later."

Bill is a member of the other half of over one million out-

of-wedlock teenage relationships that resulted in pregnancies to teenage women last year. Bill is the other half of a problem that is now considered by population experts to be epidemic. Although live births are declining in age groups 15 years to 44, children age 10 through 14 are increasing the live birthrate at a steady 4 percent a year. White teenagers are pushing this statistic to 9 percent, while black teenagers' statistics are remaining the same. (The demographics of race, class and religion of unmarried parents are increasingly white middle-class. The old rag that these problems are confined to the nation's ghettos had better be buried; it is no longer true.) Ninety-five percent of teen mothers are keeping their babies as opposed to 10 or 12 years ago, while the fathers are typically absent. If the mother and father marry, their marriage must be viewed as temporary, because the divorce rate of teenagers is five times that of adults.

The unmarried father has been a shadow figure cloaked in a fog of prejudice and misinformation. It has been the young pregnant girl who has held center stage, literally taking the rap for pregnancy, since Nathaniel Hawthorne's *Scarlet Letter*. It has been she who has received the uneasy mixture of concern, moral outrage and medical, social and educational services. Notice, for example, how the expression "unwed mother" settles easily, while "unwed father" jolts one's expectations and priorities. The burden of parentage has rarely shifted beyond identifying the father and grilling the mother.

In one way, this was possible because for years workers in the helping professions bought the dubious story that girls did not know who the father was.

This obvious lie was given implicit credence because of the worker's double-bound notions: it was the boy's fault for getting someone pregnant, but she *let* him; so it's really her fault. He was just sowing his wild oats while she's promiscuous. Often the boy is forbidden to see his girl after her parents discover her pregnancy, so his absence is interpreted as not caring. These inaccurate views are compounded with recognition of his real emotional and social immaturity and lack of marketable skills. Thus the young father has been dismissed altogether, and contact with the real person behind the true/false facade is still true today except in the proportionately small number of cases of adoption.

This situation might have totally remained this way, says one social worker who leads groups for single mothers, "if we hadn't been forced by the law to consider the father. I hate to admit it, but it's true."

The law referred to is the 1972 Supreme Court decision in *Stanley* v. *Illinois*, a ruling that established equal protection of the law to unmarried natural fathers. Prior to *Stanley* v. *Illinois*, the single father had not been a necessary party to any proceeding hearing on the custody of his child. This ruling, and similar decisions in other courts, has forced, as the social worker said, agencies concerned with the counseling of unmarried mothers to consider the rights of the father.

To fulfill the law, adoption agencies had to find the father; and in their search, they didn't know who to look for.

Identification of the unwed father was initially profiled in a book published in 1971, *The Unmarried Father,* a study done at Vista Del Mar Child-Care Service in Los Angeles by three researchers, Reuben Pannor, Fred Massarik and Byron W. Evans. This study, begun in 1963, successfully demonstrated that most unwed fathers are willing to cooperate in counseling and to face their feelings and responsibilities. In fact they wanted to, once they got beyond their fear of being blamed by the counselor and had received firm encouragement that their participation is important for both themselves and the mother and child. If the agency did not insist on seeing the father, he rarely volunteered.

The Vista Del Mar study also demonstrated that the interest and concern of the father is tangibly supportive of the pregnant girl in several ways: her feelings of self-worth were encouraged, which helped her in her decision about keeping or not keeping the baby; the father's interest helped to improve her outlook during one of the most difficult periods of her life; and the father's ability to deal with his own confusion and to integrate this experience into his later life adaptation and adjustment was reinforced.

"When I started working with natural fathers, I assumed along with everybody else that they were uninvolved and wanted out of the situation," says Chuck Wilkerson, a social worker with the Children's Home Society of California and an advocate for the unwed father. "And I discovered that I was counseling with the expectation that the fathers didn't want to contribute. I wasn't confronted with my own values until I saw some natural fathers who really wanted to get involved, wanted to see their babies and wanted contact with the adopting couples so that they could clarify why they were doing this and prevent distorted information from being passed on. I started then realizing that my attitudes—of seeing them as uninvolved —caused me to feel punitive, even if I didn't express my feelings verbally. Since then, even if I am counseling a resistant father, I can get across that I'm not going to dump on him, that he is valued, that he's an integral part of the process in the permanent planning of his baby. And I usually get a positive response from that.

"We're dealing with a sexist value system," Wilkerson continues, "in the sense that we're geared to seeing this younger unmarried father in a certain light. But the other side of it is that he also has a reality that he's been conditioned, too. He gets no support from his peers when he's faced with an unplanned, unwanted pregnancy. He's told to keep it cool by his friends if he talks to them at all about it. Boys don't have the kind of friendships that girls do. Girls feel fine about expressing their feelings and problems to girls, but this is not typical of boys' relationships with boys. Also, these fathers perceive anybody wanting to contact them as being after them. This is what their initial resistance to counseling is all about."

The Vista Del Mar study stated categorically that close relationships between the father and mother were not always apparent, and a persistent effort from social workers to seek the father for counseling was required in order to determine the relationship and offer counseling. In any event, counseling is crucial to unwed fathers' psychological well-being whether or not a close relationship exists.

But there still remains a wide gap in practice between acknowledging the importance of the father's role and seeking him out in order to include him. This gap reflects historically biased attitudes toward the father. This can be seen in agencies where not enough staff are hired to serve fathers whose babies *will* be kept. Even Chuck Wilkerson, who exemplifies the best in informed values and intent, cannot practice what he advocates. Because of time limitations, he primarily counsels boys whose babies will be adopted.

The Vista Del Mar study produced the only book published today in the United States on unmarried fathers. The study concerned itself with a small population of primarily middle-class Jewish boys. Its findings have been criticized as not applying to boys from low-income backgrounds. But another study conducted by the Youth Study Center, a part of the juvenile division of the Philadelphia County Court, is a dramatic refutation to this criticism based on socioeconomic backgrounds. Individual interviews of teenage fathers in a detention facility concluded that at least 75 percent of the youngsters did not wish to desert, be detached from or abandon their girlfriend or children. Although their immediate reaction was defensive and carried a certain John Wayne bravado, once they began talking, they opened up a flood of anguish and doubt about their self-worth. They were confused about what was expected of them and what to do. Most of these boys had no concrete ideas about what the responsibilities of fatherhood are.

Consider the dialog between Bill and Colette. They are talking about their plans for their baby. Bill says of his unborn child: "My mom raised me where I do what I want and be in on a certain time. So I feel he or she [his new baby] will go out and be with who they want to be with. I'm not going to put a judgment on them. I don't really know about when it's really little. Like if we have to go to work, the baby will be with my mom."

Says Colette, "It's scary at first."

Bill agrees, saying, "I helped to take care of a friend's baby. . . . It's hard, but you have to do it."

Colette comments, "I don't want to spoil it, 'cause then it will always want things."

Bill admits, "We've never really talked about it."

Bill and Colette also never talked about contraception. To their way of thinking, spontaneity is the essence of romance. Colette says that she once thought of taking the Pill but didn't think at 15 she'd be able to get a prescription without her mother's consent. Bill's face turns red at the mention of condoms, and it's suddenly obvious that *spontaneity* is another word for embarrassment. Imagine kids convinced of their falling in love at first sight, in the midst of their cuddling, negotiating the mechanics of contraception. It's like demanding of a two-year-old who has just been given a candy bar to write a check and show an ID to the grocery clerk, while all the kid wants to do is continue tearing off the wrapper and eat the candy.

The overwhelming majority of social research on teenage sexuality has focused on females. "Sexual and Contraceptive Knowledge, Attitudes and Behavior of Male Adolescents," by Mandelon Finkel and David Finkel, broke this record in a study in the spring of 1974. The Finkels surveyed 421 male high school students (approximately one-third black, one-third white and one-third Hispanic), whose median age was 16.3 years, and whose ages ranged from 12 to 19 years. The Finkels wanted to know what the source

of young men's sex information is and the extent of their knowledge about sex and contraception and attitudes toward sexual activity.

The main source of sex information for all groups was their own male friends. The extent of sex knowledge also did not vary according to ethnic group, *nor did it increase with age.* Only 50 percent of the questions asked concerning ways to avoid pregnancy and VD were answered correctly. Students who had taken some health courses that included sex education scored higher on the questions.

The majority of students believe that teenagers have a more difficult time obtaining contraceptives than adults. Over half felt that "only the female should use birth control." A third of the group, corroborating the idea that males have a difficult time sharing with one another, "would not want friends to know I used condoms," although over half affirmed that a "male who uses a condom respects his partner."

Responses on sexual experience revealed a mean age of 12.8 years for first coitus, although sexual activity appeared to be erratic and was calculated to occur three times a month with one or two partners.

A significant finding in the area of contraceptive use reported that over half the students relied on the inadequate methods of withdrawal, douche or no method at all to prevent pregnancy. Because of the mean age of 12.8 years for first coitus, the Finkels suggest inschool sex education at the junior high level and easier access to contraceptives. (The Population Institute, an international education organization, is considering the possibility of handing out condoms like programs at rock concerts in an attempt to educate youth to use condoms comfortably and confidently.)

Since the popular and reliable methods of birth control such as the IUD and the Pill are designed exclusively for female use, this promotes an honest awareness that women have the most to lose by becoming pregnant; but the effect is also to further disassociate boys from what is an undeniable partnership.

Despite the epidemic proportions of teenage illegitimacy and the inherent far-reaching problems produced by the birth of a half-million unwanted babies who are growing up without decent parental guidance and adequate financial support, there remains enormous resistance to implementing sex education programs throughout the country's high schools, much less junior high schools where they most properly should be initiated. Everything points to the fact that parents and the educators with clout to implement such programs would prefer to stop sexual intercourse, not illegitimate births.

It is difficult to believe that moral outrage and Band-Aid social services are preferred over preventing pregnancy. But the Child Welfare League of America, for example, held a regional conference in March 1977 sponsoring 74 workshops discussing child welfare and not one program focused on how to prevent adolescent pregnancies. Not one workshop solicited recognition for the young father of kept babies. Vituperation and services after the fact are demonstrably inadequate and vengeful.

The United States is near the top of the world statistics on live births to adolescents. Out of the total birth population to adolescents, the figure is 20 percent in America compared with 1 percent in Japan, a country that has never introduced the Pill and relies on condoms for birth control. In other countries of comparable economic status to the United States, the births to adolescents is 5 to 8 percent. In countries with the highest birthrate—Guatemala, for example—

Illustration by Joe Heiner

births to teens is approximately 23 percent. How is it that the United States is neck and neck with underdeveloped countries in births to children? Why aren't our schools, our social services, our parents dealing effectively with the pressures on children 10 to 14 years old who are the one age group that is increasing in live births?

It is certainly not the malevolence of boys toward girls. Nor is it their lack of feeling. Boys, not the girls, appear to be the most romantic and hopeful about love. The boys, given a chance to express themselves, seem to be the most unreal in their romantic expectations. As Bill says, "Colette's always going to be there—I know she'd never run out on me. I always wanted someone close to me without having to worry that I would come home without having somebody to talk to.

"I don't think that our life is going to be too hard. At first it might be, but as long as I have money . . . even if I don't, my parents will back me up.

"I know I can take care of myself and take care of her and the baby. No matter what. Because I still feel that I got her into this—well, she helped—it takes two, but I feel I have to do more. In a way, we both wanted the baby because we both wanted a part of us. It was more than just being forced into getting married. It was curiosity. We wanted to see if we were really in love with it [the baby]. Who wouldn't? We both so much wanted a part of us in case something did happen to us—like if one of us did die or one of us moved apart. 'Cause then we could look back on our child and say, 'There's a part of us.' I couldn't see myself getting married again in case I did lose her. I couldn't see myself liking another girl. She feels the same way. Some people say that's stupid, but I don't think loving one person is too stupid."

Bill and the one million others like him should have the opportunity to transfer their romantic innocence to a reality that benefits themselves, their partners and their children. This can only be accomplished if they can participate in an environment that educates the emotional, social and physical facts of life in a nourishing and humanistic manner. ⬛

We need your advice

Because this book will be revised periodically, we would like to know what you think of it. Please fill in the brief questionnaire on the reverse of this card and mail it to us.

CHILD PSYCHOLOGY: CONTEMPORARY PERSPECTIVES

I am a ____ student ____ instructor

Term used _____ 19 ____

Name _____

School _____

Address _____

City _____ State _____ Zip _____

How do you rate this book?

1. Please list (by number) the articles you liked best.

_____   _____   _____   _____   _____

Why? _____

_____

2. Please list (by number) the articles you liked least.

_____   _____   _____   _____   _____

Why? _____

_____

3. Please evaluate the following:

	Excell.	Good	Fair	Poor	Comments
Organization of the book	____	____	____	____	_____
Section introductions	____	____	____	____	_____
Overall Evaluation	____	____	____	____	_____

4. Do you have any suggestions for improving the next edition?

_____

_____

_____

5. Can you suggest any new articles to include in the next edition?

_____

_____

_____

_____

_____

_____

_____

_____

Thank you very much

80 81 82 9 8 7 6 5 4 3 2 1